Wheeling's Polonia

WEST VIRGINIA AND APPALACHIA
Edited by Ronald L. Lewis, Ken Fones-Wolf, and Kevin Barksdale

TITLES IN THE SERIES

Never Justice, Never Peace: Mother Jones and the Miner Rebellion at Paint and Cabin Creeks
LON KELLY SAVAGE AND GINNY SAVAGE AYERS

The Industrialist and the Mountaineer: The Eastham-Thompson Feud and the Struggle for West Virginia's Timber Frontier
RONALD L. LEWIS

Memorializing Motherhood: Anna Jarvis and the Struggle for Control of Mother's Day
KATHARINE LANE ANTOLINI

Working Class Radicals: The Socialist Party in West Virginia, 1898–1920
FREDERICK A. BARKEY

"They'll Cut Off Your Project": A Mingo County Chronicle
HUEY PERRY

An Appalachian Reawakening: West Virginia and the Perils of the New Machine Age, 1945–1972
JERRY BRUCE THOMAS

An Appalachian New Deal: West Virginia in the Great Depression
JERRY BRUCE THOMAS

Culture, Class, and Politics in Modern Appalachia
EDITED BY JENNIFER EGOLF, KEN FONES-WOLF, AND LOUIS C. MARTIN

Governor William E. Glasscock and Progressive Politics in West Virginia
GARY JACKSON TUCKER

Matewan before the Massacre: Politics, Coal, and the Roots of Conflict in a West Virginia Mining Community
REBECCA J. BAILEY

Sectionalism in Virginia from 1776 to 1861
CHARLES H. AMBLER

Monongah: The Tragic Story of the 1907 Monongah Mine Disaster
DAVITT MCATEER

WHEELING'S POLONIA

RECONSTRUCTING POLISH COMMUNITY IN A WEST VIRGINIA STEEL TOWN

WILLIAM HAL GORBY

West Virginia University Press / Morgantown

Copyright © 2020 by West Virginia University Press
All rights reserved
First edition published 2020 by West Virginia University Press
Printed in the United States of America

ISBN
Cloth 978-1-949199-39-0
Paper 978-1-949199-40-6
Ebook 978-1-949199-41-3

Library of Congress Cataloging-in-Publication Data
Names: Gorby, William Hal, author.
Title: Wheeling's Polonia : reconstructing Polish community in a West Virginia steel town / William Hal Gorby.
Other titles: Reconstructing Polish community in a West Virginia steel town
Description: Morgantown : West Virginia University Press, 2020. | Series: West Virginia and Appalachia | Includes bibliographical references and index.
Identifiers: LCCN 2019039039 | ISBN 9781949199406 (paperback) | ISBN 9781949199390 (cloth) | ISBN 9781949199413 (ebook)
Subjects: LCSH: Polish Americans—West Virginia—Wheeling—History. | Polish Americans—West Virginia—Wheeling—Social life and customs. | Wheeling (W. Va.)—History. | Immigrants—West Virginia—Wheeling—History. | Poland—Emigration and immigration—History. | United States—Emigration and immigration—History.
Classification: LCC F250.P7 G67 2020 | DDC 975.4/140049185—dc23
LC record available at https://lccn.loc.gov/2019039039

Book and cover design by Than Saffel / WVU Press

Contents

List of Illustrations vii
Acknowledgments ix
Abbreviations xv

Introduction 1

1. "Wheeling Might Appropriately Be Called a Polish City":
   A Local Look at the Polish Migration, 1870–1915 17
2. "There Has Always Been a Tough Element in That Section":
   Work, Culture, and Society in South Wheeling and Benwood 41
3. The Heart of the Community: Polish Catholics
   at St. Ladislaus Parish, 1890–1917 70
4. Finding a Good Job and a Good Union for Polonia: Polish Workers
   within Wheeling's Labor Movement, 1890–1915 97
5. Proving Their Loyalty: Wheeling's Polish Immigrants
   during World War I 124
6. Struggling for Economic Security: Polonia during the
   1919 Steel Strike and the Roaring Twenties 147
7. Polonia Adapts to the "New Era" of the 1920s 171
8. Moonshiners and Bootleggers: New Immigrants and the
   Selective Enforcement of Prohibition in Wheeling 197
9. Polonia in the Great Depression and the Rise of the
   CIO at Wheeling Steel 217

Conclusion 239

Notes 245
Bibliography 305
Index 321

Illustrations

FIGURES

I.1.	Wheeling Board of Trade Brochure Map	6
1.1.	Lakomy Family, ca. 1920	19
1.2.	City of Wheeling Map	30
2.1.	View of Center and South Wheeling	51
2.2.	Flood in South Wheeling, early 1900s	57
3.1.	Fr. Emil Musial, ca. 1926	77
3.2.	Interior of St. Ladislaus Church	85
3.3.	1920 Graduating Class of St. Ladislaus School	91
4.1.	Benwood Steel Mill and B&O Bridge	103
5.1.	1918 Liberty Loan Parade	141
6.1.	Advertisement for Stanley Duplaga Businesses	169
7.1.	Benwood Mine Disaster, Mass Burial	175
7.2.	Mary Kuca May Queen and Father Emil Musial	185
7.3.	Helen Kazmierczak in South Wheeling	195

TABLES

1.1.	Ethnic Diversity of Polish South Wheeling	33
1.2.	Home Ownership of Poles in Ritchie District	34
1.3.	Places of Employment for Wheeling/Benwood Poles	37
3.1.	Baptisms by Father Musial and Assistant Pastors	81
3.2.	Financial Records of St. Ladislaus Church, 1911–1919	89
3.3.	Souls at St. Ladislaus Church, 1911–1920	90
4.1.	Midterm Election Totals for Ritchie District	115
4.2.	Voting for City Council in Wheeling's Eighth Ward	117
7.1.	Souls at St. Ladislaus Church, 1920–1930	191
7.2.	Financial Records of St. Ladislaus Church, 1921–1930	193

Acknowledgments

Growing up in the upper Ohio Valley, I have always been intrigued by Wheeling's unique history, whether I was attending the annual ethnic festivals, getting my undergraduate degree from Wheeling Jesuit University, working on historic preservation projects throughout the city, or just buying a Coleman's Fish sandwich in the historic Centre Market House. Choosing to complete a long-term project on the city's diverse and colorful immigrant history has been a wonderful experience. Telling a story that examines the contributions of working-class Americans is a labor of love for me. Historical writing itself is always a collective enterprise, and while my name appears as the sole author of this book, I have been blessed along the way through the work, assistance, and friendship of numerous people.

The ideas for this project germinated among the stimulating conversations I had with professors as an undergraduate. Joseph Laker of Wheeling Jesuit University encouraged me to think seriously about the importance of microhistory as a viable method of historical analysis. Thanks to him, I decided to pursue local history as a way to examine the larger themes of U.S. history. John Cox got me fascinated in eastern European history and culture. His influence is seen throughout, especially his analytical wit.

Throughout the course of this project, I have worked with and become indebted to a vast array of librarians and archivists. My home for research and writing since 2007 has been the amazing West Virginia and Regional History Center at West Virginia University. I have been aided countless times by the knowledgeable archivists at the collection, and I always enjoyed our discussions and shared love of West Virginia's history. I want to thank Christy Venham, Lori Hostuttler, Kevin Fredette, Catherine Rakowski, Michael Ridderbusch, Anna Schein, Stewart Plein, Harold Forbes, and curator John Cuthbert for making the collection a crown jewel of the university. At the Ohio County Public Library in Wheeling, Sean Duffy has always been a great collaborator on all things Wheeling as well as an amazing writer and historian in his own right. Erin Rothenbuehler and Laura Carroll have been incredibly helpful to work with in finding maps and photographs and promoting the city's unique history. Thanks are also due to the large staff of the library who assisted me cordially the many times I ran out of paper at the microfilm readers. Also I want to thank the archivists at the Archives of the Diocese of Wheeling-Charleston, especially Ryan Rutkowski and Jon Erik-Gilot for helping me weave through the collections, even while the archives' location moved several times. I am grateful to Jon for helping me find new treasures and photographs for both research and presentation purposes. I also want to thank the staff at the West Virginia State Archives, especially director Joe Geiger and Randy Marcum who have both been so kind with their time when I have stopped in Charleston. In addition, I want to thank the staffs at the Ohio County Courthouse and the Historical and Labor Archives at Penn State University for their assistance over the years.

It has also been a pleasure working with the amazing staff at the West Virginia University Press. Derek Krissoff has made the process of publishing a first book easier than I ever could have expected. Abby Freeland has been helpful, especially with the marketing for the book. Than Saffel was very helpful in guiding me through the best strategy to provide graphics and maps for the book. Charlotte Vester has been patient answering all my questions about formatting and finalizing the manuscript. I also wish to thank the outside readers who provided such pointed and impressive comments on the manuscript. It is great to receive such deep, positive critiques from fellow colleagues. I especially want to thank Donna Haverty-Stacke, whose detailed comments and recommendations have made this book a much better final product.

I have also benefitted from friendships with other historians who have read my work, provided feedback at academic conferences, and allowed me to help them with their own research projects. Jim Green, one of the nation's preeminent labor historians, has been a constant friend and inspiration. Early in graduate school, I was asked to help Jim with his upcoming book on the West Virginia Mine Wars. We spent many happy hours discussing the story and trying to locate photographs and other original sources. I will always remember our drive along the route of the 1921 miners' march through rural Kanawha, Boone, and Logan Counties. His passing has left us without a needed champion for the rights of working people. Appalachian historians Ronald Lewis, John Hennen, and Dwight Billings have also provided helpful feedback on my work. John has been a great convener for several academic panels I asked him to participate in over the years as well. Lou Martin has been more than an academic mentor; he has been a true friend. When I first arrived at WVU, Lou was finishing his PhD on the working-class history of Hancock County, West Virginia. He took a young master's student under his wing and has continued to be a helpful resource in navigating problems. We have had numerous dialogues about how to write working-class history, traded sources, and had a fun time riding to and from the Appalachian Studies Association meeting in Boone, North Carolina, and bowling at Sycamore Lanes in Morgantown. Our overlapping interests have led us to appear on many an academic panel together, and I predict that will continue well into the future. All are inspirations reminding us that scholarship on the Appalachian region is needed today more than ever.

At WVU, I am truly blessed to pursue my passion every day with amazing colleagues and mentors. From the start of the research process, Robert Blobaum's knowledge and expertise in nineteenth- and twentieth-century Polish history was invaluable in providing a transnational perspective for this work. I am also grateful to him for helping to refine my writing and forcing me to dig deeper into research questions that I often did not consider. Elizabeth Fones-Wolf has been a reassuring and consistently helpful guide through my years at WVU. More than anyone else, she has helped me mature as a historian and a person by aiding in all my academic and nonacademic concerns that have come up since I arrived in Morgantown. I am forever in her debt. Finally, since my arrival at West Virginia University in 2007, Ken Fones-Wolf has taken the time to lead me along this maze that is the academic world. Words cannot express my gratitude to him for being a helpful sounding board. He has listened to my concerns, answered my research questions, and helped show me how to form my arguments in a more orderly fashion. Ken has always encouraged my research interests even when I doubted whether I was on the right track. I am truly grateful for his constant encouragement and collegial company in our department.

I would also like to thank my colleagues throughout the history department who have recommended important books and articles, made stylistic and argumentative suggestions, talked with me about teaching and advising, and engaged in great conversations: Katherine Aaslestad, Josh Arthurs, Tyler Boulware, Krystal Frazier, Michele Stephens, Tamba Mbayo, Macabe Keliher, Jack Hammersmith, Mark Tauger, Joseph Hodge, Brian Luskey, and Kate Staples. I want to especially thank Melissa Bingmann, Jenny Boulware, and Jennifer Thornton for discussing public history with me, letting me talk with their students, and even working on some local projects. I also wish to thank Matt Vester, James Siekmeier, and Charles MacKay, with whom I worked closely in advising our undergraduate students for years. Now as director of undergraduate advising, working with our majors is truly a highlight of my everyday interactions. Lastly, the two most kindhearted people I have known in the history department are our amazing secretaries Martha May and Becky Warnke. Their knowledge of how things actually work at the university has saved me on countless occasions. They have also been reassuring friends in times of crisis.

While a graduate student, I was blessed to have the support of a great group of fellow students who were always happy to discuss and assist each other with academic concerns. Several have been of great help in good times and when I doubted my abilities or the success of the project. Allison Fredette, Krista McCart, Shannon Tinnell, Ginny Young, Jinny Turman, and Jay Smith made my initial arrival at Morgantown happier than expected. Ginny Young and Jinny Turman are amazing scholars and kindred spirits in our shared love of the Appalachian region. All continue to serve as great colleagues and friends no matter where they may be in the country. I helped Godriver Odhiambo with some computer issues related to her own dissertation years before I ever started my own. Fellow doctoral students Billy Feeney, David Goldberg, and Joel Christenson served as exemplar role models for being a good teacher and scholar. Nilanjana Paul and I always had a great time discussing cultural and religious questions. Blake Perkins and I shared many academic interests, leading to helpful conversations on research. Adam Zucconi and Chuck Welsko will be great scholars of the Civil War, and hopefully will look more into West Virginia's past, thanks to some prodding from me. Throughout my time at Morgantown, Jake Ivey was a dear friend. Even though we study two different continents, he is a wonderful teacher, friend, and fellow football enthusiast. In particular, Henry Himes has been a good sport in discussing working-class history, especially the United Steelworkers of America, and I appreciate his interests in engaged labor education. All have helped make my time in Morgantown memorable.

In my life I have been privileged to have an amazing group of friends. While I cannot name and thank everyone, all of you have touched my life and career in ways you cannot imagine. From my earliest years, Susie and Mike Baker and their three boys Michael, Matthew, and Marc have been a second family to me. I am proud to still be close friends with them and see all the great work they do for the youth in Marshall County. During the summer of 2012, I received a WVU graduate education fellowship to work on a guided walking tour of South Wheeling's industrial history. During my time then and since, I developed close friendships with the team at the Wheeling National Heritage Area Corporation (now Wheeling Heritage). Jeremy Morris, Chris Villamagna, and especially Bekah Karelis are constant supporters. They took time away from their busy schedules to take me along with them to learn about historic preservation efforts throughout the city. I can say that I learned more from them than they did from me. They are a happy-go-lucky group of preservationists crucial to the reinvigoration occurring throughout Wheeling. New executive director Jake Dougherty is carrying on the torch, and I look forward to future collaborations with Wheeling Heritage. I have also been blessed to work with the South Wheeling Preservation Alliance. Ginger Kabala and Fr. John Byrd have been great friends. They have let me speak at their monthly meetings and aided my efforts in writing a walking tour guide for South Wheeling. Their efforts have helped redirect attention to that part of the city that "made" Wheeling historically significant. Margaret Brennan, Wheeling historian extraordinaire, has been a great friend over the years. She has always encouraged my efforts to re-create the working-class history of the area and help disseminate it to the broader public. Finally, my friends in Wheeling help make me a better human being. They have listened to my research, helped me in difficult times, helped me laugh at myself, and led me on some interesting adventures at times. I am thankful to have been a part of the cultural renaissance in Wheeling over the last few years. As my friends would say, even though I do not live in Wheeling, my heart will always be there. Special thanks in particular to Liz Paulhus, Marcie Panutsos-Rovan, Ryan Norman, Chris Rouhier, Beth Collins, Jenna Derrico and Phil, and Andrew Croft, Patricia Croft, and Jocelyn Carlson (the Rhode Island art-loving, community-gardening triumvirate). I also want to thank my Bethesda, Ohio, cohort. Ryan Hudak-Hill and T. J. Hudak-Hill have been jolly friends who are always intrigued by my historical musings and conversations. Thanks also to my travel companion Kristin McCombs. You have provided more relaxation and peace of mind during this process than you know.

Early on in this project, I realized that I would need to talk with former members of St. Ladislaus Parish. While I thought this would be quite difficult, I was happy to have assistance from members of my own family and the Moundsville community. I would like to thank Billie Louise Gorby for her help in introducing me to former parish members. I want to thank John Mysliwiec for his help in translating a Polish anniversary book from 1926. I would also like to thank those community members of South Wheeling who agreed to talk with me, especially Herman Werfele, Ed Gorczyca, Mary Martinkosky, and Blanche Resczynski. Finally, at a late stage in the process, Paul Cihy was very generous in providing access to his family's old photo albums, which document growing up in South Wheeling.

Finally, I would like to thank those four people to whom my mere words here can never express my gratitude. I thank my grandmothers, Doris Ballauri and Mildred Anderson, whose working-class experiences and hard lives during the Depression years have always been an inspiration. Both have encouraged and helped me out in hard times. While both are no longer with us, I am hopeful they would be proud of the final product. My father, Bill Gorby, told me once that history had been his least favorite subject. However, he also tells people that he knows more about history and loves to learn new things thanks to his son. Dad has always told me to be proud of writing a history of ordinary people. His working-class experience as a glassworker at Fostoria and belief in the benefits of community, family, and God fill the pages of this book. For my mother, Sherry Gorby, I am forever thankful. Since I was a young boy, she has instilled in me a love of history and social justice. She has also been my greatest proofreader, best critic, and best cheerleader. She has helped me schedule research trips and book hotels and kept me straight as I have become ever more absentminded. Her life continues to be an inspiration to me.

Abbreviations

AAISW	Amalgamated Association of Iron and Steel Workers (also the Amalgamated Association)
AAISTW	Amalgamated Association of Iron, Steel, and Tin Workers
ACA	American Constitutional Association
ACTU	Association of Catholic Trade Unionists
AEF	American Expeditionary Forces
APA	American Protective Association
ASL	Anti-Saloon League
CIO	Congress of Industrial Organizations
IWW	Industrial Workers of the World
NCWC	National Catholic War Council
NCOISW	National Committee for Organizing Iron and Steel Workers
NGAA	National German-American Alliance
NLRB	National Labor Relations Board
NWLB	National War Labor Board
OVTLA	Ohio Valley Trades and Labor Assembly
PAP Club	Polish American Political Club
PAVA	Polish Army Veterans Association
PNA	Polish National Alliance
PRCU	Polish Roman Catholic Union of America
SWOC	Steel Workers Organizing Committee
UAW	United Automobile Workers
UMWA	United Mine Workers of America
USWA	United Steelworkers of America

Introduction

Thaddeus Janeczko was born in the village of Grębów in the Russian Empire on December 12, 1880. In 1906, he married Maryanna Gonsior, the daughter of a wealthy family in Gościeradów. The following year, he emigrated through the port of Antwerp, arriving at Ellis Island on March 15, 1907. His wife and daughter Helen joined him two years later. By 1910, the family had relocated to Wheeling, West Virginia, where Janeczko found work at the Benwood tube works in the lap pipe finishing department. The family, which grew to include eleven children, lived at 2619 Locust Street near the heart of the Wheeling factory district. The house was modest with front and middle rooms, a long kitchen area, three upstairs bedrooms, and a dirt basement where the family stored coal to heat the furnace. By 1930 it was valued at four thousand dollars. Thaddeus, whom his grandson later recalled "always building or fixing something" about the house, instilled in his children a strong work ethic. Several of his daughters worked at the Warwick China Company as teenagers stamping decals on finished ware. Another worked for the Wheeling Tile Company while his son Edward worked at Wheeling Machine Products. The family did their grocery shopping almost daily at Visnic's Grocery Store, owned by a Serbian family, on Twenty-Sixth and Market Streets. For the Janeczko's children and grandchildren, the streets nearby served as a place of pickup games and general socializing for years among a mixed community of Germans, Italians, Greeks, Serbians, Lebanese, and African Americans.[1]

The Janeczko family lived closer to St. Alphonsus Catholic Church but attended Catholic mass at St. Ladislaus at Forty-Fifth and Eoff Streets. Ethnic celebrations and religious sacraments were significant events. In 1922, Edward and Stella Janeczko were part of the confirmation class, while sister Martha was in one of the largest confirmation classes in May 1928 of 249 Polish American children.[2] Marriages were also grand events in the life of St. Ladislaus. Helen Janeczko married Matthew Borgacz on August 27, 1927, and her sister Martha married Henry Baranowski on June 11, 1938.[3]

The majority of Poles living in the multiethnic city of Wheeling, West Virginia, would have agreed with Wheeling novelist Keith Maillard's fictional hero, who said of his South Wheeling childhood community, "We just called it Polish Town, but the old folks called it *Stanisławówo*, you know after the church, and they got that right because St. Stanislaus was pretty much the center of everything."[4] The description conjures up much of the ethnic solidarity that

Polish South Wheeling experienced on a daily basis in the early twentieth century. Ed Gorczyka recalled how from Fortieth Street south to Benwood there were over fifty small businesses that catered to the specific needs of the ethnic Poles of the area.[5] At the same time, they shared urban space with a multi-ethnic working class. Here they saw the birth of the state's Socialist movement and, in the 1930s, the Congress of Industrial Organization's industrial union drive.

Following the late eighteenth century, settlers and early industrialists looked to Wheeling as a transportation hub on the Ohio River for commerce moving west as well as a source of early innovations in iron, glass, tobacco, and brewing production. Transportation improvements funded by the federal government and outside capital led to the building of the National Road, the Wheeling Suspension Bridge, and the Baltimore & Ohio Railroad. By the time of the Civil War, Wheeling was already a thriving industrial hub with the most diverse immigrant population in Virginia. Once the war was over, the region's industries continued to expand along the Ohio River and east along the National Road, but topography placed limits on that growth. From 1850 to 1880, Wheeling's population rose from 11,435 to 30,737 as the city became the center of cut nail production and the capital of West Virginia. After 1885, the city lost the state capital, and the cut nail industry fell into decline; however, the city's investment capital and manufacturing infrastructure enabled businesses to diversify and adapt, making Wheeling and the surrounding region leaders in steel production. Beginning in the 1890s, the city attracted a wide array of southern and eastern European immigrants to labor in the factories, mines, and other industrial plants. This helped make Wheeling the center of the state's Catholic population. In addition, its long industrial history made it the center of the state's oldest central labor council.[6]

These "new immigrants," especially the Poles, left a world where it was becoming difficult to persist on the land. Poles began looking across the continent for higher wages. Making seasonal labor trips to the industrial core of western Germany and the factories around growing cities like Warsaw and Lublin, Polish peasants also embarked more permanently to the United States. While settling in many of the largest cities in the United States, a sizable number arrived in Wheeling. Here they lived in the heart of the city's factory district and, after 1900, also the center of the vice district. Often neglected and despised by city leaders and the local labor movement, Poles were left to create their own life in Wheeling.

Arriving in Wheeling, Polish peasants had to form a self-sustaining ethnic community if they were going to endure. This was difficult since ethnic and regional differences divided them. By 1900, Wheeling's Polish immigrants formed their community through the grassroots efforts of an active laity and their young, energetic priest Father Emil Musial. They built the parish of St. Ladislaus in the heart of South Wheeling. Through a mixture of religious piety and cultural nationalism, the community's parish, social halls, and homes helped them to develop a distinct identity and promote a strong family economy while living amidst a diverse immigrant population.

The 1910s and the subsequent decades were critical for the community. The solace provided by the parish was a natural counterweight to the largely negative response working-class Poles received from the local labor movement. While received negatively at first, the Polish working class proved their solidarity by joining in a variety of labor strikes and organizing campaigns. World War I likewise served as another testing ground for the Poles' loyalty to their new home country. Foreign-born Catholics saw the hyper-patriotic war climate as the best chance to prove their support for their adopted nation at war. Even though German Americans were targeted with suspicion, the Poles were able to thrive. They were widely praised by civic leaders for their support during Liberty bond campaigns, as well as for the large number who served in the American Expeditionary Forces (AEF) and the Polish Army in France.

Once the war ended, Poles and other new immigrants were vital to the postwar labor strikes, especially those against the Wheeling Steel Corporation. However, solidarity would fall apart by the early 1920s, leading to much animosity and surveillance of the Polish quarter. In particular, these working-class immigrants would suffer from the selective enforcement of Prohibition. The postwar years also saw growing fears within the community about the relationship of the second generation to those who remained tied to the old Polonia. The 1920s witnessed a golden era of expansion of the institutional aspects of St. Ladislaus Catholic Parish. At the same time, younger Polish Americans increasingly interacted with those from other ethnic communities in the region, forging a distinctive Americanized culture. Through attending similar schools, playing on the same football and basketball teams, and working together in the mills and mines, these interethnic relations helped provide the background for the union organizing drives of the 1930s and 1940s.

Polish Immigration and the Medium-Sized City

To understand the total lived experiences of Wheeling's industrial workers, *Wheeling's Polonia* investigates the Polish immigrants who settled in Wheeling.

While living in the industrial core of the city, Poles branched out and interacted with other immigrant neighborhoods throughout Wheeling. Poles and their immigrant neighbors did not compartmentalize their ethnic, religious, or class feelings. Core values of cooperation, equality, and mutual assistance were vital. Catholic historian Leslie Tentler has argued persuasively that "ethnic religiosity provided essential resources both for individual and family survival. . . . Religion provided them with perhaps their richest resources for shaping the world of everyday living."[7] Still the question remained: which way would these working-class ethnic communities go? Would they follow their ethnic Catholic traditions promoted by parish leaders, react to the class animosities promoted by the labor movement, or reach out to the corporate, Americanized culture? In many respects, they chose a little from all three, often balancing a left-leaning view of a moral economic order with a love of their Polish heritage and Catholic religion but all the while enticed by the mass consumer culture in the United States.

Wheeling challenges our traditional understanding of immigration during the height of industrialization. Studies of metropolitan areas are common, but I argue it is imperative to view immigration from the perspective of medium-sized industrial centers like Wheeling. The city had multiple ethnic groups, large-scale mass production (steel), and several medium-sized forms of production (tobacco, canning, tile, meatpacking, tobacco, glass, and brewing)—all of the variables available in a large city but on a manageable scale. Larger studies often focus on a snapshot image and samples from ethnic neighborhoods. *Wheeling's Polonia* alters the focus, exploring the community from a more intimate level of analysis.

Turning our attention to smaller urban locales dramatically alters our understanding of the lived experiences of working-class immigrants. Late nineteenth- and early twentieth-century Detroit, Chicago, Pittsburgh, and New York provide fascinating case studies of working-class life, but Wheeling offers some differing perspectives. Overemphasizing larger metropolitan centers downplays factors distinct to each place, such as "the cultural values of particular groups living in a city, the economic character of specific communities, or the distinctive political cultures of localities."[8] Most Americans also did not live in cities over several hundred thousand people. This study contributes to a growing urban history stressing the peculiarities of place and cities of varying sizes. Only by taking city geography seriously can historians understand how local factors assisted or constrained class formation. By 1900, working-class communities were very diverse. In West Virginia they included small, isolated coal and timber camps in the rural counties and smaller manufacturing cities like Wheeling.⁹ Smaller cities still need more investigation. There, one can get a more intimate assessment of the lived experience of working-class people while not relying on abstract samples of a couple blocks of metropolitan immigrant neighborhoods. In smaller cities like Wheeling, the daily life of walking to work past a set of row houses, around the corner saloon, and past the Catholic parish, ducking to avoid a passing streetcar, and arriving to labor in a dangerous steel mill can be more richly described. Thus, smaller cities lend themselves to a deeper level of analysis of how urban space impacts class, ethnic, and religious identity formation.

Wheeling's history made it a unique urban setting, thus contributing to its distinctive social stratification and working-class culture. Industrialization throughout the U.S. never occurred quite the same way based on geographic differences, access to raw materials and transportation networks, and the racial and ethnic makeup of the potential workforce. The Northern Panhandle and upper Ohio River Valley is just such a place, where there were various experiences of industrialization. Louis Martin examined the creation of this rural-industrial working-class culture during the twentieth century among the steel and pottery workers at the top of the Northern Panhandle in Hancock County's small factory towns of Chester, Newell, and Weirton. Native-born, European, and African American migrants developed a culture stressing local control over unions and government, a fear of distant bureaucracies, a strong attachment to place, and a culture of "making do" to provide self-help activities (such as canning, gardens, and hunting). Since Hancock County lacked industry prior to 1900, its late entry into industrial work set workers on a different post–World War II path, as compared to union members in large metropolitan areas, in their view of the Democratic New Deal coalition and Congress of Industrial Organizations (CIO) unionism.¹⁰

Wheeling was also part of a wider regional story. According to Allen Dieterich-Ward's *Beyond Rust*, Pittsburgh served as a hub for a metropolitan Steel Valley, connecting different industrial firms via a massive web of railroad track. However, a variety of municipal and state boundaries fractured the Steel Valley's integrated economy between smaller regional centers (Steubenville, Ohio), mill towns (Homestead, Pennsylvania), and rural mining regions (eastern Ohio). Industrial cities grew using urban capital to exploit rural peripheral areas, even while labor power was centralized in the urban core.¹¹ Likewise, Wheeling was a smaller central hub for the upper Ohio River Valley and crucial to the area's diffuse industrial development. With mills spread out throughout Wheeling—but also across the river in Martins Ferry, Mingo Junction, and Yorkville, Ohio—along with coal mines to the north and east of the central city,

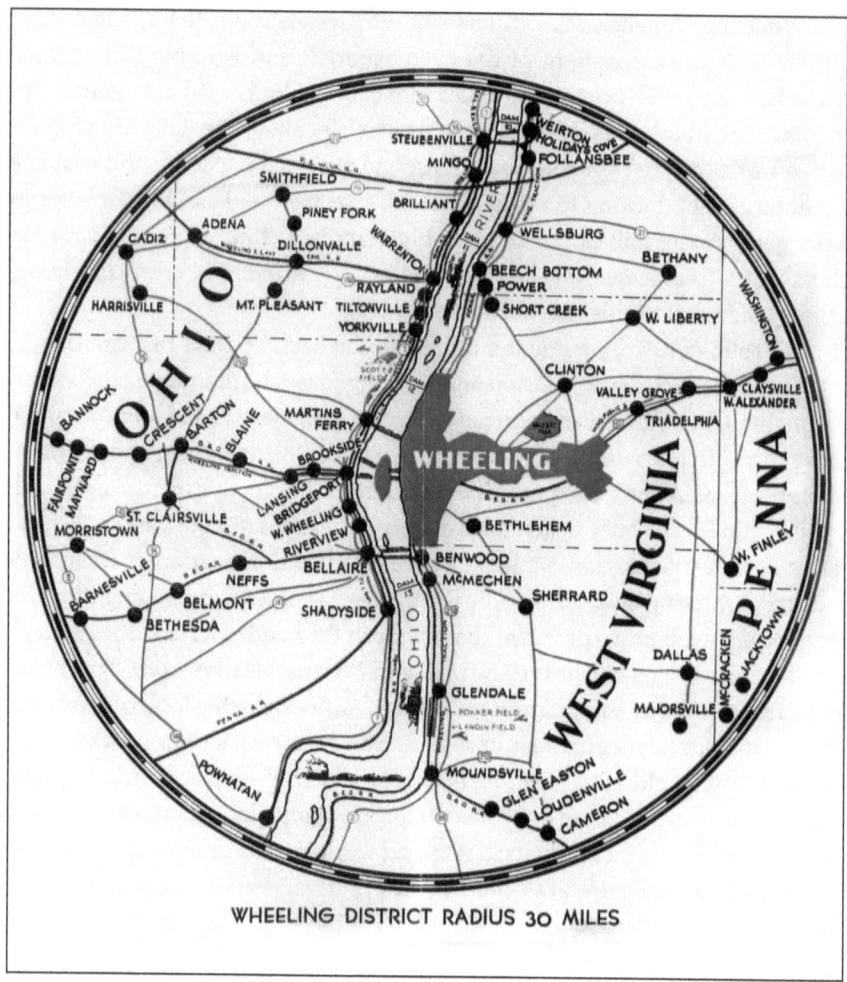

Fig. I.1. Wheeling Board of Trade Brochure Map, 1937. Courtesy of the Ohio County Public Library Archives, Wheeling, WV.

Wheeling's local economy had a wide reach. Polish immigrants had to negotiate not only with other immigrant groups in the city but also with the various mills and smaller communities on both sides of the Ohio River Valley.

Locality can influence the development of new ethnic identities and class formation among immigrant communities. This story was true of the upper Ohio Valley's industrial development, where starting in the 1880s and 1890s multi-plant steel mills and coal mines needed to act as a capital hub for future business growth while encouraging new forms of cheaper labor, like Polish immigrants, to relocate to the area. Wheeling thus served as a unique borderland to an extent, a highly urbanized and industrial zone surrounded by a large rural countryside. At the same time, the city was also within the larger industrial orbit of Pittsburgh, from which it could draw capital investment and a ready supply of labor power if needed.[12]

Polish immigrants arrived in Wheeling with prior experience migrating from rural eastern European farms to find work in the mines and manufacturing centers of Germany and the Austro-Hungarian Empire. Studying a smaller Polish community like Wheeling highlights the regional and often village connections that linked immigrants back to Europe. Whatever their host society, Polish immigrants were already quite active in the public sphere, engaging in political, religious, and labor organizations. Once they arrived in Wheeling, Poles retained strong bonds to their villages and, through the influence of St. Ladislaus Parish and the rest of the ethnic community, developed a strong attachment to being "Polish" and later American.[13]

Looking at Wheeling's Polonia highlights how Polish community-building in the United States was quite diverse. Many Poles settled in rural areas or cities of one hundred thousand people or fewer, locales similar in size and culture to the places rural Polish migrants left in eastern Europe.[14] Wheeling's Polish community helps break what has become a "Chicago-centric" focus in understanding Polonia. Larger Polish enclaves witnessed intense rivalries between the Polish Roman Catholic Union (PRCU) and the Polish National Alliance (PNA) in defining Polish identity. However, Wheeling's Poles held membership in various fraternal lodges, and these groups shared members and leaders, and worked together to promote Polish cultural events.[15]

Polish immigrant enclaves led similar community building efforts, but local conditions and the size of the city dictated differing responses to social tensions. Take Wheeling and Toledo, Ohio, as examples. In both, Polish Catholic parishes were vibrant, and wedding ceremonies, religious processions, and Catholic social events were crucial parts of everyday life. Poles in Toledo likewise were clustered in several working-class neighborhoods, working mainly in the automobile plants. However, Poles there benefitted from institutions not present in Wheeling. Toledo had the *Ameryka-Echo* newspaper, "the self-appointed voice of Toledo's Polonia," whereas Wheeling's Polonia was too small to support a regular newspaper. Editor Antoni Paryski's support for the Republican Party and criticism of labor strikes fostered tension within the majority working-class Polish community. Even so, Toledo's Polonia remained supportive of labor unions and tied to local Catholic parishes.[16]

Local community structures were crucial to class formation among immigrants to Appalachia as well. As glass companies relocated out of Pennsylvania and Ohio in the 1890s, new glassworker communities developed in Moundsville, Fairmont, and Clarksburg, West Virginia. Skilled immigrants exerted a class consciousness that depended on the strength and staying power of craft unions against labor-saving technologies.[17] As studied by Deborah Weiner, small towns were key sites as well for the eastern European Jews, who filtered into the coalfields of central Appalachia from their base in Baltimore. There, Jews acted as peddlers to the various coal camps while setting up communities in county seat towns like Williamson, Beckley, and Welch.[18] Thus, Wheeling serves as an excellent case study to examine the various connections between immigrant culture, the labor movement, and the importance of place in a modest-sized urban hub of manufacturing industries surrounded by a rural-industrial countryside.

Working-Class Religion

Historians have a difficult time grappling with the mixing of cultures that shaped Wheeling's Polonia, which alternated between sacred and secular, insular and inclusive, conservative and progressive. Often these contradictions are used to explain ethnic and religious fragmentation that limited working-class solidarity. For most studies of the urban ethnic working class, the parish and the union hall are on opposite sides of a great chasm that constrained the options for those who toiled in factories and sweatshops.[19] When discussed, immigrant working-class religion is often a negligible part of the narrative.

Wheeling's large Catholic population makes it an attractive site to explore working-class religion. The integration of religion has largely remained a sidenote in describing working-class experiences. For most labor historians, the Catholic faith often appears as an amorphous and contradictory belief system. Jefferson Cowie and Nick Salvatore noted that "these men and women could be deeply Catholic, active, even militant, trade unionists, and reject much of secular, liberal thought, while they simultaneously supported core economic aspects."[20] Catholic history gives many insights into an aspect of people's lives where social and political issues are often discussed in a religious context. The philosophical teachings of Catholic social justice apply directly to addressing the social wrongs suffered by an oppressed people under industrial capitalism. Although a counter to more radical socialism, Catholicism provided people with the means to live a moral life. Moreover, looking at the religious meaning of *place* and *parish* assists in understanding the economic development and class diversification of an ethnic community.

This book weaves religion into the narrative of working-class life. Newer scholarship no longer views labor and religion as totally opposing forces. This new work, as highlighted in *The Pew and the Picket Line*, shows that the "intricacies of working people's beliefs and practices" play a greater role in rates of unionization than historians previously thought. Working people "have often resorted to the institutional, social, and spiritual dimensions of their faith in their quest to overcome the inequalities of industrial capitalism."[21] Such was the case in Wheeling, where Polish workers drew on their experiences in the parish and community institutions as preparation and spiritual inspiration during labor strikes.

Religious beliefs and practices have stimulated rural and urban working people to organize labor unions. For Protestant workers in the early twentieth century, a rural producerism merged easily with Pentecostal and Holiness teachings stressing the power of a redemptive God. For rural coal miners in eastern Kentucky and Polish Catholic immigrants in Wheeling, religious life was intricately linked to their material concerns. All industrial workers dealt with unsafe working conditions, and Pentecostal, Holiness, and ethnic Catholic worship practices provided real healing in a culture where death always lurked under the next slate fall, blast furnace explosion, or passing railroad car. Thus, a wide variety of workers relied on their faith as moral justification to support union organizing.[22]

Even with this exciting new research, there is still a dearth of attention given to Catholic workers in nonmetropolitan locations. This leads to making sweeping generalizations about the role of faith on labor and working-class formation. Working-class Catholics viewed their religion depending on their ethnic backgrounds, church structures, and neighborhoods. Matthew Pehl has found that in Detroit the United Automobile Workers (UAW) grew concerned about the "reactionary potential of working-class religion" among the religious experiences of the city's ethnic Catholics, African American evangelicals, and southern white revivalism. In the 1930s, a pro-labor Catholic coalition developed in the parishes and local unions seeking to undercut the views of radio priest Fr. Charles Coughlin and the Communists. Ethnic Catholic autoworkers' support for the Association of Catholic Trade Unionists (ACTU) helped them espouse a plan for promoting "Economic Democracy" that was both anti-fascist and anti-communist.[23]

Wheeling's Polonia thus disputes the notion that ethnic culture was always a deterrent or always led to support for labor activism. Rather, this Catholic "religious consciousness" was remade over time and helps explain the tendency of ethnic Catholic workers to join the labor movement. This religious consciousness developed in the industrial neighborhoods of Wheeling and larger cities like Chicago. For example, Heath Carter has examined how Protestants and Catholics responded to the "labor question" in Gilded Age Chicago. There the Social Gospel "emerged from below" to balance egalitarian Christianity with the wrenching inequalities brought on by industrial capitalism. While clergy subverted the gospel to the desires of the wealthy, working people developed their own religious critiques of a hypocritical church led by "scab ministers." While Protestant clergy might denounce the right to strike from the pulpit, they also feared a massive "working class attrition" from their pews, as seen when working people struck from attending churches during the 1894 Pullman Strike. The Catholic Church did much better attracting working-class support. Concerned about the rise of socialism and motivated by Pope Leo XIII's encyclical *Rerum Novarum* (1891), Catholic priests could condemn socialists while advocating for a living wage and the right to bargain collectively. Catholics championed conservative trade unions led by the American Federation of Labor, whose membership was overwhelmingly Catholic.[24]

By the early twentieth century, Catholic religious consciousness comprised, as Pehl notes, an "evolving 'life-world' [of] informal folklore, articulated belief systems, meaningful ritual, and social structures . . . forged by the fires of conflict."[25] Crucial changes occurred by the 1930s as part of the Catholic Action movement, emphasizing a deeper level of participation by the laity to apply faith to all phases of life. Catholic Action could be fostered via lay-lead societies, Catholic Action clubs, or groups like the ACTU. In dioceses like Detroit's and even in the smaller Diocese of Wheeling-Charleston, Catholic Action built on the more communal nature of their religious practice, and members easily justified that organizing a labor union at a local steel mill or auto plant was part of "making" Catholicism.[26]

Ethnic Catholic workers shared what Max Weber called an "elective affinity" between their religious beliefs and the labor union. Michael Löwy has noted a "special dialectical relationship" between "radical secular utopian beliefs" and "redemptive religious thought." Both maintained their independence, yet there existed a "convergence, a mutual attraction, [and] an active confluence." Steve Rosswurm argues persuasively this elective affinity existed between the Catholic Church and CIO in particular.[27] Catholics during the late nineteenth and early twentieth centuries came to distrust liberalism's emphasis on the individual, freed from his or her obligations, cultural traditions, and the family. Catholics thought hierarchically. They were part of the "Mystical

Body of Christ" and, building off the papal encyclicals and Thomistic theology, stressed a sense of subsidiarity to one's community. Thus, labor unions like the CIO "required the subordination of that autonomous individual to the common good," as Rosswurm notes. For Poles, this elective affinity was quite strong, stemming out of their shared lives in Polonia and common morality learned from the religious culture of the parish.[28]

The best place to view this elective affinity is the immigrant Catholic parish in a city like Wheeling. Leslie Tentler criticizes those who argue that only after workers broke away from their backward, priest-ridden Catholicism could they move away from being doomed to a "truncated consciousness." In fact, creating ethnic Catholic identity and institutions "was probably a necessary antecedent to the development of class consciousness."[29] Joseph McCartin notes the broader problem as a "tendency to privilege instances of conflict, resistance, and working-class organization over the more mundane." McCartin sees this view doing injustice to working people: "Workers' religious identities are as real during moments of conflict as they are during periods of accommodation, but the role of their churches and religious practices is perhaps more visible and central in the latter instances, the very periods that our 'committed' approach encourages us to see as of secondary importance."[30]

Wheeling's Polonia likewise brings the parish to the center of the story since it was central to the worldviews of eastern European immigrants. In her pathbreaking book *Ballots and Bibles*, Evelyn Sterne argues that parishes were the "central institution in the city's working-class neighborhoods" and were necessary for workers to "secure their rights" and "reshape ideas about citizenship and Americanism." The Catholic Church in Providence, much as it did in Wheeling, "functioned in a Habermasian sense as a 'mediator between society and state,' an arena in which information was exchanged and public opinion developed."[31] With the church as a public square, parish, diocesan lay organizations, and charitable societies became schools for citizenship against coercive Americanization.[32]

Polonia and Americanization

The migration to and process of creating Wheeling's Polonia helped Poles to begin to self-identify as "Polish." Coming from diverse villages and urban regions with more localized identities, Polonia first united the entire community as Polish. This process builds off Benedict Anderson's notion of "imagined communities," in which nationalism develops out of social constructions forged by elite members of society. Often these "imagined" national identities assist in larger battles over the formation of who can be a member of the body politic and that entity's social, cultural, religious, and literary traits. Thus, "ethnicity" itself was a constructed identity forged from within ethnic communities.[33]

Dominic Pacyga's study of Chicago's Polish immigrants provides an excellent sociological model for this process. Poles did not totally phase out their old-world traditions but responded to their situation in a two-step process.[34] First, in the "communal response, they established small inward-looking communities that fostered stability and strength." This in turn led to an "extra-communal" response, whereby they reached out slowly to other immigrants in a common cause against poverty and unfair labor practices. It was the maintenance of old-world communal traditions that gave them guidance. The power of Polish religious identity protected peasant culture while also giving Poles a place to analyze the abuses of the industrial capitalist system. Only by understanding such practices as parish-building can one ascertain the lived realities of how immigrants used ethnic cultural institutions to organize as a working class.[35]

While fostering their own communities, Polish immigrants had to negotiate competing notions of "Americanization." One version was a top-down process that fluctuated throughout the twentieth century. At times, a racial nationalism emphasized exclusionary tactics, setting up a disciplinary state to guard U.S. borders, conduct surveillance of radicals, and forcibly Americanize the growing foreign population. On the other hand, a civic nationalism stressed an inclusionary polity based on cultural pluralism, freedom of expression, and universal political rights of citizenship.[36] Too much attention is often placed on these coercive forms of Americanization, making the process appear as a top-down endeavor imposed on immigrants by native-born elites. What needs more study is the process of Americanization from the bottom up to show how immigrants learned about the benefits of unionism and shared class grievances.[37]

Working-class formation occurred on the shop floor of Wheeling's factories but also within multiethnic neighborhoods, recreational spaces, and Catholic parishes. As James Barrett suggests, Americanization was "the gradual acculturation of immigrants and their socialization in working-class environments."[38] An earlier generation of Irish and Germans were the key Americanizers in the labor movement, working-class communities, and the Catholic hierarchy. This process was as true in Chicago as it was in Wheeling. Thus, Americanization took place via formal and informal social networks, occurring throughout urban centers, including city parks, street corners, street processions, club meetings, movie theaters, and saloons. The process built on already established working-class institutions and ethnic cultural sites.[39] While some older craftsmen might promote exclusionary behavior at times, the truth is they could not readily afford to alienate recent immigrants. In Wheeling, Socialists and union leaders often translated strike demands into many immigrant languages and had translators available.

World War I was a major turning point. Labor organizers stressed their own version of Americanism, promoting civil liberties, free speech, the right to organize, and the right to safe working conditions. A broad notion of "industrial democracy" motivated wartime workers and fueled their demands during the industrial union drives. However, the war witnessed the use of corporate and state power to repress labor while forcing conformity to a set ideal of citizenship that was native, middle class, and largely non-Catholic.[40]

This has led to disagreement on whether immigrant families retreated back into their communities during the interwar period. John Bodnar argues eastern European immigrants' "nexus of concerns" narrowed to support "realism," abandoning "loftier goals of earlier protests." Slavic workers were more pragmatic and always sought to protect the needs of the family. Taking low-wage industrial jobs provided a level of job security and allowed for the preservation of the family unit and the purchase of a home.[41] Other historians disagree about this immigrant working-class realism by comparing the first and second generations. Many second-generation ethnics desired to break away from the controlling nature of their parents. During the interwar period, this second generation "became American" through higher educational attainment and participating in a more Americanized consumer culture. Lizabeth Cohen argues in *Making a New Deal* that contact with mass culture did not fully supplant the ethnic communities but instead showed how 1920s ethnic institutions and cultures were dynamic and not a static protector of traditions. Out of their experiences, workers supported what Cohen calls a "moral capitalism," which created standards for how companies should behave. This moral capitalism explains why workers did not forge a radical movement to overthrow the capitalist system since their ideology developed from their Catholic beliefs and a culture promoting private property rights. All of this fostered a unified life experience among those who were the backbone of the industrial union drive of the 1930s and 1940s.[42]

My focus on Wheeling's Polish Catholic immigrant community will not view them in isolation but will use their shared experiences as a window into interethnic interactions and the divides within the community along class, gender, and generational lines. I argue their ethnic Catholic religion and tendency to support home ownership created a tighter class consciousness than other groups and helped them in actively supporting the local labor movement. Second, this study examines how the Poles could address both the pull of a class-based appeal as well as the pull of popular religious traditions. Which held more sway and when? By the 1910s, the Poles were a large group but had to interact with other ethnic communities. Over time, the Polish community vacillated between being insular in its relations with others by choosing to build their own religious and fraternal institutions and more outward looking in reaching out to other groups. In a smaller city like Wheeling, interaction was unavoidable and led to earlier and greater cooperation with politicians, trade unionists, and leaders in the Catholic diocese. In going to work, getting a drink at a local saloon, taking the family to a local park, and laboring in the mines and blast furnaces, Poles had direct contact with a wider number of immigrant groups. While this could lead to ethnic rivalries, by the 1920s the Poles were part of a wider eastern European community that held annual street festivals and ethnic cultural events and worked together within the Catholic diocese. The common experiences of dealing with the yearly flooding along the Ohio River and dangerous workplaces also bridged the cultural divide between the Poles and neighboring Ukrainians, Croatians, Italians, Lebanese, and Greeks.

I follow Dominic Pacyga's interest in reconstructing the "communal response" of the Polish Catholic community. Looking at how ethnic Catholics spent their money, went to school, and interacted with other groups, I argue that immigrants' Catholic religious culture had the most pull in shaping their views of themselves as working class. For this reason, much of my study revolves around St. Ladislaus Polish Catholic Parish and neighboring Catholic parishes. Evelyn Sterne argues that "Catholic parishes were the most accessible and important institutions in ethnic neighborhoods in the late nineteenth and early twentieth centuries . . . [they] functioned not only as sources of spiritual solace but also as dispensers of charity, promoters of upward mobility, and centers of neighborhood life."[43] Since parishes provided the one institution where most men and women congregated for spiritual and political purposes, they serve as a main focal point for understanding the creation of Wheeling's Polonia.

This story begins in chapter 1 by setting Polish migration in the context of the global movement of peoples in the late nineteenth century as well as the social geography of Wheeling at the time. The rise of the steel industry and growth of new urban spaces helped attract Poles to certain city neighborhoods. The pace and composition of the migration evolved over time but by 1910 made South Wheeling the center of Polonia. Chapter 2 explores how Poles, once in Wheeling, dealt with the struggles of living and working in South Wheeling and Benwood's factory district. By 1900, Wheeling had serious urban problems. The Poles' arrival coincided with growing concerns over the area's "wide-open culture" and efforts to segregate vice and crime in the factory district. Thus, these problems of corruption, the saloon, and crime were increasingly seen as immigrant problems. With city neglect, Polish immigrants slowly came to terms with the new industrial environment while adapting to their surroundings and other immigrants.

Chapter 3 highlights the Poles' communal response through the creation of the ethnic, national parish of St. Ladislaus. Through the efforts of an active Catholic laity and an energetic priest, Fr. Emil Musial, the Poles developed a unique culture on the South Side. Part of the reason for forming insular communities around the parish was, as seen in chapter 4, the tepid reaction the Poles and other Slavic immigrants received from the local labor movement during the 1890s depression. In the early twentieth century, Wheeling saw a spike in labor strikes. Slowly, the Ohio Valley Trades and Labor Assembly (OVTLA) began reaching out to immigrants and, at the same time, increasingly promoting socialist principles and political candidates. The attractiveness of this form of politics further exacerbated the tug-of-war between the socialists and the Catholic Church for the "hearts and minds" of working people.[44]

A key turning point came with World War I. Chapter 5 shows how the Diocese of Wheeling-Charleston and many foreign-born Catholics saw the wartime climate as a chance to promote their loyalty to the American war effort. While the Germans attracted suspicion, the Poles were able to flourish. The period allowed for a certain level of "pluralistic Americanism," stressing that those embracing immigrant culture and ethnic Catholicism were loyal as long as they did not promote subversive activities. While many served and donated to the cause, other Poles were critical of the war abroad, leading to intense surveillance of the factory districts by agents of the Bureau of Investigation to search out draft dodgers and potential radicals.

Polish workers also factored into the postwar union organizing campaigns. As chapter 6 shows, by the steel strike of 1919 they were increasingly supporters of trade unionism. However, this solidarity fell apart when a strike against the Wheeling Steel Corporation in the early 1920s faltered. In reaction to labor's decline, Poles turned back to the parish. Some did well; however, most still worked in dangerous and low-wage jobs as the Polish population dispersed out among the Ohio Valley's coal mines and steel mills. These economic trends led to a growing incentive to build up the institutional aspects of the community. Chapter 7 shows the pull of ethnicity remained strong in the 1920s. Following the Benwood Mine Disaster of 1924, the region saw an increase in large ethnic festivals displaying dances, food, and culture for the wider community. Imbued by strong nationalistic beliefs and intended to maintain the loyalty of the second generation, these events contributed to the heyday of Wheeling's Polonia. The era also saw an increasing level of interethnic interaction, mainly among the second generation. Attending public schools with the children from other ethnic communities and playing on integrated football teams helped bridge some of the ethnic divides in the region.

These successes, however, came during the heightened tensions arising from the selective enforcement of Prohibition. Drinking had long been a key aspect of ethnic Catholic working-class culture throughout the city's neighborhoods. Wheeling, with its legacy of organized vice, became a key concern first for state then federal enforcement. The narrow Northern Panhandle between Ohio and Pennsylvania made bootlegging not only more profitable but also easier to practice and escape detection. Chapter 8 looks at how Wheeling's Polish immigrants, among other ethnic groups, were overwhelmingly targeted by enforcers of the prohibition laws as many made moonshine in their homes to supplement their meager incomes.

The story concludes in chapter 9 with a brief look at how far the Poles had come by the 1930s and 1940s. Polish immigrants, their children, and members of other ethnic communities played a key role in fostering CIO unionism in the upper Ohio Valley. They joined local lodges and strikes and took advantage of new grievance procedures available for the first time in union contracts. There was an elective affinity between the organizing of the CIO and fostering a vibrant ethnic community, and by the 1940s the latter had provided a training ground to assist the second generation in fighting for a better livelihood while still maintaining close ties to their Polish heritage.

The story of Wheeling's Polish Catholic community fills an important gap in the discussion of America's immigration and labor history. Told from only the perspective of large metropolitan areas, the immigration narrative is left glaringly incomplete. Thousands of immigrants worked daily, scraped together enough money for their families to survive, preserved their cultural traditions, and worshipped God in a variety of medium-sized places. While available sources can make it more difficult to tell this type of account, the richness of their everyday experiences provides a fine example of how so many people found a better life on our shores. Here in Polonia, one finds the types of working people who continue to remake America for the better.

CHAPTER 1

"Wheeling Might Appropriately Be Called a Polish City": A Local Look at the Polish Migration, 1870–1915

Born in Lublin in 1890, Alexander Oszustowicz grew up in a world being drastically altered by economic forces. With the expansion of railways into portions of the once untouched countryside, the growth of modern urbanized cities like Warsaw and Krakow, and the seasonal migrations of Polish men to the agricultural fields of Prussia or coal mines of Rhineland-Westphalia, Alexander was part of a global pattern of migration that drew workers from the economic periphery of eastern Europe to work in the industrialized core. Arriving in Buffalo, New York, in 1907, he worked for several years until finally relocating to Wheeling, West Virginia, in 1910. Once there he fell in love with U.S.-born Frances Mogielski, whose marriage to a foreign national cost her her United States citizenship. Both she and Alexander settled in the industrial hub of South Wheeling at Forty-Fifth and Eoff Streets in the epicenter of a growing Polonia.[1] While there were many industrial jobs in the steel mills, glass factories, and tobacco plants, Alexander was drawn to Wheeling because of its rich cultural and musical traditions. Playing for a while in the Wheeling Orchestra, Alexander soon formed his own symphonic orchestra, the Moniuszko Orchestra, and eventually the regionally popular Polish American Rhythm Kings, whose regular Sunday program was a mainstay on Wheeling's WWVA radio.[2]

While immigrants made individual economic choices when they migrated, often they traveled via well-established kinship and village networks. As a result, Polish urban communities often contained many people and whole families from one or two towns or villages. Like Alexander Oszustowicz, Anthony Gorczyca was also born around 1890 in the village of Jastkowice southwest of Lublin in Congress Poland. He emigrated in March 1910. Unlike Alexander though, Anthony had no musical talents. He and his wife Katie (who grew up in the village of Pysznica, three miles to the southeast of Anthony's village) worked in agricultural labor around Lublin, and Katie even worked for a while in a sugar factory to make extra cash. As a peasant laborer whose life was changed by the incorporation of this peripheral region within the expanding industrial core of the Russian Empire, Anthony migrated seasonally to find work and eventually landed in Passaic, New Jersey, one of many Russian Poles and Ukrainians in the area. Anthony's small family remained in Passaic until 1913, during which time Anthony made seasonal trips to find work in the steel mills of Wheeling. He worked for some time in the blast furnace, but when it relocated to Mingo Junction, Ohio, he and his family moved to South Wheeling. Finding work in the local coal mines at Boggs Run, the Gorczycas rented and eventually purchased a house at 4706 Wetzel Street, only several blocks from Alexander Oszustowicz in the middle of Wheeling's Polonia.[3]

This chapter will focus on the European backgrounds, migration stories, demographic trends, and various push-and-pull factors that attracted Poles to Wheeling. The social and economic changes occurring during the late nineteenth century affected areas of Europe at differing times. Each of the Polish partitioned territories under the German, Russian, and Austrian Empires sent Polish migrants to western Europe and America at different times and for a plethora of reasons. As a result, Poles arrived in Wheeling over an extended period from the 1870s until World War I. As each specific group arrived, they constantly remade Wheeling's Polish community, extending its geographic base beyond the core in South Wheeling. After addressing the social and economic changes in Europe, personal stories of migration will attest to the variety of factors influencing out-migration from the rural Polish countryside. The rest of the chapter will examine the social, residential, and occupational backgrounds of the Polish immigrants. These findings highlight how groups from each partitioned land held only a loose affiliation to a Polish national identity and possessed stronger village or regional identities and affiliations.

Incorporation of the Polish Lands in the World Economy

Historians increasingly see immigration not as a single move but rather a series of calculated individual and economically stimulated moves by proletarian workers within a developing global economy. Scholars such as Dirk Hoerder and Ewa Morawska emphasize how international labor migrations between developing and industrialized regions are "a part of a global circulation of resources within a single system of world economy." Mass migrations from southern and eastern Europe between 1880 and 1914 occurred because of the evolving market relations of former peasants. A people's distance from the industrial core, their country's policies, and cultural and kinship traditions all factored into the decisions to migrate.[4]

Fig. 1.1. Group photo of the Lakomy family, ca. 1920. Courtesy of the Diocese of Wheeling-Charleston, Wheeling, WV.

The stories of Alexander Oszustowicz, Anthony Gorczyca, and Wheeling's other Polish immigrants began in Europe. Polish migrations developed in response to many factors shaping Europe in the late nineteenth century. Without a state since the late eighteenth-century partitions by the Prussian, Austrian, and Russian Empires, the Polish people benefited from the emancipation of serfs throughout eastern Europe between 1807 and 1864. This gradual process of emancipation forced Polish peasants to adjust to protocapitalist forms of agriculture. The peasantry entered the globalizing market economy of the late nineteenth century, which altered standards of living, traditional household economies, land distribution, and immigration trends.[5]

For those from the Prussian partition, political repression on culture and landholding drove migration. Polish peasants in Prussia were emancipated in 1807 without receiving land in the early nineteenth century, fostering an early impetus to migrate for labor. German unification in the early 1870s promoted a spirit of Germanization. The 1871 German constitution made no provisions protecting minority rights, and Otto von Bismarck's "Iron Kingdom" viewed the Poles as *Reichsfeinde* (enemies of the Reich). The subsequent *Kulturkampf* sought to Germanize Polish culture and undermine the influence of Polish priests. For example, authorities banned the Polish patriotic hymn "Boze, cos Polske" ("God, Protector of Poland"). In economic terms, the Germanization campaign spurred migration first to western Europe and then abroad. Seeking to purchase Polish agricultural land for German colonization, the Prussian partition saw rampant land speculation and spiking prices well beyond what small farmers could afford. According to one estimate, Prussian land policies increased land values by over 250 percent from 1888 to 1906. Brian McCook finds this trend one of the greatest ironies of German history since these policies to "Germanize" the Polish lands actually spurred a "Polonization" of parts of Germany.[6]

For Poles living in Congress (Russian) Poland, the principal factor driving migration was the massive population explosion across eastern Europe along with the difficulties in rural landholding in the late nineteenth century. Polish peasants emancipated in 1863 and 1864 received large allotments without having to pay redemption payments to the state, and they got legal title to their landholdings. However, problems developed over time for rural Poles. First, fragmented and dispersed plots set in "checkerboards" (*szachownicy*) remained widespread as former peasants gradually moved to a system of crop rotation. However, this coincided with a worldwide depression in agricultural prices in the 1880s and early 1890s, when farm incomes fell by one-third.[7] Second, the population explosion in the countryside during this poor economic period led to the subdivision of existing family plots. This subdividing of land and the scattered nature of peasant holdings among their heirs resulted in the number of peasant landholdings increasing. As a result, the average size of each plot naturally fell. In response, the Russian state eventually encouraged consolidation and land improvement by offering financial credits. By 1900, however, around 72 percent of peasant landholders were still "dwarf and small holders." At the onset of the Stolypin agrarian reforms within Congress Poland in 1906, 90 percent of the landholdings averaged 12.4 acres or fewer. Many Poles strapped for cash and living in provinces bordering the German Empire migrated for farm work in Prussia to earn enough money to then purchase more land.[8]

Finally, emancipation and the demographic boom of a "landless peasantry" resulted in a large rural proletariat. In 1900, landless wage-earning peasants accounted for nearly 3.5 million Poles. In Congress Poland, landless peasants swelled from 13.2 percent (1864) to 18.1 percent (1901) of the rural population. In rural Galicia, the peasantry's conditions were worse. Birth rates increased by 35 to 40 percent. Unlike the Russian partition, Galicia had a low degree of urban-industrial development, intensifying rural overpopulation and landlessness even more.[9]

Despite these drastic changes, by the 1890s many Polish peasants increasingly engaged in the market economy. Improving literacy and the creation of mutual benefit societies made opportunities more available. As they learned to read and came into contact with agents of the Russian Empire, Polish peasants became aware of modern political systems. Increasing numbers of peasants in local agricultural societies and agricultural circles also provided the peasantry an entry into modern "populist" discourse over agricultural technologies to help with grain yields but also to provide more diversified goods to sell for extra cash. Populists viewed the economic advances of peasant agriculture as a vital part of forming a more modern yeomanry within the larger nation-building process. These findings in Congress Poland show how Polish peasants anticipated market changes while becoming active in grassroots politics.[10]

As Polish peasants became more market oriented, they also became integrated within the world economic system. Because of the large numbers of landless peasants and the lagging economic infrastructure in much of the rural countryside, the emerging Polish proletariat became the key source of labor in extractive industries, textiles (Russian partition), and agricultural cultivation (German and Austrian partitions). The Polish lands rested on the boundaries of the core industrial region of western Europe. The distance to this core region largely determined the character and duration of Polish labor migrations. German Poles, for instance, migrated to the agricultural fields of Prussia and coal mining areas of the Ruhr and Westphalia regions of Germany. Despite local anti-Polish sentiments, they entered into the labor movement and played a key role in coal strikes around 1900.[11] Russian Poland, in contrast, served as a center of textile manufacturing for Russian markets. Because intellectual elites actively promoted a national identity, seasonal migrants in Congress Poland took hold of this idea of "Polishness" but in a way that catered to their own developing working-class identity. Polish textile workers were often a part of a fragmented ethnic labor force, which played Russians, Poles, Jews, and Germans against one another. It was this working-class conceptualization of Polish national identity that aided these workers in labor strikes.[12]

The rural peasants of Austrian Poland forged a peasant national identity during their seasonal migrations. Like Congress Poland, the Galician peasantry became more incorporated into local and regional peasant agricultural movements. Galician Poles used agricultural circles, meetings with local officials, and the increasing appeals from Polish intellectuals to craft their own expression of

Polish nationalism. Power relations based on older class arrangements faded with the emancipation of the peasantry after 1848, and various groups fought over what constituted a proper Polish identity. Polish intellectuals often misunderstood how the experience of serfdom, the Austrian state, the Polish Catholic Church, peasant ideologies, and regional loyalties (i.e., rural Carpathians versus Krakow's urban dwellers) were vital to peasant class consciousness. Later cultural attempts to forge a united vision of Polish Galicia only reinforced these class differences dating back to the failed 1846 revolt in Galicia.[13]

Over time, Galician peasants developed their own conception of Polish nationalism, combining older rural traditions alongside a revitalized Polish Catholic religiosity. This peasant conception of Polish national identity emerged with the assistance of village administrators, local schoolteachers, and populist Catholic priests. Literacy spread throughout the region with the promotion of primary education in the 1860s and 1870s and, beginning in the early 1880s, the expansion of popular school societies and public reading rooms in many rural towns. The Catholic Church also promoted higher levels of literacy through organized parochial schools while fostering a revival of Catholic religious practices throughout the late nineteenth century. Priests trained in the Krakow seminary became zealous proselytizers. In addition, Polish women religious increased by a factor of six between 1875 and 1914, forming a cadre of women going into the Galician villages to provide social services to the poor. These nuns also served as "catechizers" for intensifying the piety of Catholic villagers. The increase in devotional associations and use of prayer books, medals, and holy pictures helped spur pilgrimages to religious sites such as Częstochowa. William Galush argues that these religious transformations helped in "sacralizing travel and certainly accustomed peasants to associating piety with movement" in Europe and abroad. Some priests dispensed tools for religious instruction abroad, especially scapulars and holy pictures, to provide visual aids of their faith in a strange land.[14] This complex process of creating a national Catholic identity was vital to the "re-creation" of key aspects of the Polish village once in the United States.[15]

Personal Stories of Migrating to Wheeling *Za Chlebem*

After the turn of the century, global market forces and state policies shifted the source of Polish migrants to North America. Beginning in the 1860s, economic modernization expanded across central and eastern Europe. The ruling empires exported many traditional agricultural staples and raw materials to help develop a modern industrial sector. This development fostered a core–periphery pattern, creating large unindustrialized agrarian regions and industrial locales like Warsaw, Łódź, Białystok, and Lublin. Railroad building lagged in the Polish lands, standing at just 635 kilometers of track in 1862. However, extension projects increased the rail lines to more than 2,000 kilometers by 1887. This railroad construction connected Warsaw with Kiev, Moscow, and St. Petersburg to the east and Berlin and Vienna to the west. Periphery regions in the Polish lands included Galicia and much of north-northeastern Congress Poland. Industrial capitalism drew thousands of rural peasants in Congress Poland, Galicia, and eastern Ukraine to seek higher wages in factory work in American cities like Wheeling. Business agents at first enticed potential workers, but after 1885 steamship companies in Hamburg, Bremen, and Liverpool did most of the recruitment. Many came from multiethnic lands dominated by Poles with significant numbers of Ukrainians, Lithuanians, and Jews.[16]

Political factors also increasingly played a role. Polish migrants leaving Russian Poland spiked following the Russian defeats in the Russo-Japanese War of 1904–1905 and the failed revolution in 1905. The war closed Asian markets for manufactured products coming from the Russian Empire, which led to a stiff economic recession. Opposing war mobilization, social protests spread throughout Russian Poland, especially in Warsaw and Łódź, where most of the revolutionary activity and strikes took place against czarist control. Many of these rural Poles had already migrated to the textile mills of Łódź and Warsaw. The Russian government also began shifting industrial production to Russia, which only intensified the economic problems for Poles. Those who had migrated first from the rural countryside to the industrial centers now faced rising unemployment, which spurred many to join the migration to America.[17] Polish men arrived in chain migrations over time to work in Wheeling's steel mills. Stanislaus Fazalkowski came from Lutocin, a village in east-central Russian Poland about 120 kilometers northwest of Warsaw, on May 2, 1899. Over a decade later, Tranciszk Tayalowski arrived from Lutocin on July 16, 1910. Ignacy Klesczkewski hailed from Oleorydki and emigrated some time later. A more thorough story of these close village ties was that of Władysław Galkowski. He was born on January 1, 1897, in Skępe, a small town about forty kilometers from the village of Lutocin northwest of Warsaw. In the county seat of the Gmina Skępe, Galkowski worked as a day laborer on a farm in his teens. It is unknown whether he migrated for industrial work in the region, but he finally decided to go abroad in the summer of 1913. Leaving Hamburg, Germany, aboard the steamship *Pretoria* on June 21, 1913, he arrived in New York on July 5, 1913. Galkowski's trip was like that of many Polish migrants on the Hamburg-American Line as he spent his time in steerage (*zwischendeck*). He did not travel immediately to Wheeling, but by 1919 he found a job as an ironworker in a Wheeling Steel mill and was living at 4527 Wetzel Street when he applied for naturalization.[18]

Congress Poland's economic development was quite sporadic, leaving thousands of landless and desperate small farmers. Areas near the major factory centers could absorb this population, but those in more remote rural regions suffered terribly. The northern sections of Congress Poland were economically depressed throughout the late nineteenth century. Up to 1904, most of the migration to America from the Russian partition came from the provinces of Płock, Suwałki, and Łomża. Many Poles left the region from the 1880s through the start of World War I. This was the case for Konstanty Lapinski, born on January 27, 1894, in Łomża about 145 kilometers from Warsaw. As a boy, Lapinski worked as a day farm laborer. With the worsening economic conditions in the region, he left just before the start of World War I. Traveling on the Hamburg-American Line SS *Graf Waldersee*, he arrived in Philadelphia on June 6, 1912. Laboring in various industrial centers, Lapinski did not arrive in Wheeling until the early 1920s and by mid-decade was a millworker living near Forty-Fourth Street.[19]

Poles in rural Galicia had to make similar migration choices as the region was even more underdeveloped. During the 1850s, extensive railroad building for the Krakow-Lwow line introduced wage labor to the region but on a relatively small scale. This continued with the construction of the Krakow-Zakopane and Jaslo-Rymanow lines. However, most of these railroads connected the rich agricultural lands of Galicia with the urban centers in the Austro-Hungarian Empire, such as Vienna, Prague, and Budapest. The region suffered from overpopulation, rising land prices, and indebtedness. Industrialization provided little economic outlet for rural migrants. In 1880, Krakow's population was 59,830 but by 1910 increased to 127,592. For those migrants who did find work, unskilled work in the metal industry only paid twenty to forty cents a day with a weak labor movement to protect them.[20]

Because of the limited options in Galicia, many peasants and day laborers used the railroads to seek work in Russian and German lands. In 1900, reporter Jan Turski noted the crowds at the Krakow railroad station bound for Germany: "The reason for the emigration . . . is the higher pay by the owners of German estates for Galician workers." Working two hundred days of seasonal labor earned Poles about $96 plus room and board. Over time, Galician Poles began to learn about the better options in the United States, where average daily wages for a Polish laborer were from $1.25 to $2.00 a day with cheaper food and housing costs.[21]

Some Poles left the rural countryside following obligatory military service. Sergeant Wincenty Front left with his wife Kunegunda in 1906 after serving in the Austrian Army. Front was originally from Zawoja, a rural village in southern Poland fifty-two kilometers southwest of Krakow, and the earlier railroad construction tied his hometown to broader markets. Located in Sucha County, Zawoja was in a mountain valley. Connected by railroads to regional industrial centers like Krakow, the villages of the present Lesser Poland Voivodeship sent many migrants abroad but also to western Europe. According to a study done by the Diocese of Krakow at the height of the Galician out-migration in 1907, Wincenty's Zawoja saw 2,200 people leave. While the return rates are hard to determine, the United States was not often the top choice. Only 200 (about 9 percent) left for the United States. The vast majority went to Saxony (1,500), the industrial regions of Prussia and Silesia, and the factories in Wrocław (500). The patterns of return migration were seen in the village of Zaborów. Seasonal journeys were a way of life in the village of 160 farms. From 1882 to 1938, a total of 2,168 seasonal laborers returned, 721 nonseasonal migrants returned, and only 782 never returned to the village (about 21 percent).[22]

Rural Maszkienice shared some similarities to Zawoja, as out-migration picked up after individuals started traveling to the United States, rather than the coal mines in Ostrava, in the 1890s. Front, his wife, and others from southern Poland could travel overland from villages like Zawoja and Maszkienice northeast to Krakow. There they could take the train to one of the border stations set up after 1894 to monitor the health conditions of migrants streaming into Germany. These stations were run by two of the larger German ship companies, Hamburg Amerikanische Packetfahrt Actien Gesellschaft (HAPAG) and Norddeutscher Lloyd (NDL). From the border station, the train traveled northwest to Breslau then, depending on their embarkation point, west to Leipzig and north to Hamburg or northwest to Berlin-Ruhleben and west to Bremen.[23] Wincenty Front traveled this route, but he chose to disembark from Liverpool, England, sailing on the SS *Cedric* to Ellis Island on June 24, 1906. The couple initially lived with relatives in Lorain, Ohio, before moving to South Wheeling, where Wincenty got a job working at the Hoffman Tannery at Twenty-Eighth Street.[24]

Many migrants made numerous moves between the old country and the United States thanks to the extension of railroad lines and the speed and cheap fare of transatlantic steamships. One such emigrant was Michal Sawa, born on October 8, 1876, in the city of Zabaraz, northeast of Tarnopol, to Albert Sawa and Mary Mazur. Zabaraz had a long history beginning as a Ruthenian fortress city in the thirteenth century. Located in the multiethnic part of eastern Galicia (now part of Ukraine), the town was predominately Ruthenian Catholic and Jewish. Sawa was Polish and left the region during difficult times in the first decade of the twentieth century. Sawa first arrived in America via the Hamburg line (HAPAG) in April 1906 on the SS *Amerika*. He found work in Jamaica, New Jersey. Several passengers traveling with him from similar Galician villages sought work in Brooklyn, Jersey City, and Bayonne, New Jersey. After a short time, Sawa returned to Zabaraz but migrated again via the Hamburg line to New York. Returning this time on the SS *President Grant* on December 3, 1909, Sawa and another Zabaraz native Anton Bajarczuk traveled to Paterson, New Jersey, where there were sizable Polish and Ruthenian communities working in over three hundred silk and textile mills. The textile mills of Paterson and the Northeast saw an average daily wage of $1.15 during this time. Sawa eventually left Paterson around the start of the city's historic labor unrest in February 1913. The strike got quite violent aided by the Industrial Workers of the World (IWW) in organizing a general strike of thousands of eastern European immigrants. During the strike, Sawa traveled west and later that year began work as a laborer at the National Tube Company in Benwood.[25]

While most stories of Polish immigration tend to highlight single males coming *za chlebem* (for bread), young women also considered the decision to migrate. Some came to meet relatives already in America, while others came to reunite with their sweethearts. In many cases, husbands disembarked several years earlier and, after earning enough for the passage and rail fare, wrote to their wives on how to make the passage. Such was the story of Leokadia (born in 1878) and Antonia Jasienska (born in 1875). Both came from Gozdowo, the principal town of a rural community in Sierpc County located about 106 kilometers northwest of Warsaw. After marrying in 1891 and living in Gozdowo for some time, Leokadia's husband Władysław immigrated to the United States in 1903 and found work at the Riverside Mill. In little over a year, he sent for his wife and three young boys, Jan (born 1896), Stanislaus (born 1898), and Josef (born in 1903). The trip became a larger family out-migration from Gozdowo as Leokadia was joined by sisters Antonia and Michalina along with Antonia's three young girls Stanisława (born 1898), Lesława (born 1900), and Anastasia (born 1903). After traveling across Russian Poland, which often entailed slipping past border guards, they sailed from the port of Rotterdam on the SS *Amsterdam*, arriving at Ellis Island on February 18, 1905. Shortly thereafter, the large Jasienska crew joined Władysław and Jan where they were renting at 4526 Jacob Street in the heart of Polonia. The difficulties of keeping such a large family unit together in the railroad trains across central Europe, on the steamship, and on the train from New York shows the strength and the fortitude of Polish women to reunite their families in industrial America.[26]

The Jasienska experience suggests the commonality of family chain migrations from certain key villages, particularly in Galicia. Some were couples already married, while many more came independently and later met those from common villages. Most of the Russian and Galician Polish couples were married at St. Ladislaus Parish in South Wheeling. By 1910, a large number of South Wheeling Poles hailed from the villages in and around the city of Brzozów northwest of Przemyśl. Antoni Bober was born in 1882 in Golcowa, a rural village in the mountains ten kilometers north of Brzozów. Working as a farm laborer amid the increasing lack of land and agricultural crises led Bober to join his brother Joseph already in Wheeling. Making his way to one of the German border stations west of Krakow, he and another Golcowa farmer Josef Obloj took the train ride north to Bremen. Obloj worked from 1902 to 1904 in Wheeling with Joseph Bober and Frank Bober, who arrived in New York in September 1903 and came back to get Antoni. Both benefited from steady prices of steamship tickets as a result of the continual price wars between the major passenger lines, especially those from Hamburg and Bremen. By 1899, a steerage ticket on the Bremen line cost between $36.50 and $38.50 and averaged around a total of $30 thereafter. Both traveled on the Norddeutscher line SS *Kronprinz Wilhelm*, cruising into New York on January 11, 1905. After settling himself and getting a job as a laborer at the Top Mill in North Wheeling, Antoni "Tony" Bober met his future wife Agnes Laboj, who also emigrated from Golcowa. In a ceremony on June 1, 1909, the two were married by Fr. Emil Musial at St. Ladislaus Parish.[27]

By 1910, several trends were obvious. One was a steady stream of migrants from villages between Krakow and Brzozów and further east near Jaroslaw, creating a strong southern-southeastern Galician regional identity in Wheeling. Second, most Polish marriages included people from the same villages or regions. Of a sample of thirty-seven marriages from 1908 to 1909, at least fourteen were couples from the same village or county. Even more striking was most came from the area bounded by Rzeszów to the north, Jasło to the west, Brzozów to the south, and Jarosław to the east. This suggests that initially regional identities and cultural heritages were stronger than any unified notion of "Polishness" among Wheeling's Poles.[28]

Early Polonia Migration to Industrializing Wheeling

The transatlantic labor migrations of Poles led directly to the growth of Polonias in U.S. cities like Chicago, Detroit, Buffalo, and Pittsburgh. Whether drawn by circulars from the major manufacturing plants or by stories from friends and family, Poles flocked to urban areas, including Wheeling, West Virginia. Although much of the Mountain State remained agricultural in the last third of the nineteenth century, the Northern Panhandle consistently remained a manufacturing center. Wheeling benefited from its antebellum roots in the making of nails, iron, and glass, and the region continued to attract businesses as a stronghold of the Republican Party. With the rising political power of Gilded Age Republicans like Stephen B. Elkins and Wheeling glass manufacturer Nathan Scott, who promoted what historians call the "development faith," there was a hope for wider manufacturing growth throughout northern West Virginia. The Republican platform promoted infrastructure improvements, tax breaks, and incentives for railroads as well as protective tariffs to promote U.S. manufacturers, the gold standard, and a high-wage economy. Throughout the industrial core from the Northeastern textile mills to the coal and steel areas of western Pennsylvania and across the Midwest, the Republican Party's platform fostered manufacturing growth. On the southern fringes of this industrial core, only the Northern Panhandle of West Virginia attained the level of "development" that the "captains of industry" desired.[29]

During the Gilded Age, Wheeling blossomed as a manufacturing hub within the Appalachian region. With close ties to Pittsburgh's steel industry, Wheeling grew by leaps and bounds. The city possessed a diversified economy with iron and steel mills interspersed with glass factories, slaughterhouses, and cigar manufacturers. By 1890, Wheeling had fifty-three industrial establishments employing thousands of skilled artisans and unskilled industrial laborers, but just fewer than two thousand worked in the iron and steel factories. With the expansion of production, Wheeling's population grew to 41,641 by 1910.[30]

Much of this growth resulted directly from the influx of European immigrants from 1880 through 1917. Prior to the Civil War, Wheeling had a population of 11,435 with many Irish and Germans living in the North End and in South Wheeling. The influence of both groups added to the city's culture, religion, and architecture. Foreign-born Germans continued to arrive in Wheeling, particularly skilled artisans, puddlers, glassmakers, and brewers.

These immigrants helped maintain one of the region's strongest labor federations, the Ohio Valley Trades and Labor Assembly. With this ethnic influence in local labor unions and politics, these "old immigrants" supported many of the efforts of Republican politicians like Stephen Elkins and Nathan Scott. The two key issues for Wheeling's Irish and Germans were the protective tariff and immigration restriction on those "new immigrants" from southern and eastern Europe.[31]

Slavic immigrants first took up residence near the smokestacks of the steel mills south of the bustling, cosmopolitan downtown. In particular, the Poles settled within Ritchie District, the last division in Wheeling. In 1910, Ritchie District boasted a population of 7,947 due to the growing concentration of the Polish community there.[32] A decade earlier, the Polish contingent was spread throughout South Wheeling. According to the census, in 1900 both the foreign-born Poles and their native-born children in Wheeling totaled only 505 persons.[33] This figure is low due to the census not taking thorough account of whether a person from Austria, Germany, or Russia was really Polish. However, by 1920 South Wheeling contained a vibrant Polish community of 1,836 Polish speakers along with many more who spoke a variety of languages.[34]

The earliest Poles arrived in Wheeling as part of the German migrations in the 1870s and 1880s. Most were unskilled but blended into Wheeling's German artisanal culture in the years after the Civil War. The earliest mention of Poles living in South Wheeling dates from the late 1870s. Theodore Warsinsky, born in 1853 in German Poland, came to America on an earlier trip in 1865 before returning to central Europe. Warsinsky then arrived in Baltimore aboard the SS *Leipzig* (via Bremen) on March 27, 1876. Finding work as a laborer and living on Fourth Street, he married in 1879 and had at least ten children. By 1900, he moved his family to Benwood in Marshall County. He rose in the steel factory from a laborer, to a fireman, to a skelp weigh man, and eventually to a foreman at the Wheeling Iron & Steel Mill. By 1910, three of his sons worked as semiskilled or skilled workers in the Benwood mills.[35]

Some German Poles arrived with craft knowledge and quickly rose to occupy skilled jobs. August Kubkovski (Kubsky) was born in 1868 in the German partition and came to Wheeling around 1888 with his wife Minnie and another relative Chas. August worked as a molder's apprentice, probably at the Top Mill in North Wheeling. Living first at 454 Market Street and then on Fifth Street, by 1890 he was a skilled iron molder. By 1892, Fred Kubsky and his son arrived, moving to Pike Street in North Wheeling where the father worked at Wheeling Pottery. The chain family migration increased so much that by 1896 there were seven Kubsky men living and working in North Wheeling. Two were

Map of the City of Wheeling, ca. 1910

Catholic Parishes (P)

P1 St. Ladislaus / 4501 Eoff St.
P2 St. John's (Benwood) / 622 Main St., Benwood, WV
P3 St. Alphonsus / 2111 Market St.
P4 Immaculate Conception / 51 36th St.
P5 Our Lady of Perpetual Help (Ukrainian) 4136 Jacob St.
P6 Our Lady of Lebanon / 2216 Eoff St.
P7 St. Joseph's Cathedral / 1300 Eoff St.
P8 St. Anthony's / 124–126 18th St.
P9 Sacred Heart / 1st and Main St.
P10 Corpus Christi / 1514 Warwood Avenue (Warwood)
P11 St. Joan of Arc / 42 Joan (Fulton)
P12 St. Michael's / 127 Edgington Lane (Woodsdale)
P13 St. Vincent de Paul's / 179 Kay Avenue (Elm Grove)

Steel Mills / Foundries (S)

S1 National Tube Company (Benwood) Marshall St. (North Benwood)
S2 Wheeling Steel & Iron Co. (Benwood)
S3 Wheeling Steel & Iron Co. Belmont Mill 25th–27th Streets, Main and Water Streets
S4 La Belle Nail Mill/Tin Plate 29th–31st Streets (30th and Wood Streets)
S5 Wheeling Corrugating/East Wheeling East End 17th St.
S6 Top Mill (North Wheeling) North end (city limits)
S7 Wheeling Mold & Foundry Peninsula & Raymond (Fulton)

Factories (F)

F1 Northwood Glass Company / 36th and Wetzel Streets
F2 Hazel Atlas Glass / 19th and Jacob Streets
F3 Wheeling Tile / 3107 Eoff St.
F4 Schmulbach Brewing Company / Head of 33rd St.
F5 Uneeda Brewing Company / 3100 Jacob St.
F6 Wheeling Can Company / 48th and Eoff Streets
F7 Bloch Brothers Tobacco / 41st and Water Streets
F8 F. Schenk Meatpacking plant / (Fulton)
F9 Warwick China Company / 2140 Water St.

Businesses (B)

B1 Cooey Bentz Company / 36th and Jacob St.
B2 South Side Bank of Wheeling / N.E. corner, 38th and Jacob Streets

Cultural Life (C)

C1 Polish American Political Club / 4410 Jacob St.
C2 Polish Club / 4414 Wood St.
C3 Ukrainian Hall / 27 42nd St.
C4 Arion Hall / 10–16 20th St.
C5 Meyer's Hall / 3721 Eoff St.
C6 L. C. Driehorst Saloon / 60 45th St.
C7 John Prezelenski Saloon / 4500 Jacob St.
C8 Paul Rudzinski Saloon / 4526 Jacob St.
C9 August Dueker Saloon/Hall 2601 Chapline St.
C10 Fulton Grocery Store (Stanley Duplaga) 154 National Road (Fulton)
C11 Centre Market / 22nd and Market Streets
C12 Ohio Valley Trades and Labor Assembly Hall 1515 Market St.
C13 Pulaski Field / 4608–4618 Jacob St.

Education (E)

E1 Wheeling High School / 2101 Chapline St.
E2 Wheeling Central Catholic High School 75 14th St.

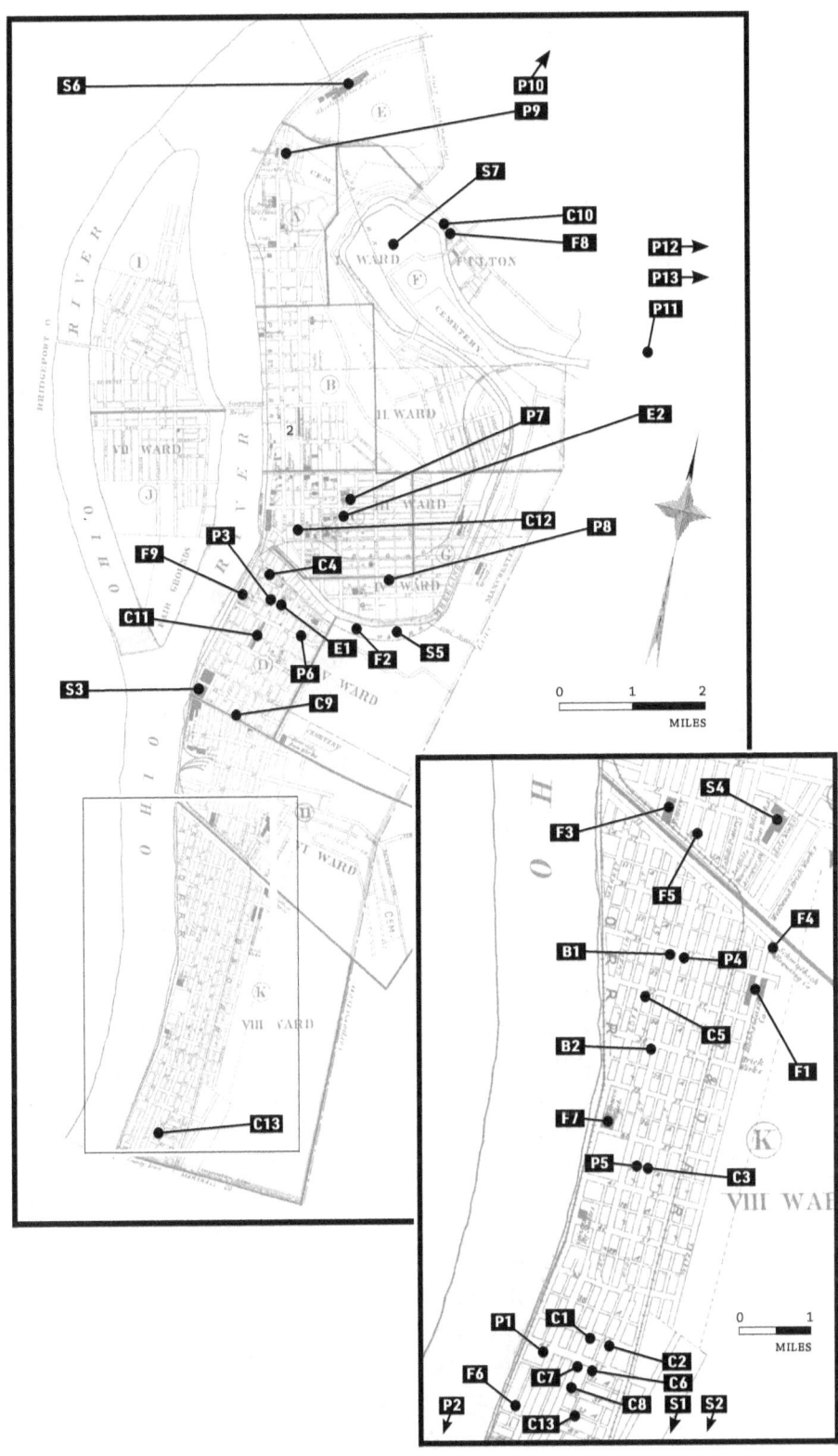

potters, and four were laborers or mill hands at the Top Mill blast furnace while August worked as a stove molder at Joseph Bell Stove Company on Fourth and Main Streets.[36]

Over the next few decades, the composition of Wheeling's Polonia changed drastically as more Poles arrived from Congress Poland and Galicia along with Ruthenians and Lithuanians. Polish migration to the United States, and Wheeling, decreased sharply with the economic depression from 1893 to 1897. With the American unemployment rate jumping from 3 percent in 1892 to 12 percent in 1893 and remaining in the high teens until 1899, immigration fell to a trickle.[37] Poles thus made seasonal moves to western Europe to find work as agricultural laborers or in the coal mines in the Ruhr and Westphalia regions of Germany. Polish migrants balanced their migratory patterns in relation to what was most cost effective, as more than three times as many Poles per year (between 300,000 and 600,000) traveled to western Europe rather than overseas (which only accounted for about 100,000 to 200,000).[38] Census records show that Polish immigrants coming to Wheeling dropped from 1892 to 1896 but then spiked upward in the late 1890s.[39]

By 1910, a growing number of Poles came from Galicia in the Austro-Hungarian Empire. Many emigrated after the "Galician Misery" as Polish farmers could no longer compete with their Hungarian and Czech competitors in the southern portion of the empire.[40] Thus, the years from 1899 to 1910 saw a massive out-migration of Poles escaping the economic underdevelopment of Galicia. In addition, census records show that between 1903 and 1906 a spike of 118 Polish immigrants to Wheeling reflects the arrival of many Russian Poles coming over during the economic recession affecting Russian Poland during the Russo-Japanese War (1904–1905) and the failed revolution of 1905.[41]

Table 1.1 highlights the changes in the ethnic composition of the Polish community up to 1920. Poland's division between three European empires for generations significantly limited the attachments of seasonal migrants to a shared Polish identity. Wheeling's contingent identified with particular villages or towns, the result of kinship networks. One of these was Brzozów in the Podkarpacie Province of southeastern Galicia. Josephine Franczak immigrated from Brzozów on September 4, 1911, aboard the SS *Berlin*. She was one of six siblings among other villagers to leave the rural countryside and settle in Wheeling.[42] As seen in table 1.1, by 1920 immigrants from Austrian (Galicia) Poland became the dominant regional group. In 1914, Josephine married a German Polish immigrant Michael Klamuta. After his death in 1927, she married Joseph Bargiel, who immigrated from Harbutowice, a small village near

Table 1.1. Ethnic Diversity of Polish South Wheeling, 1900–1920

	1900	1900	1910	1910	1920
Ethnicity	Foreign Born	Native Born	Foreign Born	Native Born	Foreign Born
Austria-Polish	27.83%	16.25%	41.56%	34.40%	40.93%
Polish	–	–	–	–	33.64%
German-Polish	37.11%	68.75%	8.13%	13.76%	1.12%
Russian-Polish	35.05%	15%	50.31%	51.83%	24.30%
Totals	97 (100%)	80 (100%)	320 (100%)	218 (100%)	535 (100%)

Note: This sample comes from the Eighth Ward in South Wheeling. The 1920 totals include the Poles living in northern Benwood, as the community extended further south.

Source: Manuscript Census Schedules, 1900, 1910, 1920 Ohio County, and 1920 Marshall County, West Virginia Regional History Collection.

Krakow, in 1913.[43] During these decades, the number of new immigrant families and U.S.-born Poles greatly increased and even spread across the Marshall County line into Benwood.

New inhabitants had a difficult time finding a place to live. Early on, most were unmarried males or husbands who came to earn enough money to pay for their families' later passage to America. These men lived in arrangements that Dominic Pacyga referred to as a "workers' commune," where several males rented a house and had either one of the men's wives or a housekeeper cook and clean for them.[44] Some single men also boarded together in the house of a widow or of a married couple also of Polish descent. Table 1.2 highlights the evolving household demographics with sizeable numbers of boarders and rental rates by 1920.

Table 1.2 shows how the Poles of the Ritchie District proliferated in a short period. Overall, boarders never accounted for more than 15 percent of the population. The small number of boarders for all of Ritchie District in 1920, along with almost a third who owned their homes, shows how many were slowly becoming economically secure.

Table 1.2. Home Ownership of Poles in Ritchie District, Wheeling, 1900–1920

Demographics	1900: Ritchie	1910: Ritchie	1920: Ritchie and Benwood
Total population	177	627	1299
Boarders	21 (11.86%)	96 (15.31%)	92 (7.08%)
Workers	64	249	403
Home Ownership (Total number of households)	–	115	239
Owns	–	29 (25.22%)	69 (28.87%)
Rents	–	77 (66.96%)	170 (71.13%)
Unknown	–	9 (7.83%)	0

Source: Manuscript Census Schedules, 1900, 1910, 1920 Ohio County, and 1920 Marshall County, WVRHC.

This large data set from Wheeling's Polonia needs to be compared with a smaller sample to highlight how certain blocks compared to the core area. Precincts Six and Seven of Ritchie District (Eighth Ward) covered the northern fringe of the region above St. Ladislaus.[45] Of the 68 Polish or Ruthenian households, 17 (25 percent) owned their homes.[46] Polish families rented out rooms in larger two to three story homes to pay off mortgage payments, thus creating a common pattern of owner-occupied homes shared with renters. This process did not last as long, for after a few years homes were fully paid off and boarders moved out. As parents aged, their children would pick up the work load. Only 16 households (24 percent) got by with the earnings of the family head, 29 housed boarders (43 percent), and 23 (33 percent) saw children or other family members working. Those having boarders averaged 2.7 per household. This wide variety of family economies is intriguing considering that 74 percent of all household heads labored in unskilled, low-paying jobs. Eleven household heads (16 percent) were in semiskilled or skilled jobs, and only seven (10 percent) could be considered white collar.[47]

The use of boarders and other relatives in an overwhelming number of households suggests the economic struggles faced by Polish families. This was particularly the case with child laborers. While there were three times as many boarders as children working in the sample, their early entrance highlights how crucial their labor power was to the family economy's success. Most were teenagers, and none were younger than fourteen. Occupations were highly gender specific. Six female laborers worked as packers or pickers at Bloch Brothers Tobacco Factory located between Thirty-Ninth and Forty-First Streets. Polish teenage girls working at Bloch Brothers often acted as unofficial agents of the company, attracting other Polish female friends and relatives. On the other hand, the boys either worked in the steel mills or served as gatherers, carry-in boys, or laborers at the Northwood Glass House near Thirty-Sixth Street. Some households mixed both forms of supplemental labor. For example, the Januszewski family rented their home at 4403 Wetzel Street, and the father worked at the Riverside Mill. Contributing to the family income were his two daughters—Katherine (nineteen), a tobacco packer at Bloch Brothers, and Mary (fifteen), a laborer at the Northwood Glass House—and a boarder named John Mieske (thirty-eight), a Riverside laborer. The Januszewski daughters needed to continue working and stay with their parents to help provide for the family's four young children, all under twelve.[48]

The census also reveals the gradual emergence of an ethnic middle class. While some rose to prominence by hard work in Wheeling, most arrived in this country with some business trade or skill. Like those analyzed by John Bukowczyk, most of these men, especially those from German Poland, were merchants who followed trade networks to this country to open up businesses. For example, John Raszkiewicz arrived as a grocer in 1907 and established his store at 91 Forty-Fifth Street. There were two types of Polish businesses—small artisan or retail shops (bakeries, butcher shops, saloons) or those businesses meeting specialized ethnic needs (printers and funeral parlors).[49] This middle class provided many of the community's needs, especially during mill layoffs and strikes.

Wheeling also offered possibilities for upward mobility. Frank Lewandowsky changed occupations many times, first arriving in Wheeling in 1904 as a coal miner, which was his occupation until he opened his own painting business in 1921.[50] Stanley Zarnoch illustrated the ebb and flow of opportunities Polonia could offer. Born in 1888 in Dąbrowa, he arrived at the port of Baltimore in September 1907. After migrating back and forth, Zarnoch settled permanently in Wheeling in September 1911 as an unskilled steelworker. While initially out of work in 1917, by June he had risen to be a pipe cutter at the Wheeling Steel & Iron's Benwood Works. Once World War I was over, he was out of work again, but he was rehired by 1921. In the mid-1920s, Zarnoch labored as a coal miner at the Hitchman Coal Company. After saving some money, he tried to open his own pool hall in 1928. However, the onset of the Depression forced him back into the mines as a coal loader.[51]

Although Wheeling's Polonia was an overwhelmingly blue-collar community from 1900 to 1920, there were some members who climbed into the ranks of skilled workers and even a few who were able to ascend into the middle class. Most Poles and their sons remained unskilled laborers in the steel mills, although some entered semiskilled positions. Some even entered skilled union positions as pipe cutters, machinists, boilermakers, and miners. At the top of the community was a steadily growing contingent of businessmen.[52] Many were proprietors of their own stores or served as clerks, bartenders, butchers, funeral men, pool house men, musicians, jewelers, or teachers. This middle class grew over time with about an equal number of them being of the first or second generation. Table 1.3 gives a breakdown of the sectors employing a sample of Wheeling's Poles. Despite the diversification of Wheeling's industries at this time, the Polish immigrants overwhelmingly represented the bulk of the unskilled labor force in the steel mills.[53]

The Changing Nature of Wheeling's Polonia

As industrialization expanded through the city and beyond, so did the Polish settlement process. Poles tended to cluster near work environments, leading to the mass concentration from Forty-Third to Forty-Eighth Streets and south through North Benwood near the massive steel mills. However, after 1900 large Polish clusters grew in two other sections of Wheeling where there were blast furnaces. One of these was in the multiethnic working-class neighborhood across from the Belmont Mill, located between Twenty-Fifth and Twenty-Seventh Streets. The Belmont Works dated from 1849 when it produced cut iron nails. In 1874, a blast furnace was built on the site, which was remodeled and expanded in 1893. After several downturns during the 1890s depression, owners updated the site with a continuous rolling mill operated by newer machinery and furnaces.[54]

After these 1903 renovations, the Belmont began recruiting a multiethnic workforce. The region from Twenty-Third to Twenty-Seventh Streets was increasingly populated by some Slovaks and Serbs, but the majority were Italians, Greeks, Lebanese, and Poles. Most of the latter were from Congress Poland and began arriving after the failed 1905 Russian Revolution. In the core of what residents dubbed "Little Poland," a sample shows that at least

Table 1.3. Places of Employment for Wheeling/Benwood Poles, 1910–1920

	1910: Ritchie	1920: Ritchie	1920: Benwood
Steel Mills	188 (74.60%)	154 (62.60%)	100 (71.94%)
Mill	69	–	11
Tube mill	90	–	42
Plate Mill	13	–	3
Other-Mill	16	–	44
Coal Mining	8.33%	8.54%	10.79%
Can Factory	0.40%	6.50%	2.88%
Glass Factory	1.98%	2.44%	0.00%
Tobacco works	2.38%	0.00%	0.00%
Other Industry	2.78%	1.22%	5.04%
White Collar	9.13%	15.45%	9.35%
St. Ladislaus	0.40%	3.25%	0.00%

Source: Manuscript Census Schedules, 1900, 1910, 1920 Ohio County, and 1920 Marshall County, WVRHC.

110 Polish immigrants lived there in 1910. Of that number, eighty-four (76 percent) were Russian Poles, and 81 percent of those arrived after 1905. Unlike the core area around St. Ladislaus, this neighborhood was even more blue collar. Of those working, 76 percent were unskilled laborers or blast furnace workers at the Belmont. The rest were unskilled laborers at the Hoffman Tannery at Twenty-Eighth Street or skilled machinists and chargers at the mill. Only 4 percent of the sample were small businessmen, including two grocers and a saloonkeeper. Little changed by 1920. With about 125 residents, the community had many more stable families as opposed to single male boarders. However, 80 percent of the families rented their homes. Even so, the area saw some occupational mobility. Of thirty household heads, ten (33 percent) were unskilled steelworkers and five (17 percent) were coal miners, but twelve (40 percent) were now in semiskilled and skilled positions in the steel mills. This included several heaters, catchers, and doublers. However, there was only one head who was not in a blue-collar factory job, an older German Polish woman serving as a midwife.[55]

The neighborhood was long viewed negatively among native-born residents and even Poles living farther south. "Little Poland" was also renowned as "Fighting Poland" for its boisterous and heavy crime activity. Poles and other immigrant groups lived in large boardinghouses facing the Belmont Mill going toward the hillside. The police heavily patrolled the region arresting many Polish, Greek, and Italian men for disorderly conduct. Most common were street fights and "booze fests" that could get out of control. As seen in the next chapter, this area was also very close to the Centre Market House and the growing prostitution district.[56]

The peak immigration period also saw the emergence of a separate but closely linked Polonia in the Fulton area just northeast over Wheeling Hill. Like the Kubsky family migration in the 1880s, many German Poles first worked in North Wheeling at the Top Mill. While long a state-of-the-art nail factory during the Civil War, in the mid-1870s the plant expanded when a Bessemer steel blast furnace was constructed and then remodeled several times between 1888 and 1894. Many eastern Europeans labored there, the plant producing one hundred thousand tons of Bessemer steel annually. However, most were Slovaks and Croats according to census records.[57]

The Polish settlement in the area expanded in several spurts between 1900 and 1920. This growth occurred after the expansion of meatpacking establishments and more so after the construction of the Wheeling Mold & Foundry complex on the peninsula east of Wheeling Hill. In 1901, Charles Blue expanded his mold-making business building a machine shop and massive foundry on a ten-acre site located on a high plateau where Wheeling Creek bends around the hillside. The company produced heavy steel castings and had large contracts including the Pennsylvania Railroad's underground tunnels in New York City and the castings and mechanisms needed to finish the Panama Canal lock gates.[58] The need for men drew many Polish immigrants to the foundries but also to the Top Mill blast furnace providing pig iron for the complex. By 1910, many Russian and Austrian Poles were living on North Main Street, in corridors snaking up Wheeling Hill along Coal and Bow Streets, and eventually along National Road. The area's immigrant population diversified after 1901 to include a few Russian Poles, Slovaks, and many more Slovenes, Lithuanians, and especially Austrian Poles.[59]

The Polish immigrants mainly arrived from Galicia between 1906 and 1914. At about twenty families in 1920, their population continued to expand.[60] In 1920, sixteen of the twenty families rented their homes, but most were small families with an average household size of fewer than four people. Andrej Wojewadka was born in Domaradz in Galicia in August 1891 and arrived in the United States in May 1910 traveling to meet his brother Francisiek already working in Wheeling. His wife Marianna arrived two years later, and they took up residence on Bow Street as Andrej worked as a butcher's helper at the nearby F. Schenk & Sons meatpackers.[61] John Jawrilowicz and his wife came from Poland in 1906, but as illustrative of the many smaller moves in the immigration process, he and his young family spent time from 1906 to 1914 in New York and later from 1915 to 1917 in New Jersey, probably during the early war years in the steel works and Polish enclaves of Bayonne and Paterson. They arrived in Wheeling sometime near the end of World War I.[62] Stanisław Kryc was another Galician Pole, born in 1886 in Wieliczka, who arrived in America in 1913. After working initially in Ambridge, Pennsylvania, and Buffalo, New York, he came to Wheeling in October 1916 to work as a mechanic at the Wheeling Mold & Foundry.[63]

The Fulton area was also home to Stanislaus (Stanley) Duplaga, who was also born in Brzozów in Galicia on December 10, 1890, and immigrated in March 1910. He soon became one of the key leaders in the local Polish community. During the war years he established the Fulton Grocery to cater to the Poles and other ethnics of the Fulton and National Road area. While he was one of several white-collar storekeepers, 68 percent of the Polish men were unskilled laborers. Although the Top Mill blast furnace remained a large employer of Poles in 1910, by 1920 many more labored at the foundry or were unskilled workers and butchers in Fulton's various meatpacking plants.[64]

Selective service registration cards also shed light on the changes to Wheeling's Polonia. From a sample of ninety-nine young Polish immigrants from Ohio County, sixty-one lived in South Wheeling (between Fortieth and Forty-Eighth Streets), and thirteen lived between Twenty-Seventh and Thirty-Ninth Streets with the third largest concentration living in Fulton (eleven). With the core still in South Wheeling and Benwood, the community began to expand north to Warwood and east along National Road.[65] The draft cards also provide a glimpse into where these men came from in eastern Europe. While it is difficult to locate some of the more obscure villages, the majority of the data shows that a growing plurality hailed from Russian Poland (forty-two). The sample reveals that many of these Wheeling immigrants came from the areas around Warsaw, Lublin, and Kolno. Others hailed from the small villages in Galicia (ten).[66]

These Polish immigrants made up a significant portion of the unskilled labor force fueling the industrial war machine. Of those sampled, sixty-eight worked in the various steel mills around Wheeling, with the majority (thirty-four) employed at Benwood's National Tube Company. Nine men worked in the coal mines, five were unemployed, and ten held various unskilled jobs. Only six were considered white-collar proprietors, and many of them requested exemptions. Despite some gains, in 1917 the Poles remained at the bottom of the labor force.[67]

Conclusion

In the first two decades of the twentieth century, South Wheeling's Polonia was a microcosm of the evolving world economy. Becoming market oriented allowed many Polish peasants to engage in seasonal migrations to western Europe and the United States. Wheeling was a prime location on the fringes of the manufacturing belt that possessed a long immigrant history and drew Poles from all three sections of the Polish partitions to its growing industrial community. These Poles arrived with village and regional allegiances in the years before World War I and thus held only a loose understanding of a unified Polish identity. The predominance of new waves of migrants arriving from differing parts of Polish-speaking eastern Europe constantly remade the growing Polonia. However, what faced Polish immigrants upon their arrival was adjusting to the social problems caused by rapid industrialization in a crowded, medium-sized industrial city. Confronting these challenges would slowly erode their parochial identities and foster a unified understanding of what it meant to be Polish in the industrial United States.

CHAPTER 2

"There Has Always Been a Tough Element in That Section": Work, Culture, and Society in South Wheeling and Benwood

Life in South Wheeling was rough. Because of industrialization throughout the nineteenth century, Wheeling grew and attracted a wide variety of workers from around the globe. Industrialization caused growing pains as largely agricultural eastern European migrants had to traverse the many difficulties of life in urban America. Family and kin networks were crucial for survival, but the dangers of everyday life made it difficult. Finding hard, irregular work at low wages, many new immigrants suffered from constant workplace dangers and frequent economic insecurity. As a result, most were forced to live near the largest factories in old or decaying housing stock. Crammed together in grimy brick row houses and wood-frame structures, these immigrant families endured constant flooding and unhealthy conditions.

Polish immigrants suffered the worst in their new surroundings. In November 1893, a local reporter investigated a brick row house in North Wheeling. Housing laborers for the nearby Top Mill blast furnaces, the row structure was two hundred feet long, forty feet high, and two-and-a-half stories, where lived "promiscuously about seventy-five Polanders." The reporter wondered "how they live[d]" since they were unemployed for six months and "hunger [was] abroad among them."[1]

Describing the scene, the *Wheeling Register* noted the dreadful living conditions: "The apartments were dimly lighted by candles and wood fires. Wandering in the darkness, over ash barrels and other rubbish, the reporter managed to get to a large room. In this were probably forty of the foreigners. They were all poorly clad, and most of them sat on the floor. There were among them the old gray-haired man and the babe, the men and women of various ages. Throughout the room, a heavy fog of Hungarian cigar smoke hung in the air."

Common of depictions of immigrant poverty, the reporter ridiculed the "Polanders'" eating and drinking habits. Commenting on how they substituted beer for food, the reporter writes: "Pretty soon quite a racket was heard and [a] big, powerful Polander rushed in with a beer keg on his shoulder.... Some seemed so thirsty that they made a dive for the tub, and began to drink like a horse from a trough." The scene turned joyous when a large amount of "strong smelling meat" mysteriously arrived. They "attacked" the meat with knives, forks, and fingers and gobbled it up in a "hideous" frenzy. Following the meal, the Poles "danced and sang in their native manner." Finally, they "ascended a rickety stairway" to the second story, where fifty "stretched out on the floor." With bleak work prospects, the merriment over a keg of beer and some decent meat distracted these Poles for a night from the grim prospects of a harsh upcoming winter.[2]

This chapter focuses on the precarious nature of working-class life for new Polish immigrants. By the turn of the twentieth century, Wheeling had serious urban problems. Most blamed the power of brewmasters, saloonkeepers, and prostitution madams, dubbed "Schmulbachism" after the city's leading symbol of political corruption, the prominent brewer Henry Schmulbach (1844–1915).[3] Poles crammed into South Wheeling's neighborhoods at the height of the "wide-open" culture. They arrived just as public outcries against prostitution led city officials to regulate vice by creating a segregated "Tenderloin District" in the area of South Wheeling becoming populated by recent immigrants. Thus, the period represents a shift in the social history of the city. Issues of political corruption, organized vice, saloon culture, and criminality appeared in the assumptions of many native-born residents who read the daily newspapers as general problems caused by the immigrants. This unfair association led many residents to neglect the real problems caused by industrialization, dangerous working conditions, and unhealthy life in immigrant neighborhoods.

One must understand the social conditions immigrants confronted before viewing how they built ethnic Catholic parishes, joined trade unions, or entered local politics. Immigrants did not shed their old-world ways but, through a gradual acculturation process, came to terms with the new industrial environment. Most immigrants learned about city problems while tending the blast furnace or loading coal, drinking in a neighborhood saloon, assisting immigrant families during a spring flood, encountering yeggs and street toughs, and chatting with neighbors on the front stoop.[4] However, these sites served as direct threats to Polish family and religious culture. Re-creating this social history serves as a reminder not to ascribe too much agency to those immigrant poor who had limited choices in life.[5]

Precarious Nature of Working-Class Life

Recent immigrants arriving in Wheeling entered a mechanized and dangerous work environment. Undercutting machines had replaced highly skilled colliers. At the Elm Grove, Richland, Hitchman, and Wheeling Steel mines, immigrants became fast-paced machine tenders and conveyer loaders. The same fate met those in the steel mills, tending blast furnaces, working in railroad yards, and moving raw materials. The growth of "nondescript, unheralded" labor came just as mass immigration from eastern and southern Europe heightened. The adoption of the continuous flow of production in Wheeling's steel mills, coal mines, and glass factories deprived new immigrants of control over the pace of their work.[6]

Following the 1890s depression, Polish and Slavic immigrants' main employer was the Wheeling Steel & Iron Company and the National Tube Company's Riverside Works in Benwood. The latter mill complex in North Benwood employed anywhere from 2,000 to 2,500 workers; however, in good times it employed as many as 4,000. The Wheeling Steel & Iron mills, along with Wheeling Corrugating, Wheeling Can, and the American Tin Plate Company's mill at the LaBelle Nail Works, employed 1,951 in 1895. By 1905 their total employment nearly doubled to 3,724 steelworkers, and in 1908 they employed 4,300. Bloch Brothers Tobacco, Northwood Glass Company, and the Wheeling Pottery and Tile Factories employed many young female immigrants. Throughout the 1890s to the 1910s, Bloch Brothers employed nearly 500 workers; the Wheeling Pottery Works had anywhere from 350 to 500 workers. Bloch Brothers tended to hire Polish and Slavic women in the tobacco stripping department and the finishing rooms. Young Polish women also did machine work at Wheeling Stamping and the Wheeling Can Factory at Forty-Eighth Street. By the 1910s, Polish immigrants found work at the Wheeling Mold & Foundry in Fulton. Assisted by contracts for work on the Panama Canal and munitions in World War I, the factory's employment grew from 209 (1905) to 360 (1907) and eventually 815 (1919). Finally, many Slavic and Italians found work in the B&O railyards, which by the 1920s employed over 500.[7]

During this time period, skilled workers increasingly lost control to mechanized mass-production processes. A number of labor historians have described how managers demanded a faster work pace and greater standardization, but Polish steelworkers often took time to adjust to this system of regulated time on the factory floor. As a result, immigrant workers endured higher rates of workplace accidents.⁸ With this process underway by 1900, corporate managers kept costs down through recruiting a large pool of common laborers from eastern and southern Europe. As "Hunkies" and "Polanders" filled the jobs tending large furnaces, loading coal underground, and stripping tobacco, employers set common wage-labor rates low. Constant levels of immigration along with women and child laborers helped to further subsidize this low-wage, unskilled economy. Edward Slavishak found Slavic immigrants working in the Pittsburgh mills earned on average 16.5 cents an hour in 1910, barely enough to support a large family even with the male head working six twelve-hour days.⁹

Periodic unemployment plagued common laborers. The boom-and-bust nature of the business cycle often led to periods of seasonal unemployment and larger downturns, like during the "Banker's Panic" of 1907 that ushered in a widespread economic depression devastating the industrial Midwest. This made attaining an economic foothold increasingly difficult. In Pittsburgh, steel tonnage fell by almost 40 percent from 1906 to 1908. Most steel companies laid off masses of unskilled workers. Conditions in Wheeling were bad by early 1908, as an observer noted how awful it was "to see children of the city running about with no shoes or stockings on their feet. Their fathers . . . being unable to provide for their wants."¹⁰

Unskilled laborers suffered the most. The panic produced a sluggish economy from late 1907 through early 1910 followed by another recession from 1914 to 1915. During both panics, immigrants responded in similar ways, with 1908 and 1914 seeing some of the largest return migrations to Europe. Many secured tickets from steamship agencies operating out of the Bank of Benwood.¹¹ Hundreds stayed, suffering from a lack of relief services and near-starvation conditions during the cold winters.¹² Things seemed to brighten in January 1908 when several factories reopened on the South Side. The Wheeling Pottery Company's Chapline Street and La Belle departments rehired 250 and 400 workers respectively. Warwick China rehired 60 to 70 employees, Northwood Glass Company brought back 400 hands, and Bloch Brothers Tobacco employed 300 more in its packing department. However, the steel mills remained closed.¹³

The plight of immigrant steelworkers and their families filled the local press coverage. The *Wheeling Register* noted the high numbers of Poles "in bad straits" who seemed to be "almost starving." Reporters also remarked how foreign saloonkeepers could no longer provide aid and free lunches for needy men.¹⁴ Conditions were worse in Benwood. Although one observer, imbued by his own class bias, claimed that the "foreigners, on account of their thriftiness and ability to live cheaply, are in much better shape to weather the panic," in reality their suffering was much worse because of meager wages and the poor condition of rental housing.[15]

One of the reasons they survived was not their thriftiness necessarily but because of the support of private institutions like the Catholic Church. The middle-class women of St. Joseph Cathedral's Immaculata Guild, located in East Wheeling, reached out to fellow Catholic families providing food and clothing for those near starvation. As the center of the Catholic diocese and with the most abundant financial resources at the time, groups operating out of St. Joseph provided assistance throughout the city's working-class wards. One of the worst cases was a Polish family living on Twenty-Fifth and Market Streets near the Belmont Mill. The Catholic society found the Lokiski family living in a "mere shamble of a dwelling... a veritable hovel scarcely fit to quarter an animal" without even a "crust of bread in the house." Unable to speak English, the men of the house were unemployed, and the youngest children went without necessary winter clothes. The Catholic women provided groceries to ease the suffering of the malnourished. Most families were "too proud to ask for aid," desiring to take care of themselves. In Benwood, the Knights of St. John joined in as well assisting the poor near St. John's Catholic Church.[16]

The unnamed descriptions of immigrant families highlight the variety of suffering:

> Two widows living on South Jacob street, sons unable to secure work, suffering from cold, and without provisions.
>
> Afflicted family on Chapline street, Eighth Ward, entirely destitute.
>
> Family of father and five children living in Riverside block, Eighth ward, father rheumatic, need food and clothing.

Conditions in Benwood reached crisis conditions as almost 90 percent of the men there were unemployed for months. Local ethnic grocers stopped extending credit for destitute families. Lacking the money to purchase coal, families nearly froze to death in their cramped quarters. Conditions turned worse when a large flood surprised the working-class sections of South Wheeling and Benwood in mid-February.[17] Economic conditions did not improve until the large Benwood mills reopened in June 1909. The good news attracted several thousand immigrants who "poured into Benwood and South Wheeling ... clamoring for employment" outside the mill gates every day for weeks.[18]

Another economic depression occurred in April 1914 when the National Tube Company closed down furnaces A and B throwing thousands out of work. The situation intensified after the Wheeling Steel & Iron Company plants closed in December 1914. One local charity official commented that "conditions among the poor [were] worse than they [had] been for years." What made the downturn of 1914–1915 unique was that many more immigrant families sought relief for the first time. Settlement house workers noted that most cases were of "industrious and deserving men and women who [were] idle through no fault of their own." The desperation continued during the winter of 1914–1915, especially with an increase in the number of "tramps." By January 1915, there were at least four hundred unemployed men sleeping each night at city hall. Many "wanderers" from other cities asked the local police to arrest them. With some warm shelter in the city jails, police turned many away after lodging for a night or two. The police also arrested many young female "street walkers" roaming the streets whose numbers spiked with "new recruits from the shops, mills and factories."[19] When things finally improved, the men flocking to the mill gates also quickly filled the tenement apartments on Harmony Hill and in North Benwood leading to massive crowding on South Wheeling's streets for months.[20]

Even when there was employment, working in South Wheeling's factories was inherently dangerous as steelworkers toiled near treacherous machinery. In one grisly incident at the National Tube Company in the fall of 1907, an immense iron flywheel, eighteen feet in diameter, went to pieces killing a foreign laborer John Bedosck. The incident occurred in the die shop on a "large elevated platform suspended about eight feet from the floor." The description of what transpired was terrifying: "Another piece of the wheel fully as heavy as the one that struck the die shop went through the roof of the tube building, soared over the storage house and buried itself in the ground about eight hundred feet distant."[21] Bedosck's demise occurred when he was "struck on the head by a piece of metal and instantly killed; skull split open and brains and flesh oozed out."[22] Six others were also injured, suffering broken arms and legs and bruising.

The nature of these industrial accidents did not strike all workers equally but tended to find unskilled eastern European immigrants. These men often lacked prior industrial experience, and managers placed them nearest the deadly machinery. The almost passive reportage of workers' deaths, argued a writer in the *Amalgamated Journal*, showed that managers treated immigrants like a "bedbug or cockroach or a troublesome mosquito . . . so much vermin" that was expendable.[23] Where one worked on the shop floor was dictated by skill, nationality, and the possibility of fatal injury. The Riverside Tube Works was an industrial war zone. One man, John Polis, died after being "struck by a B&O passenger train." Another "well-known foreigner" Jacob Levock had "a heavy piece of iron" fall on his head, almost fracturing open his skull.[24]

The numerous accidents and deaths in the steel mills meant that immigrants were taking their lives into their own hands. One horrific accident involved a Lebanese immigrant Joseph Judge working at the La Belle tin plant in August 1906. Joseph, age fifty, "fell headforemost into a seething pool of acid." Fellow workers were so terrified they could not budge to assist him. When rescued, Joseph presented the "most revolting spectacle imaginable" as the acid burned off his moustache and eyebrows and burned his skin from his head to waist.[25] Most mill accidents occurred in the blast furnaces and in the loading yards near the railroad tracks. Often reporters noted that "accidents galore" occurred near the Benwood steel mills, especially involving discharges from furnaces A and B. Steve Visnic operated the furnace around the gas producer; however, on one occasion flames burst forth, badly burning his face and chest. Of even more danger were runaway coal cars that intersected the mill yards. A sixty-eight-year-old worker, Frank Szcemski of Forty-Eighth Street, was "horribly mangled" when he was run down by a B&O train.[26]

The intense heat of the furnaces and constant steel production often killed men on the spot or drove them mad from fatigue. Mike Coleric died an hour after collapsing at the Riverside Mill from the intense heat. A "Polander" working there, Peter Rodonic, became so "mentally unbalanced as a result of overwork and the intense heat" he ran "amok" through the mill. This intense fatigue was common for the newest arrivals, who came to Benwood with no prior factory experience. Rodonic, who died within the week, did not understand the labor gang's work rules since he labored a series of continuous turns without resting or eating his meals. The desperation of men injured physically and psychologically led some to commit suicide. Slavic miner Anton Ambrose hanged himself from a rope in the closet of his room in the Hitchman Row boardinghouse in early 1914. Ambrose labored for years at the Hitchman mine, and its dangerous conditions proved too much for him to take. Leaving some letters, Ambrose despaired that he would never get to see his wife and children still living in Europe again.[27]

Work in the nearby coal mines and coke ovens were also full of peril. From 1890 to 1912, West Virginia's mines had the highest death rate in the nation. While the southern coal fields were the deadliest, several Wheeling-area mines were also dangerous. Polish miner Frank Bartula almost lost his life working too fast digging coal and was crushed against the floor by a heavy fall of slate. Many Polish and Slavic miners knew they walked into a proverbial battlefield every day below ground. The Hitchman Coal & Coke mine in Benwood was the most notorious. Many older Polish miners died like John Compass. He met his demise digging coal from the face when a two-foot piece of slate fell on him.[28]

The upper Ohio Valley's coal mines attracted thousands of Slavic-speaking immigrants to the region. On the Ohio side, immigrant coal miners congregated in Bellaire, Bridgeport, Martins Ferry, and especially Lansing. On the West Virginia side, miners settled in South Wheeling and Benwood as well as in Warwood and Triadelphia. Many of the miner settlements outside Wheeling were derisively dubbed "Hunkie Hollows" for the high proportion of Polish, Hungarian, and Croatian immigrant miners. Often these "company patches," two to three miles from Wheeling, allowed for better control over the diverse workforce.[29]

Immigrant coal diggers lived a precarious life. John Kogut's father Andy arrived in the United States in 1908 and settled in Lansing, Ohio. The company charged Kogut three dollars a month for rent taken directly from his wages. By the 1890s, most local coal mines had a strict ethnic divide as southern and eastern Europeans were mostly coal loaders and scrappers, while native-born, Irish, Welsh, and German miners ran mine machines or served as foreman. With the increase in fatal accidents, the Department of Mines in racially and class-biased language blamed the conditions on the "heterogeneous mass of humanity," which lacked the proper knowledge to mine safely.[30]

The mechanization of area factories also led to the hiring of scores of young boys for certain unskilled work. Boys assisted relatives as coal loaders. Many teenage boys entered the steel mills where their additional wages were crucial to the family economy. August Oglinsky emigrated with his parents from a rural Polish village in 1909, and his father found work in the mines near Lansing, Ohio. Recalling family expectations, Oglinsky remarked, "Everybody, when they got to the age of about 14 . . . [was] looking for a job to help their parents." Oglinsky remembered that, without the children's paychecks, "you didn't eat." After graduating from the eighth grade, he started looking for work in 1921. By 1923, the sixteen-year-old (five-feet, two inches tall and weighing 112 pounds) went with a neighbor to meet the foreman for the Wheeling Traction Company. Seeking work on the track gang, the foreman asked whether he thought he could "do a man's job." After working all day with a pick and shovel crew, the foreman learned that August was the "best man in the crowd." He returned home, proudly telling his mother "I've got a good job now," and worked with the company for the next fifty-two years.[31]

Young boys also dealt with dangers. Steelworkers worked the twelve-hour day beginning at 6:10 in the morning until about 6:30 at night. Their youth and inexperience could lead to accidents. One foreign boy's leg was badly mashed in Benwood's tube mill requiring amputation. Another Polish teenager Joseph Chynat met a terrible death at the Hitchman mine in August 1914. Working since age fifteen, he died from electrocution deep below ground.[32]

While immigrant men clustered in the blast furnaces, rolling mills, and coal mines, many young children supplemented the family income working unskilled jobs in smaller machine factories, tobacco plants, and glass houses. Younger immigrant children provided extra supplies often by scavenging for food and, even more so, for coal in the cold winters. After Christmas 1897, constables arrested a Polish family after catching them stealing coal falling from the B&O train cars. This was a common problem for the railroad as they reported losing fifteen tons of coal in South Wheeling and Benwood to families who had "their coal houses stocked with enough coal to last all winter." More often, Polish boys were run over by B&O trains as they sought to provide fuel for their needy families. Many local factories actively recruited young workers. Wheeling Can Company employed many young boys and girls over fourteen to work the canning machinery, while some boys did yard work at Wheeling Mold & Foundry.[33] Northwood Glass Company was another key employer. After taking over the former Hobbs, Brockunier Glass factory in 1901, Northwood needed a ready supply of young boys ten years old and older to work as "snapping up boys" and to carry in ware. One Northwood ad needing fifty young boys claimed they could earn 80 cents to $1.20 a day and hopefully have a chance to learn the skilled trade. Walter Reuther's childhood shows the dangers of work in the glasshouse. Walter and his brother Ted worked at Northwood around the corner from their home. With no state child labor laws at the time, the company employed children sporadically for five-hour shifts. At age nine Walter wandered into Northwood and was struck near his eye with a hot blowpipe, with molten glass on the tip, leaving a terrible scar. Because of their youth, inexperience, and small stature, many children were maimed terribly. Many worried daily if they would be like one young girl who lost two fingers caught up in a press at the Wheeling Can Factory and "crushed to a pulp."[34]

As a result, the low wages promoted a unique family economy, where all members of the immigrant household contributed to the family's survival. This "working class realism," as John Bodnar calls it, made up the principal "calculations in the working class economy." Most families had a unique "nexus of concerns," forcing them to be pragmatic in protecting their family above all else.[35] Polish households reflected this trend, exemplified by Joseph Kowalski, who lived at 2628 Market Street in "Little Poland." Born in 1866 in German Poland, he immigrated with his wife in 1892. By 1910, they had six children between ages two and sixteen. With their father out of work, Kowalski's three oldest children worked outside the home. Daughter Frances (sixteen) was a house servant, and his son Mike (fifteen) worked at the La Belle nail factory, while his daughter Rose worked as a sorter in another nearby factory. To help pay their rent and other family needs, Kowalski allowed eight boarders to live with them. Between the ages of nineteen and forty-four, all but two arrived after 1905. Given the lingering economic recession at the time, only five were employed as unskilled laborers at the nearby Belmont Mill, and one was employed as a farm hand. When conditions remained poor and the male breadwinner was out of work, this family economy sustained many Polish households.[36]

Arrival of Immigrants into Crowded and Environmentally Hazardous Industrial Zone

For South Wheeling's new residents, social class "had a distinct spatial dimension" as they fought a daily battle against the potential dangers lurking around every corner. Poor sanitation, crowded housing, and bustling streets posed a daily challenge in survival.[37] The problem was acute for new immigrants encountering South Wheeling's streetcars and railroads. As early as the 1890s, Polish immigrants died as the result of speeding B&O railroad cars. In what the *Wheeling Daily Register* callously called "the same old story of stepping out of the way of one train right in the way of another," a young Polish laborer at the Riverside Tube Mill named Lewandowsky was hit by a train backing up between Fortieth and Forty-First Streets. Knocked down onto the tracks, the "engine passing over his legs . . . mangling them in a horrible manner."[38] The worst incidents involved young children. One Polish boy needed both arms amputated after being hit by a Hempfield Division train near the Riverside Mill. The most gruesome story was the death of ten-year-old Anton Cienkurski. During another cold winter, young Anton was picking up loose coal near the B&O yard at Twenty-Seventh Street near the Spears Axle Works. While "industriously engaged" in collecting the fuel, Anton's foot got caught in the track, and his body was "cut in two, across the abdomen." In one of the most agonizing scenes imaginable, the boy's mother ran from nearby and "gathered up the upper part, the head and the chest and carried it to the house in her apron." Worse yet was there "seemed to be a spark of life left" when she arrived. Another woman brought home the other portion of the little body.[39] Labor leaders protested that the city "filled the streets with

Fig. 2.1. View of Center and South Wheeling from Ohio, ca. 1900. Courtesy of the Wheeling National Heritage Area Corporation, Wheeling, WV.

railroad tracks with complete disregard for the common people compelled to live in the vicinity." Most lived nearby dangerous industrial machinery. A sample of eighty households near the Belmont Mill from the 1920 census shows ten different immigrant and racial groups in the area. Of the sample, 37.5 percent were Polish; 18.8 percent were white native-born Americans; 11.3 percent were African American; 10 percent were Irish; 8.8 percent were German; 5 percent were Greek; and 7.5 percent were Slovak, Syrian, or Italian. Of the sample, 73.8 percent rented, and only 26.3 percent owned their homes next to the Belmont Mill from Twenty-Fifth to Twenty-Seventh Streets, where dangerous explosions and fast railroad cars endangered all.[40]

South Side streets were appalling. Most were still brick and kept in a dreadful "shameful condition" while dirt alleys were common. One angry resident chided the *Wheeling Register*, the supposed "champion of the oppressed," to force the city to do something about the "noise evil" that made living in these regions almost unbearable. Every day, residents competed with the "rumbling and creaking of the traction car," business wagons, "vehicles of pleasure," and the "cackling" of a young woman and the "exultant crowings of her proud and happy consort." These caused a "nerve-disturbing" public to wish that South

Side factories would be more considerate of the thousands of people crammed into the small region.[41]

By 1900, Wheeling had a modern and extensive streetcar system, extending south to Moundsville, north to Wellsburg and Weirton, and across bridges to Bridgeport and Bellaire. These connections allowed some South Wheeling workers to travel quickly to downtown shops, the steel mills on Wheeling Creek, Fulton's Wheeling Mold & Foundry, and mills in Martins Ferry and Yorkville. In 1899, the formation of the Wheeling Traction Company consolidated the various electric car lines, extending an interurban line with Wheeling's suburban communities to the east. By the 1920s, the company operated seventy cars on a system of 101 miles of track.[42]

The Traction Company was a focus of working-class discontent. The company's rates changed arbitrarily, and most believed that it bribed local city councilmen. Animosity toward the streetcars could also erupt into violence, as seen during the bitter streetcar workers' strike in 1899. In early April, an angry mob set fire to the company's barn in Benwood, and workers antagonized those riding the cars throughout South Wheeling during the strike.[43] The B&O railroad's lines also presented many hazards since they ran down the middle of streets. The B&O's major railroad terminus was located near the river between Twenty-Seventh and Twenty-Ninth Streets with spur lines connecting to near the various factories on the South Side and running to the Benwood Roundhouse. This dense network of railroad and streetcar traffic and the close proximity of factories made daily life noisy, dirty, and precarious.[44]

Working-class immigrant families contended with another major problem—the prevalence of deadly diseases. In a river town like Wheeling, its physical geography made the spread of pestilence a concern. The low-lying region south of Wheeling Creek through Boggs Run was in a floodplain. These neighborhoods laid in a narrow stretch of land flanked by the steep hillsides to the east. By 1900, the potential for epidemics grew as a result of overcrowding, pollution, and industrial waste. Almost half of all disease deaths came via tuberculosis. From 1903 to 1912, between forty-seven and ninety-four people died annually from the disease. Many cases went unreported. By 1912, about 75 percent of those reported infected died from tuberculosis. Charles Yergovich, already weak in health, hoped to return with his wife and son to Poland after earning enough money. However, watching his son die from typhoid fever led to his own breakdown. Diagnosed with tuberculosis, Yergovich longed to "die back home."[45] Poor garbage collection made the problem worse. Without a crematory most garbage was partially burned and then thrown on the hillsides above Center and South Wheeling. Already clear-cut of trees, the soil was polluted even more by garbage. During the summer the garbage would smolder and "fill the air with noxious gases." Moreover, most houses and tenement apartments were not fumigated after people died of small pox, scarlet fever, or consumption.[46]

The spread of typhoid fever was a dire concern. Without indoor plumbing in most of the frame homes and brick rows in South Wheeling, many residents drank water directly from the river or hillside wells. In addition, most used "dry vaults" or simply dumped human waste in backyards or street gutters. According to the City Health Department, between 1873 and 1913, 1,583 people died from typhoid fever out of at least 15,000 cases reported. Discovering infected water north of town, one observer from the health department warned: "Now we are drinking the filth of the upstream cities from Pittsburg to Martins Ferry. No wonder it is bad!" Most times the river appeared clear; however, it could be very colorful from industrial wastes. During the summer of 1909, shocked residents witnessed a horrid sight as a "scum" gathered on the river, giving it almost an orange color "only broken up by the thousands of dead fish" passing by Wheeling. With this constant problem, most working-class residents had to boil their water.[47]

City wells tested for high levels of the deadly *coli bacillus* (*E. coli*). The highest contamination was found at the five city handpumps near the Centre Market House. Health inspectors blamed this on the close proximity of "privies and cesspools." In the Fifth Ward alone, there were 135 outside privies within a few blocks of the wells. In a heavy traffic region used daily by about 1,150 people, this contamination endangered many families.[48]

The daily worry of contaminated drinking water contributed to the popularity of working-class saloons. Channeling this fear, local brewers stressed notions of "cleanliness" and "purity" in their advertisements. The local Pabst Brewery claimed their Blue Ribbon Beer as a "clean food" and noted how sterilized tubes and pipes with hermetically sealed tanks prevented "any possible contamination." Likewise, Schmulbach Brewery dubbed their prime lager "the beer of the home" and the "highest in healthfulness." The company encouraged working fathers to order their beer as the "ideal family beverage," healthier than the local water or milk.[49]

Like the efforts of middle-class reformers and activist municipal governments in larger cities, growing public complaints over dangerous streets and poor sanitation pressured Wheeling's city government to take action. These concerns found an advocate in Mayor Charles Schmidt (1905–1912). Elected as a Democrat in 1905 in a heavily Republican city, Schmidt immediately pushed for structural reforms to city government to provide better municipal services for the growing working-class population.⁵⁰ He supported raising tax revenues for street cleaning, stricter building codes for housing, a bond issue for a city water filtration system, and a new crematory. Schmidt was especially angered at poor garbage collection; he received about seventy complaints a day that garbage remained on the streets for up to ten days. He vigorously urged that city council take action since the "present antiquated eyesore is entirely too small and inadequate to the task."⁵¹

Concerns about municipal sanitation reached a breaking point following the 1907 spring flood. City Health Officer W. H. McLain warned there were 226 deaths in the year's first quarter (an annual death rate of 20.26 per 1,000 people). This number had been spiking. For 1905 it was 15.94 per 1,000, and in 1906 it was 17.04 per 1,000. He blamed the high death rate on the lack of an efficient crematory, no process of fumigating homes, poor garbage collection, and the poor inspection of impure milk.⁵² Through the City Health Department and the Associated Charities, the city began inspecting impure milk in 1907. Immediately, the number of children's deaths dropped by 50 percent in 1908. By 1912, almost 90 percent of all milk tested by the City Health Department was below dangerous levels. A greater success was garbage collection. Until June 1910, refuse was collected through a private contract system. Garbage often piled up in the streets, further polluting water. After 1910, Health Department policy required garbage to be drained and wrapped in paper, and city wagons went semiweekly to all residences.⁵³ Even with improvements the city's mortality rate remained highest for those living in the working-class wards. For 1912 and 1913, the Eighth and Sixth Wards ranked first and second most for all disease deaths, and immigrants showed a spike in disease deaths from thirty-five (1912) to forty-three (1913).⁵⁴

Like other progressive reforms, municipal sanitation targeted immigrants. Many middle-class progressive reformers in Wheeling subscribed to the views of social scientists stressing the foreign born's dirtiness. As a result, local officials used coercive health ordinances to force immigrant cleanliness. Antone Postovitch and Frank Kukay received fines for violating a law in 1912 against throwing decaying animal carcasses (in this case a dead cat and "putrifying [sic] meat") in the streets and gutters in an alley near the "Little Poland" neighborhood at Twenty-Sixth Street. According to the local judge, "the foreigners evidently thought they could do in Wheeling what they do in their own countries."⁵⁵ Poles were continually in police court and grew angry at sanitary officers patrolling their homes. Bronick Chasitaski violated three ordinances relating to keeping outside vaults and water closets. Felix Swakvoarke failed to comply with a quarantine on his home and family after a child contracted scarlet fever. When several Poles testified against him, Swakvoarke alleged, "If sent to the workhouse I will give all the prisoners scarlet fever."[56] While health reforms improved Wheeling's quality of life, recent immigrants came to see themselves overly targeted by reformers to change their lifestyles, and this perception intensified class and ethnic tensions in the city.

For the new Polish and Slavic immigrants arriving in South Wheeling, the most pressing environmental crisis was flooding. Lying in a low floodplain, and lacking proper flood walls along the river, immigrants were constant victims of spring thaws. Rapid industrialization negatively affected the environment, especially the clear-cutting of trees and smog-like pollution that covered the valley. Because of the late nineteenth-century building boom, the overlooking hills (Chapline, Mozart, and Harmony) were clear-cut for housing, further disfiguring the land. Throughout the state, excessive timbering led to soil erosion and forest fires. Soil often washed from the hillsides or fell into Wheeling Creek and other streams polluting well water. With the timber cut from the tops of the high hillsides, the ground was exposed to wind and heavy rains causing springs to dry up. As the water and waste ran off the hillsides, it picked up drainage from the meat packers, tanneries, coal mines, glass factories, and steel mills located along Wheeling Creek and near Caldwell's Run at Twenty-Ninth Street. With this soil destruction, the watershed could not hold the heavy rain water in early springs.[57] Thus, the first fifteen years of the twentieth century saw an increase in the number and strength of floods as well as terrible droughts.[58] Often these floods came with little notice. To understand the devastation, it is necessary to briefly look at the two worst floods in March 1907 (50.1 feet) and in late March 1913 (51.1 feet).

In the early morning hours of March 13, 1907, the Ohio River began rising rapidly. Following a strong and steady rain for forty-eight hours, starting at 16 feet at 6:00 a.m., the river eventually reached a height of 50.1 feet. Floodwaters struck South Wheeling most viciously. Most major steel mills were below flood stage (i.e., Benwood mills were at 34 feet).[59] In addition, transportation routes were completely blocked, isolating South Wheeling. For those out of the direct path of the floodwaters, terrible damage occurred because of numerous mud slides on Chapline and Mozart Hills overlooking South Wheeling. According to some observers, "tons of earth rolled down" including "huge rocks, trees, brush, and other debris." The sewer located under the B&O railroad track at Forty-Eighth Street became clogged with debris and flooded all of North Benwood. No matter where one lived, the flood took a heavy toll.[60]

Stories of immigrant suffering filled the newspapers during both the 1907 and 1913 floods. The South Side was "the heaviest loser of all the water-infested portions." Some, thinking they were further away from the river, were surprised when river water backed up from Caldwell's Run. The main street traffic stopped along Jacob Street from Thirty-Ninth all the way to Forty-Eighth Street. In 1907, four feet of water covered this region, suspending operations at Bloch Brothers Tobacco Factory and the Wheeling Can Factory. In 1913, most streets were flooded from two to eight feet. Immigrants sat looking out second-floor and third-floor windows as they were "held captive by the swirling Ohio." Benwood was "practically inundated" and a "scene of direful desolation;" most residents could only navigate by small boats and skiffs. On Harmony Hill, the dual effect of landslides and rising water left "the foreign inhabitants of this locality . . . almost terror stricken as several houses have been caved in by large masses of earth falling against them from the hill." At least eighteen to twenty-four inches of mud covered the streets for days. In 1913, the worst in need were the hundreds of new immigrants who lived in "small shacks close to the river banks." Most of these wood-frame houses were small and nearly knocked off their foundations by the high currents. In the Polish neighborhood starting at Fortieth Street, the river extended "clear to the hills and [was] several miles wide."[61]

Unable to cash or collect their paychecks, unemployed immigrants found relief as several relief organizations distributed free lunches and the Board of Public Works enlisted gangs of immigrant men to clear the mud and debris from the streets. During the 1913 flood, Mayor Harvey L. Kirk (1913–1917) organized relief boats and helped avert a bread famine for those living on Wheeling Island and in South Wheeling. Police used motor boats to reach the hungry and patrolled the South Side to prevent looting and arrest those overcharging people to haul their personal possessions and families. In addition, city officials and private charities converted the Webster School at Twenty-Sixth Street and the German Columbia Club near St. Alphonsus into temporary relief stations to house hundreds needing shelter and warm food. Even so, Benwood and much of South Wheeling remained entirely cut off since streetcars could go no farther south than Twenty-Seventh Street. The only humorous flood stories occurred for the "denizens of Wheeling's red light district." The "gay times" included stretching pontoon bridges and docks about the houses, allowing for merry boat rides. Of course, business continued as a result of these modifications.[62]

The most horrific sight occurred on the night of March 15, 1907. *Wheeling Daily News* reporters graphically recounted the human suffering. In a story titled "River is Yielding Up its Dead" following a devastating fire and explosion at the Warwick Pottery Company, police and concerned family members flocked to Center Wheeling looking for survivors. Thirteen people died immediately,

Fig. 2.2. Flood in South Wheeling, early 1900s, from the William O'Leary Real Photo Postcard Collection. Courtesy of the Ohio County Public Library Archives, Wheeling, WV.

---

four others drowned, and another six were reported missing as a result of the panic that spread among the immigrant neighborhood near the factory. Almost all the dead, mainly "Syrians,"[63] lived on Twenty-Second and Main Street near the factory. Many Lebanese died in the ensuing chaos by diving from the high windows of a foreign boardinghouse near the river and quickly drowning in the rapid current. A *Daily News* reporter summed up the horrific conditions: "There in the water, darkness, which appeared hideous blended with the lurid glow from the pottery fire, a terrible fight for life was witnessed by a dozen [or so] persons who were powerless to take action." Philip Cushman, his wife, and their four small children all died during the explosion. Mike Bretries leaped from the boardinghouse and perished holding his nine-month-old son in his arms. A boat capsized, drowning two infants as their mothers shrieked. Fast, swollen currents also took Polish immigrant Rosa Luswic (age nine) and Petar Sutti (age twenty-four) along with an Italian John Festicci. Many policemen struggled to help the immigrants holding onto telephone poles and windowsills "screaming piteously for help." The most unforgettable sound was the constant "dull splash" of people diving into the water, sealing their fate.[64]

Most working-class immigrants found solace from their fellow countrymen and Catholics. Lacking the money to replace their destroyed furniture, families moved in with neighbors, found temporary housing, or moved elsewhere. At an impressive service downtown at the cathedral at Thirteenth and Eoff Streets, Bishop Patrick Donahue delivered a touching address in front of hundreds of grieving residents. While they represented a variety of nationalities, Donahue spoke of how the dead and the living in the region "were bound together by the 'link of Catholicity.'" He spoke of the relief organized by the middle class and elite laywomen of St. Joseph's Cathedral. Even in these difficult times, the Catholic Church was the key institution seeking to care for the newly arrived immigrants' many needs.[65]

Even kind words and support could not change the plight immigrant families faced. In Benwood, virtually the entire town between the two large steel mills was flooded above the second story with many houses completely under water. The scenes were "pitiful":

> Hundreds of the foreigners who are employed in the mills and reside in the city fled with what early [sic] possessions they could grab, at the first signs of a record-breaking flood and with terror-stricken hearts took up their abodes on the rough hillsides, sheltered by any kind of tent or shack which could be quickly raised over their heads . . . they are still hovering about the fires on the hills, discussing their plight in their native tongue . . . a stranger would pass the encampment under the impression that a band of gypsies had been flood bound.[66]

The image of the immigrant working class as a "band of gypsies" presented them as a horde of foreigners, largely unprepared for the danger, while also suggesting a level of sympathy for working-class families who lost all their possessions and their modest homes.

The floods of March 1907 and 1913 left many working-class immigrants with important choices to make. Some could return to their homes only to spend weeks clearing away mud and debris. Others risked contracting disease as an "extreme dampness" covered everything south of Wheeling Creek. Finally, building and loan companies advertised the fact that many working-class residents should "buy a lot at Mozart, high and dry." Following the 1907 flood, developers began encouraging people to move out of the floodplain. Completed homes cost as low as $900, and 30-foot by 120-foot lots sold between $100 and $600. These inducements for building on the hillsides and interior valleys led to a gradual out-migration of the native-born and old German families, leaving eastern and southern European immigrants to continue living in the cheaper housing in South Wheeling and Benwood.[67]

"Wide-Open" Wheeling and the Politics of Vice South of the Creek

Just as Polish and Slavic immigrants settled in Center and South Wheeling, evolving city policies contributed to that region being associated with vice, prostitution, and crime. The developing vice culture occurred for several reasons reflecting the larger social forces remaking the city. Wheeling and its surrounding industrial suburbs and towns had greatly expanded since the 1890s. As David Rose has argued, this social transformation bred many negative attributes: poverty and prostitution, decaying housing stock, inadequate sanitation, and impure water supply. Wheeling lacked proper urban services for lower-class people, and crowded conditions bred many neighborhood hostilities. According to the City Health Department in 1911, the leading cause of death was "violence," which included "industrial accidents, homicide, and suicide." By the early 1900s, the city appropriated more money for police surveillance so that there were thirty-eight mainly German and Irish policemen.[68] The city also saw a rise in all types of crime. Arrests for disturbing the peace rose from 359 in 1900 to 468 in 1902. Assault and battery arrests rose from 7 in 1900 to 57 in 1901 and to an astounding 121 in 1902. Larceny also saw a spike from 10 cases in 1900 to 71 by 1902. By 1914, Wheeling had a real crime problem with 634 arrests for disorderly conduct, 410 cases of loitering to commit prostitution, 71 arrests for street fighting, 149 arrests for gambling, 70 cases of petty or grand larceny, and 90 arrests for pistol toting.[69]

By the 1890s, Wheeling's reputation as a "wide-open" town was renowned, and its vice trade was vital to the local economy. David Rose vividly recalls Wheeling's "subterranean economy of vice" dating back to the siege of Fort Henry and Wheeling's riverboat and transportation hubs bringing thousands of young men to the city seeking pleasure. The earliest vice districts dotted downtown Wheeling near the upper market house and in East Wheeling along Wheeling Creek. From a practical perspective, Wheeling's political leaders saw the saloon and vice trades as something to be "contained" in segregated districts, and they followed the policy of other larger cities in monitoring it through police surveillance, a licensing system to collect vital city tax revenue, and court fines when flagrant abuses occurred.[70]

Around 1900, various Protestant ministers coalesced into a reform movement known as the "Committee of One Hundred." This type of organization was not unique, as in other cities these religious-led anti-vice campaigns helped spur much of the Progressive Era reform impulse. Protestant ministers pressured the administration of Mayor Andrew T. Sweeney (1899–1905) and the chief of police to strictly enforce a range of local ordinances against the "vice trust." Led by Rev. R. R. Bigger of South Wheeling's Third Presbyterian Church and Rev. J. L. Sooy of the Fourth Street Methodist Church, the committee attacked "the liquor interests [who] . . . are organized in Wheeling for political aggrandizement and public plunder. They have bartered votes and never neglect to protect groggeries and low dens."[71] Ordinances included bans on slot machines in saloons, high prices on liquor licenses, Sunday closing laws, and the closure of "houses of ill fame." Reformers worried that these vices were spreading throughout Wheeling.[72] Especially problematic were the "fake hotels," where saloons and restaurants allowed prostitutes to receive men on the upper floors or even in adjoining "stalls."[73]

The fake hotels' expansion occurred in Wheeling's "Tenderloin" just south of the creek near the Warwick China Company and Wheeling Stamping Factory. A *Register* reporter noted how the region became populated by an "undesirable class of tough men and women" occupying the many tenements facing the alleys. After 1904, "Cyprians of a low class" rented out rooms selling their wares. Reformers merged moralistic arguments with an economic one stressing the "corrupting power of trusts." In Wheeling the close connection between saloons and the "fake hotels" seemed to confirm this attack. "Red-light" districts were marketplaces, and the vice trust, working with the beer trust, "bought and sold prostitutes to fill district brothels." The connections between the brewers and the vice trade reinforced their power over local politics.[74]

These reforms neglected the real causes of the vice trade. Prostitution occurred in Wheeling's working-class districts in East Wheeling, Alley C near the upper market house, and near the Fifth Ward market house. There, prostitution was a form of low-wage work, an occupational opportunity for young women when low-pay factory jobs and domestic work were limited. While a reporter noted that "these harpies find it frequently necessary to despoil their victims" of all their wages, many did not notice the low-class position of the harpies themselves. In the areas near the Market House, prostitution became virtually integrated into the local market trade for "commercial sex" for out-of-town farmers bringing goods to market and for single factory workers seeking a "thrill" on their Saturday night paycheck binge. Even worse, with the increasing number of female wage workers in South Wheeling's tobacco, glass, stamping, and pottery factories, many "virtuous" women had to walk to work through the Tenderloin's back alleys. One reporter graphically noted the actions of "harpies" near the pottery: "the sight of these depraved creatures dressed in negligee clothing of flimsy material and gaudy pattern, with the don't-care appearance of a person who has had a good time, has a tendency to make these hard-working girls dissatisfied with their lot and easy victim for the tempter."[75] While written in compelling language, descriptions such as this masked the class bias of the newspaper's middle-class audience, neglecting the economic struggles and exploitation that forced these working-class women to engage in prostitution.

The exploits of Wheeling's most infamous madam, Alice Bradford, led to the eventual segregation of vice in South Wheeling. Bradford rented out a series of houses along Alley C from the early 1890s through 1903. However, after some conflicts with city council and police raids, she became the center of a heated trial in the summer of 1904. Bradford took three Pittsburgh minors and forced them into prostitution in Alley C, sparking a public outrage. The *Wheeling Register* encapsulated this sentiment: "The whole district should be cleaned out as the moral cess-pool and pestilence breeder it is. It has far too long been a sort of Augean stables, a blot on the city, the shame and disgrace of Wheeling. Away with it!"[76] With the upcoming municipal elections in January 1905, Police Chief John Ritz's closure of the Alley C brothels in November 1904 led most prostitutes to relocate to the growing "lower-class" slum near the Centre Market House over the next few years. Citizens realized the city had no intention of closing down prostitution in Wheeling. In fact, as Rose argues, Ritz essentially continued the policy of municipal control by "redrawing the boundaries of its containment."[77] This municipal policy occurred just as Polish immigrants began congregating in the neighborhoods of Center and South Wheeling. Over time, the continued concerns of crime and vice would be linked in the public's mind as problems caused generally by the immigrants living in these regions.

A related concern was the proliferation of saloons. At its height in 1904 and 1905, there were fifty-two saloons south of Wheeling Creek and around two hundred in Wheeling proper. In the early 1890s, Benwood had a population of 3,000 and twenty-one licensed saloons (one for every 135 people). By 1906, Benwood had forty-five licensed saloons.[78] South Wheeling's saloons were distinctively immigrant working-class spaces. One local negatively summarized their clientele as "foreign vandals . . . viciously and remorselessly tramping American law under foot."[79]

However, for recent Polish immigrants the saloon had more positive functions. Historians studying other urban areas note how Protestant reformers' preoccupation with closing down these spaces flew in the face of ethnic Catholic workers' cultural norms. Most immigrants saw these reforms masking an "ethnic insult" leading them to actively evade temperance laws.[80] Saloons were sites of an evening of moderate drinking and socializing for Italian, Polish, Hungarian, and Croatian immigrants in Wheeling's factory districts. For new migrants to the city, the saloons served as informal employment bureaus advising immigrants on how to bribe factory foreman to get an unskilled position. During hard times, the foreign-owned saloon could provide aid and assistance for unemployed workers and even a "free lunch." The common prices of a nickel for a drink and lunch and a dime for a fill of a "growler" pail and meal were common. John Ramsky opened his establishment in 1893 with a "grand free lunch." Conrad Utermoffen's saloon at the corner of Thirty-Sixth and Wood Streets, near the Hobbs, Brockunier Glass Works, served a free lunch every day from nine to twelve in the morning. These free meals were sorely missed during periods of long unemployment, such as during the 1907–1908 recession.[81]

In South Wheeling and Benwood, saloons were as varied as their clientele, and the two main types of saloons were "universals" and "ethnocentric" saloons. The first were run by Irish and German saloonkeepers catering to a wide immigrant clientele. These "universals" were usually located near factories and transportation hubs. Examples included the Last Chance Saloon near the mouth of Boggs Run adjacent to the Benwood steel mills and even the La Belle Saloon at Thirty-First Street just across the street from the gate of the La Belle nail and tinplate works.[82] Second was the neighborhood "ethnocentric" saloon. These were often run by Germans, Poles, Italians, Croats, and Czechs and often found in the center of ethnic neighborhoods and near Catholic parishes.

Two examples highlight the ethnocentric saloon's relation to other ethnic spaces. Julius Lohse, a German dealer in imported and domestic wines and liquors, operated an ethnic neighborhood saloon at 2145 Market Street. This location was ideally situated in the middle of the German neighborhood near the Centre Market House. His saloon was located on the same block as Menkellmeyer's Drug Store and St. Alphonsus Catholic Church along with a variety of German-run candy stores, livery stables, grocers, druggists, meat dealers, and cigar stores.[83] A similar pattern of ethnic saloons developed in Polish South Wheeling. By 1905, there were several Polish-run neighborhood saloons: one run by Paul Rudzinski at 4526 Jacob Street and another at John Scherwinski's place at 4504 Jacob Street were close to St. Ladislaus Catholic Church at Forty-Fifth and Eoff Streets. Immigrant saloonkeepers often had trouble maintaining their business. Several years later, John Przelenski took over Scherwinski's saloon space. Both Polish saloonkeepers maintained neighborhood saloons until the enactment of statewide prohibition in 1914.[84]

The saloon underwent a significant change during the 1890s. In Wheeling and throughout industrial America, the older neighborhood saloons run initially by lower-middle-class Irish and German immigrants became less independent. Rapid industrialization and the growing separation of work and leisure time led to the growing commercialization of saloons.[85] Beginning in the 1890s, the saloon business became more difficult to enter because of the high price of liquor licenses and the cost of beer. At the same time, Wheeling's brewing businesses grew through consolidations to become one of the city's most prolific industries. Henry Schmulbach (1844–1915) was Wheeling's premier brewer. His dominating style, command over much of the city's brewery business, membership with the Board of Public Works throughout the late nineteenth and early twentieth centuries, and controlling interest in a local empire of street railways, bridges, and the telephone company earned him a role as a political boss. Reformers dubbed his control "Schmulbachism," a system of machine politics tied to the saloons but also linked to gambling houses and prostitution.[86]

The brewers and neighborhood saloons provided a friendly environment for working men to relax, have a cheap beer, and even enjoy public amusement. Mozart Park, opened in 1893 by Schmulbach, provided the most affordable leisure for South Wheeling's immigrants. Competing with Anton Reymann's Wheeling Park, Schmulbach catered to workers by providing cheap amusements and easy access via an incline railway. There was a dance hall capable of holding five thousand people, a roller coaster, casino, bowling alley, outdoor stage, bicycle track, and concession stands to sell large mugs of Schmulbach beer for five cents and large kaiser-roll sandwiches also for five cents. The park hosted German singing societies, vaudeville shows, a parachute jump, and a zoo.[87]

Wheeling's saloons were often subsidized by one of the city's largest brewers. Even though expensive liquor licenses made it increasingly difficult to operate, many saloonkeepers took advantage of the "tied-house" system. After making an arrangement with one of the breweries, the brewer contributed to the rent and license fee and sometimes supplied the bar fixtures and artwork. In exchange, the saloonkeeper agreed to sell no other brand of beer and reimbursed the brewer by having to pay a special tax added to each barrel of beer. This created a reciprocal relationship, and brewers often assisted with fighting city council's attack on the saloons.[88]

The brewers' power was seen in the battles over liquor license renewals. For years the state legislature dictated highly priced licenses; however, city council often lowered the fees or issued tax credits. Because of the brewers' influence on city council members, in 1905 the Reymann and Schmulbach Breweries saw their average taxes cut by about five hundred to six hundred dollars a year. This support also helped immigrant "coffeehouse" owners get liquor licenses. In 1903, council approved 120 such licenses including "coffeehouses" and social halls run by Polish and Greek immigrants.[89] Dry advocates criticized this corrupting influence. In 1900, several saloonkeepers forced to explain their "reputation" were caught trying to bribe city officials for up to five hundred dollars each.[90]

By assisting some working-class Polish and other new immigrants' move up the social ladder, these questionable relationships with the brewers only added fuel to the criticisms of progressive reformers. Throughout industrial America, middle-class professionals and religious leaders in reform groups like the Committee of One Hundred in Wheeling argued a group of vested interests were corrupting local politics. New York City's Committee of Fourteen, formed in 1905 with the help of the Anti-Saloon League, likewise collected data on saloons, called for stricter licensing, and pressured mayors to take tough action. For these groups, rather than providing efficient city services in an equitable manner, a small group of wealthy brewers ran a system that maintained urban blights like the saloon.[91]

The Committee of One Hundred, frustrated by city council intransigence, endorsed George Laughlin's Liquor Bill in January 1901. This bill would have placed the liquor license renewal in the hands of a circuit court judge preempting the city council. The city brewers, wholesale liquor dealers, and saloonkeepers fought the bill by starting a "petition against it in the saloons, the consideration for signing being a free drink." The bill failed, and things continued as usual. In the spring of 1902, against Mayor Sweeney's ordinance that all license applicants must have an individual hearing, council overrode him and approved all the liquor licenses en masse. This led to the largest number of licenses ever issued in Ohio County—340.[92]

Finally, the anti-saloon forces urged strict enforcement of the Sunday selling ordinance. Beginning in the 1890s, police constantly harassed violators. Most of the saloons targeted were located in South Wheeling and were run by immigrants or catered exclusively to working-class immigrants. Some saloonkeepers found themselves indicted numerous times. Eberhard Hofreuter's saloon at 3501 Jacob Street was charged with Sunday selling an amazing twenty-five times from 1895 to 1902. They also went after saloons that acted as halls for local labor unions such as L. C. Driehorst's saloon at 4421 Jacob Street. John Przelenski, who ran a saloon in the heart of Polonia at 4504 Jacob Street, received five indictments in 1901 and 1902 alone.[93] The overt targeting of ethnic working-class social spaces only infuriated immigrants. The anti-vice crusades set a precedent of reformers and government agents investigating the working-class districts of the city, and this surveillance would continue during the anti-immigrant fears of World War I and the Red Scare and the enforcement of statewide and later federal prohibition.[94]

Reformers attacked the perceived rowdy and violent character of saloons. With the closeness of tenement houses, saloons, and the steel mills in Benwood, shootings were common. Waso Linewitcj learned this the hard way as he returned from work at the National Tube Company. Upon arriving at the appropriately titled Last Chance Saloon, Waso was shot at from the hillside near Boggs Run. He was lucky in just being hit in the hand.[95] Stories of "Hunkies" wreaking havoc in local saloons catered to the newspapers' native-born audiences.[96] In crowded, dirty, industrial neighborhoods, the availability of beer seemed to confirm the saloon's negative effects on immigrant families. However, this hid the nature of the city government's collusion in "regulating" saloons and prostitution houses. Providing tax revenues, while not improving sanitation, the politics of vice exacerbated the struggles that new Polish immigrants faced upon arriving in Wheeling. With this vice district and saloon traffic heaviest south of Wheeling Creek, immigrants were unwillingly included as part of the crime problem, which only served to neglect the dire living conditions they experienced.

Street Fighting and Immigrant Turf Battles

Living in dangerous and often environmentally hazardous neighborhoods fostered ethnic tensions in South Wheeling and Benwood. Frustrated by the lack of services, low wages, and poor working conditions led some working-class immigrants to fight their neighbors. Poles encountered public (i.e., streets) and private spaces (i.e., social clubs and saloons) with other ethnic groups. These interactions most often led to crime and street fighting.

Most engagements occurred at boundaries between immigrant neighborhoods or within multiethnic areas. By the 1910s, Poles settling along with Syrians and Greeks working in the nearby steel mills and stamping factory lived in a region from Twenty-Third to Twenty-Seventh Streets associated with vice and gambling. Those in the "Greek colony" often bore the brunt of this cultural association with "organized crime." The police targeted the Greek coffeehouse district arresting those caught playing card games and betting on sporting contests.[97] Many ridiculed the rows among the Greeks. In one vivid encounter titled "When Greek Meets Greek," a reporter replayed a battle between warring Greeks in the Sixth Ward, highlighting their perceived riotous tendencies: "The fight was in the Greek colony in Alley B below Twenty-fifth street [sic]. Several of the sons of Sparta were engaged in a game of cards, when one accused another of cheating. Then the war commenced. Bottles, chairs and other implements were thrown promiscuously around, and a keg of salted fish that was in the room was overturned adding zest to the melee."[98]

After 1900, the migration of newer immigrants into older Irish and German neighborhoods made them a center of gang activity. Rival urban street gangs fought to maintain their own ethnic turf through intimidation and violence. The Irish "Dirty Dozens" gang of Goosetown often crossed over into the Fifth and Sixth Wards to attack Italians. In South Wheeling, gang activity was even more pronounced. The Dirty Dozens' archrivals were the "Fightin' Irish" and the "Howleytown Gang." They clashed with the Syrians, Greeks, and Italians between Twentieth and Twenty-Seventh Streets near the Belmont Mill and the Centre Market House. To the south, gangs clashed with the established Polish neighborhood. They even fought with the African American community between Twenty-Ninth and Thirty-Third Streets, which saw black migrants arriving during World War I to work for the foundry and B&O in South Wheeling.[99]

All of this interaction made the Sixth Ward region from Twenty-Third to Twenty-Seventh Streets and the industrial district from Twenty-Ninth to Thirty-Seventh Streets a "rowdy" stretch. Irish "street toughs" patrolled "about that end of town doing as they pleased," accosting many new immigrants taking a stroll through the neighborhood or on their way to work. Young Irish and Polish "yeggs" mugged workers for their paychecks and stole women's purses in South Wheeling's factory district, especially near the Twenty-Ninth Street streetcar interchange.[100]

Newer immigrants living in crowded neighborhoods filled weekly court dockets. Most of these foreign-born workers fought at the boundaries between ethnic neighborhood turfs. For example, Polish immigrant John Majesky of the "Polish colony" at Forty-Fifth Street was arrested for a "cutting affray" with two Russians near the Forty-Eighth Street boundary with Benwood. Because there was no discernible physical boundary, Forty-Eighth Street became a contentious site. The start of World War I increased violence between immigrant groups. By the fall of 1915, frequent street fights occurred on the imaginary boundary often "over bitterness between the Austrians and the Russians."[101] One example was an attempted robbery and murder of Croat Mike Kostolich a week before Christmas 1915. Operating a small confectionery near Forty-Eighth Street and being a community leader during the floods and frequent unemployment of the period, he was killed by two German men living in a nearby boardinghouse.[102]

Frustrations over dire working and living conditions merged with resentment against the racial epithets applied to new immigrants. James Barrett and David Roediger have argued that terms like "Hunky" and "Polander" were applied by the public and factory managers to those new immigrants laboring in the blast furnaces and mills. "Hunky," a corruption of Hungarian, became a pan-Slavic slur applied indiscriminately to all eastern European immigrants. As a result of the constant workplace dangers, and ridicule from native-born workers and foremen, Slavic immigrants developed a defensive attitude.[103] Management used their own anti-immigrant viewpoints to justify why certain ethnic groups worked in specific trades. The blast furnaces in steel mills were staffed by Slovak, Hungarian, Polish, and Croatian laborers, who worked according to one investigator in jobs that were "too damn dirty and too damn hot for a white man." These practices also worked to segregate workers on the shop floor to prevent labor solidarity.[104]

Coverage of the Polish immigrant "colony" in the press magnified these racially "in-between" classifications. These newspaper accounts of Wheeling's Poles were crucial in shaping a largely negative perception of the ethnic community as a whole at the turn of the century. Some stories stressed "Polanders'" docility at times, while others emphasized their aggressive tendencies when having "a warm old time" in odd disturbances in South Wheeling and Benwood. In one example, several "Hunkies" got on the "outside of two or three quarts of tangle foot" and had a wild time in their boardinghouse near Forty-Fifth Street. After hours of the group's raucous laughing, the police arrived whereupon the "Hunkies" threw a lamp and some furniture from the window before being taken downtown. Sometimes Polish immigrants engaged in attacks among each other. One big fight near Boggs Run put one man "out of business." It appeared that as the men were walking home, for no reason, "they began pelting each other with stones." The wounded man was hit by what the reporter called vividly "a well directed stone thrown by a husky son of Kosciusko." This description highlighted several perceived stereotypes of the Poles—their propensity for aggression and their large, husky appearance. These unsavory views of Polish immigrants explain, in part, why the Polish community was rather insular at this time and focused on carving out a distinctive space for themselves, away from such prejudice, which was centered around the Polish parish.[105]

A propensity for fighting was also applied to the Poles' most numerous neighbors, the Croats. They predominated in unskilled jobs at the Wheeling steel mills and coal mines competing directly with Polish immigrants for jobs. This competition naturally carried over to the neighborhoods. In what one reporter dubbed a "free for all fight among the Croatians," a riotous mob wielding clubs, stones, and even pistols led Benwood police to make a round of all the foreign saloons and boardinghouses.[106] However, immigrants could unite against overbearing police activity. In one incident the police officer patrolling the Riverside Works arrested "two Polanders for attempting to create a disturbance." As the officer took the Poles to the lockup, "a horde of foreigners swept down upon him, threatening, gesticulating wildly and flourishing clubs" including fifteen to twenty Croats, "Polanders," other Slavs, and Hungarians. The "unsettled state of affairs" led officers to continue to monitor the "foreign colony."[107]

Tensions ran high as well during immigrant weddings. After weddings at the local parish, Poles would return to a large social hall or saloon for the reception. The presence of such a large amount of drinking and merriment often led to fighting. Mike Koloski, a coal miner, "out of the largeness of his heart donated his home" for a Polish couple's ceremony. However, the guests enjoyed the "booze and hilarity" so much that they began destroying Mike's fine chinaware. After going after a "strapping big Polander," Mike went to jail after he missed and hit the man's wife with a glass pitcher.[108] Even more dangerous were fights when the groom's countrymen tried to kiss his young bride. During Antonio Lonstack's wedding near the Hitchman row houses, a group of foreign miners got into a melee after hours of heavy drinking, celebrating, dancing, and singing when one man kissed Lonstack's new wife. After some time, the entire street was full of men fighting to the point that the "street was covered with blood."[109]

Even with all the negative press perceptions, there were supporters of the immigrant working class. In a negative rebuke of South Wheeling, the *Wheeling Register* chided: "The numerous bloody brawls of foreigners in this vicinity are periodical reminders of the undesirable character of this class." Coming to the defense of the "abused foreigner" was Fr. John W. Werninger of St. John's Catholic Parish in Benwood. Werninger criticized the press for never living among the immigrants and concluded that "when a number of violations of the law are chronicled against them, you draw the conclusion that all are disturbers of the peace." He spoke of the thousands of Hungarians, Croats, Slavs, Czechs, Poles, and Italians living in South Wheeling and Benwood as "industrious" people. As one living "in the midst of them, [who saw] them every day upon the streets," he deemed them respectable people. Even though Father Werninger admitted, as Catholic immigrants, "few are burning and shining lights," the area's Slavic immigrants were due respect. Werninger placed most the blame on the saloons as the cause of the many brawls in South Wheeling "fomented by the greed of liquor sellers."[110]

Conclusion

Father Werninger's editorial was not unusual for the time. Although divided by ethnicity, he and other Irish and German Catholic leaders heartily defended their immigrant parishioners because of their shared Catholic heritage. Industrialization drastically increased Wheeling's Catholic working-class population. As immigrants struggled to find ways to respond to the trials of industrial life, they found an ally in the Diocese of Wheeling-Charleston. By 1900, the arrival of many former peasants from southern and eastern Europe gave the Catholic Church more social and political influence but also sparked debates over whether these "new immigrants" would worship in Irish- and German-dominated territorial parishes throughout the city or in newly created "national parishes" seeking to maintain old-world traditions.

CHAPTER 3

The Heart of the Community: Polish Catholics at St. Ladislaus Parish, 1890–1917

Caroline Lakomy's best memories of life in South Wheeling came from the functions associated with St. Ladislaus Parish. In much the same way that the Polish village revolved around seasonal Catholic holidays, South Wheeling's cultural climate reflected the social and cultural traditions of its largest ethnic group. Prior to Lent, the Poles held a renowned three-day festival, the Paczki Ball. From Sunday through Tuesday, the ladies of the St. Hedwig's Society and the Rosary Society made the traditional pre-Lenten feast while, for three successive nights, dances were held in the St. Ladislaus school auditorium. Immigrant parents would teach their children the polka but also the livelier oberek. Decades later Mary Martinkosky could vividly recall the pomp that occurred each May with the annual May processions as the local children marched throughout Polonia in the traditional Polish garb. She also could recall the solemnity of the Polish mass and the veneration of the Black Madonna, a revered icon of the Virgin Mary dating back centuries that is located in Częstochowa, Poland, as crucial aspects within traditional religious devotionalism. Mary Pietras Robbins and Rebecca McGuire also reminisced about the significance of religious holidays for Polish American children. No matter the occasion, South Wheeling's Poles held a strong attachment to their Catholic religiosity.[1]

Experiencing what historian Robert Orsi refers to as "popular lived religion," these immigrants found solace at mass on Sundays but also during their festival times. When walking down any of these streets, observers seemed transported to a Polish village in Europe with the air full of smells of native foods such as cabbage dishes, kielbasa, and of course fresh-cooked pierogies. During the Lenten season, visitors saw scores of Catholic immigrants marching in processions re-creating home traditions from as far back as the sixteenth century. These Poles relived part of a cultural past in their new homes. These hard-pressed workers recast their reality within a religious context with celebrations in honor of the Holy Mother of Częstochowa and their patron St.

Ladislaus, the minister of the Poles' social welfare and architect of national parishes.²

This chapter examines how the first generation of Polish immigrants created their own distinctive cultural and religious identity in South Wheeling. Father Emil Musial led the development of an inward-looking Polish community, which possessed the necessary social, financial, and cultural institutions to survive on its own. By 1917, St. Ladislaus was the epicenter of a re-created and unified Polish community, or Polonia. Musial maintained this close-knit community by uniting the German, Russian, and Austrian Poles together around a shared Polish Catholic nationalism, merging popular religion with a structured Polish ethnic education.

This chapter will address two aspects of the growth of ethnic communities. First, how did the process of creating a community bring all of its various groups together? As noted by Dominic Pacyga, Chicago Polish immigrants initially in their "communal response" forged small, inward-looking communities that were distinctively Polish.³ This chapter will examine three important aspects of this development: the building of the church and hiring of Father Musial, the purchase of the Polish Hall, and the building and staffing of a school. Second, this chapter will consider the benefits and drawbacks of this process. Musial's plan succeeded in creating a strong, thriving ethnic community, but it also isolated the Poles. This process created intense ethnic rivalries, especially with the Irish and Germans in the Wheeling diocese. Constant battles occurred between Father Musial and Bishop Patrick Donahue over allocating resources to build a Polonia in South Wheeling. Musial and the Polish community's efforts to foster a distinctively Polish parish was a common goal of many ethnic parish priests during this era. In larger cities in particular, they debated about the power and influence of Irish and German Catholics over dioceses. Irish American Catholic leaders wanted to help the church respond to growing fears about secularism and modernity. Their central goal was to promote Americanization through English language instruction, more uniform religious practices and devotions, and constructing territorial parishes that would bring together multiple ethnic groups and thus help unify Catholic immigrants. As seen in Wheeling, this process often did not go as planned with continued demands for ethnic, national parishes.⁴ The process of community formation also made more noticeable class divisions that already existed among the Polish people. South Wheeling's Polonia was majority working class, but the need to create an inward-looking community required the skills and services of an ethnic small-business class who benefited materially from the growth of St. Ladislaus and its institutions.

Father Musial and St. Ladislaus Church

In the urban north, Catholicism and its "parish boundaries" form the long-term attachment of ethnic groups to their communities. A shared sense of collective ownership fosters a genuine and vigorous support for community cohesiveness.[5] Wheeling novelist Keith Maillard, who grew up in the 1960s, sheds light on these topics while also providing a vivid physical description of Polish life in South Wheeling. Maillard's narrator, army veteran Jimmy Koprowski, describes the timeless feeling of his childhood community: "Our neighborhood is a narrow strip from 43rd Street down to 48th Street where Millwood [Benwood] starts. One set of railroad tracks runs along the river, and then there's three Streets and another set of railroad tracks and, bang, you're slapped up against the side of the Hill. That's South Raysburg [South Wheeling]. We just called it Polish Town, but the old Folks called it *Stanisławówo*, you know, after the church, and they got that right because St. Stanislaus was pretty much the center of everything."[6]

The increasing numbers and varied backgrounds of Polish immigrants in South Wheeling made it necessary to establish a strong ethnic community to meet their pressing interests. The Diocese of Wheeling-Charleston saw the need to construct a Polish parish by the 1890s with the Poles spread out over South Wheeling, Benwood, and elsewhere. Many Poles from the Prussian partition began arriving around 1880. As a result, they migrated toward the center of Wheeling in the vicinity of St. Alphonsus German Catholic Church.[7] Despite the stigma of worshipping in services with German-language homilies and a culture that politically dominated their homeland, the small number of Poles pressed on through the 1880s.

By the early 1890s, Polish immigration to Wheeling swelled to such a point that the Poles pressed for their own ethnic church. The process of ethnic parish construction reflects the direct actions of immigrant laypeople. Unlike in Europe, where the state often subsidized churches, American parishes often faced financial troubles since most of their funding derived from lay initiative and members' contributions. For most immigrants the process of coming together collectively to build the church was their first religious action as a community in America.[8] The process usually included the formation of religious societies for the men and sodalities for the women, which along with honoring patron saints from the home country reflected a strong ethnic religiosity.

While many attended St. Alphonsus uptown, other Wheeling Poles sought spiritual assistance from Immaculate Conception Church located on

Thirty-Sixth Street. As the Polish began congregating near the Benwood steel mills in South Wheeling, the largely Irish Catholic parish began holding regular missions for the Polish population. Father Joseph Mullen brought in a Polish priest to minister to the Polish Catholics during the Lenten season and then on a regular basis. This priest, Fr. Ladislaus Miskiewicz from St. Adelbert's Parish on Pittsburgh's South Side, started ministering to the Poles in the early 1890s. In 1892, a St. Stanislaus Society observed the feast of St. Stanislaus in early July, which was hosted at Immaculate Conception. Without a Polish national parish of their own, the St. Stanislaus Society allowed Polish immigrants to celebrate their Polish Catholic religious practices and, like other fraternal societies, helped to provide practical assistance for adjustment to life in the United States. The society also worked to organize efforts to raise money to get a Polish church constructed. Father Mullen advised the Poles to continue forming the necessary ethnic societies to attract assistance from first Bishop John Kain (1874–1894) and then Bishop Patrick Donahue (1894–1922). Thirty men formed the St. Ladislaus Society, while the women later formed as the St. Hedwig's Society.[9] By 1896, Father Miskiewicz still conducted missions for the Polish and Slavic populations, which had grown to the point that it would not "be many days before the congregation [would] be compelled to secure the services of a Polish priest." By 1901, the St. Stanislaus Society acquired title to three lots on the southeast corner of Forty-Fifth and Eoff Streets measuring seventy-five feet long and one hundred feet deep and costing $1,900. The *Church Calendar* praised the Wheeling Poles as "a thrifty and industrious people" who had "been very loyal" to achieve their own community.[10]

Bishop Patrick Donahue also played an important role in St. Ladislaus's development. During his tenure, Donahue focused on building parishes for the rapidly expanding Catholic immigrant population in the state, including the Polish community in South Wheeling. However, he also began his service as the bishop of Wheeling in 1894 at a time when the state and nation suffered from anti-Catholic nativism.[11] Donahue fought vigorously against the American Protective Association (APA), the leading national anti-immigrant group of the 1890s, and its attacks on immigrants across West Virginia. Nativists criticized the growing number of immigrants from eastern and southern Europe and the perceived undemocratic influences of the Roman Catholic Church. Donahue used his influence to gain concessions from state politicians. Complaining that some schools disseminated nativist literature, Donahue convinced Democratic Governor William MacCorkle to reject any "criticism of the Catholic religion" and to order "that the dissemination of any such intolerant doctrine should [not] be tolerated in any institution of the state."[12]

To blunt the influence of the nativists, Donahue acted as an influential adviser for politicians in both major political parties. He cultivated a close friendship in the Republican Party with U.S. Senator Stephen B. Elkins, who ensured that state Republicans did "not sympathize in any way with the A.P.A. movement." Elkins hoped to secure the Republican victories in 1896 and even used Donahue to appeal to Catholic voters.[13] Likewise, the Democratic Party hoped to use Donahue to their electoral advantage. In the 1906 midterms, state Democratic Party Chairman John T. McGraw urged Donahue to "get the Catholic vote" in Harrison, Lewis, and Marshall Counties for the party's congressional candidate. For Catholics tending to vote Republican, McGraw argued that "a word in the right channel from you" would secure their switch to the Democrats.[14] Donahue, in turn, espoused the diocese's contributions in the monthly *Church Calendar*, the state Catholic newspaper, which countered the secularism of the local papers, attacked socialism, and fostered the "nourishment of the soul."[15]

Disputes between Polish Catholic clergy and the largely Irish American-led hierarchy at the turn of the twentieth century were also a concern for Donahue. In November 1901, he received a circular notice from the Executive Committee of the Polish Catholic Congress. Polish priests had met in Buffalo, New York, in 1899 and 1901 to urge the U.S. Catholic hierarchy to help in halting the growth of Polish independent churches, which declared full freedom from ecclesiastical authority. The circular addressed the national dilemma caused by these schismatic Polish clergy, who argued that the Roman Catholic archbishops and bishops of America were taking virtually no action to improve the growing Polish population's economic position or meet the group's spiritual needs. Most prominent in this movement was Fr. Francis Hodur, who was a well-known priest among Polish anthracite coal miners in Scranton, Pennsylvania. His disputes with Irish American Catholic leaders led to a schism and the creation of the Polish National Catholic Church in 1897, which actively competed with the Roman Catholic Church in larger Polish ethnic communities in America. This independent movement criticized a church that had not one Polish bishop. The Polish Catholic Congress asserted that "the Irish and German Bishops object to it, because they consider[ed] the Poles unfit for such dignity." This schism was a problem for Donahue since he was an Irish Catholic bishop. While the committee did not advocate selecting a Polish bishop, they suggested the hiring of more ethnic Polish priests, the formation of more Polish societies and sodalities, and building more Polish ethnic parishes.[16]

Because of lay initiative and pressure from broader church issues, Bishop Donahue supported the construction of a Polish church and initiated a search for a youthful and energetic Polish leader. Like any new church, regardless of faith tradition, there are many difficulties and snares that arise along the way. Budding religious bodies require a clergyman who can guide the new church and settle any disputes. These disagreements may be between the bishop and the parishioners or the common conflict between various factions within the parish.[17] As a result, an intense search process of the various seminaries, particularly in the Midwest, resulted in Donahue selecting young, twenty-seven-year-old Emil Musial.[18]

For Wheeling's Poles, Father Musial was the heart and soul of their community at St. Ladislaus. Born in Zaborze, German Silesia, on October 3, 1873, Musial came with an "inborn stubborn persistence and set purpose of mind."[19] At the time of his Diamond Jubilee, celebrating his fifty years of continuous service at St. Ladislaus, Musial described how he built the church by the sweat of his brow along with many others. He reminisced about the community's vibrancy and lamented that the "old family ties that once held people together have disappeared and instead [they were] living as individualists." For many of the first generation, Musial's fears of subsequent generations of Polish Americans losing their cultural and ethnic heritage were very relevant.[20]

Keith Maillard's novel also gives a personal and amusing biographical sketch of Musial. Gleaned from personal knowledge of Musial, Maillard's narrator Jimmy recalls:

> Our priest was old Father Joe Stawecki [Emil Musial]. He was a little guy with a face like a bulldog, and he used to brag that he could say mass faster than any priest in the Ohio Valley, and he wasn't kidding—in and out of there in twenty minutes flat. He'd get cranked up, he'd be going faster than a hillbilly auctioneer.... You go make your confession to him, same thing—in and out of there, bingo, five minutes tops.... He preached short and sweet too, all in Polish, and he'd get real personal sometimes. "Hey, I heard Stas Rzeszuski's been stepping out on his wife again. He better stop that." No parish priest today could get away with that.[21]

Father Musial emerges as a parish priest intimately connected to his parishioners with a personality that could be at times cajoling and also humorous. He was the perfect type of priest to exert the strength and fortitude needed to start and lead a primarily working-class congregation.

Maillard's account also suggests a man whose understanding of his place in life developed out of his experiences in Europe. A Polish-language history from 1926 explains how one aspect of Musial's character—his toughness—was developed. As a young man still learning to be a priest, he had worked as a private tutor in Prussia. However, because of so much constant traveling, doctors discovered that his blood was very diluted, causing him to suffer from weakness. With the help of a German doctor, a treatment was devised that more than likely toughened young Musial. To thicken his blood, doctors tied him to a tree or column three times a day and then poured near-frozen water over him for a half hour at a time. This odd treatment must have worked because the history notes that he was made strong enough to "easily turn a mill."[22]

Born within the German partition of Poland, Musial hit several roadblocks as he tried to achieve his goals. Early on the Prussian school system, which often slighted young and intelligent Poles, hindered his academic progress. After beginning his preparatory studies in Krakow in the 1880s, Musial was drafted into the Prussian army in his late teens. As a true Pole, he was sickened by the possibility of serving the occupier and "predatory army" of his country and perhaps fighting against Polish rebels. As a result, Musial cast his eyes for the famed freedom he had heard of in the United States. In the middle of the night, he fled, leaving his family to seek a life doing "pastoral work." After going off to Torino to finish his philosophical and theological studies in the 1890s, he went in service of "Polish castaways" in need of a spiritual guide, and in 1900 Musial entered the SS. Cyril and Methodius Polish Seminary of Detroit.[23]

From the scant writings on Musial, a picture develops of him as a benevolent leader who overcame considerable odds to provide a church for Wheeling's Poles. However, this generalization blurs the true historical picture somewhat. While he showed great zeal upon arriving in 1901, Musial almost chose not to serve in Wheeling. In a long correspondence between Bishop Donahue and Emil Musial from the spring of 1901 through his appointment in November 1901, Musial shared his reservations. Writing from seminary, Musial expressed that he wanted to minister to the many Poles in Wheeling but that his only difficulty was that he did not speak English well enough. Then in June, while preparing for his exit examinations, he delayed going to Wheeling as he assisted the Detroit archdiocese with an outbreak of smallpox.[24]

Musial surprised Donahue on September 5, 1901, by informing the bishop that it would be "virtually impossible for me to labor as a priest in the diocese of Wheeling" since he learned in Baltimore that "the Poles are very much scattered in W.V. on which a polish [sic] priest is obliged to be always on missionary journey."[25] Even after being told he was misinformed about Wheeling's Poles, the disheartened Musial inquired whether Bishop Donahue would ever decide to set him free from the Wheeling diocese.[26] However, for what remains a mystery, Musial changed his mind, decided not to join the Baltimore diocese,

Fig. 3.1. Portrait—Father Emil Musial, ca. 1926. Courtesy of the Diocese of Wheeling-Charleston, Wheeling, WV.

followed his vow of obedience, and was ordained in Wheeling on Thanksgiving Day 1901. On August 2, 1902, Musial was on hand for the laying of the cornerstone of St. Ladislaus Church at Forty-Fifth and Eoff Streets in South Wheeling with exuberant processions taking place the entire day.[27]

Musial's appointment to the Diocese of Wheeling was mired in confusions developing between the chancellery in Wheeling and the Archdiocese of Baltimore. During the months leading up to his ordination in Wheeling, Musial was the focal point of a dispute between Bishop Donahue and Reverend Morys of St. Stanislaus Church in Baltimore. In mid-November 1901, Morys claimed that upon his last visit Musial personally saw the archbishop of Baltimore and that application procedures and acceptance were already under way.[28] Later, Morys seemed quite befuddled by the fact that Musial was somehow "tied" to the Wheeling diocese by a secret contract he signed in Wheeling. In September, Morys informed Donahue of Musial's acceptance to the Baltimore diocese. Morys obviously assumed that Musial would serve in the Baltimore diocese since he had discussed with Musial his possible role as a coeditor for a local parish weekly newspaper in Baltimore. Even so, Morys agreed to part with Musial on the condition that Donahue forward him the sixty dollars for payments that Morys had already given to Musial for training and expenses.[29]

While Musial decided against working in Baltimore, what remains uncertain is what changed his mind. Was he bargaining with both Wheeling and Baltimore to see which diocese would provide a better opportunity financially and for his ministry? Did he simply feel more needed in founding a new parish rather than working for an established Polish church? Or did Donahue, Weber, and the Wheeling diocese recognize Musial's future promise and actively work through the Detroit seminary to ensure his appointment? Donahue received a notice in 1900 of the schism created by the Polish Catholic Congress and its desire to have more ethnic Polish priests to minister to the steady arrival of Polish immigrants. According to the 1926 parish history, Musial's mocking colleagues argued that his life would be wasted "buried in the wild Virginia mountains." That still failed to dissuade him from ministering in Wheeling.[30]

Perhaps more important was Musial's training at the SS. Cyril and Methodius Seminary. Founded in Detroit in 1886 by Fr. Joseph Dabrowski, this seminary functioned as a primary bulwark against the full Americanization of the Polish ethnic clergy. It was one of the few schools of theology in America that actively promoted an ethnic education and the unity of Polish Catholicism with Polish nationalism.[31] Musial's success as a student led Father Dabrowski to hope he would remain as a professor to instruct other young Polish priests.[32] Musial's negative experiences in German Poland, his devout Catholicism, and his ethnic, nationalist training all shaped his personality and his understanding of what constituted a Polish national identity.

Emil Musial acted as an intermediary to assist in attracting Polish ethnic clergy to the Wheeling diocese. As the first Polish-appointed priest in West Virginia, Musial recruited other seminarians from SS. Cyril and Methodius. This process was a key extension of his ideology of fostering strong, inward-looking ethnic communities. By attracting young Polish clergymen sharing his ideological beliefs, Musial hoped to promote his goals on a diocesan level.

Musial was selective in choosing other Polish priests for the diocese. After recruiting several fellow seminarians, he and Bishop Donahue learned that these students had engaged in an "open rebellion against the authority of the Seminary."[33] They were among the thirty students who openly protested for the removal of the vice-rector of SS. Cyril and Methodius and threatened to use the newspapers if Dabrowski took no action. Viewing these men as poor stewards of Christ, Dabrowski removed them from his seminary. In January 1903, Donahue, with the tacit consent of Musial, accepted the resignation of the recruits because he wanted respectable young priests to serve the growing numbers of immigrants in his diocese. Musial likewise wanted Polish priests sharing his ideological views and willing to act properly so that their loyalty to their congregations would not be questioned by the Polish laity and the diocese.[34]

Following the removal of the Polish seminarians, Father Musial continued to attract Polish clergy to the diocese. In 1904, Dabrowski's successor praised the abilities and sensibilities of Master Leo Dzicek, who recently arrived in Wheeling to serve the diocese. Father Musial informed him of Dzicek's appointment, and he talked of his good, moral behavior as a young priest.[35] Over the years Musial assisted in attracting many more priests in line with his efforts to promote other Polish communities. As he became well known throughout the entire diocese, Musial achieved a position of authority in assisting not only the religious but also the social and political needs of Polish Catholic immigrants. As a member of Bishop Donahue's council and later serving under Bishop John Swint, Musial became an important Catholic figure.[36]

Musial's authority in the diocese and knack for often conflicting with the policies of the Irish hierarchy stemmed from his early activities in the Ohio Valley. While hired to serve as the parish priest at St. Ladislaus, analysis of his travels in his first decade in Wheeling show him serving a much more significant role. Musial was the first Polish priest stationed in West Virginia and the upper Ohio Valley. Therefore, he not only ministered to his own flock but also traveled around the region observing religious holidays, administering the sacraments, and officiating at weddings and funerals for any and all Polish immigrants. The constant traveling by both streetcar and the B&O railroad must have taken a toll emotionally and physically on Musial and confirmed what he thought in 1901 that any new Polish priest would be constantly on "missionary journey." In February 1906, Musial wrote the bishop asking for a "Central Passenger" ticket book or a note that would allow him reduced rates on the railroad.[37]

Musial spent much of the first decade of the twentieth century traveling. From his ordination in November 1901 till the opening of St. Ladislaus in February 1903, Musial served as an assistant to Fr. Joseph Mullen at Immaculate Conception caring for the many Poles attending there.[38] When finally built St. Ladislaus served all the Poles located in Wheeling, Benwood, and Fulton. Musial also received numerous calls for assistance to minister to the missions for Poles and even Ukrainians and Slovaks throughout the Ohio Valley. One way to track Musial's movements is through the parish's baptismal records. Because of their working-class status, most Poles outside of Wheeling could not afford the travel fare to go to St. Ladislaus to have a child christened. As a result, Musial often took a week or two to travel the region and baptize many Polish babies. Table 3.1 shows some of the locations of these baptisms.

While most of his traveling was in the adjacent communities in Marshall and Ohio Counties, he also traveled extensively in Ohio, primarily to the mill towns and smaller coal mining camps. For example, after 1904 Musial traveled to the Polish enclaves in Neffs and Lansing, Ohio, where many Slavic coal miners worked. After 1907, he traveled to even smaller mining camps in places like Short Creek, Glens Run, Pipe Creek, Rayland, and Rush Run.[39]

Musial's duties expanded as did industry in the upper Ohio Valley. After 1900, Polish immigrants came to work in steel mills outside of Wheeling clustering in Steubenville and Martins Ferry, Ohio, and Weirton, West Virginia. Others found work as unskilled workers in the booming pottery factories of Chester and New Cumberland. Musial found hundreds of mostly unmarried Polish and Slavic men living in a "secluded neighborhood" on a "lofty ridge" two miles from New Cumberland. The men earned $1.50 a day, with 50 cents deducted for boarding in a makeshift "barracks." Bishop Donahue appointed Rev. Julius Javorek to minister to the Poles in a new mission. This assistance allowed Father Musial to focus his attention to community building in the core of Polonia in Wheeling.[40]

However, his overextended schedule often meant that Musial upset other priests. A fine example of the animosity toward his inability to be in all places at once was with Fr. William Sauer of the Church of the Sacred Heart in Chester, West Virginia. His parish was located near the growing Polish enclave

Table 3.1. Baptisms by Father Musial and Assistant Pastors from St. Ladislaus, 1901–1910

City	1901-2	1903	1904	1905	1906	1907	1908	1909	1910
Wheeling	25	47	72	89	82	88	90	98	111
Benwood	0	3	15	34	26	49	21	24	13
McMechen	0	3	3	7	3	8	6	3	5
Moundsville	0	0	0	0	1	0	3	3	3
Bellaire, OH	0	2	1	0	0	0	5	9	5
Martins Ferry, OH	1	0	0	0	0	2	1	4	2
Yorkville, OH	0	3	5	3	3	3	4	1	3

Source: St. Ladislaus, Baptismal Records, December 22, 1901, to September 2, 1923, Microfilm Roll 10, DWC.

working at the pottery factories and steel mills in Hancock County. Unable to properly minister to them, Father Sauer consistently requested Father Musial's assistance. From 1904 to 1907, Sauer grew increasingly angry with Musial and all Polish priests in numerous letters to Chancellor Edward Weber. When Lent and Easter season came, Sauer informed the bishop that "Rev. E. Musial of Wheeling promised to come by last Christmas but did not come. He disappointed both the Poles and myself."[41] In addition, he noted the "Poles all work in the mill and could not very well get off during the week." By Easter 1906, Sauer again said Polish steelworkers had "to stay up all night to go to Communion after one oclock [sic] in the morning. Many go to work at four O'Clock in the morning and these poor fellows complained that it was too hard for them to stay up all night and work hard the next day."[42] Without regular sacraments, these Poles could fall to secular temptations. Sauer apparently did not think it important that "Father Musial was to do a funeral at Clarksburg the day before" coming to Chester.[43] By April 1907, Sauer was so fed up trying to rely on Polish priests that he started learning Polish but noted sarcastically that "I could learn the hogs' language about as soon as the Polish."[44]

Unlike his absences that upset Father Sauer, Musial played a greater role in the development of the Sacred Heart of Mary Polish Church in Weirton. With the growing number of Polish immigrants flocking to this new industrial city after 1909, Weirton's Poles required an ethnic priest who could appreciate their culture and language. After several other priests, Donahue appointed Fr. Andrew Wilczek on October 15, 1916, to lead them in erecting a church. On October 24, 1920, Emil Musial served as celebrant and assisted Donahue in consecrating another addition to the Polish faith in the Northern Panhandle.[45]

Once committed to Wheeling, Musial and his Polish laity embarked on a two-decade-long campaign to forge a strong center for the Polish Catholics. Over the years, the parish allowed them to meet their spiritual and economic needs but also provided a place to discuss their homeland, politics, and labor activities. During an interview in the 1950s, Musial remembered how his community around 1900 only numbered about eighty families living between Forty-Third and Forty-Eighth Streets in South Wheeling.[46] With such a small support base, one wonders how the construction of the church ever got off the ground. Part of it was the determination of the local Polish ethnic working class. However, much credit goes to Father Musial, who put in long hours and sweat, which consequently earned him the gratitude of not only the Poles but many city officials and city organizations. Parish histories note how he helped organize not only Polish and Catholic drives for moral issues but also citywide religious groups that held a wide influence in Wheeling.[47] Moreover, Musial was adept at avoiding the rivalries and conflicts that often afflicted ethnic parishes resulting from merging peoples of differing class and regional origins.[48] Musial appears to have experienced only minor conflicts of opinion with parishioners and was, for the most part, a beloved person.

Building the Parish

On February 22, 1903, the South Side witnessed the exuberant festivities that went along with the founding of a Catholic church. With a massive march starting at the Cathedral on Thirteenth Street and proceeding all the way to St. Ladislaus on Forty-Fifth Street, Wheeling witnessed a lively parade headed by Musial, followed by the St. Ladislaus and St. Stanislaus societies, the Knights of St. George, the Mullen and Parke Divisions of the Ancient Order of Hibernians, the Grand Opera House Band, the city's four Croatian societies, and ending with Bishop Donahue and the clergy. The ceremony also brought leading Polish clergymen from as far away as New York City and Providence, Rhode Island.[49] While a Polish celebration, the event also highlights how Musial was able to avoid ethnic conflict by bringing together different Catholic groups.

Father Musial's success and his parish's long devotion to him for sixty years stems from Musial putting the needs of the Poles in South Wheeling and elsewhere ahead of the Catholic Church in general. While he contributed necessary funds to the diocese for regular curia and special diocesan collections, he often ran afoul of the local diocese. Before the dedication in February 1903, Musial was struggling to complete the necessary building projects with limited funds. On December 31, 1902, with most of the building complete, the debts of the church were $13,402. Musial owed large sums of money to the South Wheeling Bank and the Fahey Brothers as well as to his own St. Ladislaus Society. Musial's list of debts also included two individuals, Vincent Ciak and Stanislaus Klos, who loaned him a total of $2,900 with interest.[50]

This sort of outside borrowing became characteristic of Musial's financial philosophy. Assistance from his laity and private institutions fostered a level of ownership, which tied the Polish Catholics intimately to their church. In 1994, an older Polish American parishioner spoke candidly on this relationship while angry over St. Ladislaus's proposed closure: "Everything belongs to the diocese. . . . We built it, yeah, our parents and all built this church, mortgaged houses and all to build this church, but it ain't ours, no way."[51] She was disappointed the diocese ignored this strong sense of collective ownership around their local Polish parish.

Musial's financial practices often exasperated diocesan leaders. Using some diocesan funds, in the spring of 1902 Musial contracted through Fahey Brothers for the principal ironwork and carpentry for all of the church's facade and set the price at $5,644.[52] By the fall Musial increased the church's overall price with his plans to add a tall steeple, but Donahue stipulated that he could only spend up to one thousand dollars.[53] Then during the Easter season of 1904, Chancellor Weber wrote to Musial requesting that he send his obligatory Good Friday collections as well as the interest on his loans.[54] These records are vital to understanding not only the financial difficulties of the church in its early years but also the things Musial saw as necessary for his parish.[55] Musial saw fit to stretch the money he collected and borrowed as far as possible to help create a church that was beautiful in appearance and effective in acting as a spiritual and community meeting place.

Musial made several other plans to expand his church's influence in South Wheeling. The first was a better parochial residence for himself located directly across the street from St. Ladislaus. This convenience eased his burden as a renter and gave him a larger residence where he could host parishioners.[56] He also hoped to expand the church's influence by expanding its parish school, which he led in the parish's basement with less-than-standard equipment.

In 1906, however, Musial delayed these plans until he paid off his growing debts. While exploring further purchases for the community around St. Ladislaus, Bishop Donahue finally addressed his spending habits. Expressing his position strongly, Donahue instructed Musial "it is my will that you borrow no more sums of money from parishioners or other people or from any private persons or banks or corporations of any kind." Although willing to help, the bishop wanted a detailed account of Musial's "indiscriminate" spending for 1905 and the interests and loans of all parties involved.[57] This letter illustrates the tensions between Musial and the diocese over his efforts to seek collateral from Poles and private financiers. Disputes over expenditures by ethnic, national parishes were not uncommon for the time. Bishops faced quarrels with German, Italian, French Canadian, and a variety of other immigrant groups. However, Polish parishes had a greater tendency for conflict with bishops and dioceses. Hoping to preserve the community's Polishness, Musial desired to build a strong economic base so that the church could function with almost complete self-sufficiency, even when it meant conflict with the bishop.[58]

Social Life of St. Ladislaus Church

As Musial's church gradually grew in numbers, St. Ladislaus also became the center for the social and cultural life of the surrounding area of the city. Sponsoring numerous religious societies and sodalities, these organizations added a Polish flavor to Wheeling's Catholic culture. Musial maintained Polish identity by having the mass said and many of the songs sung in Polish, and he worked at passing down various ethnic and cultural experiences at St. Ladislaus. Common events included the Polish Catholic processions, which became a fixture of the Wheeling cultural scene after the Polish community achieved a critical mass of people around 1900. Often starting around St. Ladislaus, processions webbed through the wider South Side neighborhood where other German, Ukrainian, and native-born residents lived. Over time Polish lay societies also marched in parades through downtown Wheeling (especially during World War I). Spotlighting the solidarity of the Polish community, while also speaking to the city's dominant German and Irish Catholic population, such processions were often the clearest way for the entire city to witness the unique religiosity of the ethnic parishes. These processions spoke their own language, creating a cultural production that could be passed down

Fig. 3.2. Interior view—St. Ladislaus Church, ca. 1950. Courtesy of the Diocese of Wheeling-Charleston, Wheeling, WV.

from year to year and highlighting how this public space throughout South Wheeling was crucial to the values and identity of the Polish Catholic community.[59] Delores Skrzypek recalled vividly how the first generation of Polish immigrants taught many of the children how to dance the polka bianca while wearing the native Polish garb. Another important annual event, especially for the children, was the May processions. Children joyously marched around the school and neighborhood in white dresses carrying flowers to crown a statue of the Virgin Mary and a May queen while celebrating the Lenten and spring seasons. Like the adult members of the community, these May processions also provided a public display of the Poles' religious-ethnic identity. While celebrating the coming of spring in the traditional European rite, May processions were often used as a way to teach children about moral purity and also the dangers of socialism.[60] The community came together and maintained religious customs involved in infant christening, marriage, and even funerals. No matter the occasion, these events always centered on St. Ladislaus.

One of the largest events for the Polish community were weddings, which helped tie together families and even united lovers separated by the migration process. A great example is the marriage of John and Katie Klocon at St. Ladislaus on May 6, 1905. The "pretty romance" extended over several years, and their courtship story "reads more like fiction than facts." First meeting in 1902 "among the hills in southern Austria," John was prevented from marrying his love. Emigrating from Galicia to Benwood for work, he spent the next three years "struggling as a common laborer in the mills to save a sufficient amount to bring his girl lover to this country." When able he wrote and gave her money and instructions on how to reach him. Making the entire journey alone and unable to speak English, she arrived to meet her lover. The romantic event led the "foreign colony to turn out in mass" to celebrate.[61]

After a wedding at St. Ladislaus and festive street processional, families and friends would return to the home of the couple and have a raucous celebration. According to one observer, "A Polish wedding is the signal among those of that nationality for prolonged jubilation, generally lasting two or three days." The party atmosphere was full of singing and dancing. In fact, "Without dancing a Polish wedding is not complete, and the assembled guests danced till they were exhausted only to renew it all again."[62] A native-born observer noted how participants were "whirling around with a quickness and gracefulness" foreign to outsiders. This resident was amazed at how they "jigged and waltzed, skipped and twirled . . . until one would imagine that the participants were machines in the hands of a skillful mechanic regulating his revelry apparatus." Some wedding receptions lasted as long as a week. While long wedding parties often led native-born residents to criticize them as primitive, these cultural events connected the Polish migrants with their homeland peasant traditions.[63]

The church's religious societies and sodalities proliferated with the growth of the church to assist in the moral and civic duties of the parishioners. As in many Catholic parishes at the time, these groups particularly gave the women in the parish a strong place of authority. Priests could provide spiritual guidance but needed the help of laypeople to raise funds, run societies, and organize parish events. Because of the rapid growth in the Catholic population, dioceses often relied on nuns and laypeople to manage parish and diocesan charities. Over time, the hierarchy and religious orders often sought to take back some control over these diocesan organizations, but laywomen still maintained a large amount of autonomy at the parish level.[64] A pamphlet celebrating St. Ladislaus's twenty-fifth anniversary lists prominent parishioners during the church's first generation; among the fifty-two people mentioned, twenty of them were women.[65] Women were crucial in managing the parish's female Catholic societies. The Women's Rosary for adults and the Blessed Virgin Mary's Sodality for young girls both provided moral uplift but also brought working women together for the social welfare of the Polish community. Since its inception one of the parish's largest events was the making of pierogies for the annual bazaar held to benefit the community and raise necessary funds for the parish's upkeep. As remembered by Jane Murray, these events led by the women of the St. Hedrick's Society were vital for women during the Lenten season and the Forty Hours Devotion fast times.[66]

The men and women of St. Ladislaus also promoted Polish Catholic community building outside Wheeling. On June 26, 1904, 150 men of St. Ladislaus traveled on a B&O train to Fairmont and then to Monongah. They marched in an ethnic processional with their own Polish band, joined by the band from the newly formed Stanislaus Kostka Parish. Along with the St. Ladislaus and St. Stanislaus societies, the Monongah and Wheeling Poles showed a strong regional level of Polish Catholic identity and ethnic solidarity. Even Bishop Donahue encouraged the Polish congregants' activity "while not in the least surrendering their own language, customs, and observances." The ladies of St. Ladislaus arrived in advance of the ceremony to assist with the preparation of the celebration and food.[67]

Many of these societies promoted social engagement, but the primary purpose was for spiritual uplift. Especially important were the young people's sodalities, which according to Leslie Tentler addressed issues surrounding what many parish priests at the time saw as a "sexual revolution." The Catholic Church condemned any form of birth control in the early twentieth century, and many priests stressed themes of purity in their homilies and during confession. St. John's in Benwood, the neighbor parish of St. Ladislaus, most directly addressed this issue by creating the St. Aloysius Abstinence Society in 1905. This society, along with that parish's Blessed Virgin Mary Sodality, sponsored many activities for teenagers such as bowling, roller skating, and dancing without the threat of "serious scandal."[68]

As St. Ladislaus grew in numbers and influence during the 1910s, many other organizations formed to unify the community religiously but also along ethnic and political lines. Musial was in the middle of these actions, which often involved the efforts to pay off the debts incurred in building St. Ladislaus. Church building caused financial difficulties for many Poles as they mortgaged their homes and held fund-raisers to pay off their debts. Musial made sure to allocate money each year to help pay off the church's construction. In 1915, all the early debts were paid in full. This did not mean that Father Musial halted his efforts. Instead, he became more aggressive in solidifying the community by purchasing the Polish National Assembly building (later the Polish American

Club) in 1916 at a cost of $19,130. Table 3.2 tracks the financial highs and lows of the parish during the 1910s.

Many outside donors from the community and city loaned money at the start, but most of the money after 1910 came from parishioners in the form of pew rents and other collections. There are no exact records of how much money certain families paid in pew rents in the 1910s; however, later anniversary books show this was a time of social mobility within the community. Prospering families probably paid more, but the inward-looking nature of the church community tried to downplay any class-based struggles.[69] Finally, Musial felt that purchasing the Polish National Assembly building would more adequately serve the men of the community if it came under church control.[70] This purchase assisted in the continued growth of the fraternal lodges of the Polish National Alliance (PNA) and the Polish Roman Catholic Union of America (PRCU).

The PNA sponsored a Boy Scout troop during the 1910s known as the "Harcerze," which differed from its U.S. counterparts by conducting all activities in Polish. By February 1920, the Boy Scout troop numbered around 175 boys, and Musial himself praised the organization's efforts "to show him [the Polish American youth] what a truly great country he is permitted to call his own." In addition, the PNA held many Polish folk dances and supported a baseball team.[71] The PRCU also sponsored sports teams, including semiprofessional Polish baseball and basketball teams. Many of their functions took place in the new Polish Hall. Both the PRCU and Musial used this social space in the 1920s to show silent films and organize wedding receptions, communion breakfasts, and even political rallies. Later during the Jazz Age, Polish Hall became renowned for its pre-Lenten "Paczki Ball" as well as the performances of first the Mamushka Orchestra and later the American Rhythm Kings. With the additions of these social spaces in the 1910s, Father Musial provided his parish with religious and social venues to keep intact his flock's ethnic heritage.

Fraternal organizations also provided monetary assistance. As far back as 1897, several Polish men led by Jan Malkowski formed the Tadeusz Kościuszko Society of the PRCU. This early fraternal unit suffered from poor organization and lost members. In 1902, Father Musial helped reorganize the group renaming it the St. Stanislaus Society. However, it was also split by political infighting and disputes so that in 1914 sixty-eight members formed the St. Joseph Society, Group 213 of the ZPRK (Polish Roman Catholic Union). Very quickly the society provided accidental and death insurance. By 1926, 416 men and women took out insurance worth over $275,000. These plans provided some of the most reliable insurance premiums for immigrant families. For example,

Table 3.2. Financial Records of St. Ladislaus Church, 1911–1919

	Receipts	Pew Rents	Expenses	Debt
1911	$7,599.14	$438.90	$6,988.01	$7,600
1912	$8,074.74	$2,993.25	$7,160.80	$6,600
1913	$8,817.70	$600.50	$8,817.70	$2,600
1914	$6,707.37	$505.00	$5,268.92	$1,600
1915	$7,613.03	$2,860.65	$6,328.59	$0
1916	$29,984.78	$2,936.70	$29,612.90	$19,130
1917	$16,490.29	$2,569.20	$16,134.09	$18,650
1918	$24,544.00	$2,668.90	$24,512.65	$14,400
1919	$11,446.56	$2,794.60	$11,295.43	$13,200

Source: St. Ladislaus Annual Reports, 1911–1919, DWC.

in 1916 the society set up a sick and disease fund that would pay seven dollars in weekly assistance checks for the cost of fifty cents a month to members. By 1926, this program paid out $7,037. After 1921, the St. Joseph Society branched out by establishing the St. Alojzy Department for Youth to provide young people with sick and accidental death insurance.[72]

Musial also made Polish Catholic education a priority. Before 1910, he conducted some classes in the parish basement. However, the steady increase in students, seen in table 3.3, encouraged Musial to seek better school facilities and encourage families to send their children.

To meet demand, Musial sought the assistance of the Felician Sisters of Detroit. In 1911, four nuns arrived providing the necessary staff to educate children of all ages. The parochial school played a critical role in the Polish Catholic experience as immigrants hoped that their cultural traditions would remain sacred for their children. To hold onto these "ethnic truths," Catholic orders trained teachers to embrace and instruct their pupils in Polish language, religion, culture, and history.[73] Delores Skrzypek recalled that the Felician Sisters, who took care of the interior of the church, visited the sick and provided an exemplary parochial education: "we studied Polish and English up to the eighth grade. You had your Polish religion and English religion, Polish history,

Table 3.3. Souls at St. Ladislaus and Children in Parochial School, 1911–1920

	Souls	Students
1911	1200	153
1912	1200	185
1913	1500	215
1914	1500	216
1915	1500	205
1916	1500	265
1917	1200	245
1918	1500	315
1919	1450	295
1920	1300	336

Source: St. Ladislaus Annual Reports, 1911–1920, DWC.

English history."[74] By 1920, the rising numbers of students forced the parish to purchase a three-story building with eight classrooms.[75] With this parochial institution, the Polish Catholics possessed a fully self-sustaining community.

Ethnic Interaction and Early Class Divisions in Polonia

During the first decade of the twentieth century, Wheeling's Poles established a thriving ethnic community on the margins of the Friendly City. However, a major component of their life in South Wheeling revolved around living in close proximity to other immigrants. To the north the Polish intermingled with Germans, Austrians, and Bohemians, while Hungarians, Croats, and Serbs congregated to the south in Benwood. Although ethnic animosities traveled with immigrants from Europe, the relationships were more complex in the United States. Dominic Pacyga argues that Chicago's Poles faced more ethnic conflicts with their Lithuanian neighbors than with the larger ethnic groups.[76] Other scholars highlight the range of racial animosity felt by

Fig. 3.3. Graduating class—St. Ladislaus School, ca. 1920. Courtesy of the Diocese of Wheeling-Charleston, Wheeling, WV.

Polish immigrants, particularly toward African Americans. Poles, like other Southern and eastern European immigrants, sought to position themselves within the city's ethnic diversity.[77]

Arriving later than the Irish and Germans, South Wheeling's Poles were relegated to an inferior position when obtaining work. Like other newer immigrants, they had advantages over African Americans who congregated near the Belmont Mill from Twenty-Fifth to Twenty-Seventh Streets and from Thirty-First to Thirty-Third Streets, both near the Poles. However, due to Wheeling's small African American population, the larger tensions occurred principally between Wheeling's ethnic groups. In 1904, Bishop Donahue asked all priests to send him a survey of their parishes' ethnic compositions. Father Musial's response suggests the ethnic tensions between the immigrants near St. Ladislaus. The document lists the two major divisions within the parish—542 Poles and 325 other Slavs. The document then notes that Musial did not want Hungarians or Croats in his parish. He is even more forceful with his request that he absolutely does not want any Italians.[78]

This document suggests that Musial's primary goal was to provide a solid religious, social, and cultural base for Poles and Poles only. Although not unique for its time, this reflects a desire to maintain the ethnic purity of his community. Another problem was interethnic marriages. From the start of his appointment, Father Musial worked to facilitate marriages between people of Polish descent. According to the parish's marriage book, from 1902 through 1907, of all marriages where both participants' background is known, 87 percent united persons from the same Polish region.[79] At least in the first generation, Musial wanted to keep his flock ethnically intact, reflecting his desire to keep his community unified as they tried to gain the necessary economic and political footholds to advance as a group.

Musial's efforts to maintain a traditional community mirrored those of many ethnic parish priests as they contested the growing influence of Irish and German Catholics within local dioceses. As Irish leaders sought to alter the church to the needs of "modernity," they crafted an institutional structure of social, fraternal, and religious societies to "Americanize" and unify all Catholics. Territorial parishes promoted Catholic Americanization, such as St. John's in Benwood. Father Werninger opened a school in the fall of 1906 to teach English noting "they must be able to read and write Teddy Roosevelt's English before they can qualify as citizens."[80]

While it did lead to some ethnic tensions, the Irish American brand of Catholicism also stressed a surprising degree of social justice and ethnic tolerance. The Catholic hierarchy reached out to immigrants and the impoverished by fostering lay societies. Most ran through St. Joseph's Cathedral and had a distinctive "Hibernian" feel. However, they provided assistance to the growing immigrant population. The most important was the ladies' Immaculata Guild from St. Joseph's Cathedral. Created on December 8, 1903, to honor the Feast of the Immaculate Conception, the Irish American women's society sought united action to "devise practical means of assisting and helping the poor."[81] In always seeking to "soften the hard lot and relieve the wants," the ladies sponsored charity events and donation drives to collect clothes for the "deserving poor." Operating in a nonsectarian fashion, the women gave out hundreds of garments and food every winter. Throughout the early 1900s, the guild and the St. Vincent de Paul Society were the only lay organizations whose sole purpose was alleviating the local poverty and sickness that "grows heavier each year."[82]

The Immaculata Guild played a major role during the March 1907 flood. The women quickly formed a Cathedral relief station and sent committees to investigate needs in each city neighborhood. Many were appalled to see foreign families on the South Side "scantily clad." One case that drew particular sympathy involved a Polish widow and her two small children who lost everything they owned in the flood. The ladies discovered them all sleeping on a wet mattress covered with rags. Upon receiving a consignment of food and a clean mattress, the Polish mother gratefully "tempted to kiss the feet of her benefactress." For several years the guild commented on the increasing "misery and distress" as men could no longer find employment to care for their families.[83]

This Catholic reform impulse expanded in the first decades of the century to meet the growing concerns of the poor. While not necessarily catering to immigrants, these institutions reflected the Church's willingness to care for the material not just the spiritual needs of its members. One example was the creation of a home for the aged. Bishop Donahue was particularly worried with the growing numbers of "old people thrown upon the world without a roof over their heads" with no assistance to care for them in their most vulnerable time.[84] Also, the reach of the diocese's orphan home in Elm Grove was expanded as were the efforts of the Sisters of the Good Shepherd home on Edgington Lane.[85]

As the Irish-dominated seat of the diocese, St. Joseph's Cathedral gave Bishop Donahue a venue to host meetings, bazaars, and entertainments (including black minstrel shows) to reinforce the tenets of a Catholic Irish American modernity. During the 1910s, the cathedral hosted the annual Holy Name Society rallies, distributed diocesan literature against socialism, and organized charity efforts by the Knights of Columbus and the Catholic Women's League for Protective Work. The latter served to protect "young [immigrant] girls coming into Wheeling."[86] Female-led reform organizations also fostered Americanization. Donahue appointed several Sisters of St. Joseph to teach English to an initial class of thirty-nine girls of Hungarian, Bohemian, Slavic, and Polish descent.[87] Even within the cathedral, there were physical metaphors emphasizing the "supremacy" of the Irish American brand of Catholicism. On November 16, 1913, Cathedral members were told that "the Chapel in the basement of the church is for the use of the Italians and for no one else; hence you are requested not to intrude." This came after many references to Italians who were continually coming upstairs during masses.[88]

Despite this interethnic squabbling, starting around 1910 Musial increasingly felt the need for South Wheeling's Poles to work together with different ethnic Catholics. The primary vehicles for this were parish-level Holy Name Societies and their annual Holy Name parades. The Holy Name Society included all men in a parish, and they worked to regularly attend confession and communion services as well as show unified reverence to the "name" of the Lord.[89] Over time these conservative Catholic societies began to express a more overtly political message, protesting the social wrongs committed overseas and particularly the plight of the working class. While one of the Holy Name Societies' primary purposes was to counter socialism, these groups actively pushed for social justice so workers would not opt to follow radical anti-Catholic doctrines. The annual parades were a chance for Catholic communities to unite in processionals against the evils plaguing society. On October 13, 1912, a massive Holy Name parade coursed through the streets of Wheeling, stopping at the cathedral. Marching, without caring about "class divisions," the men sang hymns and listened as Bishop Donahue spoke about the evils and terrors he saw while visiting the southern coal fields of West Virginia, where "there is bitterness and strife between man and man, and between class and class."[90] St. Ladislaus Parish gained a prestigious position as the second parish marching behind the bishop. In these acts of Catholic unity, working-class Poles could reaffirm the tenets of their faith.

Likewise Musial attached his parish to the bishop's political agenda. Donahue used many of the lay societies and the *Church Calendar* to espouse the church's disdain for socialism. His popularity, political influence, and public rhetoric forced other ethnic priests to support his position. Early in 1909, he spoke around Wheeling of the "two great perils looming of the future," socialism and divorce. Following the church's social teachings, Donahue also argued that the right to private property was sacred. While there was a growing concentration of wealth, "private property is necessary so that wages may secure *their true value*."[91] He saw that "Christianity . . . is made opposed to Socialism as light to darkness. . . . They are totally irreconcilable!" Moreover, he emphasized how the Socialists were incorrect in saying that the church was always "arrayed against the weak and the indigent" in unwavering support of capital and power.[92] Donahue served on a commission investigating the Paint Creek and Cabin Creek strikes and drafted the main report on miners' conditions throughout the state. He condemned both the repressive mine guard system but also the radical leadership of the United Mine Workers of America (UMWA). Bishop Donahue thus drew on the papal encyclical *Rerum Novarum* (1891), critiquing the excesses of both capitalism and the dangers of socialism. Donahue noted that labor "has no right to coerce by threats or violence anyone to become affiliated with it." He also highlighted "the abundant evidence before us that a reign of terror was attempted to be organized in the strike district," suggesting that socialists were responsible.[93]

While the Holy Name Society helped bridge some of the divides between Wheeling's ethnic Catholics, a more positive force for social interaction was St. John's Parish. Located in Center Benwood, between the two large steel mills, the parish was long dominated by the Irish. Beginning in the 1890s, St. John's developed differently from St. Ladislaus by serving as a territorial parish catering to a diverse group of ethnic groups. As the Slavic population grew, Father Musial and the South Wheeling Poles worked with St. John's Parish. In the spring of 1905, a Polish priest from Cleveland arrived in Benwood to assist both parishes to confirm the applications for membership in the "Polish church and the Slavish society." The priest received over five hundred applications leading to a "busy day" of work at the formal ceremony at St. Ladislaus.[94]

Musial relied on a small but growing Polish business class to help him thwart the appeal of secular working-class organizations. However, by the 1910s, the ethnic community also exhibited early signs of class divisions. Rising Polish businessmen like Stanley Duplaga, John Raszkiewicz, and others arrived in the late 1900s and early 1910s, presumably already possessing some retail experience from eastern Europe, and carved out niches for themselves within Polonia. During World War I, the increasing number of Poles entering the small business class showed the successful opportunities Polonia could offer. Marcel Olszta and his sons opened a successful funeral parlor and monument business operating near the parish at 4510 Jacob Street.[95] Down the street was Stanley Owoc, who ran a barbershop near the Polish Hall and later acted as editor of the *Polish West Virginian*.[96]

One indication of the influence of this ethnic business class involved the collection of pew rents. From 1915 through 1919, pew rents averaged between $2,500 and almost $3,000 annually.[97] These increasing sums must have been critical to Musial's efforts to neutralize the socialist threat and offer Catholic social spaces that could rival their secular counterparts. Mutual benefit associations, small businesses, and the Polish American Club all became vital institutions during this period. The Polish American Club was itself purchased in 1916, probably with the financial assistance of many of the rising businessmen who later became its principal leaders.[98]

Finally St. Ladislaus subtly endorsed this emerging business-class leadership. The parish promoted local small businesses in their pamphlets and church circulars but also in their anniversary books. In this way the parish used their example as another way to counter the appeal of socialism. This advertising reflected a direct link between the parish and those community leaders who gave higher amounts of money to the parish and assisted in purchasing buildings like the Polish American Club. Musial fostered these connections even more after 1915. Anniversary books highlight the relative social status of particular businessmen. Successful Poles like Stanley Duplaga, the Lukaszewicz Brothers (they owned a bakery and a service station), and Frank Lewandowsky all bought full-page ads. Duplaga's advertisement came on the second page of the anniversary book. In contrast, the Olszta family undertakers, Louis Merge, and John Raskiewicz purchased only quarter-page ads.[99] All of these men by 1926 had been in their respective businesses for some time; however, some could purchase larger ads than others. Small businessmen like Stanley Owoc and Louis Loges, who both changed occupations or took on second jobs, bought eighth-page advertisements. All other parishioners received a small block among twenty others on a page.[100] These advertisements reveal how immigrant parishes relied on close economic ties with ethnic small businesses.

Conclusion

By the 1910s, South Wheeling had a thriving Polonia centered around St. Ladislaus. The wider area was shaped by the social, economic, and cultural traditions of the neighborhood's largest immigrant group. New arrivals to Wheeling had a place to seek spiritual fulfillment, celebrate Polish Catholic holidays, and have their children receive a rigorous education while preserving old-world traditions. The Poles, led by Fr. Emil Musial, fashioned an inward-looking neighborhood that could provide the services new Polish immigrants needed to adjust to life in industrial Wheeling. Through this process of community formation, the parish was able to bring together Poles who had a variety of local and regional ties back in eastern Europe. Through fraternal organizations, the parish school, and the Polish American Club, St. Ladislaus was able to create a shared understanding of what it meant to be "Polish" in America.

The decade also marked a transition for St. Ladislaus's first generation. Throughout the 1910s, Polish working-class immigrants were increasingly drawn, like many other workers in Wheeling, to the class-based appeals of the labor movement and the Socialist Party. While it seems Father Musial's vision for the Polish community was triumphant, there was a legitimate fear that without a structured, moral community, Poles might drift toward socialism under the increasingly desperate and intense working conditions in Wheeling and Benwood's factories. Even with the strong attachment to an ethnic cultural nationalism, the rising importance of the labor movement in the lives of these blue-collar immigrants provided a more secular avenue for moral regeneration in industrial America.

CHAPTER 4

Finding a Good Job and a Good Union for Polonia: Polish Workers within Wheeling's Labor Movement, 1890–1915

Waking up to the sweltering heat of July 23, 1915, Wheeling's South Side appeared ready to erupt as five hundred workers of the Wheeling Can Company discussed a strike. Tensions finally reached their breaking point when management demanded that employees work added overtime and fired those refusing to comply. Angered by the unfair demands, the can workers organized themselves by passing out flyers as they left the factory at 6:00 p.m. That evening they held a mass meeting at Scherwinski's Hall at Forty-Sixth and Jacob Street, just several blocks from the plant. Most of the strikers and hundreds of others listened intently as Walter B. Hilton, Socialist editor of the *Wheeling Majority*, and L. M. Greer and Smith Calvert of the Ohio Valley Trades and Labor Assembly helped the strikers draft their demands. They sought a nine-hour day, time and a half for overtime, a return to the wages of 1912, pay for lost time caused by machine break downs, union recognition, reinstatement of the fired employees, and the weekly payment of wages.[1] The next morning the strikers set up a picket line around the plant at 7:00 a.m., shutting down the plant for that day. Another mass meeting occurred that night at Polish Hall on Wood Street below Forty-Fifth. This "meeting was larger and more enthusiastic than the last one" as the largely immigrant audience agreed to hold out. After management supported all of the demands except for union affiliation, another meeting at Scherwinski's Hall led to a "loud and unanimous demand for affiliation with the American Federation of Labor." While members of the local Socialist Party and the Trades Assembly were present, "none of these spoke" so that the workers' decision "could not be twisted by the Can Factory Management into a claim that 'the agitators' had influenced them against their will."[2]

The role of recent Polish immigrants in this strike makes it all the more intriguing. During the meeting at Scherwinski's Hall, when the strikers sought AFL affiliation, Charles Ajmar of Bridgeport, Ohio, translated the demands and meeting minutes into "Polish for the benefit of a large number of girls" who worked at Wheeling Can. Enthusiastically the women "flocked to the front and paid their initiation."[3] That these recent female Polish immigrants vigorously supported organizing efforts by the local Trades Assembly and prominent Socialists surprised the local Catholic leaders, especially since they met in spaces usually reserved for Polish social functions and the Catholic religious festivals of the Polish St. Ladislaus Parish. The strikers also promoted a lawn fete in expectation of selling over three thousand tickets for "probably the biggest [fete] ever held in the Eighth Ward."[4]

The "radical" use of Polish Catholic social spaces contrasted greatly with the goals of Fr. Emil Musial and much of his Polish Catholic laity. As seen in chapter 3, for Musial, the successful formation of a thriving Polish community was tied to Polish popular religious practices and Polish cultural nationalism. By disseminating these ideals through the parish, social halls, fraternal organizations, and the parochial school, Musial sought to unite the Poles scattered throughout Wheeling to combat the trials of life in industrial America. But Musial was no reactionary. While rejecting socialism, his brand of Catholicism offered a moral critique of economic individualism and reinforced a working-class activism based on the social teachings of *Rerum Novarum* (1891) and nourished by Catholic culture and religious practices within ethnic parishes.[5] Ultimately, these two visions of how to best promote the needs of the Polish community—one advocating class solidarity, the other Catholic ethnic solidarity—clashed in the streets of South Wheeling in 1915.

The complexity of the competing facets of Polish working-class life often created a tangled identity for Wheeling's Poles. This chapter will explore immigrant class formation by focusing on their work and political experiences before World War I. Poles and their immigrant neighbors in South Wheeling developed a unique "subculture of opposition" that did not compartmentalize their ethnic, religious, or class feelings.[6] Each tugged on their loyalties, sometimes one more than the other. Class consciousness developed slowly for the Polish and Slavic immigrants because of the early antagonistic treatment they received from skilled workers. In the early 1890s, native-born Irish and German tradesmen mostly viewed the Poles with contempt for accepting lower wages, acting as strikebreakers, and working in ever-dangerous conditions in the new and expanding factories of the Wheeling district. Many saw them as a danger to the gains made by the Ohio Valley Trades and Labor Assembly (OVTLA), which formed in the early 1880s to address the changing conditions of work for the area's skilled tradesmen. Early on the assembly stressed craft unionism and supported immigration restriction while suffering defeats and lockouts by companies implementing mechanization.

The labor movement's position toward these newer immigrants only changed with the rising influence of the socialists within the OVTLA, the devastating depression from 1907 to 1910, and the fact that an increasingly large number of unskilled immigrants, women, and children made up Wheeling's labor force by World War I. Continued defeats by the local labor movement, especially during the U.S. Steel strike of 1901, gave credence to the criticism of the OVTLA by more leftist members, like Valentine Reuther. They argued that the Trades Assembly's narrow support for skilled workers was foolhardy, especially as employers continued to hire new types of immigrant workers. The Poles and other ethnic groups were also becoming more politically involved during this period. Socialists forced the assembly to slowly support a version of industrial unionism and organized campaigns to promote interethnic solidarity lest they lose the support of the Polish working class to the pro-business Republican Party or even the more radical Industrial Workers of the World (IWW). These political realities helped overcome the previous nativism Polish workers faced when they started entering the mills and factories in previous decades. Labor leaders, especially German American socialists, began meeting immigrants on their own terms, sponsoring cultural events, providing foreign-born interpreters and organizers, and helping organize around key safety and quality of life concerns facing the Poles living in cramped South Wheeling. By the early 1910s, they may not have succeeded in converting all the Poles to socialism, but Polish Catholic workers had become one of the most active new immigrant groups in supporting the goals of organized labor and joining labor strikes throughout the Wheeling area.

Polish Position within Local Labor Struggles

For the Irish and German craftsmen who dominated city politics and the labor movement, maintaining their economic foothold was becoming increasingly difficult as the arrival of new immigrants threatened their privileged status. Wheeling was transformed by the restructuring of the steel industry beginning in the 1890s. With the move to tin-plate production, the Wheeling steel mills needed unskilled eastern European immigrants in their local steel mills, coal mines, and blast furnaces.[7] However, skilled craftsmen still maintained their power on the South Side. Outside firms, like the American Tin Plate and the National Tube Company, owned many local mills but required skilled rollers and heaters. Owners paid tonnage rates to crew leaders, who in turn paid their helpers. Heaters placed steel bars in furnaces until they glowed red and then passed them to "roughing" crews that sent the bars through a series of rolls flattening them "like rolling pins flattening bread dough." Heaters reheated the sheets, and then roller crews sent them through a complex process of folding until the sheets reached the correct "gauge." Heaters used much practical knowledge that machines could not yet replicate with furnace temperatures judged "by the heaters' eye."[8]

According to the state commissioner of labor in 1890, "In Wheeling we find the standard of living of the working people nearly on a parallel with that of their employers, while their personal independence is maintained at all times."[9] Labor leaders, however, increasingly looked with contempt at new immigrants who "degrade the character and dignity of citizenship, and in the end become a burden and expence [sic] on the community." The commissioner did warn of what unrestricted immigration would do to Wheeling: "It is a fact that where this class is introduced in large numbers, the standard of living among laborers descends to a low grade, and the morality of the people is affected from the fact that these foreigners seem to live as if they had no hope in this world."[10]

Rank-and-file workers also stressed their anti-immigrant anger. When asked about the most pressing concerns for the state's labor movement, most workers stressed needing a "good trade union" and supported the "single tax," high protective tariffs, child labor and mine safety laws, the eight-hour day, and weekly payment of wages.[11] However, virtually every working man queried raised the problem of foreign-born labor. The strongest criticisms came from those where mechanization was deskilling the labor force and replacing it with foreign single male workers. "Foreign labor is the downfall of all good wages," stated an ironworker. A carpenter took it further by declaring that "immigration has effect on all trades." At the growing steel mills in Benwood, a steelworker objected to being "invaded by certain classes, that come over here and stay a few years and then go back." Many probably shared the views of a foreman at Bloch Brothers Tobacco Warehouse, who said bluntly: "The government has shut out the Chinese, but we have amongst us a more deadly viper in the shape of criminals of Italy, Poland and Hungary."[12]

The devastating economic depression of the 1890s stoked many of these fears and animosities. Conditions worsened in many factories in the summer and fall of 1893. Several firms failed, most notably Hobbs, Brockunier Glass Works on the South Side. All the pent-up anger against foreign workers finally reached its breaking point among the city's steelworkers. Throughout the

1890s, every time a mill closed and laid men off, when conditions improved, they immediately hired a large number of new immigrants. For several weeks in late August through September 1893, Benwood residents noticed the quiet arrival of these "strange faces" coming from McKeesport and Homestead seeking work. Soon a "swarm of Hungarians and 'Polanders'" were at the gates of the skelp mill and the Riverside Tube Mill seeking work.[13]

The resumption of the large steel mills started a decade-long trend in the Wheeling area and in other steel mill towns of small "riots" between native-born and immigrant workers over the latter's willingness to work at reduced wages.[14] The blast furnaces in Benwood first saw this change in the workforce. In 1892, a sheet roller noted how the Wheeling Iron & Steel Company employed "ten Huns and Italians to one American." He claimed they were paid eight dollars per month and about forty lived in an "old barracks of a building." The Wheeling firm contracted these men directly from Germany, and this fact aroused many working men about hurting local "free labor." The trend continued in the fall of 1893 when the Riverside Tube Mill, the largest employer in the region, announced it would rehire workers at a 10 to 15 percent wage reduction.[15] For the next month or so, the local press reported on a variety of "pitched battles" and "rows." On September 18, 1893, a reporter claimed that gangs of Hungarians, Italians, and Polanders arrived at the mill's gates in "squads" and "practiced drilling." When over two hundred immigrant workers tried to bolt into the factory complex, they were repulsed by a crowd of fifty American boys with bricks, iron pieces, and other projectiles. The boys tied a flag to a pole and charged at the immigrants, routing them from the mill. Observers noted the boys "evidently had declared war" on the immigrant "gangs" because they (particularly the "Polanders") had agreed to work as laborers for only ninety cents a day. They even agreed to bribe the foreman for ten dollars. Another war commenced at the start of the shift turn, but the "two factions battled for over an hour" to a stalemate. After police arrested several "Polanders with unpronounceable names," the locals thought they had won. However, "the foreigners again formed" near Boggs Run and viciously attacked the boys.[16]

Often these "crowd actions" functioned as a form of lower-class politics in which native-born workers attempted to defend neighborhoods and assert democratic rights. These disturbances, along with increasingly bloody labor confrontations like the Homestead strike of 1892, were used by employers, however, to support their very different arguments about the volatile nature of the working class. Employers took advantage of this intraclass rivalry to advance their own anti-union agenda, one at odds to the nativist union workers who fought immigrants in the streets. Eastern European immigrants became the primary symbol of social instability in newspapers, magazines, and even vaudeville plays. Dubbing these incidents as "riots" or "mob battles" worked to further discredit labor unions. It also painted the average striker as part of an alien, savage mob lacking restraint. After the melee near the Riverside Mill, many assumed the Poles would attempt "more serious trouble." These fears seemed confirmed as rumors spread about the danger of the Poles, Hungarians, and Italians who were "getting hungry." A reporter went to a boardinghouse and noted that "For dirt, filth, and stench it goes beyond imagination." Angry citizens had warned of the presence of this "filthy element" even before "500 Polanders gathered on the [streetcar] track and stopped the running of the cars." Later, labor bosses fired many Poles to assuage the growing fears.[17]

Growing desperation with unemployment and stiff labor competition drove this "war." But not all workers bought into the employers' explanation that the unskilled immigrant was to blame. An iron puddler named Justice wrote an editorial in the *Wheeling Daily Register* highlighting how the future was "rather discouraging." From his point of view, "Oppression and depression [had] brought a dark cloud of misery and destitution to iron workers in general." With manufacturers cutting labor costs, desperate working men were constantly forced to accept reductions "when bread [was] needed on the family table." These efforts coordinated by mill owners throughout the Ohio Valley and Pittsburgh would eventually force the craftsmen "down to European starvation wages." The producerist perspective of this skilled worker suggests that some workers realized that their increasing loss of control derived more from the power of monopoly and big business consolidations than a mob of five hundred Poles.[18]

The debate over what happened at the Riverside induced the immigrants to respond. In a series of editorials, "Austrians" and a "Hungarian" argued over the mindset of the foreign workers in the area.[19] The "Austrians" claimed that none of their countrymen offered to work for eighty cents per day nor bribed foreman for jobs. The writer blamed a laborer named Nicstosic, who was "known as a troublesome man . . . and [had] been guilty of inciting trouble in the old country." Most Slavs acknowledged they could "barely exist upon the present wages as paid" without becoming "pauper labor." The "Hungarian" asked native-born critics "to show [him] where [his] people ever did anything to the workingmen of this country that was not right and fair."[20]

Nevertheless, throughout the 1890s depression, native-born workmen fought new arrivals. Desperate for work, John Borluski went to the National Tube Company's offices offering to work for seventy-five cents a day. When an

Fig. 4.1. Benwood Steel Mill and B&O Bridge (Benwood Works), ca. 1903. Page from scrapbook of Wheeling landmarks, 1903, by W. T. Nicoll, Nicoll's Art Store. Courtesy of the Ohio County Public Library Archives, Wheeling, WV.

angry group of men threatened the "Polander," he picked up a brick and struck one of them. After knocking him down, many of the young boys, who had been involved in the vicious fights with new immigrants for months, "took a hand by beating and hurling bricks at the foreigner, who was unable to rise." Few seemed to notice the plight of Polish men who traveled to Wheeling with families. A Polish man named Goiske also went to the Riverside Mill because his family was very much in need of money for food. Immediately Goiske was hit hard in the head with a cinder block cutting a gash on his head and almost severing an artery. After stumbling back as far as Boggs Run in a faint condition, Goiske was attended to by a doctor.[21]

Skilled workers faced a dire situation by the turn of the century that contributed to some of this violence. In response to mechanization, workers also went on strike in increasing numbers to force better wages and working conditions. While solidarity was strong among craftsmen, they were faced with what to do with the growing divisions of the workforce by age, gender, and nationality. Craft unions gained their strength from the continuing levels of power skilled men held over the labor market. Unions sought to protect their members from the intrusion of new workers, halt or slow the effects of automation, and provide an avenue for political organizing. This was an era of heightened strike activity. Most involved coal miners and streetcar workers, trades with more autonomy on the job. Also common were those workers in the larger factories, where strikes resulted from the breakdown in collective bargaining agreements. More semiskilled workers also struck over lack of union recognition and reduction in piece rates. These workers were most affected by the industrial changes in Wheeling after the decline of the cut nail industry. Glass blowers, potters, tobacco rollers, machinists, iron puddlers, rollers, and heaters all struck for concessions to the changing management systems. Their attempts suffered from trying to organize employees often divided along racial and ethnic lines.[22]

The steelworkers' struggles highlight this growing tension. During the era of the Knights of Labor (KOL), skilled employees fought against any inclusive style of unionism and affiliated with the Amalgamated Association of Iron and Steel Workers (AAISW). In the late 1880s, a split occurred between the lodges and the KOL assemblies over who claimed workers at the steel mills of the Riverside in Benwood and Bellaire as well as the Belmont and LaBelle nail mills. The disputes stemmed from the Riverside Lodge No. 12 of the AAISW placing the Riverside Mill on the Trade Assembly's boycott list for furnishing steel for nonunion nail plants. They alleged the KOL controlled the mill and were helping in the underpaying of steelworkers. Bellaire's AAISW lodge also claimed the KOL's wage rates at the Riverside undercut their own contract. The Benwood KOL Assembly 2323 tried to defend its actions to represent all the workers in the Benwood mills even though more denunciations followed. In response, Nail City's lodge had to revoke its contract over the Riverside Mill. After further arguments between KOL and AAISW lodges over wage scales in the mills, by May 1888 Washington Assembly 638 (Benwood) and Fidelity Assembly 2065 (Bellaire) withdrew from the Trades Assembly.[23]

These divisive stands came at a poor time for steelworkers at places like the Riverside Mill. Skilled nailers held great power over the production process since the plant's opening in 1872, but things changed when the factory retooled in 1886 to build a Bessemer steel plant, along with the tube works. Management abandoned the nail works in 1888 shortly after the disputes between the KOL and AAISW. This change enabled the business to manufacture steel steam, gas, and water pipes. With this shift from nail to steel tube, the Riverside operations expanded to over ninety acres by 1902. Several large blast furnaces were added, which led the Wheeling Iron & Steel Company's Benwood plant to shift to producing steel tinplate. By the early 1890s, most Wheeling iron factories had opened tinplate mills. The Bessemer converters gave control of the process to managers, who then expanded by creating continuous rolling mills.[24]

Excessive competition in the industry led to a series of corporate mergers from 1898 to 1901. In March 1899, the National Tube Company purchased the Riverside Mill, but by the spring of 1901 its new owner was the U.S. Steel Corporation. Increasingly, larger mills needed the strong backs of hundreds of unskilled immigrants. However, the tinplate and other finishing mills still required many skilled heaters and sheet rollers in the hot mills and tin houses.[25]

Most of the labor disputes at this time were "control strikes" by the skilled employees over wage rates, standardization of production processes, and longer work days. Several large walkouts occurred in the Wheeling mills from 1898 to 1900. In early 1898, Wheeling Iron & Steel Company's plate mill forced its hourly day laborers and all the tonnage men to take a reduction in pay. Immediately there were calls for solidarity. This was the second wage cut since the summer of 1897 reduction of 10 to 25 percent for all employees. Assured that wages would return when the business climate improved, skilled workers grew angry when the company appeared disingenuous. For example, President C. Russell Hubbard chose to miss a scheduled meeting with the workers to meet with the company's stockholders instead. Setting all workers on the tonnage rate hurt the unskilled. The "first helpers" got $2.00 a day under the old scale, but would earn only $1.60 a day on the tonnage rate. The company also stipulated that a "turn" would be extended from five to six heats. While the wage reduction raised the most enmity, the increase in turns reflected a broader problem. The Benwood mill made five heats in seven and a half hours. At the Riverside Mill, steelworkers labored for seven and a half heats per day; at the Belmont and LaBelle Mills the daily turn was a rigorous ten heats.[26]

The success of the Wheeling Iron & Steel Company's scale reduction spread throughout Ohio Valley's companies for the next few years. The mill immediately asked that their coal miners in Benwood accept a cut from 40 to 33⅓ cents per ton. At the Riverside, the company cut tonnage wages from 10 to 40 cents per 100 tons. Unlike the across-the-board cut of all employees in April 1897, this reduction only targeted the heaters, rollers, shearmen, vessel makers, and other skilled workers. The Riverside plate mill again cut wages in the fall of 1900 leading to another strike; however, the issue at hand was also the company's refusal to recognize the Amalgamated Association in negotiations.[27]

The key turning point for the AAISW came with its strike against the U.S.

Steel Corporation in 1901. The Amalgamated Association sought to extend their union contracts to cover the nonunion mills of the subsidiary companies comprising U.S. Steel. When the union threatened a strike in July 1901, corporate executives asked for a conference to mediate the dispute as the public grew angry about the monopolistic nature of the company. When negotiations broke down, first after a conference in Pittsburgh and then with J. P. Morgan in New York, union president T. J. Shaffer called for a general strike against the "United States Steel Trust" on August 6 as the "central fight for unionism."[28]

Wheeling was a center of the strike, and organizers focused on the large Riverside Mill. This focus seems unique considering that most of the plant's three thousand employees were immigrants. For months prior the AAISW sent several "missionaries" to educate them about the benefits of unionism. These men, who before were chastised for wanting to "scab," now were willing to join the union in its fight. With the Benwood plant as the "storm centre of the strike," the union set up an organizing center at Bischoff's Hall on Forty-Third Street in South Wheeling and began recruiting members. Early success came with organizing the United Lodge of four hundred skilled men of the steel and plate mills of the Wheeling Steel & Iron Company in Benwood.[29] Shaffer spoke to a mass meeting of strikers on Wheeling Island. A parade of the local lodges webbed its way through town cheering as they passed each factory. There was much popular support for the strike among other skilled workers, the OVTLA, and citizens worried about the power of the trusts. Even state officials condoned the strike. Labor Commissioner I. V. Barton informed Governor A. B. White the strikers had the "approval of all law-abiding citizens" and in "conducting a peaceful campaign" there was no need for police assistance.[30]

While generally peaceful, rumors of imported strikebreakers sparked fear on the South Side. The AAISW set up shifts of men to watch the railroad depots. They worried when about two hundred soldiers returning from the Philippines arrived fearing they would be used to suppress the strike. While the union initially tried to organize the entire Riverside Mill, they quickly changed their strategy to focus on the eight hundred skilled men. For some time, the Riverside's steel department continued to operate along with the blast furnace crews. To protect their gains, more pickets were set up around the mill and to guard the railroad depots.[31]

The strike situation seemed to be turning in the union's favor. On August 10, the skelp millworkers "drop[ped] their tools" in solidarity. With the prospect of the rest of their workforce joining the cause, over 1,300 attended a mass meeting in South Wheeling stressing the "weight of moral influence" on the other men about the need for organization. At this point only the 1,000 men of the steel works and blast furnace remained at work. Vice President Walter Larkins was surprised by the speed of organization at the Riverside, where prior union efforts failed. Later the *Pittsburgh Press* reported "Strikers Win Big Victory" in tying up the entire Wheeling District. However, the press noted the unskilled blast furnace men still worked.[32]

The ultimate failure of the blast furnace workers to organize suggests that many Slavic immigrants did not join the union's cause. However, many new immigrants worked in other departments. Workers living in the city for some time were more willing to support the union cause. During the strike the AAISW attempted to build worker solidarity. At a meeting at the Blue Ribbon Hall in Benwood, several hundred men attended an entertainment where "music, songs, and witty stories beguiled away the hours." The union organized committees to solicit money for the general strike fund. South Wheeling and Benwood were divided into two sections. Prosperity Lodge No. 5 of the LaBelle Tin Mill covered above Forty-Third Street, while Wheeling Lodge No. 5 of the Riverside went south of Forty-Third Street. Several Polish and Slavic men contributed. A steelworker S. Kolonsky gave one dollar, Croatian leader John Lubic gave one dollar, John Schlanski gave fifty cents, and tin worker Fred Warceski gave twenty-five cents. The saloonkeepers gave financial contributions and organized a charity baseball game between themselves and the bartenders.[33]

These moments of class solidarity were fleeting. By late August union leaders learned that "strange Slavs" were brought into Benwood to operate the Riverside Mill. Union officials also intercepted a group of Benwood Slavs solicited to go to a Pittsburgh mill on strike. Through their efforts, "the foreigners were persuaded by more than a forcible argument" to return to their boardinghouses in the "brick row" of Benwood. A few days later, strikers learned twenty-five Slavs who arrived on a B&O train had snuck into the Riverside led by a Slav who formerly worked at the factory. Cots and mattresses were brought into the LaBelle Mill for scabs as well. By the end of the month, a foreman at the tube works reported "A sufficient number of men have arrived here to-day by the Ohio River road to operate the mill." The strike failed in the Wheeling District because the union did little to build solidarity with newer immigrants.[34]

The 1901 strike's failure fit within a broader craft union policy of the Ohio Valley Trades and Labor Assembly. One early critic was Valentine Reuther, who emigrated from Germany in 1899. Upon arriving in South Wheeling, Valentine lived in "a very proletarian boarding house jammed with immigrants" located at 2600 Jacob Street.[35] Through the help of a relative, he got a job as a laborer at the Riverside. He worked the "long turn" of seventy-two hours, six days of twelve-hour shifts, and earned just $1.50 a day. After coaxing the shop foreman to let him learn the heater's trade, Valentine got his first taste of trade unionism attending meetings of the local lodge of the Amalgamated Association. However, he grew concerned at how this craft union overtly discriminated against eastern Europeans. Reuther tried to bridge the cultural divide reaching out to the new arrivals by speaking several languages. He vigorously protested this exclusionary form of unionism. During the 1901 strike, "Val" walked the picket line encouraging immigrants. In the end the strike made him an enemy of both the company and the union.[36]

For many years the Trades Assembly was very anti-immigrant. Like the AFL, the assembly supported a brand of working-class republicanism defending the democratic rights of producers. This approach fueled immigrant exclusion. Hearing about Italians working on a Wheeling & Hempfield Railroad project in the late 1880s, the assembly lashed out at "the manner in which the Dagos lived." Heated debates about immigration restriction legislation often divided unions in the assembly. During the 1897 coal strike, delegate T. L. Lewis of the steelworkers' union "traced the evil effects that had followed the displacement of English-speaking labor by an illiterate foreign element." Companies cut wages by half, and immigrant laborers were "in charge of the English-speaking foreman." When it came time to vote, the assembly overwhelmingly endorsed immigration restriction by a vote of thirty-six to nine. The assembly also endorsed enforcement of the Chinese Exclusion Act and sent petitions to West Virginia congressmen to pass literacy tests for potential immigrants.[37]

Another divisive issue for the labor movement was the role of immigrants in local politics. During the 1896 presidential election, skilled steelworkers, mostly Democrats living in the Irish-dominated Sixth Ward of Wheeling and in Benwood, complained about how for weeks in September the Republicans sent a Polish and Slavic organizer from Cleveland canvassing the Eighth Ward and Upper Benwood to elicit his countrymen to register and vote for their "little god [William] McKinley." Throughout the campaign the Riverside hired many "unmarried aliens" while skilled "Americans" lost their jobs. Days prior to the election a "Riverside Laborer" accosted the Republican mill owners for employing the Polish operative from Cleveland whose job was to "speak to the Polanders and tell them they must vote for McKinley or lose their jobs." Angered by this tactic of stealing Polish votes, he called upon his fellow Americans to act as "free men" and not allow their jobs to be given to "Polanders." Although the "Riverside Laborer's" reaction was rooted, in part, in nativist hostility, it may also have reflected his anxiety over a political reality.

Unlike in many urban locations where Polish workers maintained their ties to the Democratic Party and were drawn to Bryan's campaign because they saw the Republican Party as anti-Catholic and anti-labor, in smaller industrial towns, which were ravaged by the 1890s depression, Poles turned slightly to support McKinley's "Full Dinner Pail."[38]

But, even given this general pattern, it is quite difficult to determine precisely how Poles in Wheeling voted in 1896 and 1900, and therefore it is also hard to ascertain whether the Riverside Laborer's anxiety was rooted in truth or prejudice. In 1896, seventy-seven eastern European immigrants officially naturalized. Their naturalization petitions suggest Republican operatives seemed more active in targeting South Slavic groups. Hungarians (twenty-one), Austrians (twenty-five), and Croats (eighteen) registered in the highest numbers. In fact, most Polish naturalization came during the 1892 (twelve) and 1894 (twenty-one) election campaigns. Many of these Polish immigrants lived in distinctively Democratic precincts in the Irish-dominated Sixth Ward. In 1894 these registrants included Mike Gredovich, Stanislaus Klos, and Joseph Kowalski, all German Poles living in a boardinghouse at 22 Twenty-Sixth Street near the Belmont Mill, along with Frank Dunbrowski of 2636 Main Street. Furthermore, many Polish migrants of the 1890s were quite independent and could just as often lash out against Polish authority figures, whom they perceived as bossing them around too much, as they would against Democratic organizers. A Polish labor boss at the Riverside Mill, Joseph Kolinski, was struck with a pick in the head after two Polish workers "became incensed at his manner" toward them.[39] The Poles' political independence, therefore, may have unintentionally fueled the nativist critiques hurled at them by other workers that, in turn, added to the difficulty of building solidarity among all of Wheeling's workers.

Politicization of the New Workforce

Interethnic working-class solidarity was thus challenged by the anti-unionism of the employers, the mainstream press, and the labor nativism during the 1890s, but there were competing forces that also helped foster the politicization and class consciousness of Wheeling's Poles during the early twentieth century. Immigrant communities provided mutual assistance during periods of economic want, but by 1908 Wheeling's immigrants pushed for more substantial changes. The city's Polish and other eastern European immigrants were increasingly politicized "from the bottom up" in response to their poor living conditions.⁴⁰ Although low levels of naturalization and voter restrictions limited immigrants' political voice in national and state elections, some cities allowed them to vote in municipal elections. Wheeling's 1907 city charter, its first since 1836, granted the vote to all males living in the city limits for at least one year, without any reference to state citizenship, and to all nonresident males owning at least two hundred dollars of city property.⁴¹ These voting restrictions disenfranchised many recent immigrants, but they did not negate all Polish voting. In a 1910 sample of South Wheeling's Polish households, about one-quarter owned their own homes.⁴²

Local political machines canvassed immigrant communities, like Wheeling's Eighth Ward. Of particular emphasis for the Poles were the efforts by the Democrats and the Socialists of the Trades Assembly. A number of historians studying Polish American politics find that Poles often supported the Democratic Party in the early 1900s because the party had close ties to the Catholic Church and opposed prohibition and immigrant restriction.⁴³ Similarly, Wheeling Socialists were vital to the growth of an immigrant political consciousness on the South Side. Socialist literature was distributed and discussion groups were started in several of the city's iron factories as early as July 1897. The predominately German Socialists criticized the failures of craft unionism and the corrupt nature of Wheeling municipal government. As early as 1900, members of the Eugene V. Debs branch of the Social Democracy of America and Germans, including assembly president Albert Bauer, openly criticized the "accursed competitive system that places the value upon dollars instead of humanity . . . that would drive Boys, Girls and Women into mills and factories." Bauer argued persuasively that conditions for these new types of workers would not be ameliorated "until we recognize the fact that labor is entitled to all it produces and arrange our labor organizations with that object in view, organizing ourselves on the political field as well as on the economic." He advocated for the public ownership of all means of economic production to halt the trusts' power.⁴⁴

For several years, the socialists focused their attack on local political corruption and the poor urban services affecting thousands of working people. In May 1901, the Trades Assembly criticized the Board of Public Works "against the filthy and disgraceful condition of the streets" that needed a system of cleaning and garbage collection. Labor leaders also expressed anger at the collusion between the city and street railway companies over unfair franchise rates that hurt working men's pocketbooks. By 1902, leftist delegates in the Trades Assembly resolved: "That we the delegates of the Ohio Valley Trades and Labor Assembly believe it would be to the interests of the City that the Assembly take a more active part in Municipal Affairs."[45]

Educating the working class was vital to the growth of class consciousness in Wheeling, and these educational efforts were crucial in understanding how Socialists sought to win workers' hearts and minds. During a machinists' strike in 1903, the Trades Assembly provided aid, and the local Socialists sponsored speaking events, headlined by Frank and Katie Richards O'Hare. In August, they gave a series of open-air lectures attended by hundreds, if not more. At the Centre Market House, they spoke about the history of "Capitalism and its effects on the conditions" it had created. Following a "miniature war" near the Riverside Mill in August 1903 between union and nonunion members, when over one thousand gun shots were fired, over 1,500 attended another rally at the market house. F. C. Roberts of the AFL highlighted the horrible conditions at the Riverside, where, for ten to fourteen hours a day, every two dollars earned in worker wages earned twelve dollars for the company. Katie O'Hare spoke on the corporation's power to import strikebreakers and detectives and implored all who "should forget race, sex, creed, political beliefs" to work to meet the interest of all the working class.[46]

Immigrant workers were increasingly receptive to unionization as they suffered the most from the dangerous working conditions. The summer of 1903 saw numerous injuries to Polish and Slavic workmen at the Riverside including crushed limbs and broken bones.[47] This led organizers to reach out to firms employing large numbers of immigrants. Such action occurred during the UMWA's strike in the Fifth Ohio Subdistrict (eastern Ohio and Northern Panhandle) in April 1906—especially in the campaign against the Hitchman Coal & Coke Company in Benwood, which opened several years earlier and employed 165 to 190 men. Organizers attended a meeting to hear grievances from miners organized as UMWA Local 1825. Hitchman recently attained the contract to supply the Baltimore & Ohio Railroad engines at their yards in Benwood. Mr. John Zelenka, a Slavic UMWA organizer from the subdistrict, helped the miners draft their strike demands. After workers refused to return to work at the old wage scale, manager W. H. Koch requested a court order to force the miners, mostly foreign born, to vacate the company's housing. The men held firm to the union demands. Setting the stage for the precedent that would be established in the *Hitchman Coal & Coke Co. v. Mitchell* Supreme Court decision (1917), manager Koch expressed a willingness to sign a new wage scale but refused to recognize the union.[48] The failure of the strike and the company's stand on forcing miners to sign "yellow dog" contracts to refuse to join the UMWA during their time of employment led many immigrant miners to seek work elsewhere.

The "Banker's Panic" of 1907 and the subsequent economic depression also boosted the Socialists' local political influence. Foreign-born and unskilled workers suffered the most from the economic downturn, and many former Socialists noted years later how much easier it was to recruit among the disaffected Wheeling working class in 1908. Capitalizing on workers "seriously questioning the value of capitalism," the Trades Assembly and local glassworkers, stogie makers, and miners' unions advocated for an independent United Labor Party.[49] The Trades Assembly appealed to immigrant workers' disillusionment with the Republican Party's support for protective tariffs and corporate mergers. The Wheeling Socialists also presented their class-based appeals in "religious rhetoric." Through their weekly newspaper, the *Wheeling Majority*, the Socialists spoke of how Jesus Christ was a worker: "The working man of today who tries to preach an uplift doctrine to fellow workers is . . . set upon by the hired thugs of Privilege, enjoined by Judge Dayton and eventually surrounded by troops and arrested. So was Christ—all except the injunction, and the Federal Judge is of a newer birth."[50] Thus, the local Socialists hoped to tap the sentiments of Catholic social teaching and *Rerum Novarum*, which they assumed were important to Wheeling's Catholic working-class populations.

Over time, the Socialist Party gained many new members in Center and South Wheeling, which were the center of much labor unrest, especially during the U.S. Steel strike of 1909–1910. Beginning in July the Wheeling District was the center of resistance against the "open shop" drive. U.S. Steel shifted production, imported strikebreakers, and hired company agents to entice skilled workers to break the picket line touching off considerable violence in Wheeling. More unrest occurred as a large crowd surrounded and then beat up U.S. Steel agent William Eagan as he left the LaBelle Mill. This attack led to an injunction from Judge Alston Dayton against any interference with the persons or property of the American Sheet and Tin Plate Company or the placement of pickets near their South Wheeling mill. Later the threat of an armed mob of over seven hundred across the river in Martin's Ferry raised the fear that strikers "were looking for another Homestead." As for scabs, the *Majority* jokingly remarked how in "Wheeling some scabs . . . fell down and hurt themselves in different parts about town."[51] While it is uncertain if the strike directly led individual workers to embrace socialism, given this level of resistance to the strike and the attack on scabs, it is clear a deeper class consciousness was growing among workers in Wheeling.

Socialist Party leaders thus linked the declining economic conditions for wage earners to the unfair political system corrupted by corporate power. One of its key leaders was Valentine Reuther, father of future UAW leader Walter Reuther. After the failed U.S. Steel strike in 1901, Reuther got a job driving a beer wagon for the Schmulbach Brewery. As he immersed himself in the German working-class culture of South Wheeling, he organized brewery workers, helped halt the construction of a Carnegie library in downtown Wheeling, and became president of the Ohio Valley Trades and Labor Assembly. Building off his earlier advocacy of industrial unionism, Reuther saw that with the power of the trusts, the blacklist, court injunctions, and boycotts: "It becomes apparent that labor must organize politically and elect such men who will carry out the wishes of the people. . . . Whenever the workers become class conscious and unitedly cast their ballot in support of the workers' party then the ruling of the trust owned courts and the enaction of corporation laws will vanish from the so-called land of the free and home of the brave."[52] Reuther's viewpoints reflect the Wheeling Socialist Party's goal to unify the local working class by providing tangible economic benefits. These changes could only come by electing independent pro-labor politicians to provide equitable public services and undermine the benefits traditional politicians gave toward large corporations.[53]

The defeat of unions in Wheeling owed much to the influence of the city's business community. They feared that labor radicalism would force U.S. Steel to move capital investment from Wheeling. American Sheet and Tin Plate officials warned leading businessmen that the company was withholding two hundred thousand dollars for improvements to Wheeling's plants. Realizing that the "difference between capital and labor has probably kept Wheeling back twenty years," Wheeling businessmen promoted more cooperation between the community, business, and city government.[54] The Wheeling Board of Trade, which helped form the Municipal Improvement League to promote "progressive" notions of civic betterment to keep Wheeling beautiful, became business-friendly. Adopting the slogan "Wheeling Means Business," the league and the Board of Trade publicly promoted the new Market Auditorium, public playgrounds, parks, and anything else "to make Wheeling brighter and more attractive" and to show the "substantial growth of that civic pride and local patriotism which after all is at the bottom of all civic advance."[55] Board of Trade Secretary R. B. Naylor highlighted that "Upward of 500 letters were sent to prospective industries . . . inviting them to consider Wheeling's advantages and resources." According to Naylor, "there [had] been some unfavorable features in our industrial situation . . . [but] Wheeling [was] in the procession of progress."[56]

While the Board of Trade downplayed the level of labor unrest in 1909 and 1910, the lingering economic conditions still plagued the city's working class. Particularly troubling was the high cost of foodstuffs and other consumer goods. Also inefficient municipal entities failed to provide necessary services during the spring of 1910. Especially pressing was the rehabilitation of the municipal lighting system. While the public had been "paying for the fun at the rate of more than $20 per day," local Socialists quipped that the Board of Control's recommendations were sidetracked by the undue influence of the Electric Light Goods Trust and political cronies working for the "political boss of this bailiwick, the defender of the Steel Trust and Senator [Nathan B.] Scott."[57]

As a result of the economic crisis from 1907 to 1910, the Socialists made a more concerted effort to enter into politics by targeting key municipal issues vital to the livelihoods of working-class Polish immigrants. Early in 1910, the Socialists informed the public about excessive taxes on electricity and supported a bond issue for the completion of a new filtration system to break up the business influence on the Board of Control.[58] They also set up a viable trade union ticket for the 1910 midterm election, running *Majority* editor Walter Hilton for state senate and Valentine Reuther for the state house of delegates. They pushed a strong platform, advocating for home rule, the initiative, referendum, recall, short-term franchises for public utilities, direct labor employment, the eight-hour day, free textbooks for public schools, opposition to the use of private detectives, and other issues.[59]

Voting returns from South Wheeling's Ritchie District, the center of Wheeling's Polish community, show the relative growth of the Socialist influence among the immigrant working class. Table 4.1 shows that even though the party's trade union candidates lost, the Socialist vote swayed many races in the 1910 election to the Democrats. This election demonstrates the degree to which Democrats and Socialists mobilized the working-class vote. Although the Poles were not the major ethnic group in the ward in 1910, their close proximity to local party leaders and the organizing of both parties forged networks that only grew as more Poles arrived.[60] The Ohio County Democrats won the race for Congress and the state senate and elected four Democrats to the House of Delegates.

The threat of a rival Polish Socialist subculture became viable during the early 1910s. Socialist organizing intensified throughout Ohio County with the creation of twenty local branches by 1911, including various party branches in South Wheeling. Local organizers divided wards into sections where members distributed literature, particularly during city council elections. Ritchie

Table 4.1. Midterm Election Totals for Ritchie District, 1910

	Congress: Pre. 7–9	Congress: Total Ritchie	State Senate: Pre. 7–9	State Senate: Total Ritchie	House of Delegates: Pre. 7–9	House of Delegates: Total Ritchie
1910						
Republican	35.9%	40.9%	33.4%	37.6%	33.1%	35.8%
Democrat	36.7%	37.4%	36.0%	37.7%	38.2%	41.1%
Socialist	26.2%	20.9%	28.7%	23.6%	27.1%	22.0%
Prohibition	1.3%	0.8%	1.9%	1.0%	1.6%	1.1%
Total (N =)	474	1296	467	1273	1854	4954

Note: These returns represent the total percentage of votes cast for the members of the given political party.

Source: *Wheeling Register*, November 9, 1910. Precincts Seven through Nine reflected the concentration of Polish immigrants.

District Socialists formed a branch of about fifty members with L. C. and C. W. Driehorst as the financial secretary and primary party organizer.[61] L. C. Driehorst was a local saloonkeeper, whose establishment on Forty-Fifth Street was a key social and political center for the German and Polish Socialists.[62] In February a meeting with Polish Socialists from Pittsburgh garnered much attention. During a meeting at Driehorst's Hall, comrades H. Machalski and Peter Morawsky welcomed several new Poles within the local as the promoters saw "that the prospects [were] bright for good progress in the movement among the Polish people of Wheeling."[63] By that summer Wheeling had a viable, dues-paying Polish Socialist local. As they organized for the upcoming 1912 election, the state Socialist Party praised its many diverse ward and ethnic locals in Wheeling, where the future of a Socialist subculture seemed promising.[64]

The Democrats also made a concerted effort to attract immigrant voters by routinely canvassing in South Wheeling. In the Progressive Era, the party increasingly conducted a politics of "class" in their daily newspapers and in their organizing tactics.[65] Democrats consistently espoused an egalitarian, producerist critique of industrialization and monopolization competing for supporters of radical third parties.[66] Wheeling's Democrats followed a similar policy. In 1910, congressional candidate John W. Davis came to Mozart Hall on Thirty-Eighth Street to argue that Republican tariffs had not prevented another depression like that of 1893 to 1897 and the Democrats would not close the steel mills in the Wheeling District.[67] The Democratic *Wheeling Register* effectively attracted working-class votes from the Socialists by appealing to the most pressing local situation—soaring unemployment. The Democrats posed a simple answer to the question "What's the matter with business in Wheeling?" With 11,300 men unemployed in all of the district's local industries, they argued that the Republicans and their protective tariffs were to blame. For unskilled immigrants, the key to material advancement remained the ability of men to work consistently to have enough money for necessary items but also to save for the purchase of their own home. The *Register* blended these immigrant needs while showing that anti-working-class policies and the corrupt power wielded by Republicans, led by Wheeling industrialist and United States Senator Nathan B. Scott, were to blame.[68]

The votes in Wheeling municipal elections during the 1910s (seen in table 4.2) highlight the disaffection with Republicans and their policies in the predominately Polish Fifth Precinct of Wheeling's Eighth Ward. In 1909, Republicans benefited from news that Thomas Beattle of the National Tube Company's Riverside Mill, which was the largest employer of Poles, would restart production after being idle since November 1907. This gave hope to the over 8,000 inhabitants of South Wheeling, of whom 80 percent of its 2,500 industrial workers had been periodically unemployed.[69] However, as the 1910 midterm election indicates, when Republican promises failed to quell rising unemployment, this immigrant community voted for the Democrats and Socialists. The relatively high turnout for the Socialist Party continued for the 1911 municipal and 1912 general elections. The *Intelligencer* chided in 1912 that city and county Republicans had "no idea that the growth of the [Socialist] party was so large in the county."[70]

While local politicians were confused by the success of the Socialists, the Catholic Church worried about the power of this secularist appeal. As seen by his efforts in chapter 3 to effectively mobilize against Socialism, Father Musial needed to offer his working-class parishioners something more than church services. Fortunately for him, these years saw Catholic leaders speak out against unrestrained capitalism. They promoted a corporatist alliance between capital, labor, and the government, building upon the encyclical *Rerum Novarum* (1891). Catholic social teaching stressed the importance of the wage contract and private property but reminded employers that the Catholic worker who "places at the disposal of others his skill, his strength, and his industry"

Table 4.2. Municipal Voting for City Council in Wheeling's Eighth Ward, 1909–1913

	First Branch Council: Precinct 5	First Branch Council: Total (%)	First Branch Council: Total	Second Branch Council: Precinct 5	Second Branch Council: Total (%)	Second Branch Council: Total
1909						
Republican	58.4%	66.1%	975	60.0%	69.7%	3747
Democrat	41.6%	33.9%	501	40.0%	30.3%	1632
Socialist	–	–	–	–	–	–
1911						
Republican	36.8%	53.8%	618	38.3%	53.0%	2370
Democrat	40.6%	26.4%	303	35.9%	24.9%	1113
Socialist	22.6%	19.8%	227	25.7%	22.1%	990
1913						
Republican	41.5%	54.6%	860	45.0%	56.0%	3454
Democrat	54.8%	39.9%	628	50.7%	39.0%	2404
Socialist	3.8%	5.5%	86	4.2%	5.0%	309

Note: The vote totals for the Second Branch Council reflect the relative totals for all the candidates on each party's municipal ballot, which in this case usually included four prospective councilmen for each party.

Source: *Wheeling Register*, May 28, 1909; *Wheeling Intelligencer*, May 26, 1911; *Wheeling Register*, May 23, 1913.

expects "not only the right to his salary, but also a strict and rigorous right to use it as he sees fit."[71] In addition, Irish American Catholic leaders sought a wider political voice by linking the church more closely to the Democratic Party and diocesan organizations to "Americanize" Catholics.[72]

Musial and the diocese's efforts reached their height in the mid-1910s, at the peak of the local Socialist Party's growth. The Wheeling can strike was a turning point. During the height of the strike, the Wheeling Socialists subtly called out Musial and the church's duty to the female can workers, whose "Sunday work roused no church to opposition," and to the Eighth Ward's population whose "distress [was] known to all."[73] For six weeks the Socialist press spoke fiercely of the can workers' gendered discrimination on the shop floor, the unsafe working conditions, and the "locked" exit doors that eerily reminded readers of the disastrous Triangle Shirtwaist Fire in 1911. Finally, using the emerging rhetoric of "industrial democracy," the Socialists asked readers to "pause long enough in our demand for peace in Europe to demand industrial peace in the Eighth Ward."[74]

"Organize the Unorganized"

By the 1910s, Polish Catholic workers were more active in union organizing campaigns. This increased support for the local labor movement coincided with the increased organizing by the Socialist Party and the local Trades Assembly. As James Barrett suggests, working-class "Americanization from the bottom-up" occurred through "the gradual acculturation of immigrants and their socialization in working-class environments" often by Irish and German Americans in the labor movement.[75] The Trades Assembly and leading Socialists continued their support of municipal reforms and better services in the working-class neighborhoods where new immigrants lived and labored. By 1913, they demanded more—that the city government provide public playgrounds, food and factory inspections, tenement sanitation, free public concerts, modern water filtration systems, and streetcar regulation. During this time, many trade unionists and "evolutionary" socialists denounced the more radical aims of the IWW by advocating for improvements to everyday concerns. Walter Hilton, Socialist editor of the *Wheeling Majority*, attacked the backward nature of city government: "Wheeling today is struggling along with the laws of a village . . . our factories can maim or sicken the workers with impunity, landlords can crowd as many tenants into as miserable and dirty quarters as their greed will allow."[76]

The Trades Assembly sponsored labor reforms in the state legislature, especially the state Workmen's Compensation Act of 1913. The bill provided a uniform system of compensation to injured workers while relieving employers of liability in individual cases. It paid funeral expenses of the deceased and a stipend to the widow and children, and, in case of partial or permanent disability, the employee was paid a certain percentage of his salary. The system was financed by a tax on the employer and employee. Sponsored by State Senator Jesse Bloch, of Bloch Brothers Tobacco, the bill reflected a similar company program in effect since 1896. The company's health plan paid workers three dollars a week if sick or maimed. Workers were eligible to join an Employee Relief Association by paying a two-dollar fee and then twenty-five cents weekly dues thereafter. Bloch Brothers' plan included a one-thousand-dollar life insurance policy (extended up to two thousand dollars for employees with a certain level of seniority) and paid unemployment benefits for up to thirteen weeks a year. The company's benefits, which were widely praised, were the result of collective bargaining with the Tobacco Workers International Union Local 2.[77]

Unfortunately the coal interests lobbied to limit the law's effectiveness. The "compulsory" clause was removed, placing the burden on workers to take the claim through the legal process. However, the Trades Assembly assisted many workers in the process of filing their claims and making sure companies paid appropriate benefits. New immigrants directly benefited from these reforms. In the awards distributed in late September 1915, many of the beneficiaries were unskilled immigrant steelworkers. Frank Woske, a laborer at the Wheeling Mold & Foundry, received compensation for several days missed. John Szeligowski, a laborer at the Wheeling Iron & Steel Mill, got a substantial award following an accident of $54 for medical costs and compensation of $480 for 120 weeks. The assembly worked on the behalf of Mike Stanko, who died of overwork at the American Sheet & Tin Plate Mill at Twenty-Ninth Street (La Belle). When the state denied his heirs the right to compensation, they wrote directly to Governor Henry Hatfield and the State Workmen's Compensation Agency. However, many immigrants, especially coal miners at Hitchman Coal & Coke, never got benefits or received meager sums. In addition, many continued to suffer from the physical effects of their injuries. Woske and his family were still struggling in 1920, renting their home at 314 Coal Street in North Wheeling as Woske worked at the Top Mill blast furnace. Szeligowski died tragically at age forty-six on April 9, 1918, after trying to return to work at the Riverside Mill in Benwood.[78]

The actions of the radical IWW in 1912 and 1913 helped spur a new organizing campaign by the Trades Assembly. Committed to providing tangible benefits, the assembly denounced the actions of IWW organizer Joseph Ettor, who was working among the coal miners of Bellaire advocating a general strike and direct-action tactics. *Majority* editor Walter Hilton referred to the IWW as a collection of "every freak and bug." As conservative Socialists, Hilton and others argued industrial unionism would only come by organizing semiskilled and mostly unskilled workers through education and by using the existing craft unions.[79]

Soon thereafter Wheeling's Socialist Party planned a massive organizing campaign in the spring and summer of 1913. Building solidarity would be difficult, but as Hilton argued "The fact that the skilled men have in the foolish past failed to protect the unskilled has resulted to the injury of the skilled." While the education campaign to reach new workers was crucial, the bigger problem would be convincing the craftsman that he must "adapt himself" to the fact that mechanization was yielding an "ever increasing army of the unskilled," especially recent immigrants. Of grave concern were young girls and boys. After investigating factories using child labor, especially the Wheeling Can Factory, Northwood Glass Works, and many cigar factories, the Socialists warned that this work was "stunting them" and contributing to the subsidizing of ever-lower wages and, in time, these girls and boys would be "crushed into a 'slum proletariat.'"[80]

Women workers were the main focus of the organizing campaign. An investigation conducted by the *Wheeling Register* found that by July 1914 the city had at least four thousand women working in small factories, offices, and department stores. This meant about one in five wage earners was a female. While many entered wage work with the "desire for economic independence," the main factor was the city's rapid spike in the cost of living after 1900: "So many are the homes that are pinched by poverty that it is necessary for the children, both the boys and the girls, to add to the family income." Many small factories employed large female contingents, especially Wheeling Can Company (200), Wheeling Stamping Company (204), and Bloch Brothers Tobacco (177), all on the South Side. As the opening story of this chapter suggests, these factory women were aggressive union supporters. This was true of the four hundred to five hundred girls in the city's tobacco plants. When the plans for the union drive began, the most enthusiastic union was the Tobacco Strippers' Union. The "union girls" canvassed several neighborhoods and factory sites encouraging girls to meet to talk about joining their respective unions.[81] Most of the organizers were from German immigrant households. At a get-together at the Odd Fellows Hall, the "militant girls" gave talks and played music. One of the girls was Elizabeth Bozenska. Born in 1897 in Prussian Poland, she lived on Twelfth Street and worked at the Pollack Cigar Factory. Later she worked at the Wheeling Can Factory following the strike by Polish girls there in the summer of 1915.[82]

The campaign promoted solidarity by reaching beyond the factory gates. Organizers encouraged meetings near the "Street corners, Factory, Churches, Halls and if necessary in the Homes . . . even to call on [a] man's wife and induce her to take a union card." Communications were sent to all preachers and priests in Wheeling, especially Bishop Patrick Donahue, to allow ministers to speak from their pulpits on a certain date about the moral importance and "aims and object of the organized Labor movement." They also asked that parishes observe "Child Labor Sunday" held on January 18, 1914. The Socialists realized the importance of reaching into the churches, since "invariably the Church [will] be filled with people that would not go to the Union's Hall." The stress on morality also attacked commercialized vice in Wheeling, but the

Socialists shifted the focus. Hilton stated it directly: "The ABOLITION of commercialized vice is impossible.... The places are not in themselves the cause so much as they are the effect." Those who blamed the victims should be ashamed, according to the Socialists, for the "environment which they were not strong enough to overcome, shaped and fashioned their lives into the hideous thing it is today."[83]

Initial organizing meetings went quite well. Machinists' Local 818 and members of the Molders Union at the Wheeling Mold & Foundry attracted many unskilled workers. Their ability to appeal to these workers was important since many Polish men labored in its foundries. The Butchers' and Flint Glass Workers' Unions were more reluctant to hold meetings. Skilled workers stressed key benefits of unionization, including "the saving of arms and legs, of lives and of widows," the end of night work, and the eight-hour day. The most useful organizing technique was meeting men on their own terms in clubs and fraternal organizations and the tobacco "union girls'" efforts to visit the homes of factory girls. The organizing committee also printed materials in at least four different languages.[84]

The cultural efforts of the organizing campaign to attract foreign-born workers proved vital. Socialists and skilled workers sponsored meetings, cultural events, and amusements to show the new immigrants the benefits of unions. The Polish were one of the most targeted groups. At first, the assembly sponsored union rallies in popular theaters and vaudeville houses, which many Polish immigrants on the South Side attended for entertainment. A protest meeting was held in the Victoria Theater downtown, led by Mother Jones, against the "human exploitation in the coal mines of this state." Marco Roman spoke at first in Italian followed by UMWA international organizer Frank Ledvinka. The latter talked for some time in "Polish, translating for the benefit of the Polish people present."[85]

Unions increasingly met in ethnic social halls for entertainment and organizing events. One of the key sites in South Wheeling was the Polish Hall on Forty-Fifth Street. While the venue mainly served the functions of the St. Ladislaus Parish and Polish fraternal organizations, by 1914 unions held regular events in the space. Molders Union No. 364 from the Wheeling Mold & Foundry held its third annual ball on April 3, 1914. The molders had been promoting solidarity for some time with the unskilled Polish foundry and furnace men, and meeting in the center of the Polish community highlighted that growing support. The hall also hosted a more humorous event for Brewery Workers Union No. 53 titled a "Good-By Ball." With the passage of the Yost

Law, German brewery workers wanted to celebrate legally, asking all to join them "filling with joy and jest."[86]

The Trades Assembly had much to worry about regarding Wheeling's Polish immigrants if they continued to exclude them. Coal miner and leader of the Polish Socialist local Peter Morawsky informed the assembly of the condition of his countrymen and other foreign workers in the city's steel factories. While the unorganized campaign had made tangible gains, Morawsky criticized the assembly for not reaching out to the largest unskilled workforces at the Wheeling Iron & Steel Mill, the Riverside Mill in Benwood, and the Wheeling Mold & Foundry in Fulton. He acknowledged that many Poles were "anxious to organize" but that the "I.W.W. having availed themselves of the opportunity had been working among the men for years . . . and the I.W.W. [would] organize."[87]

The Trades Assembly took his warning seriously, and throughout 1915 and 1916, the two most successful organizing campaigns involved plants with large Polish workforces. One was the Wheeling Can Factory strike of the summer of 1915. As noted at the start of the chapter, Polish women were quite active in working the picket line and calling for AFL recognition. The strike was successful, and the employees earned a minimum wage of $1.00 a day, a ten-hour day, $1.25 for overtime hours, and time-and-a-half for holidays. The company also refunded the money they should have paid into the state workmen's compensation fund.[88]

The other successful campaign led by the Trades Assembly and involving Polish workers took place against the city's largest meat packers in late 1915 through 1916. The strike also suggests the growth of ethnic solidarity within the local labor movement by this point. With growing demands for processed meat nationally and the start of World War I, the large meat packers F. Schenk & Sons Co. and Paul O. Reymann Company, both in Fulton, refused to negotiate with the butchers in a "deliberate attempt to destroy unionism." The Amalgamated Meat Cutters and Butcher Workmen asked for wage increases for all butchers, meat cutters and packers, coopers, drivers, and laborers. All new workers, including immigrants, would earn no less than two dollars for a nine-hour day with overtime and holiday pay. After the companies refused to discuss the proposal, butchers and all other workers went out on strike in December 1915. When the strike expanded to include smaller meat packers, the larger firms tried to seek a court injunction to prevent picketing and imported an "undesirable class" of strikebreakers.[89]

What worried union men the most was how Albert Schenk apparently told these imported men there had been "antagonistic nationalities at the plant" and that he discharged them to be replaced with "good Germans, and Austria-Hungarian races." It seems that no man could work there that was not a "good German." While trying to replace the strikers with Polish men from northern cities, the union found that most were reluctant to come as scabs. When company officials tried to "cause a split among the strikers on racial lines," they were unable to induce the foreign-born men, mostly Polish and "Austrians," to break the picket line. When the company tried to get a former popular saloonkeeper Alois Smalzer to organize a meeting among the Polish and Bohemian strikers, the men sternly refused to go, instead informing the Amalgamated Meat Cutters about the underhanded tactics. After a month, 300 of 325 strikers voted to remain out for their demands. Walter Hilton spoke to the men along with Bohemian butcher Mike Teufel and Andy Kissel in Polish. They remarked about the horrible living conditions in the Schenk company boardinghouse for many immigrant workmen. By the end of the successful strike, the German American Butcher Workmen praised the unskilled Poles "standing as firm as a rock."[90]

Conclusion

By the start of World War I, Wheeling's Polish immigrant working class, male and female, were slowly becoming members of the labor movement. That was a long cry from the days when "Polanders" were accosted for working at near starvation wages. Thanks to the OVTLA and local Socialists' educational and cultural outreach campaigns, the Poles and their families were further Americanized within the blue-collar neighborhoods of Wheeling. However, the First World War brought new trials. With the nation caught up in the wartime patriotism, Wheeling was afflicted with anti-German propaganda and renewed animosity toward immigrants plagued the city. Public schools ceased teaching German as a second language, and banks and institutions took the word *German* out of their titles.[91] The first generation of Polish immigrants worked to balance their support of Catholic ethnic institutions tied to St. Ladislaus Parish with their blue-collar identity as junior members of the city's labor movement. However, by 1917, the primary threat would be an attack on the Poles' loyalty to a conformist Americanism.

CHAPTER 5

Proving Their Loyalty: Wheeling's Polish Immigrants during World War I

Following almost three bloody years of global war, the United States ended its "neutrality" in early April 1917. With Germany reinstituting unrestricted submarine warfare and the threats posed by the Zimmermann Telegram, Congress heeded the president's call for a declaration of war. For the next nineteen months, U.S. military involvement aided in the victory of the Allies against the Central Powers. Of equal significance was the mobilization of the American home front as the Wilson administration instituted propaganda and sponsored war bond campaigns while also strengthening the federal bureaucracy's control over U.S. citizens. Jeanette Keith in her study of rural southern resistance to the wartime draft sees World War I as the rise of the "American surveillance state," which increasingly monitored citizens' activities.[1]

The coming of the war had an immediate impact in Wheeling. Scanning the *Wheeling Intelligencer* shows the declaration's effect on many differing groups. Successful entrepreneur and German immigrant George Stifel and his German and Austrian clerks declared their "loyalty" to America. Sheriff Howard Hastings's proclamation, reprinted in seven languages, promised protection to immigrants, who need not "fear any invasion of his personal property right so long as he goes peaceably about his business." In a public display, three Austro-Hungarian immigrants applied for naturalization on April 9, 1917. From February 1 to May 1, 161 immigrants filed their declarations of intent to become U.S. citizens. On June 5, 1917, immigrants reported before their local draft board for the first time.[2] Wheeling's Catholic population of around twelve thousand mobilized after the editors of the *Wheeling Intelligencer* questioned Catholic patriotism: "No American flags have been nor will be placed inside any of the Catholic churches. The church is a universal organization and does not allow the flag of any nation on inside walls." Spurred to react following Easter Sunday the Carroll Club Council and Knights of Columbus issued plans for an American flag rally and street parade with over three thousand children from the city's Catholic parochial schools participating.[3]

While patriotic groups "convinced" many immigrants of the need to show their loyalty, Wheeling's Polish community gave its consent in grand fashion at a rally at the Polish Hall in South Wheeling. In a statement to the press, the two thousand in attendance affirmed: "We American citizens of Polish descent . . . considering that not birth alone, but loyalty to American ideas makes men Americans—declare our united allegiance to President Wilson and to the government of the United States of America, and pledge ourselves by word and example to teach and impress upon our children and fellow countrymen the duty of a loyal citizen and obedience to the government."[4] The loyalty meeting was preceded by a mass street procession including the Polish Falcon members in military uniform. Marching from the Polish Hall, they stopped at the city hall downtown. Joseph Rozanski gave a patriotic address, and men placed a wreath of flowers on the Soldiers and Sailors Monument. Back at the hall, the Polish choir sang patriotic numbers and Prosecuting Attorney David McKee praised the "Polish people for their spirit of loyalty." Later Fr. Emil Musial addressed the crowd in Polish saying "Poland should be a free state . . . and that there [would] not be peace until Poland receives her freedom." He urged young Poles to take up arms for the United States. In this effort he "could see the freedom for all Slavic-speaking people."[5]

This chapter focuses on the tensions within Wheeling's Polonia as it confronted both promises and dangers during a time of war. The war years produced a brand of conformity stated in terms of a "civic nationalism," promoting the greatness of American political ideals and the benefits of citizenship.[6] However, the war also saw a more fluid "pluralistic Americanism," promoting the inherent benefits of immigrant culture. As long as Poles supported the country and did not engage in subversive activities, there was no reason they could not be good Americans and good Poles at the same time. Nationally, Polonias witnessed divides between the conservative Polish Roman Catholic Union (PRCU) and the secular, radical nationalist Polish National Alliance (PNA) over support for the re-creation of the Polish homeland.[7]

In Wheeling there was more cooperation between fraternal groups and across class backgrounds as Wheeling's Poles showed their loyalty through a variety of cultural displays and public actions. Street parades, public meetings, Polish Catholic events, and organizing for the Polish Army in France suggest a form of politicization that was often not fully understood by the 100 Percent Americanizers. While presenting a strong pro-war loyalty, their actions hid a subtle critique of coercive Americanization, giving Poles ways to celebrate and promote their multiple identities as Polish and Catholic. These actions provide an illusion of total consent while allowing immigrants to create space to support alternative worldviews. Wheeling's Poles could fight for America and "Polishness." Thus these everyday acts allowed for the continued growth of an alternative subculture in Polonia promoting the community's multiple identities.[8]

Making the Home Front Safe for Polish Catholic Americanism

By 1914, Fr. Emil Musial, the Polish Catholic laity, and the rise of an ethnic middle class all contributed to the stability of South Wheeling's Polonia. The onset of hostilities abroad created new challenges. The war pushed southern and eastern European immigrants into a closer relationship with the federal government. From the propaganda of George Creel's Committee on Public Information to war mobilization, military conscription, and the selling of war bonds, immigrants were bombarded by the efforts of a government and middle-class Protestant society to shape them into loyal, patriotic Americans. Through the mobilization of public school advocates, businessmen, political speakers, and even ethnic priests, World War I ushered in a new period of political identification for recent immigrant groups.[9]

Wheeling's Polonia weathered these outside pressures by long advocating citizenship and political participation. As early as 1904, the "Polish race" organized a meeting of the Pulaski Polish Association held at St. Ladislaus to promote Polish political action in the United States. In 1909, the Sokol Society of "Americanized Polanders" held a dance at Mozart Hall at Thirty-Eighth and Jacob Streets and also presented a "fine American flag to the Polish Catholic church." Contingents attended from South Wheeling, Upper Benwood, and Bellaire, Ohio. During a parade, one marched with a brass band riding horses draped in red, white, and blue.[10]

One crucial Americanizing element in the Polish neighborhood was the Polish Falcons. A militant, fraternal organization connected to the PNA, they advocated physical fitness and Polish cultural pride. Increasingly the Falcons linked Polish hopes for an independent state with Americanism by promoting Polish American cultural heroes such as Kościuszko and Pulaski. While supported by the middle-class elites within Polonia, working-class Poles took an active part in the emphasis on sporting events and popular Polish nationalism. The Falcons were crucial to bringing the different classes and regional groups together and encouraging a shared ethnic consciousness as "Polish."[11]

In 1911, Wheeling's Polish Falcon Society built a new clubhouse on Wood Street near Forty-Fourth Street at the cost of fifty thousand dollars. A large celebration was held at its dedication, including Falcon lodges from Pittsburgh, Bellaire, Steubenville, Bridgeport, Neffs, and Dillonvale, Ohio. In full uniforms a party of over 1,500 marched through the South Side. Blessings by Fr. Emil Musial and the local officers were followed by the keynote talk by Father Skaryanci of Pittsburgh. Afterwards the entire group sang the Polish national hymn. Founded by the first generation of immigrants, this club helped foster Polish and American political consciousness in the years before World War I while sponsoring athletic events. The club housed a poolroom, bowling alleys, and a large social hall.[12]

The Falcons played an important role in Wheeling and the upper Ohio Valley throughout the decade. Shortly after the dedication, the Fourth District of the Polish Falcons held their annual convention at the fairgrounds on Wheeling Island. Taking place on July 4, 1912, the event honored the United States while advocating Polish independence. Local reporters called the event "Polish Soldier's Day," highlighting the militant political importance of the celebration. While the event was a strictly Polish affair, organizers opened participation to Russians, Bohemians, Slavs, and even interested Americans. The festivities commenced with a parade of between two and three thousand people marching from St. Ladislaus to Wheeling Island. Led by the Złot Sokołów in full Polish military uniform, many women and children followed dressed in red, white, and blue. A large picnic was held along with seventeen sporting contests (mile race, 100-yard dash, and shot put among others) to highlight Polish athletic prowess. The superiority of the Poles was seen in the main event, a wrestling match between Polish champion Walter Bonecki and an American. Lasting only three minutes, the American admitted that "the Pole was too strong for him."[13]

Polish Catholics also promoted Americanism through St. Ladislaus. In July 1914, several parishioners organized the Polish American Citizens' League, which aided in naturalizing the city's Polish immigrants and encouraged them to take part in politics. The group's leaders represented a cross section of mainly working-class members and some small businessmen. The president was Frank Lewandowsky, a coal miner; Secretary Paul Jurczak was a helper on a furnace at the Riverside Mill. Other organizers were Frank Templin, who worked at a tannery, and Anton Cihy (Cinkling), who ran a dry goods store and grocery in Fulton near Wheeling Mold & Foundry.[14]

Within weeks over fifty Poles joined the organization and were "making progress in solving the intricacies of the English language." The society sponsored English language and other classes to prepare immigrants for applying for citizenship. The *Wheeling Register* highlighted the key beliefs of the city's

Poles on the eve of the Great War: "The Polanders more than any other class of foreigners seem anxious to secure the privileges of citizenship once they have settled in this country.... At each term of federal court they compose by far the larger number of those admitted to citizenship. The actuating motive that is impelling such a general desire among the South Side Poles to swear allegiance to Uncle Sam is undoubtedly due in a large measure to that general characteristic of all sons of down-trodden Poland—a love of freedom in all things political."[15] The emphasis on "liberty" and "freedom" suggests how the Polish Falcons, St. Ladislaus Parish, and the quest for a free and independent Poland fostered an interest in political engagement. These political efforts would also enable them to link the fight for Polish independence to the cause of World War I, thereby promoting their Polish nationalist identity in a manner compatible with the Americanism of the wartime climate in Wheeling.

Proving Their Loyalty

Unlike other immigrant groups nationally, the Poles suffered less repression. However, they still had to prove their loyalty. Many emigrated from the German and Austro-Hungarian Empires, making them suspect. In August 1914, it was the longstanding Polish animosity toward the Russian Empire that led some residents to question whether these antipathies for the czarist state would lead the "Polish element of the city to favor the Austro-Hungarian cause."[16]

Beginning in August 1914, the immediacy of anti-immigrant reactions took America's foreign-born populations by surprise. The central issue was loyalty. How did individual immigrants prove their loyalty on an everyday basis? Those who naturalized obviously wanted to become U.S. citizens, but a large number of Wheeling's foreign population were aliens. Speaking multiple languages, worshipping differently than the WASP majority, and holding a wide spectrum of political views created obvious problems. The war years ushered in new understandings of who was a true American and created new categories of citizenship, such as the "enemy alien," and deemed questionable people as "pro-German." Wheeling's immigrants would now encounter federal structures for the first time. Appearing before the local draft board, filing an exemption, registering as a German enemy alien, and constantly carrying their draft papers helped to create the early features of the twentieth-century U.S. security state.[17]

Federal and state officials targeted the city's immigrants to ferret out subversives. Governor John Cornwell and agents of the Federal Bureau of Investigation worked to track down draft dodgers and "enemy aliens" to foster a more modern, conservative political culture in the state.[18] As chairman of the State Council of Defense, Cornwell sent a confidential message to the state's major employers warning of the many "alien enemies in this State." He wanted them to send detailed lists of all Germans, Austrians, Hungarians, Bulgarians, and Turkish immigrants and even keep track of their movements.[19]

During the war the Federal Bureau of Investigation's main local agent, John B. Wilson, led the surveillance of suspected "pro-German" immigrants. Working with local law enforcement, lawyers, and factory superintendents, Wilson and other bureau officials spent most of their energies keeping track of suspected radicals engaged in wartime espionage, looking for supposed Bolshevik agitators after the war, and monitoring the immigrant working-class areas of the city. The use of informants in local factories was a key component of this surveillance network. Wilson's chief focus was enemy aliens who had failed to sign their registration papers. One key informant was Thomas Hearne of the Riverside Tube Mill in Benwood. During May 1918 he was looking for John Schemelgeski, a German Polish immigrant steelworker living on the corner of Forty-Fifth and Wetzel Streets, who allegedly remarked that "the German soldiers were better soldiers than the Americans . . . and would win the war." When asked about his support of the kaiser, Schemelgeski asserted "he had pledged himself in the old country, and he would stick to it." Hearne visited Waston Koosnick, another Russian Pole, who blamed Schemelgeski's statements on too much liquor. It proved hard to find his location since Hearne could not locate an employment record for him.[20]

Company informants were particularly concerned with rooting out pro-German support. Later Hearne investigated Robert Stolz, who according to Deputy Sheriff Paul Jurczak stated emphatically on a streetcar that "Paul, Germany is going to rule this country." Another immigrant, Thomas Telpa, confirmed Stolz's pro-German sympathies, claiming that while talking near the Polish American Political Club, Stolz stressed the superiority of the kaiser and argued that local immigrants were "fools to take out Liberty Bonds; that the money goes into the pockets of the rich man" and "the Dutch [Germans] are going to lick the world."[21] Another case was the arrest of German Poles George and Zefia Gregofsko after they cursed the U.S. and President Wilson "for killing their people." After Agent Wilson spoke with fellow Polish acquaintances Alex Krew and William Lovonduski, and even General Manager Koch of the Hitchman Coal & Coke Company, he learned that the two "defendants [were] good, quiet, respectable people" and George Gregofsko was a "steady worker."

Koch spoke of George as an "industrious fellow, and has been a leader among the miners in promoting the sale of Liberty Bonds, and in contributing to the Red Cross." It appeared Peter Macekevich, with whom the couple had a quarrel, was using the overzealous surveillance apparatus "to get even with them."[22]

Paul Jurczak's role suggests the divided nature of the Polish community during the war. Appointed as a deputy sheriff to assist the bureau, Jurczak was actually a laborer and helper at the National Tube Company. Born in 1881 in Austria-Poland, Jurczak immigrated to America in 1900 and naturalized in 1908. While he rented a home at 4401 Wetzel Street, during the war he apparently lived in a boardinghouse near the mill so as to report on any unpatriotic speeches by his countrymen.[23] For example, Jurczak arrested Konstanty Lapinski for "alleged disloyal remarks" on August 3, 1918. Thomas Hearne talked with both Jurczak and D. W. Sieroski, recruiting officer for the Polish Army in France. It appears Lapinski accosted recruit John Pawelczak in front of the Polish Hall. Before Sieroski entered an automobile to drive around with Pawelczak, Lapinski called the other Polish men several "unpleasant names" and told Pawelczak to "put him [Sieroski] in a wheelbarrow and wheel him into the river." Lapinski also remarked angrily that before he enlisted in any army "he would kill three." Lapinski made this speech in the presence of several notable Polish men in the community, including Wojciech Swiader. Swiader immigrated in 1907 at age seventeen and upon arriving in Wheeling quickly rose to become an electrician then shop foreman for the Pullman Company. On the other hand, Lapinski was an unskilled mill hand. While the other men's backgrounds are unknown, it seems that Lapinski held personal animosities against those skilled blue-collar and middle-class Poles in the neighborhood and their patriotism.[24]

Even with bureau overzealousness, some Poles did harbor "pro-German" sympathies. This was apparent after the first draft call on June 5, 1917. Under the Selective Service Act of 1917, all male citizens (ages twenty-one to thirty) and male aliens who had taken out their first papers had to report to their local draft boards. Bureau agents focused in on the city's working-class immigrant neighborhoods. Here alien men and boys roamed the streets and crowded into dark pool halls, and law enforcement already considered them suspect for their many violations of the Yost prohibition law.[25]

Draft enforcement divided immigrant communities as well. While many followed Father Musial and other middle-class leaders' support for registering and buying war bonds, others sought a different political response. Shemek Wnuck was born in October 1889 in Niezdów, Russian Poland. Immigrating sometime in his teens, by 1917 he was working as an unskilled laborer at the Belmont Mill. Unlike those Poles who patriotically joined the American Expeditionary Forces or Polish Haller's Army, when he registered on June 5, 1917, Wnuck requested an exemption from the Ohio County draft board. However, when the time came to report, he evaded the meeting. After some investigating, special agent John B. Wilson informed the bureau that Wnuck had disappeared.[26] Wilson had the same difficulty in locating John Mozodewska, who also filed for an exemption. After going to his address at 146 National Road across from the Wheeling Mold & Foundry, Wilson learned he had moved and was thought to be in Philadelphia. Mozodewska was also a Russian Pole in his mid-twenties who only recently arrived in the United States. However, he was caught and sent to military camp as a "non-wilful [sic] deserter" on December 30, 1917.[27] Reports compiled in early 1919 show that these "disloyal" men represented an ethnic cross section of the area's population, including Polish immigrants. Lucas Daolski, Walter Andrzejonski, and Joseph Cieslek were still at large by March 1919. Some Poles were found but reclassified to Class 5 like Adam Zaniszlweki, meaning he was discharged from service.[28]

Slavic immigrants tried to evade the draft in many ways. Joseph Delenski was caught by authorities in a poolroom in Braddock, Pennsylvania, where he claimed he went for work two weeks prior. The case of Mike Szembowski suggests how coercive authorities could be toward pro-German sentiments. On June 5, 1917, registration day, he bragged loudly he planned not to register. Soon thereafter county deputies arrested Szembowski and sent him to the county jail. While Szembowski was there, patriotic and "husky prisoners . . . secured an American flag and at the evening drill forced Mike to parade about the corridor" with Old Glory on his shoulder. He was forced to do this over several nights. As a result Szembowski learned that there "are worse things than registering," and he asked to fulfill his patriotic duty soon after.[29]

While draft resistance and evasion involved native-born citizens as well, in the mill district it appeared like a problem unique to immigrants. During the second call for six hundred drafted men in Wheeling in September 1917, about 20 percent never reported to the local draft boards, and 43 percent claimed an exemption. To "promote" civic obligation, the *Wheeling Register* printed all the names and draft numbers of men who were supposed to appear. Of fourteen distinctively Polish names listed, seven claimed an exemption as "aliens," and four failed to report. Benwood's draft board noted that fourteen immigrants failed to report; most were coal miners at the Hitchman Coal & Coke Company but had since left for other coal fields.[30] By January 1918, Benwood's draft board published a list of sixty "missing registrants" in the *Benwood Enterpriser*. Almost all were Croatian, Polish, and Slovak immigrants from North Benwood and other immigrant boardinghouses near Boggs Run and the large steel mills along Marshall and Main Streets.[31]

Even with these cases of suspected disloyalty, most of Wheeling's Poles vigorously supported the U.S. war effort. They registered for the draft in high numbers and contributed more in war bonds than many other immigrant groups in the city. However, their pro-American expressions gave them the space politically to support their multiple identities as Poles and Catholics. Ordinary Poles fought for these shared identities in both the secular and sacred aspects of their everyday lives. The recruitment for the Polish Army in France and the American Expeditionary Forces (AEF) reflected this secular side, while religious processions and related Catholic events represented the sacred.

Thousands of Polish immigrants fought in the last months of World War I on the western front. Organized through the Polish Falcons and with help from the French government, what became known as Haller's Army gave Polish men another avenue to show their dual patriotism to the United States and their homeland. Wheeling served as a recruiting center for the Polish Army for the entire upper Ohio Valley. Support for the fatherland, according to the Wheeling Polish veterans after the war, was the primary motivation. Desiring to protect Polish cultural heritage, thousands of Polish men heeded the call to serve. After the war, Polish veteran societies expressed the views of those who fought on the fields of France, Poland, and Ukraine in helping make Poland a free nation again. Polish veterans in Wheeling in particular noted the inspiration they got in their adopted nation from President Woodrow Wilson's support for a Polish state and the legacy of George Washington as the leader of the struggle for independence in the United States.[32]

Many Polish men in Haller's Army continued the fight against the Bolsheviks after World War I. Allied leaders at the Versailles Peace Conference used Haller's Army in the Polish–Soviet War of 1919–1920 on Poland's eastern border and into Ukraine. However, starting in early 1919 these Polish units were criticized for engaging in pogroms and acts of violence against Jewish and Ukrainian populations in eastern Poland, thus tainting their reputation to some extent.[33] In America the army was primarily heralded for its success in repulsing the Bolshevik advance on the eastern front, a source of pride for many veterans once they returned to the United States. Like the patriotic fervor that inspired the creation of chapters of the American Legion following the war, Polish Army veterans formed various chapters of the Polish Army Veterans Association (PAVA). Their goal, as stated by Wheeling's PAVA No. 82 in 1926 was to "maintain the Polish soul and to take an active part in celebrating" their achievements and to provide mutual assistance when veterans are sick and unable to work.³⁴

Most of the "Hallerczy Boys" who volunteered for service in the Polish Army shared similar characteristics in that most came from the Russian partition and had only been in the United States for a few years. Two of the leaders of the Wheeling's PAVA No. 82 highlight these backgrounds. Jan Mirosław was born in 1890 in Wojciechów, arriving in the United States aboard the SS *George Washington* on September 21, 1912. Władysław Zdanowicz was born in 1890 in Trszebien and arrived in the 1910s finding work at the National Tube Company's pipe mill.³⁵

Many federal and state officials worried about Polish intentions. This was especially true when Lieutenant Steffen Hoffman arrived in Wheeling to set up a recruiting station for the Polish Army in November 1917. Hoffman caused sensations early on when he stated, "I am a former officer of the German army, fighting against Germany." In his Polish uniform, he set up his headquarters at the Polish Hall at 4414 Wood Street and began recruiting Polish men in Wheeling, Benwood, and eastern Ohio.³⁶

The War Department and Federal Bureau of Investigation checked to make sure Hoffman was not potentially a German army spy. Chief A. Bruce Bielaski asked John B. Wilson to check Hoffman's credentials, citizenship history, and political connections. Shortly after arriving, Hoffman successfully recruited twelve Poles to go to the training station in Canada.³⁷ Problems stemmed from the bureaucratic mess created by the Polish Army and activist recruiters like Hoffman. Based on the terms set by the Selective Service Act, General Enoch Crowder of the War Department saw no problem enrolling men under twenty-one or over thirty years of age. For draft-age men, the Polish Army recruiters could only seek Polish immigrants termed enemy aliens (i.e., German Poles) or those "in deferred or exempted classes," such as Russian Poles who were subjects of an Allied state. All Poles posed a unique problem since all were technically aliens of the German, Russian, or Austro-Hungarian Empires. This reality was a major issue for Wheeling's local draft boards. After November 6, 1917, all German alien men fourteen and older had to register, present photographs of themselves, and be fingerprinted, later along with those of the Austro-Hungarian Empire. With large numbers coming from the German and Austrian partitions, these Poles were technically considered enemy aliens. However, it appears that Wheeling's local draft boards endeavored to make a distinction between those of German and Austrian ethnic stock and Poles and other nationalities from the respective empires.³⁸ Governor Cornwell asked Crowder whether Hoffman could transport Polish draftees to the Polish

Army camp at Niagara on Lake Ontario. In November Crowder informed him he could not, as he was awaiting word on the legal issues tied up with the recruitment itself. Cornwell also inquired whether it was proper for Poles to claim exemptions as aliens in order to join the Polish Army. Hoffman did have to prove on several occasions that he was a legitimate recruiting officer for the Polish Army in France under Alexander Znaniecke of Pittsburgh.[39]

Polish men from the upper Ohio Valley signed up for months winning the praise of much of the South Side. The first group of eighteen recruits left for Canada on December 12, 1917, to a rousing send-off by Polish citizens and the Polish and Slovak bands. The volunteers along with their families participated in a mass at St. Ladislaus, led by Father Musial, followed by a dinner at the Polish Club. Following several stirring speeches, the men left by train after receiving a carton of cigarettes, fruit, and other "goodies." In later recruitment celebrations, Polish priests from nearby parishes attended, and the Polish recruits received supplies from Wheeling's Polish Woman's Association. In total 150 Polish men joined to fight in Haller's Army with fifty-six coming from Wheeling alone and the rest from nearby mill towns. A. W. Cleahoff, a Pole from Martins Ferry, summed up the sentiments of those joining: "No nation can live in peace as long as German autocracy and militarism exists."[40]

Jozef Fic (or Fitz) of Wheeling was one soldier who joined Haller's Army. Born on August 28, 1894, in Domaradz, Galicia, he arrived in the United States aboard the SS *Zeeland* on September 20, 1912, to find work in Wheeling. He came from the Brzozów area, like many Austrian Poles living in Wheeling. In May 1918, he joined Haller's Army, returning from service in the summer of 1920. Truly representative of the dual allegiances of Wheeling's Poles, Fic then enlisted at Camp Dix, New Jersey, on July 23, 1920, serving a year in the U.S. military.[41]

Polish men registered for the selective service drafts in high numbers as well. Bishop Patrick Donahue spoke often of its importance. At Mount de Chantal's graduation ceremonies on June 6, 1917, Donahue noted "the registration of millions of young men, who went to these offices like men, like patriots and caused their names to be inscribed as possible defenders of this republic." Donahue spoke of the problems faced by area residents whose foreign roots put their "heads and hearts . . . in conflict." Donahue made clear that he knew the region's foreign-born communities, even those who "have love and affection for that land for which he drew the breath of life and in which his forefathers, for generations back, lived and died," would now "cling to the land of their adoption and fight to the last breath for the 'Stars and Stripes.'"[42]

The military service of Wheeling's Polish Catholics drafted into the

American Expeditionary Forces exemplifies the highest level of loyalty they felt for their adopted country. Joining Haller's Army was one thing, but fighting with General John Pershing's AEF in France showed the local native-born population the Polish Catholics were true American patriots above reproach. Many Poles were joined by men from the region's other ethnic neighborhoods as well. Following the first draft call on June 5, 1917, the men going off to military training camps in Virginia looked like the proverbial melting pot. For example, Benwood's contingent in September 1917 included fifty-two men: sixteen were native-born with eleven Italians, ten Croatians, seven Poles, six Slovaks, and two Greeks.[43] Many Polish men from Wheeling served abroad in the AEF. Peter Templin was born in 1896, the son of Polish immigrants living in South Wheeling. Filing on June 5, Templin eventually rose to the rank of sergeant in Battery F, 314th Field Artillery, which was comprised primarily of men from Wheeling. Battery F was known by officers as the "motley crew of Mountaineers from West Virginia." Almost a dozen men in Battery F were from Benwood, which was truly a melting pot. Sergeant Templin (Polish) was joined by Privates Steve Bankovich (Croatian), Michael Brazdovich (Slovak), Michele Campagnia (Italian), Andrew Hlaszko (Slovak), and Alex Habak (Ukrainian). Other batteries in the unit had Polish immigrants, especially Battery C with eighty-four men from Wheeling and Ohio County. William Wodiske was a coal miner at the Hitchman Coal & Coke Company. He rose to the rank of corporal in Battery C. Another was Konstantz Vendlinski, a Russian Pole, who applied for naturalization after his service.[44]

These units were part of the Eightieth Division of the American Expeditionary Forces, and the whole division, especially the 314th Field Artillery, had men from Pennsylvania, Virginia, and mainly West Virginia. The division was known for being overly aggressive, even during their training at Camp Lee, Virginia. Seeing action early on, they earned the motto "The Eightieth Division Moves Only Forward." The division's artillery batteries boasted more days of straight combat engagement than any other AEF batteries. They were part of the offensives at St. Mihiel (September 12–15, 1918) and even more so during the crucial Meuse-Argonne Campaign (September 26–November 11, 1918). During that latter effort, these artillery units reached many of their preset objectives quite quickly. The use of mobile infantry and artillery attacks worked well for small penetrations, but often led to men being exposed to swift German counterattacks. The 314th experienced heavy fighting in late October into early November 1918. On October 29, they executed a harassing fire, which was met by stiff return of artillery from the Germans. In the exchange Corporal Wodiske was wounded. The 314th was later ordered to make an attack at 5:30 a.m. on November 1. The unit's First Battalion delivered a gas attack followed by zone fire; the Second Battalion, of which Sergeant Templin and Private Habak's Battery F was a part, took a position to the north for the rest of the night before to provide supporting fire against German machine-gun nests. The morning of the attack saw a heavy mist cover the field. When it lifted, the men of Second Battalion were too close to the German machine guns. Three were killed, and seventeen were wounded, including Sergeant Templin. The day's attack was successful, as several hundred German prisoners were taken. Both Wodiske and Templin survived their wounds. Upon returning to South Wheeling, Templin got work as a butcher for the Wenzel Packing Company.[45]

As the service of local Poles like Peter Templin highlights, Wheeling's Polish Catholics illustrated their Americanism in a variety of ways. Military service was the highest level of devotion that could be expressed that highlighted their hybrid identity as Polish and American. Poles from St. Ladislaus could join both Haller's Army and the AEF, since both were fighting the United States' common enemy the Germans. If the military provided the best secular avenue for promoting their dual identity, the role of the parish and the Catholic diocese during wartime provided the perfect space to emphasize the importance of the sacred to being Polish in Wheeling.

Catholic Americanism

The second area that allowed the Poles to affirm their loyalty was via the Catholic Church. During the Progressive Era, the Irish Catholic hierarchy used the church as a bridge between the sacred and the secular. Catholic parishes and lay societies were often crucial for asserting larger political goals as well. Following the Catholic social teachings laid out in *Rerum Novarum* (1891), Catholic bishops and priests sought ways to carve out a larger political sphere for ethnic Catholics during the 1910s and 1920s. The Irish spearheaded this movement, but immigrant clergy and laypeople became engaged within their local ethnic communities. Without a strong voice from political machines, ethnic Catholics used parish and later diocesan lay societies. Historian Evelyn Sterne argues that these groups utilized "the diocesan press as a mouthpiece, religious parades as statements, and Catholic doctrine as justification" for promoting the full rights of citizenship for ethnic Catholics.[46]

During World War I, the American Catholic Church and its various social arms sought to promote what Paula Kane refers to as "separatist integration."

Catholics integrated more into American society while seeking to maintain their distinctiveness. This mentality usually manifested itself among the ethnic parishes. While new immigrants were under constant attack for their "hyphenated" loyalty, the Irish-dominated hierarchy promoted larger organizational programs that protected these newcomers from being labeled subversives.[47] Taking their lead after the creation of the National Catholic War Council (NCWC) in April 1917, the Catholic hierarchy asked Catholics to "fight like heroes and pray like saints" while also urging individual parishes to form war committees. The dominant belief was that "the parish [was] the supreme testing place for the length and breadth and depth of Catholic patriotism."[48] Members canvassed the community promoting the purchase of Liberty bonds, donations of food, and various fundraising drives. These local branches of the NCWC solicited support and unity between the largely Irish and German American diocesan clubs and societies (e.g., Knights of Columbus, St. Vincent de Paul Society, Holy Name Society) with the ethnic parish societies (e.g., St. Ladislaus Society, Polish National Alliance, Polish Roman Catholic Union).[49]

The mobilization of Catholic ethnic groups during the war provided the main context within which the Polish Catholics and their Slavic brethren worked together with the distinctively "Hibernian" societies promoted by Bishop Patrick Donahue and the editors of the Catholic *Church Calendar*. With the growth and expansion of St. Ladislaus Parish, the community could finally expand its influence and work with other ethnic groups throughout South Wheeling. It also required the formation of Irish-style lay societies, which came under the control of Bishop Donahue and the cathedral, but allowed for better organization. After 1918, Wheeling became a dominant Catholic center in the region with a broad coalition of support from various ethnic groups. The diocese made efforts to forge this coalition. In February 1917, the largely Slavic St. John's Parish witnessed a proliferation of Irish American Catholicism with the formation of a Holy Name Society and addresses by the local Knights of Columbus. The latter "exhorted all young men if they wished to prosper in their lives as well materially as spiritually" to seek out the Catholic solidarity provided by the knights.[50]

The diocese emphasized the need for "absolute loyalty to the flag [and] our sympathy should not be circumscribed by territorial lines" to prevent anything that might undermine the church's broader efforts. The Knights of Columbus, the Women's Catholic League, and the St. Vincent de Paul Society met basic needs by providing clothing, food, and financial resources as a result of high wartime consumer prices.[51] Uniting a broad coalition of working-class Slavs with old-stock German and Irish laborers aided in presenting all Catholics as moral and patriotic. On April 23, 1917, shortly after declaring war against Germany, St. John's Irish Kain Club sponsored a day's worth of "patriotic" dinners and speeches to arouse the passions of the immigrant population behind the "the red, white, and blue."[52]

The Knights of Columbus also played a crucial role. They organized a meeting in the Market Auditorium on April 13, 1917, where over 2,500 ethnic youth listened attentively as Bishop Donahue and other diocesan leaders such as Charles Wingerter, John Coleman, and George Mathison urged united patriotism. Afterwards, the youth, their teachers, and the parish priests marched uptown to display "fourteen American flags to the fourteen parochial schools of the Wheeling District." Each school chose a young boy or girl, characteristic of other "Liberty Boys" and "Liberty Girls," to show the cross-ethnic support of the diocese. What is interesting is which children were chosen as representatives. Parishes with mixed ethnicities like St. Vincent and St. Michael's in Elm Grove, Sacred Heart, Corpus Christi, and even St. John's mostly chose to be represented by children of Irish or German American extraction. The most un-American name listed is actually that of St. Ladislaus's Doretty Poeljesqui.[53] While the event promoted the ethnic diversity of Wheeling's fourteen parochial schools, the knights at the same time attempted to highlight a distinctive top-down version of Americanism defined by the Catholic diocesan leaders who ran the event.

This display of Americanism emphasized the group solidarity of Wheeling's ethnic communities, but it also acted as a preemptive strike in mobilizing support.[54] Through patriotic demonstrations, ethnic Catholics challenged the nativist assumption of "100 Percent Americanism." During Holy Name parades, ethnic festivals, May processions, and other folk practices, the members of the respective communities engaged in ethno-religious celebrations that "promoted a nuanced Americanism through a complex iconography that melded sacred and secular, old world and new."[55] Marching from the parish to the parochial school and throughout South Wheeling, these displays of ethnic-religious pride projected a deeply embedded symbolism that these immigrant families saw themselves as constituent members of "many communities." By engaging in a politicized march during the war, processions, and other forms of popular religious devotion, Poles advanced democratic notions that they could be American as they remained Polish and Catholic while also establishing networks and political loyalties giving them greater autonomy in the 1920s and 1930s.[56]

As working- and middle-class immigrants maneuvered in the highly charged wartime political climate, their pageantry further reinforced the diocese's growing autonomy. On June 10, 1917, St. John's Parish sponsored a parade to honor those men joining the army. The highlight of the ceremony was the erection of a sixty-nine-foot-high "liberty pole," the flag for which was donated by the Knights of Columbus. This display was followed by the various Croatian, Slavic, and Hungarian societies marching in uniforms and military step. The parade ended with speeches by Father Schoenen, Thomas Garret of the local Holy Name Society, Dr. A. J. Noome, "who [was] always on hand when there [was] a question of a foreigner and this country," and other diocesan and local political leaders. They watched as participants sang patriotic pledges in English and various other Slavic languages.[57]

These displays show the levels of negotiation involved in shaping the appropriate political discourse during a time of crisis. While immigrants appear patriotic in raising the liberty pole, they are able to highlight their ethnic distinctiveness by wearing the dominant dress of their Polish, Croatian, or Hungarian homelands. The *Church Calendar* even mentioned how the Croats honored their ethnic pride and wore the uniforms of the Black Guard. As long as the eastern European immigrants pledged loyalty to the U.S., they had a good deal of latitude in their presentations. For these ethnic Catholics, social diversity and religious freedom were the key aspects of Americanism. Their use of American republican ideals argued subtly that immigrant loyalties and their Catholic faith were the best exemplars of wartime Americanism.[58]

The diocese used the war to entrench itself within the currents of American life. In September 1917, the diocese formed the Wheeling chapter of the Catholic War Relief Service to meet the ecclesiastical needs of over four hundred Catholic clergy in Europe. Catholic women's committees made khakis and other necessary goods for the men overseas. Each parish had a branch that worked through the leadership of Bishop Donahue and Rev. Oscar Moye.[59]

Polish immigrants had several goals in adopting a new civic role. While promoting a pluralistic Americanism, Poles were also intensely nationalistic. They hoped that their pro-war support would return a unified Poland to the map of Europe. They relished collecting Liberty bonds. During the second Liberty bond campaign in October 1917, Wheeling organized solicitation committees to collect in each city ward, as well as among the largest immigrant groups. The Poles contributed $22,100, which was more than the Greeks, Italians, and Syrians. At the ceremony held at the Market Auditorium, the crowd "cheered so loud and vehemently" upon hearing of the large Polish contribution from Dr. M. Gaydosh. St. Ladislaus contributed ninety-three soldiers to the war effort, third behind only St. Alphonsus (177) and St. Joseph's Cathedral (166).[60] The area's immigrants also raised large sums of money. While the parish contributed three hundred dollars to the Polish Relief Committee, civic leaders played off the "rivalries" between local ethnic groups showing that the Poles were third behind the Greeks and Italians for money raised.[61] Massive Liberty Loan parades reinforced this ethnic competition. In celebrating the third series of loan collections, Benwood's civic organizations and industrial plants were joined in a massive parade in early May 1918 by all the ethnic societies, showing pride in how the city had quadrupled its loan quota. How well this worked as a propaganda tool is hard to say, but immigrant groups came together to prove their loyalty.[62]

St. Ladislaus Church members espoused a strong nationalistic ethos as they actively campaigned to aid the Polish war effort. In the waning months of the war, local questions over the creation of a Polish Legion sparked various political debates. On April 7, 1918, Wheeling's Southside Poles listened to speakers of the Polish National Alliance at Polish Hall. The principal speaker was Kazimierz Żychliński, president of the Chicago branch of the PNA (the nation's largest branch). During the meeting he, along with other speakers from Pittsburgh, informed the gathering of the German atrocities against European Poles and asked for volunteers for the Polish Legion. Musial urged support from the community's youth so that "Wheeling [would] be above all other cities in responding to the call."[63] The local newspapers continued to print articles and editorials praising the efforts of the Polish and other Slavic legions. On June 25, 1918, the newspaper printed a clarification of a previous article to emphasize that this Polish Legion would be "autonomous," possessing its "own national flag."[64]

The height of the wartime drive for loyalty occurred during a citywide "Americanization" parade set for July 4, 1918. The city organized the event in a top-down fashion to show the "means and methods by which one, not an American born citizen, may become 'naturalized.'" Various civic, labor, business, and foreign-born organizations were invited by a central committee to participate. Its structure was similar to the previous Liberty Loan campaigns, with huge patriotic floats. To include up to ten thousand marchers and mammoth floats and patriotic symbols, the parade's slogan "American Citizenship Offers You Freedom, Equality and Opportunities of Progress" suggested that the area's immigrants were the target audience. With a massive float of the "Goddess of Liberty" surrounded by figures representing labor, farmers, transportation, and business, the parade highlighted the need for unity in a time of war. Ethnically the parade included 1,500 Poles, 300 Syrians, 1,500 Greeks, 500 Italians, and 150 Ukrainians.[65] The parade seemed to attain its goal several days prior to Independence Day when a "Flood of Foreigners" swamped the federal building desiring to fill out naturalization papers.[66]

Fig. 5.1. Liberty Loan Parade, Saturday, April 14, 1918, "We Are Pulling for Uncle Sam and Liberty," from the Margaret Brennan Collection. Courtesy of the Ohio County Public Library Archives, Wheeling, WV.

The parade suggests how wartime Americanization must be viewed from multiple perspectives. While some of Wheeling's immigrants violated the draft laws, other community leaders urged fellow immigrants to participate in parades and fill out their naturalization papers. Governor John Cornwell articulated this point by stressing in his speech that "No man [could] be truly loyal and patriotic until he [became] one with and of us." During a rally after the parade at the Market Auditorium, immigrants watched a reenactment of a court scene, where seven representative nationalities acted out a scene of completing their naturalization papers.[67] However, others willingly joined in the events. The *Wheeling Intelligencer* editorial the next day praised the foreign population for bringing "themselves into closer touch with the spirit of the entire community and with the ideals of our republic." Even so, immigrants still maintained their shared loyalties and identities. As the editor noted, "More than a dozen different nations, races, and creeds marched shoulder to shoulder, carrying the emblems of their own nationalities, but all with the splendid emblem of the American Republic and of human freedom." The Poles highlighted their love of liberty clearly by being the first foreign-born contingent in the parade. Following the Polish Society was a float with Anna

Ronawjcz, a stenographer in the City Clerk's Office, representing liberty along with Martha Wisniawska.[68]

Following a massive patriotic parade and rally on July 4, 1918, the Poles met at the Polish Club to publicly announce their allegiance to the United States. Father Musial read the drafted resolution to all in attendance. This document serves as yet another example of how Wheeling's Poles reworked the tenets of civic nationalism to promote a level of independence. The first two paragraphs highlight the rhetorical aspects of freedom and democracy promoted by Wilson in his Fourteen Points, in which the United States pledged "herself specifically to restore an independent Polish state, with free access to the sea." The next section directly addressed the 100 Percent Americanizers, stating that Poles have "already allied themselves morally and politically with the United States" in the present crisis. With no hints of subversion or disloyalty, the resolution then concluded by stating that all Poles and Polish Americans exempted from service in the U.S. Army would serve in the Polish Legion forming in France.[69] In a well-constructed resolution, the Poles not only refuted the negative calls of coercive Americanism but argued persuasively for how their loyalty should allow them to serve their homeland abroad.

The growing power of the diocese did not sublimate all of the ethnic tensions. The Irish and German hierarchy continued to have troubles with ethnic Catholic immigrants. At the November 11, 1917, Holy Name rally, Fr. Stanislaus Grennen, who was presiding over the ceremonies, urged the immigrant men of the diocese to continue to prove their loyalty. However, of all the churches mentioned, only St. Ladislaus did not have any members present. Later that month Bishop Donahue voiced his displeasure at the lack of parish donations to the Knights of Columbus War Fund. Donahue spoke of how "it would grieve all patriots and Catholics to think that this poor showing [only one-half of the $21,000 quota] is a real index of our charity and our faith." He added: "I do not hesitate to assert that it is binding on the conscience of every Catholic to contribute to this most urgent and sacred cause."[70]

More than most ethnic Catholics, Father Musial asserted his independence from the diocese during the war years. For example, during the 1917 Holy Name rally, Musial and much of his laity celebrated the Forty Hours Devotion in Weirton, joining in the opening of the Polish parochial school at Sacred Heart of Mary. Many Polish clergymen from the state and the Pittsburgh area were present as Musial gave a major address along with Father Michalski of St. Stanislaus Parish in Monongah, West Virginia. Praising the devotion of the Weirton Poles for building the new school, they urged the crowd to promote an ethnic Catholicism that was patriotic to the United States. Father Michalski also reinforced Polish ethnic pride by accepting appointment as chaplain to the Polish Legion, which was being recruited in the United States and Canada.[71]

This occasion shows how Musial hoped to expand the Poles' influence by promoting a thriving and independent-minded Polish community in Weirton. Musial spoke in the ceremony alongside Mr. Loeb of the Phillips Tin Sheet Company of Weirton to eulogize the magnificent efforts of Father Wilzcak and the Sisters of Sacred Heart of Mary, "who were giving their lives of love to bring the Catholic Church of Weirton to that pedestal whereon she never stood before in this town."[72] They spoke of a "boosterism": "It is a fair assertion to make at this time that if this good work goes on in less than five years the people of Weirton will learn to love the Catholic Church. The town will have churches and schools that any like village may be proud of."[73]

There is mixed symbolism in the juxtaposition of Musial, the Polish crowd, and a representative of their largest employer. One can assume that Musial is aiding the local industrialists, who hope to keep a pliable, cheap labor force happy with better schools and infrastructure. A few months earlier, the *Church Calendar* was happy that "the Company at Weirton [was] paying such good wages." A local steelworker agreed, noting "It is not the money that makes us happy . . . it is rather the kindness we receive away [from our dear ones] from the highest officials who make us feel we own the plant every time we happen to meet them."[74] These positive hopes mirror aspects of 1920s corporate welfare capitalism. As Lizabeth Cohen noted about Chicago at this time, the "enlightened corporation" sought to meet the moral and material demands of workers—better wages, company unions, incentives, and paid vacations would encourage workers to "identify their personal futures with that of the company."[75] Advocating for a sort of corporatism between the immigrants, the church, and the local industrialists promoted the benefits of an industrial society where all worked together in unison. As a result it was necessary for the community to possess strong social and religious institutions so workers would feel tied to Weirton. Therefore Musial and the other Polish Catholics were present to promote the broader goals of ethnic community development that were the core of Musial's philosophy and efforts at St. Ladislaus.[76]

The heightened animosity toward new immigrants did lead St. Ladislaus to begin contributing to the diocesan Knights of Columbus War Fund in January 1918 along with Benwood's National Tube Company. Even with support for local industrialists, Polish priests saw their goals as not counter to labor but counter to atheistic socialism. Illustrative of this emerging corporatism is how the Sacred Heart of Mary Parish continued to cooperate with the Phillips Tin Plate Company, who were "most solicitous for the moral, spiritual and social welfare of their many thousands of employees." Even Bishop Donahue urged foreign working men to contribute to the cause that U.S. business also aided. In a proclamation issued throughout the fall of 1918, Donahue encouraged coal miners to increase production and proclaimed "Coal is King! You are his willing subjects." Encouraging no strikes, the bishop acknowledged that "Every additional ton will build a fire to burn despotism to ashes. Every car [coal miners] load helps to hasten the death knell of Kaiserism." Donahue worked with parish priests and the UMWA to reprint his appeal in multiple languages for the state's immigrant coal diggers. He was the keynote speaker for the city's Fourth Liberty Loan Drive in September 1918 and noted in glowing terms the coal companies' benevolence in southern West Virginia towns like Williamson, Gary, and Pocahontas, where "patriotism [was] aflame" and miners earned anywhere from eight to fifteen dollars a day.[77]

Around the same time in September 1918 came news that Bishop Donahue appointed Fr. Emil Musial to his Board of Diocesan Consultors. This was a point of great pride for Musial. As the only Slavic clergyman, Musial possessed a larger voice in representing the needs of the Slavic immigrants in Wheeling and throughout the state. His appointment speaks volumes about the changing nature of the Catholic hierarchy by 1918 and the growing voice of Polish Catholics in the Mountain State. Donahue's act may have been placating Musial by giving him a higher position that entailed many more duties to the diocese, but the appointment also gave Musial exactly what he needed to advance the goals of the diocese's Poles.[78]

As the war wound down, Wheeling's Polish and Slavic immigrants continued to expand their influence. In early October 1918, Bishop Donahue urged the formation of local councils of the National Catholic War Council (NCWC). St. Ladislaus's council, led by Musial, consisted of a wide variety of community members. The chief organizer was Joseph Rozanski, while the head of "publicity" was grocery-owner John Marchlenski. Ironworker Frank Templin appealed to the largely working-class men working at the steel mills and took over as head of the parish's speakers. Musial also recruited the community's children to promote the war effort. Organized into "Liberty Boys" and "Liberty Girls," they were led respectively by widow Lucy Jannozewska and Felician Sister Filipina. This mixture of people fit with the bishop's goals as he hoped the councils would "inspire" pro-war support and jubilantly "Organize! Organize! Organize!"[79]

The role of parish-level and diocesan Americanization adds much to the history of the World War I domestic front. The American Catholic Church provided many avenues for achieving a sense of shared loyalty and autonomy. Its institutions allowed Father Musial and the Poles the ability to advocate for a pluralistic Americanism in the face of fears of the "foreign menace." This period also brought together ethnically fragmented groups in the hopes of appealing for broader social and economic changes. A circular distributed by members of St. John's Parish is illustrative of this point. Entitled "Just American," the patriotic prose flows in such a manner as to promote the growing solidarity felt by such a diverse community: "Just today I chanced to meet / Down upon the crowded street / One-I wondered whence he came, / What was once his nation's name. / So I asked him: 'Tell me true, / Are you Pole or Russian Jew, / English, Scotch, Serb, Rumanian, / Flemmish, Belge [sic], Swiss, Moravian, / Dutch or Greek or Scandinavian?' / Then he raised his head on high / As he gave me THIS reply: / 'What I WAS is Naught to me / IN this land of LIBERTY! / In my soul as man to man / I am just-AMERICAN!'"[80]

Polish immigrants were good Americans, good Catholics, and good Poles. This was reflected in the sorts of fraternal organizations and lay societies created after 1918. In January 1919, twenty-four Polish nationals organized the Polish American Political Club (PAP Club) "to be aware of what was happening in American politics." While members gathered on evenings to "chat, read newspapers, and useful books," they also discussed how best to "take an active part in National matters and the politics of this country" while maintaining ties to Polish politics.[81] The Fulton Local 2395 of the Polish National Alliance (PNA) continued these connections between the new world and the old by proudly displaying fine portraits of revolutionary heroes like George Washington, Thaddeus Kościuszko, Casmir Pulaski, and the 1920s Polish nationalist leader Józef Piłsudski. Finally, the Benwood Local 2353 of the PNA fully captured the essence of what the World War I experience taught the Poles: "Christopher Columbus gave us an example that we can courageously accomplish these things and not pay attention to anyone's sneering and exist in this New World. The most intelligent will not be discouraged. With determination we will strive for this purpose. We can work for someone and be able to decide if we will work in a factory, in an office, or if we want to work for ourselves. Interestingly in this place we can organize members so that we can foster approval, courage, our Urge for knowledge, and our creative talents."[82] No bishop or president could summarize better the benefits of a pluralistic Americanism.

Conclusion

For Wheeling's Poles, World War I heralded the rebirth of the Polish republic. At a meeting on January 26, 1919, the Polish Hall was adorned with American and Polish flags as men, women, and children from across the Ohio Valley celebrated "the first free election of the Polish people." Following President Wilson's call, these Poles could joyfully praise their dual loyalties as they had fought to "defeat imperialism and bring about democracy for their people and the world."[83] Having shown their loyalty to their old and adopted countries, they would now need to address the problems of industrial democracy at home. As during the war, they would unite with other nationalities and native-born workers to secure their democratic rights in the postwar strike wave.

CHAPTER 6

Struggling for Economic Security: Polonia during the 1919 Steel Strike and the Roaring Twenties

The First World War gave the labor movement the opportunity to incorporate eastern European immigrants. Government support for unions in mass-production workplaces peaked during the war. Increasingly labor councils looked for organizers from the diverse ethnic communities to educate blue-collar immigrants. Luckily the Wheeling labor movement had a Polish organizer, Joseph Rozanski, to appeal to the large Polish and Slavic labor force. Born in 1876 in the German partition of Poland, Rozanski arrived in Pittsburgh in the early 1890s and eventually found work as a plate mill laborer at Wheeling's Belmont Mill. Initially he struggled like his countrymen in finding regular employment; he was out of work for eight months in 1900. But by 1903 he was a catcher at the Belmont Mill, and he eventually became a skilled heater in the tin mill. Rozanski also became quite active in the local labor movement speaking Polish and English and appealing to the unskilled men in the mill. A popular figure, by 1906 he was one of the grand marshals for the Ohio Valley Trades and Labor Assembly's Labor Day parade.[1]

As with many leaders in the OVTLA, Rozanski still lived within his ethno-religious culture. Rozanski served as both a union organizer and a lay leader at St. Ladislaus. During the First World War, he was the chief organizer for the diocesan United War Work Campaign. Afterwards, as the Catholic Church sought to unify Catholics against nativist attacks, he was a lay delegate and Polish organizer for Wheeling's District 1 of the National Catholic Welfare Council. Organizing the men's council branch applied Rozanski's talents to bringing together Poles living throughout the city. However, his organizing talents were best used as a leader in Stogie City Lodge No. 25 of the Amalgamated Association of Iron, Steel, and Tin Workers (AAISTW). When steelworkers went on strike in 1919, and when Wheeling Steel locked them out in 1921, Rozanski, a "member of the Amalgamated Association for many a long year," was a central go-between for the union and the Polish and other eastern European immigrants.[2]

New immigrants were among the most willing recruits of the Amalgamated

Association lodges. Throughout Wheeling, immigrant workers organized in what national strike leaders saw as the most peaceful, successful, and longest lasting of the local strikes. Rank-and-file meetings of new steelworkers' lodges cropped up starting in September 1918.[3] Led by Irish and German American skilled workers from the OVTLA, these new immigrants took active roles in manning picket lines and holding out for union recognition. Why were the organizing attempts in Wheeling so successful so quickly? The efforts by the OVTLA and local socialists to promote industrial unionism in the early 1910s helped the 1919 campaign.[4] Trade unions were an effective Americanizing force, because they focused on common problems present in ethnic communities that could only be solved through a working-class led organization.[5]

Multiethnic solidarity was visible quite early. In Benwood, organizers hired foreign speakers to make strike demands and news understandable to immigrants. What is more intriguing is how the union merged elements of "industrial democracy," socialism, and ethnic culture by having one of their largest mass meetings at the Polish Hall on Forty-Fifth Street. This was the main social hall for the Poles and the Catholic St. Ladislaus Parish. For organizers to allow National Secretary William Z. Foster and the editor of the socialist *Wheeling Majority* to speak to an audience of mostly ethnic Catholics shows how Wheeling's immigrant steelworkers started bridging the gaps among their multiple identities.[6] Even as the strike began to falter elsewhere, Wheeling's immigrants held strong. At the end of November, a spontaneous street parade of around 3,500 strikers snaked its way from Benwood through Wheeling and back. Coke and electrical workers, female can workers, and steelworkers from all seven Amalgamated Association lodges in Wheeling participated along with many of their families. Vowing not to return to unfair working conditions, foreign-born strikers demanded "eight hours or nothing."[7]

This chapter examines how Wheeling's Polish immigrants factored into the local labor struggles, highlighted by the 1919 steel strike. During the war, labor organizers stressed their own version of Americanism, promoting civil liberties, free speech, freedom of religion, and the right to organize. Labor unions saw the war as a time to rally support for a wider industrial democracy. Even with these high hopes, this period witnessed coercive campaigns by corporations and state power to repress labor organization.[8] By focusing on the steel strike of 1919, and then against the new Wheeling Steel Corporation from 1921 to 1924, this chapter suggests how the Poles became key supporters of the union struggle early and even supported some aspects of labor's version of Americanism. When the strike failed and the union movement declined, Poles struggled to find a level of economic security. The family economy continued as second-generation Polish Americans found work in Wheeling's mines, mills, and small factories and helped their parents to purchase homes and even start small businesses to get by during the uneven economy of the 1920s.

The Great Steel Strike of 1919 in the Wheeling District

In the last months of World War I, AFL trade unionists agreed to organize a national campaign in the nonunion steel industry. The campaign was part of a broader working-class movement featuring organizing drives among packinghouse workers, coal miners, and railroad workers.[9] The campaign gained momentum in the Wheeling area with the increase of wartime production. Wheeling received important contracts for tinplate and tubing. The Wheeling Steel & Iron Company added six hot mills to the Yorkville tin mill early in 1917; the Whitaker-Glessner Company built a large sheet mill at Beech Bottom. Increased demand for unskilled workers forced the National Tube Company to increase wages several times by 10 percent.[10]

In the summer of 1918, the National Committee for Organizing Iron and Steel Workers (NCOISW) began its campaign, and by the time of the armistice it had made gains in Pittsburgh, Chicago, and Wheeling. Clearly, the National War Labor Board's (NWLB) endorsement of collective bargaining and President Woodrow Wilson's own wartime appeals to workers helped.[11] The organizing effort was also the direct result of a "rank and file" movement of workers dissatisfied with the traditional "turn" of seven-day weeks and twelve-hour days, falling real wages, and growing unemployment. Leading the NCOISW were Chicago labor leaders John Fitzpatrick and William Z. Foster. Combining the longstanding grievances of hourly wage workers with the patriotic atmosphere during the First World War, the committee found a large groundswell of support from new immigrant steelworkers. While its leaders urged a policy of industrial unionism, the twenty-four AFL craft unions participating and financing the campaign fought to organize the steelworkers along craft lines, which undercut solidarity. Therefore, although led by the future leader of the American Communist Party, the strike was distinctly unradical.[12]

The main organizing principle behind the strike reinforced the basic tenets of industrial democracy. Merging conservative trade union ideas and a patriotic left-leaning view of Americanism, the NCOISW's organizing appealed to many steelworkers. Starting the campaign in conjunction with the Fourth Liberty Loan Drive and the last large battle of World War I made it seem to immigrant steelworkers that joining the union was another way to prove their patriotism.

Democracy came to be synonymous with the union. One Steubenville, Ohio, steelworker summed up this sentiment best: "We are all on the firing line once more and we are going over the top as we did in 1918 over there. . . . For we are determined to lick the steel barons and Kaisers of this country as we were to lick the German Kaiser."[13] Industrial democracy also meant organizing across race and ethnicity. Organizer Matt Greer, of Crescent Lodge No. 8 (East Wheeling) of the Amalgamated Association, urged Wheeling mill men to reach out to the "English, Welsh, Irish, Italians, Slaves [sic], Hungarian, Polish, Servian [sic], Greeks, Syrians, Russians, Finlanders, and Colored men. . . . We must bury the past." Nationally Amalgamated Association lodges reflected these attitudes with names like Democracy or Liberty. However, Wheeling's new lodges reflected a more local orientation, adopting names like Mountain State, Victory, Ft. Henry, Wheeling, Stogie City, Nail City, and Ohio Valley.[14]

The intensifying rank-and-file discontent finally forced the NCOISW to endorse a national strike. While the mill towns around Pittsburgh saw outright repression by steel companies in the months following the armistice, a general feeling of discontent and impatience was common in places like Wheeling. As companies began to lay off unskilled hourly workers, steelworkers demanded a strike for the eight-hour day and union recognition. By the summer of 1919, the NCOISW started negotiations with U.S. Steel and other firms. On July 11, 1919, William Z. Foster reported, "Some action must be taken that will secure relief. All over . . . men are in a state of great unrest. In Johnstown, Youngstown, Chicago, Wheeling, and elsewhere, great strikes are threatening." After continued efforts to meet with Judge Elbert Gary, the head of U.S. Steel, and then President Woodrow Wilson failed, the NCOISW called the national strike to begin on September 22, 1919.[15]

Rank-and-file steelworkers, including much of Wheeling's Polish and Slavic working class, made tangible demands. First, they wanted the right to bargain collectively. Second, they demanded an eight-hour day, one day's rest in seven, and the end to the twenty-four hour "long turn" shift. Third, they wanted a living wage, double-rate pay for overtime, holiday, and Sunday work, and standard wage rates for all tradesmen and hourly classified workers. Finally, they wanted a check-off system for union dues, seniority lines, the abolishment of all company unions, and no more physical examinations as part of the employment application.[16]

Wheeling's foreign-born steelworkers were eager to join the Amalgamated Association. The first mass meeting for the National Committee's efforts in Wheeling was held December 6, 1918, at the Polish Hall on the South Side. Louis Leonard, a leader in the Amalgamated Association's Crescent Lodge

No. 8 and several times president of the OVTLA, led the meeting with speakers "in Polish and English." Foreign steelworkers from the Wheeling Steel & Iron Company and National Tube Company mills in Benwood and the LaBelle tin mill in Wheeling attended the meeting. Appealing largely to the Polish audience, organizers made their claim: "You have more freedom in the Ohio Valley than any other place among the nonunion mills. Why? Because we that are organized have fought for and maintained the right of free speech and free assemblage." After stressing the poverty seen about South Wheeling's Eighth Ward, organizers emphasized the union's benefits, especially the sick and accident insurance programs.[17] In the next few weeks, the union drive included all the mills in the upper Ohio Valley. A few days after the Polish Hall meeting, the union held another large rally at nearby Bischoff's Hall led by William Z. Foster. The goal would be to enroll as many as twenty thousand steelworkers in the organization in 1919.[18]

Union organizers successfully appealed to a broad cross section of immigrant workers during lodge gatherings. The union campaign was a mixture of top-down planning led by William Z. Foster on a national level and Jack Peters at the district level along with grassroots organizing by a core group of local Irish and German American organizers in each lodge. For example, Wheeling Lodge No. 18 at the LaBelle tin mill was led in early 1919 by German Americans like Harry Reibold and then Walter Ruble with Brother Glisser serving as chairman of the sick committee. Mountain State Lodge at the Wheeling Steel & Iron Company in Benwood was led by Irish and German American officers but had an Italian and Slavic rank and file. The Fort Henry Lodge at the LaBelle hot mill met in the German neighborhood just south of St. Alphonsus German Catholic Church but branched out holding a dance at Martins Ferry's Hungarian Hall. Meetings of union workers continued in the fraternal ethnic lodges, at the German Dueker Hall, and most notably the Polish Hall.[19] Organizers in the Wheeling District consistently urged nonunion men to make them a family affair: "Bring your wife and let her bring a nonunion man's wife along, so that your wife and the nonunion man's wife can both understand what the union means."[20]

Polish Hall witnessed one of the largest early meetings on January 16, 1919. A "mammoth crowd present, representing several nationalities," the meeting was organized through several AFL unions. District Secretary Jack Peters explained that the main purpose of the organization was "to educate the workers" nationally about the benefits of collective bargaining. Various union representatives spoke, providing addresses and literature in several languages. Ben Groggin of the Mine and Smelter Workers Union spoke in Italian, and

Stanley Ingersky, a Polish UMWA organizer from Pittsburgh, spoke in Polish. These were the two largest nationalities of the unskilled men living near the mills in South Wheeling and Benwood.[21]

Local organizers sought to assist steelworker families. In early May 1919, U.S. Steel shut down the National Tube Works in Benwood, laying off nearly 2,500 workers. To prevent civil unrest and disorder, Victory Lodge No. 21 in Benwood brought in a government mediator to calm the immigrant crowd. Mountain State Lodge No. 19, claiming to represent over 1,400 steelworkers, sent out a letter protesting the closing of local plants and highlighting the wartime sacrifices of "our comforts, pleasures and enjoyments of life, even life itself, for the cause of Democracy." They sent their protests to the Department of Labor for redress. When things became difficult for families after subsequent layoffs, Fort Henry Lodge sponsored a grand ball as the other lodge members mingled with their families in a multiethnic atmosphere.[22]

As the Red Summer of 1919 grew in intensity, organizers made a stronger appeal to the immigrant steelworkers. Mountain State Lodge attracted new members from the Wheeling Iron & Steel Company plant and worked to "get speakers for our Italian and Slavish brothers." Other lodges at the LaBelle Mill and Wheeling Iron & Steel plants around town encouraged members to "keep on working like the other thrifty lodges." In preparation for the annual Wheeling Labor Day parade, Crescent Lodge estimated a large contingent from the newly formed lodges: Mountain State (1,000), LaBelle hot mills and tin house (400), and LaBelle plate mill (250). Stating that the Wheeling labor unions "recognize no race, creed or color," the organizers bluntly asserted that "the good men parade and the moral coward stands on the sidewalk." Organizers gave speeches to new unionists at the Belmont Mill lodge on "Unionism and Organization," since the factory had been nonunion for years. They also found returning World War I veterans after only "one pay joined the union" to continue the "battle put on for industrial freedom."[23] By early August, there were six new lodges covering all the Wheeling and Benwood steel mills. On Labor Day, Wheeling's downtown streets were filled with the unions affiliated with the OVTLA and over four thousand Wheeling steelworkers, of whom over 75 percent were recent union recruits.[24]

As tensions built toward a strike, district committee organizers distributed thousands of handbills in at least seven different languages urging steelworkers to remain fast until the national call for action. When the call came, lodge organizers encouraged solidarity.[25] During the largest mass strike of the era, almost 98 percent (about 1,600) of the workers at Benwood's National Tube Company joined within the first few days. Wheeling, Fort Henry, and Nail City lodges joined forces to organize the LaBelle Mill. Wheeling Lodge had very quickly "organized from top to bottom . . . and even the girls who sort the tin."²⁶ Within a short time, over 15,000 steelworkers were on strike in the Wheeling District. A large meeting of strikers and organizers from the AAISTW, AFL, and International Association of Machinists instructed steelworkers to be peaceful. Jack Peters, Wheeling District secretary, warned all to be weary of believing any disinformation coming from the newspapers: "I want you to pay attention only to such information as you secure through your local union." After members were told to sleep in the next day, the meeting concluded with an address to the "foreign element by Robert Matusck delivered in the Polish language."²⁷ That a large number of the union members in attendance were Polish speaks to the fortitude of the Polish Catholic immigrants, who worked with the AFL unions and the OVTLA.

Wheeling's steelworkers advocated for mutual assistance using the language of "Americanism." At a mass meeting of over three thousand strikers at the Market Auditorium, various union leaders reinforced the strike's aims. William Roy, UMWA District 5 president, questioned that, after patriotically purchasing Liberty bonds and donating to the Red Cross, how could steelworkers now be called un-American? To him, "Americans have the reputation for going out and fighting for justice." Walter Hilton, editor of the *Wheeling Majority*, linked the wartime autocracy of Kaiser Wilhelm to "the industrial autocracy of America, ruled by King Gary's [U.S. Steel].²⁸ Mutual assistance manifested itself in arrangements to provide food, clothing, and other forms of relief to strikers and their families. The Pittsburgh headquarters of the national strike committee set up several distributing centers in the Wheeling District. Families received a commissary card for food allotments twice a week based on size. Nine thousand pounds of food arrived by early November with at least two hundred strike families applying for aid.²⁹ When Jack Peters could not find a suitable location to rent for distributing future food allotments, Catholic church officials offered the use of the basement of St. Joseph's Cathedral. The cathedral provided assistance to 350 strikers' families distributing 3,500 loaves of bread and 3,000 pounds of potatoes—in all, about seven tons of food. The choice of the cathedral seemed odd, considering the following day distribution ended at noon so strikers could go several blocks from the cathedral to listen to William Z. Foster speak. While the Catholic diocese approved of helping strikers' families, they probably disapproved of steelworkers listening to Foster's more radical ideas. Secret FBI informants noted that he spoke only of the strike, nothing of an "inflammatory character." However, Catholic leaders had reason to worry since the "foreign-born workers [were] evidently in sympathy with Foster, as they applauded loudly when he was introduced."[30]

While immigrant workers were generally peaceful, festering tensions eventually led to hostilities during the strike. As the strike wore on, there were small acts of intimidation and fisticuffs by immigrant steelworkers. Attorney James Parriott informed the governor that tensions began on November 18 as a returning soldier was "badly beaten up" by five foreign workers in downtown Benwood. Strikers worked diligently to maintain picket lines and keep out strikebreakers. The incident also suggests that local police were rather sympathetic to the strikers' cause. After the November 18 incident, the Marshall County sheriff had to dispatch several deputies after the Benwood police refused to act, whereupon they arrested Mike Rendulic and George Sikich. Later the sheriff, five deputies, and one state police officer stood outside the Riverside Mill when it reopened for a time on November 24 while strikers prevented scabs from entering, "but no licks were struck." Regardless, Parriott noted that Benwood police still seemed unable to halt strikers congregating outside the mill.[31]

The Riverside Mill was the center of much of the strike militancy. Many union organizers from the Wheeling Iron & Steel plants worked with the leading "radicals" at the Riverside Mill to coordinate strike activities. The presence of county and state police to monitor the situation, and company attempts to reopen the mill, enraged many strikers. By the last week of November, an estimated 350 men who were attempting to reenter the mill faced harassment each morning from pickets. County officials continued to press for state police until a contingent of twelve constabulary arrived. Throughout this tenuous period, state police and bureau informants alleged "that the danger of violence lies with the foreign element and not with the Americans." A worker named William Wagner was attacked on November 29 while on a South Wheeling streetcar. This incident led to a public admonishment from Sheriff W. E. Clayton urging the immediate impeachment of Benwood's chief of police and mayor for "turning a deaf ear to lawlessness" and "making absolutely no effort toward curbing attacks they have committed on mill men who want to return to work." Clayton went further, later declaring "Benwood is full of Bolsheviks." Although strike leaders urged restraint, it appeared that "practically all the insulting words such as 'scab,' 'blacksheep,' etc. come from the foreigners." In response, some strikebreakers shouted back: "You d[amn] hunkies, go back home. . . . We don't want you in America anyway."[32]

The bloody climax to these escalating tensions occurred on the early morning of December 1, 1919. In a large gun battle outside the main gate of blast furnace B of the Riverside Mill, Sheriff Clayton and a deputy were seriously wounded while an Austrian Pole Matija Baron (of Victory Lodge) was killed and John Meharlow (of Mountain State Lodge) was shot in the face. As a group of native-born workers got off the streetcar, foreign strikers ordered them to go home, whereupon several workers "were attacked from behind." According to police, Baron attacked Deputy McCardle and tried to take away his gun at which point he was shot fatally. Meharlow in response fired off a shot wounding McCardle in the hand. Officers also claimed that bricks and stones had been thrown just prior to the shooting by foreign-born strikers. Fear and panic spread quickly as authorities desperately tried to get assistance from the state police and even deputize local residents. Bureau agents learned from interviewing the wounded workers that radical foreign activities "have been very much under cover" and the crowd of immigrants numbered as many as two hundred the morning of the riot. While in Wheeling Hospital, Clayton "advised that foreigners in Benwood [were] organizing to resist and attack officers." Lawmen took precautions after several boys heard a group of immigrants in a poolroom planning to get back at the officer who wounded Meharlow. Later Colonel Jackson Arnold of the state police arrived with authority to deputize local citizens.[33]

In subsequent days, state police and bureau agents attempted to link the strikers to radical Bolsheviks. John B. Wilson interviewed John Meharlow, who denied knowing of any radical plans for the morning of December 1. He also stated he knew nothing of the Union of Russian Workers. Meharlow claimed he was only a member of "the Steel Workers Union" and the local Russian Orthodox church. After trying to entrap him, Wilson concluded that Meharlow was "more or less identified with the radicals in Benwood." An interpreter told Wilson that Meharlow previously claimed he had gotten up early on December 1 and said to his brother, "Come on and we will go out after these scabs."[34]

The events surrounding the fatal shootout suggest a situation that had gotten out of the control of local authorities. Even before December 1, strikers attacked several men on the streetcar going through South Wheeling. Most incidents occurred at the Forty-Fifth Street stop in the middle of the Polish neighborhood. The mayor of Benwood, Clark Sprouts, charged that these attacks were the result of heightened feelings created by the inflammatory Wheeling press reports over the preceding week. However, the mayor's policies leading up to the fatal shooting raised many eyebrows. After requesting assistance from unwilling locals, Mayor Sprouts "personally called upon several men of character and ability." The mayor's decision angered Governor Cornwell since several of these men "a few days ago were acting as pickets to keep men out of the mills."³⁵ Cornwell was incensed that the strikers seemed emboldened by the fact the Benwood police were "with them" and that one officer had told a strikebreaker "he would be shot and thrown into the river."³⁶ Sprouts continually denied that any policeman made the inflammatory comment to men entering the mill and that he had worked cordially with Sheriff Clayton. After the shootout, conditions quieted down as special deputies patrolled the main gates of the mill and another one hundred men returned to work.³⁷

After several days of fear, on December 4, the Polish and Ukrainian communities turned out for the funeral for Matija Baron. Officers found a passport in Baron's pockets, indicating that he had been preparing to set sail soon to return to Poland. He even had his trunk prepared to leave, but his union lodge asked him to do a turn of picket duty, which he willingly obliged. Polish undertaker L. F. Stolarski of South Wheeling administered his estate, and a large funeral service was held at St. Ladislaus. Baron left $1,500 in Liberty bonds, $884.20 in the Security Trust Bank, and $205.46 on his insurance policy. He was buried at Mt. Calvary Cemetery where nearly two thousand steelworkers attended the solemn event overseen by the Benwood Polish Society.³⁸ Victory Lodge No. 21 published a eulogy to Matija Baron in the *Wheeling Majority*, describing him as a "pure religious man" and a "worthy and most honored member of the labor movement."³⁹

The shooting in early December 1919 was a turning point in the strike. Calls for law and order prevailed as state police and deputized locals protected men desiring to go back to work at the Riverside. The AAISW held a meeting placing blame for the violence on government surveillance and criticizing most of the negative newspaper coverage of the strike, especially in the *Wheeling Intelligencer*.⁴⁰ In the following weeks, pressure grew on strikers to return to work. The Wheeling Iron & Steel Company planned to restart its Benwood mill. The *Wheeling Register* noted "hundreds of foreigners" were working at the six-inch pipe mill. Lodges representing the Benwood mill and the Carnegie Steel plant in Bellaire, Ohio, voted to return on December 9 along with the Twenty-Ninth Street tin mill of the American Sheet & Tin Plate Company. Within a week nearly 1,800 men were working at the Riverside. Mills at Aetnaville and Martins Ferry, Ohio, also planned to restart, but many immigrant strikers held fast. Mostly native-born skilled workers returned to work. While not the only explanation, the December 1 shooting and the press reaction aided in dividing the steelworkers.⁴¹

For most immigrant steelworkers, the goals of World War I were the same as those advanced by the union organizers in their stress on industrial democracy. Immigrants' commitment to the union cause and the strike came from their seeing both as a way to earn a better living for their families and, as seen during the Great War, another demonstration of their evolving sense of Americanism. Their dedication to the union and the strike became crucial to their identity as ethnic Catholic workers in promoting community solidarity and their own dignity. They were the first to crowd mass meetings and the most eager to join the union. Membership rosters showed a spike in Slavic surnames. The Amalgamated Association channeled their support by meeting immigrants on their own terms. They printed strike bulletins in many different languages, held meetings in immigrant social halls, and brought in speakers of their own nationality. It was more difficult to organize the largely native-born skilled steelworkers. Crescent Lodge attacked the Wheeling Sunday paper for calling a meeting of only U.S.-born steelworkers in Benwood "asking Americans to SCAB." From the organizer's perspective, this made it appear that "only men of foreign birth are loyal union men." He went on to criticize those who called the Wheeling immigrants "Hunkies" since "Those so-called Hunkeys [sic] are the cleanest union men."[42] Another union organizer captured immigrant sentiments: "The poorest foreign laborer . . . wants to get organized and you don't. . . . Remember this Mr. Smart non-union American that we are coming to your tin and sheet mills and take your foreign speaking men and put them into the Amalgamated Association and then they will make you come clean. They will show you what Americanism really is, one who stands up for his rights."[43] His comments reflected the reality that the Poles were increasingly involved in the local labor movement throughout the 1910s. Their earlier labor activities culminated in their very eager support for the cause of the Amalgamated Association. Years of struggling to provide for their families and forming their religious community around St. Ladislaus taught them to value solidarity. Their values allowed them to support the key aspects of the labor movement's version of Americanism during the 1919 strike.

Even so, the failure of the 1919 steel strike posed economic challenges. Since many foreign-born strikers were Catholic, local parishes struggled to provide assistance. Many at St. John's Parish in Benwood could not celebrate the feast of St. Patrick in March 1920 since "people still seem to be 'boycotted' or blacklisted" for their roles in the 1919 strike. By July 1920, men who did find work in the mills only averaged about three days a week. The lack of steady work caused many headaches for parish priests who needed to provide food and clothing aid and address those dying from influenza. By March 1920, St. John's alone had seventy funerals in just six weeks. Father Schoenen was constantly behind on his diocesan collections during the 1919 strike on account that "only four men and nine girls [were] working from [his] parish." It was difficult to maintain the parish's finances, especially in March 1920 after he took out insurance policies of five thousand dollars on the church building and two thousand dollars on all its contents.[44]

The economic despair continued into 1922 and 1923. In an illuminating and dire letter to Chancellor Edward Weber, Father Schoenen tried to summarize the conditions among the foreign working class: "You know the bad conditions of Benwood—not one hour work for over ten months, and since then three or four . . . every other week at a 60% reduction in wages. We will hope it will be better after the settlement of the miners' strike in April."[45] Predicting that many coal miners might go out on strike at the Wheeling Steel and Hitchman coal mines in Benwood, Schoenen spoke to the feeling of despair and frustration with the local labor climate. By November conditions were still poor but started to slowly improve once the National Tube Company reopened in early January 1923. For the members of this multiethnic parish, the deprivations of the long labor battle affected all aspects of their economic and social life.[46]

For the Poles of St. Ladislaus and Fr. Emil Musial, there is less direct evidence of their views of the strike. While many of the early union organizing meetings were held in the Polish Hall, by the early 1920s the space was used more for Polish Catholic events. Poles began retreating back into their own ethnic world as the strike floundered. Even the number of people claimed by the parish increased from 1,200 in 1917 to 1,500 by 1922. One suggestion of the Poles' growing economic troubles was seen in parish financial reports for the early 1920s. The parish's total receipts dropped from $24,544 (1918) to $11,446 (1919). While pew rents stayed about the same, money donated to special collections (a rather good indicator of Poles' extra income) plummeted from $11,513.98 (1918) to $4,586.65 (1919). While parish income did see improvement in 1920 and 1921, parish receipts dropped to a low of $10,290.35 in 1924.[47]

The Lockout at Wheeling Steel

The area's Polish and other immigrant steelworkers faced additional challenges from the newly created Wheeling Steel Corporation. Formed via a merger of several local firms in June 1920, Wheeling Steel became the prime economic driver in the upper Ohio Valley, employing 17,348 by 1925.[48] Following the 1919 strike, Wheeling Steel joined other corporations nationally to promote more harmonious relations with their employees while also undercutting labor unions. Using what was known as welfare capitalism, the most popular element of this strategy was the employee representation plan (ERP), which the firm began creating after the strike. To counter the Amalgamated Association, the committee at the Benwood Works set up a Relief and Beneficial Association, which in 1921 represented around 80 percent of the employees. The association provided financial assistance "in case of sickness, accident or death for which no provision is made under the Workmen's Compensation Act."[49] Under the plans, workers casted votes for candidates, who individually represented up to two hundred workers and attended regular meetings with company officials. Likewise, Wheeling Steel developed a variety of safety programs, which through frequent group meetings helped to drastically drop accident rates.[50]

The crushing of the national steel strike in January 1920, however, did not mean the union movement among Wheeling's immigrant steelworkers was dead. Many locals made tangible gains. Following the murder of Matija Baron, the management of the Wheeling Steel & Iron plant in Benwood agreed to collective bargaining with the Mountain State Lodge No. 19 a few days before Christmas 1919. The company agreed to institute the eight-hour day and not discriminate against former strikers.[51] The most vigorous organizing continued at the mills in Benwood and South Wheeling. By August 1920, union organizers won collective bargaining contracts at two of the largest nonunion mills. Covering many immigrant workers, these contracts were for Stogie City No. 25 men laboring at the Belmont Mill and Mountain State No. 19 men working at the Benwood Works in the Bessemer steel, tube, pipe, and plate mills. This was the high point of the union's postwar success, and by Labor Day 1920 the AAISW claimed contracts at eleven Wheeling Steel mills.[52]

During this period Amalgamated Association lodges continued to attract rank-and-file support, and the union's sick and accident benefits played a major role in garnering that appeal. Mountain State Lodge's sick committee consistently sought to care for a wide group of immigrant steelworkers.[53] Many men who suffered from disability also received claims. For April 1920, Pete Klochan received $15, Martin Skitarback $20, John Meharlow $65, and J. Martimiovich $35. By April 1921, Pete Klochan ($5) and Lawrence Kalaska ($20) still received assistance from Mountain State No. 19. Even union organizer Joe Rozanski filed a claim in April 1921 for $40.[54] Stogie City sent out resolutions of condolences and aid to several immigrant families. Charles Cusnik lost his wife, who had been caring for their eight children. Joe Ralbowsky, age twenty-seven, suffered from lung-related conditions for several years and finally died of consumption on December 28, 1920. His wife applied for death benefits from the local and received $100 a week after his passing. These sick and death benefits were one of the ways the Amalgamated Association tried to maintain immigrant workers' loyalty.[55]

Maintaining the loyalty of immigrant union members was crucial by the summer of 1921 as the Amalgamated Association began a long strike against the Wheeling Steel Corporation. After the formation of the company, Amalgamated Association President Michael Tighe got a favorable wage scale for the year ending July 1, 1921. President I. M. Scott stated the company would sign union contract extensions with those mills already organized prior to the merger in 1920. However, since the company was one entity, the union argued Wheeling Steel must sign scales for all lodges.[56] Wheeling Steel slowly implemented anti-union policies. As production picked up in late May 1921, the company cut the daily wages of unskilled workers at the Benwood Works from $6.00 to $3.96 for a twelve-hour workday.[57] Amalgamated Association lodges from Benwood, Wheeling, Beech Bottom, and Yorkville, Ohio, joined a massive parade on June 5, 1921, protesting the open shop. Czech-born UMWA subdistrict president Frank Ledvinka spoke eloquently and urged the solidarity of all workers to prevent the open shop's spread throughout the Ohio Valley.[58]

When the lockout began, lodges faced the full brunt of anti-union tactics. The company refused on August 5 to deal any more with the Amalgamated Association, and they hired labor spies to infiltrate the lodges and encourage workers to cross the picket lines.[59] Additionally, in July 1921, Circuit Judge Sommerville endorsed the company's request to expand an earlier court injunction to prevent the Amalgamated Association from picketing any nearby mills or the company's downtown office. The Belmont Mill on Twenty-Sixth Street was the center of much of the picketing, and on August 27 the circuit court granted a special injunction against Stogie City No. 25, targeting their leaders, especially Vice President Joe Rosanzki, in order to stop interference with those desiring to work and visiting employees in their homes.[60]

Other tactics sought to divide the strikers by nationality. Stogie City's picketing was hurt when labor bosses forged a petition saying that the strike had ended in an attempt to convince a large segment of the Polish workforce to report back to work. Stogie City Lodge held a meeting to inform immigrants about the company's tactics. A week later, Wheeling Steel obtained from the circuit court a temporary injunction against Stogie City Lodge, which included mostly Poles in the list of petitioners. Most were young, having immigrated between 1907 and 1913. Leo Sulek, one of those Poles that signed the petition, was born in 1896, immigrated in 1912, and worked as a finisher at the Belmont Mill. He signed along with his wife Rose and another relative Alexander Sulek, who was a skilled shearman. Alexander was born in Gozeff, Poland, in 1888 and worked as a roll hand in the Belmont plate mill. Władysław Swek also signed the petition. He was born in 1893 near Warsaw and during World War I was working as a laborer at the Belmont Mill.[61] While it is hard to validate the union's allegation that the company tricked these Poles into signing the petitions, it does seem that, for the Suleks and others, some were beginning to move into semiskilled and skilled jobs by 1921. They may have seen their future prosperity tied to the company. Regardless, by the fall of 1921, men began to cross the picket line. Wages stagnated, and by late fall 1921 unskilled men earned nineteen cents per hour for twelve hours. Desperate workers had few options but to return to work at such reduced wages.[62]

While Poles and other immigrants went back to work, skilled steelworkers increasingly saw black migrants as a threat. After World War I, Wheeling's steel mills suffered from an acute labor shortage with the cut off of immigrants from southern and eastern Europe. The company began recruiting large numbers of African Americans from the South. Many worked in foundries, blast furnaces, and mold shops or for the railroad, congregating in South Wheeling where houses and apartments were more affordable. Steelworkers blamed the companies for hiring black migrants at much lower wage levels. The Riverside Mill discharged two hundred to five hundred men for black migrants, who, according to an angry white union member, "work[ed] here in the winter and beat it in the Spring." The union member went on to claim, "It takes about five of them to do one good white man's work in the mills." In Wheeling as elsewhere at the time, rising racial tensions grew from economic competition over access to industrial jobs and housing with the various immigrant populations.[63] By 1920, Wheeling's African American community numbered 1,623, making it the fourth largest in the state. Since many of these black families relocated to between Twenty-Fifth and Twenty-Ninth Streets, they were segregated from the Polish and Ukrainian populations farther south. However, immigrant children were well aware of the separate racial spaces. George Janeczko remembered there were two parks for children near Twenty-Sixth Street, one for whites and the other near cinder pits and closer to the Ohio River for blacks.[64]

Many of the African American migrants arrived just as the strike commenced, but they were themselves struggling to find better economic conditions. In the early summer of 1921, a group of forty blacks from Alabama arrived at night on the B&O. Coming from the tobacco districts, one stated that "conditions in the south [were] completely dead as far as work is concerned." Some brought their families, intending to remain in Wheeling for good. At least 1,500 black southern migrants worked in the Wheeling steel mills during the height of the strike.[65] A number of black workers lived in what was called the Belmont Bunk, which was company housing built near the Belmont Mill. Many were attracted by the higher wages working in the mills. James Bumkin was just eighteen when he came up from South Carolina in the summer of 1923 after earning a rate of $1.70 per day on the railroads. John Calhoun also migrated from Donalds, South Carolina, after doing contracting work for a rate of $2.50 a day. William Collins, age thirty-one, left the cotton mills of Georgia after being hired by Wheeling Steel in June 1923. All three also joined the company's Relief and Beneficial Association once they arrived in town.[66]

Eventually Wheeling Steel's new corporate policies devastated the union by enticing new workers and maintaining company loyalty. First, in April 1923 the board of directors passed a 10 percent horizontal wage increase. Second, they ended the company's policy of twelve-hour days for most semiskilled and unskilled workers, setting the maximum at ten hours. Third, capital investments went into expanding the LaBelle nail mill and the Forty-Eighth Street can factory, further boosting employment. Finally, the company's use of employee representation plans (ERPs) seemed to be paying dividends. The Employee Relief and Beneficial Association offset the appeal of the Amalgamated Association's health and injury policies. Many new workers liked the company's generous pension plans, especially for those incapacitated by injury.[67]

By 1924, the AAISW strike was all but defeated. Polish unskilled steelworkers were desperate for money in the poor economy, and many broke ranks in need of the better wages offered by Wheeling Steel. While in 1921 unskilled workers' wages were 19 cents an hour for a twelve-hour day, by 1923 the company was paying 31 to 36 cents an hour. By August 1923, common laborers' wages increased to 42 cents an hour for a ten-hour day. Frank Buchan, who immigrated to the United States in 1891, found work at the firm in October 1922. Frank Chelminski of Forty-Sixth Street was hired on September 10, 1923, after previously working at the Wheeling Can Company. Mike and Andrew Cichowicz of 4838 Eoff Street came back to work in March and August 1923 respectively.[68] Twenty-nine months into the strike in December 1923, skilled workers looked angrily at the men laboring in the mills, "ex-scabs of three or four strikes, and first time scabs of Wheeling, together with Greeks, Syrians, Negroes and Poles."[69] The union no longer sympathized with the needs of immigrant families, who went back to work for consistent wages in an inconsistent 1920s economy. In April 1924, John Moran of East Wheeling gave a long talk at the OVTLA meeting on "the undesirables brought here to work in the Steel Mills," suggesting the final death knell of solidarity among Wheeling's increasingly diverse labor force.[70]

The high hopes of the Amalgamated Association's strikes faded in the harsh realities of the tightening economy of the 1920s. A good example was Polish union organizer Joseph Rozanski. He eventually lost his job at Wheeling Steel. In 1923 and 1924 he worked as a chauffeur for a furniture company and later as a driver for a hardware store. While he and his wife owned their home at 2804 Wilson Street, they still required the labor of their children to meet their economic needs. By 1930, his teenage daughter Rosie worked as a tobacco stripper at M. Marsh & Sons. Through the 1930s, the family also relied on their son Edward's unskilled foundry job and daughter Elizabeth's job as a packer at the Wheeling Match Company.[71]

Polonia Seeks Economic Security in the Roaring Twenties

During the interwar period, other Polish immigrants and their children adopted a similar defensive strategy to that of the Rozanskis. Poles had limited occupational choices and generally found work via family and kin networks in the steel mills. What they most desired was economic security in the form of a steady income, decent neighborhood, home ownership, and the respect of their fellow community members. Children of Polish families tended to live at home longer, substitute work for high school, and take care of their parents as they aged. As a result, many followed similar occupational tracks into metal factories, tobacco plants, and glass factories.[72]

The major change in the 1920s was Polish women's growing employment in a diverse number of factory jobs. While ethnic women had worked in Wheeling's cigar, tobacco, and glass factories in high numbers since the 1880s, by the 1920s they moved into new types of jobs in metal and steel fabricating. While this trend was slow, the 1930s saw the rapid increase of women in the iron and steel factories from 355 (1930) to 1,643 (1940).[73] Many Polish, Slavic, and Italian Americans also worked at the Hazel Atlas glass factory in East Wheeling whose piece-rate system provided women an avenue to make more money depending on their skill. Italian Pasquale DiCesare noted that men in the early 1910s could earn as much as thirty to forty cents per hour (about three dollars a day) at Hazel Atlas.[74]

For the Polish and Ukrainian children of South Wheeling, the Wheeling

Can Factory was still a major employer. The Polish girls at the Forty-Eighth Street plant were instrumental in the 1915 strike for union recognition. However, conditions declined during World War I. The AFL contract soon only benefited the most skilled men, who were union leaders and "would not give ear to grievances expressed by younger members."[75] The factory's workforce had grown to 574 (297 men and 277 women). Of the women, 121 (44 percent) were under the age of nineteen. All worked fifty-five hours a week, from 7:00 a.m. to 5:40 p.m. While most men received a scale of wages reflective of seniority, skill, and union positions, the women were paid uniformly. Of the 277 female operatives, 232 (83.7 percent) were paid 19¼ cents per hour. This gendered wage discrimination was evident in the hand-soldering department where women earned 22 cents an hour, while men earned 36 cents for the same work. Overall, girls between the ages of sixteen and eighteen, representing almost 50 percent of the female workforce, earned just $10.50 to $12 per week, well below a living wage estimated at $15 per week per person. In essence, the union contracts, and the use of girls living near the factory, helped promote the company's sexual division of labor.[76]

Polish and Ukrainian American women also continued to do much of the production work at Bloch Brothers Tobacco in the heart of South Wheeling. Women working in the stemmery building fed the loose tobacco through a breaker and then wet it and hung it to dry out. The women's main job followed when the dried tobacco was sent to female "strippers" to be threshed. By the 1920s and 1930s, the company implemented treadle-like machines to increase production. Young girls worked an automated machine to check for any loose stem particles in the tobacco leaf. Women also worked cutting machines that set the tobacco off into "ribbons" before being sent off for final drying and then automatic packing machines. Young girls' employment grew as the factory became more automated.[77]

The best way for Wheeling's Polish immigrants to find economic security came through home ownership. Polish families valued the security of homeownership over social status. They were determined against all odds to purchase a lot, build a home, and mortgage their assets to assist in paying off a wood-frame or brick row house. The fluctuations of the 1920s economy intensified a "working-class realism," manifested in the practice of paying off the mortgage over time with the additional labor of male and female children in factory jobs.[78]

Unlike larger cities where Poles had their own building and loan associations, Wheeling's Poles relied more on loans from local banks. By the 1920s,

Wheeling's working class went to one of the city's eighteen commercial banks, which served as the financial center for the upper Ohio Valley. Immigrants could send money back home or convert their currency to dollars by going to one of the foreign exchanges, either downtown at the Wheeling Bank and Trust Company at Twelfth and Market Streets or the South Side Bank & Trust Company at Thirty-Eighth and Jacob Streets. Immigrants became more comfortable keeping their savings accounts and mortgages in banks, as most saw an increase in savings deposits after the war. Many of Wheeling's banks tried to entice the working class by offering 4 percent interest on their savings accounts. Crucial as well were Polish small businessmen who gave loans and helped fellow Poles learn the banking process. In this regard middle-class Poles acted as intermediaries by getting working-class immigrants to invest in the city's future. This often entailed cosigning bank loans and acting as witnesses to deeds, mortgages, and estate appraisals after a family member's death. Undertaker M. W. Olszta was listed as an appraiser for Szyman Kowalski's estate in September 1918, which included $265 in the Center Wheeling Savings Bank and two bank notes signed with Fr. Emil Musial for $200. Grocer and small businessman Stanley Duplaga also served the same function for Katherine Zombak's estate, which had $1,091.40 in the Fulton Bank & Trust Co. and $1,487.40 in the National Exchange Bank in July 1922.[79]

The long process of repaying debts emphasized a culture of doing without certain household amenities until they could be purchased and using old-world strategies of making do. Many women tended small garden plots, even in South Wheeling's crowded backyards. Families settling in Fulton tended large gardens and some livestock. Josephine Franczak kept chickens and small animals behind her family's home in Fulton. John Kogut remembered that since his family came from the "Ruski Polski section" of Poland they had experience mixing life in a coal camp with old-country farming and butchering customs. When the mines closed around Easter time, or when he only got two to three days a week underground, Kogut's father would kill some hogs he kept and dig a twenty-foot trench covered with tin sheet in his garden to make a homemade smokehouse. After smoking the meat for twenty-four hours, he then rolled together his own Polish kielbasa.[80] Finally, some men distilled moonshine in homemade basement stills for sale.[81]

Throughout the 1920s, Polish immigrants were on the path to home ownership, but they were still firmly working class. Public records and the 1930 manuscript census suggest much about their evolving status. In the Eighth Ward, the densest section of Polish settlement, 125 eastern European households were in the process of owning their homes; however, another 106 eastern European households were renters.[82] In relative terms the Poles saw some social mobility. In 1920, the same sample area had a home ownership rate of 28.9 percent. In 1920, 71.1 percent of all Polish households were rentals, but by 1930 renters dropped to 45.1 percent.[83] For those who did rent in South Wheeling, the prices were affordable, with the average monthly rent being $14.75. For 1930, values for the majority of the homes in the sample were worth on average $3,134.71, and only three homes were worth more than $10,000.[84] Most homes in this section of South Wheeling were wood frame and increasingly had indoor plumbing. Standard home prices remained somewhat more stable in this region because of the recurring threat of floods. After one in March 1924, one real estate company listed prices for available South Wheeling homes with values depending on the distance from the river and nearby factories. Some sample homes suggest their value: "Eoff Street, Frame house, 7 rooms—$3,850"; "Forty-first Street, Frame house, 4 rooms, bath—$3,600"; "Forty-eighth street, 11 rooms, garage—$8,000."[85]

The process of home ownership took many years, as evidenced by the experience of millworker Jan Zalewski. Arriving sometime in the early twentieth century, Zalewski first purchased the deed in May 1906 to an Eighth Ward lot thirty-five feet by fifty feet costing $800. After living at that house for some time, the Zalewskis agreed to purchase a house from Hannah Hoeke in July 1916. The details of the arrangement suggest the difficulties paying down their new debt. The Zalewskis were to pay $950 for the property, which included $300 in cash up front and $75 a month for six months. They also had to pay 5 percent on all deferred house payments already made and all insurance and taxes, which totaled $650. Eventually, by November 1924, the Zalewskis wanted to make sure the home stayed within the family and transferred the deed to their son.[86]

Despite increasing levels of home ownership, Polish families lacked the disposable income to purchase mass consumer goods. Those blue-collar workers in Wheeling owning radios could listen to Pittsburgh's KDKA, which commenced broadcasting in 1921, and later WWVA broadcasts from downtown Wheeling beginning in December 1926. By 1930, 46.7 percent of Ohio County households owned a radio set. However, according to the South Wheeling sample, few owned radios. Out of 235 households, only 36 had a radio (15.3 percent). Many working-class immigrant families waited years to pull together enough money to purchase consumer goods. One female press operator at Wheeling Corrugating noted that only after her father and sister started working regularly did they have the income to buy a refrigerator followed by an electric stove. Not until well into the Great Depression were they able to purchase a radio set.[87]

Attaining a small business was a very difficult process that often led to failure. South Wheeling for the first half of the twentieth century had an abundance of small grocery stores. Most catered to the working-class population living paycheck to paycheck by allowing families to "run a 'book.'" Most sold meats, bread, milk, and basic canned foods, and some even delivered to private homes.[88] But family-owned businesses survived on the edge of economic ruin. Many were undercapitalized, heavily credit-driven, and reliant on a working-class customer base that had little disposable income. Poles often waited a few years to accumulate some capital from their wages before purchasing a necessary structure to house their business along with stock and equipment. The trend for many Wheeling Poles was to pay cash up front to another businessman whose business was insolvent or recently went bankrupt. Thus, working-class immigrants could purchase necessary stock up front at a reduced price from a fellow immigrant usually willing to sell within the ethnic group. Polish grocer Wincenty Front, having worked at the Hoffman Tannery for several years, started a business in 1913 by purchasing the contents of Frank Kruszewski's grocery. Before he sold all available groceries and provisions along with shelving counter scales, and show-case displays, Front had to pay Kruszewski $600 up front and sign a promissory note for $1,000.37. Front would have to pay $100 a month until the note was fully paid, which was costly. Sometimes parties reached confidential agreements, agreeing to exchange all the contents of a store on face value for ten dollars to cover the cost of the deed. While it is hard to determine what "valuable considerations" meant in practice, it was a common legal exchange that kept stores, saloons, and other small businesses within the community.[89]

Certain locations were adapted for similar business use. In 1914, John Marchlenski purchased all the stock, merchandise, and groceries in the storeroom at 2624 Chapline Street, along with some household goods and rooms on the second floor of a brick house at 2618 Chapline for his family to live. Most of the goods were simply exchanged on payment of the deed costs. Once his business expanded and he decided to relocate farther south in the Polish community, Marchlenski sold the contents of the storeroom, cash register, refrigerators, scales, and meat-slicing machines to two prospective business partners.[90] Even when business partners put their money together to open a store, eventually one would want to get out of the business or his partner would buy him out. George Zuebel sold "all rights, title, and interest [he had] in . . . Fulton Grocery Company" to Stanley Duplaga. This sale included all the stock, merchandise, and even the businesses automobile. Duplaga's Fulton Grocery boomed during the 1920s allowing him to open the Southside Department Store at 4513 Jacob Street in the heart of Polonia in 1923. By 1928, he was able to buy an even larger home in Elm Grove.[91]

Ethnic small businesses allowed for greater economic autonomy while still being linked to the industrial working class. These enterprises helped some owners to transcend class differences within the community.[92] Frank Lewandowsky worked at the Hitchman coal mines from 1904 to 1919. After the war, he was able to operate a successful painting business among the Polish homeowners of South Wheeling.[93] Reflecting back on his father and other immigrants' lives, Herman Werfele surmised, "They had the same goals in mind. They wanted to become . . . small business owners, several of them became large business owners, [and] some of them became wealthy entrepreneurs. . . . But the majority of them had a comfortable living."[94]

While the grocery business could be very profitable, other types of businesses were harder to maintain, especially pool halls. Many Poles who operated saloons prior to Prohibition converted to operating pool halls. Born in Kamionka Strumiłowa in Galicia (now part of western Ukraine) in July 1892, Walter Prask started in Wheeling as a steelworker in 1909, but by the First World War he had opened a poolroom in the center of Polonia. In the postwar recession and following his marriage to Lekla Wisniewska, Prask went back to work in the mills only to reopen his pool hall in 1921. However, throughout the rest of the decade, Prask remained a steelworker. Stanislaus Klos had a similar history. Arriving in America in 1890, Klos and his wife Aleksandra Wyzykowska had the honor of being the first couple married at St. Ladislaus on February 23, 1903. Working at the Belmont Steel Mill, Klos eventually saved enough money to open a restaurant in 1915, which in 1917 he converted to a pool hall. Like Prask, he had to close his business during the postwar recession and went back to work as a skilled heater in the steel mill, briefly reopening a restaurant in 1921. Until 1928, he continued working in the mills and saving his money so that he could reopen the pool hall. By 1930, Klos's business was next door to Prask on the 2600 block of Main Street. Both owned homes with some value in the mill district where most rented. Prask's home was worth eight thousand dollars, and Klos's was worth seven thousand dollars. However, to keep his business going, Klos's children still lived at home and worked in local factories to supplement the family's income. Unlike Prask, Klos could retire by 1940 and did not need to work in the mills in his old age.[95]

Fig. 6.1. Advertisement—Stanley Duplaga businesses (from parish history), ca. 1926. Courtesy of the Diocese of Wheeling-Charleston, Wheeling, WV.

Conclusion

The postwar strike wave held high hopes for Wheeling's immigrant communities of raising their standard of living and providing a modicum of industrial democracy. By 1920, the Polish retreated back to the stability and strength provided by their Polonia centered around St. Ladislaus. While there was a certain modest level of social mobility in the 1920s, the Polish community remained predominately blue collar. The decade also witnessed the flowering of the community and its institutions and saw renewed attempts for interethnic cooperation, which would provide the basis for revived unionization during the 1930s and 1940s.

CHAPTER 7

Polonia Adapts to the "New Era" of the 1920s

During the 1920s, Wheeling's Polonia faced many new challenges and opportunities. In the age of mass culture, some blue-collar immigrants saw a rise in their status and standard of living. A great example was Wojciech (Albert) Swiader. Born in January 1890 in the village of Grodziszko in southern Poland, Swiader came to the United States in 1907 and settled in Wheeling in 1912. Starting out with the Pullman Company, he rose through the ranks eventually becoming an electrician and for many years a shop foreman. By 1920, he owned his own home valued at four thousand dollars less than a block from St. Ladislaus Parish.[1]

Swiader's blue-collar background and social striving helped him become a leader within Wheeling and the upper Ohio Valley's Polish community. Starting in 1917, Swiader was a key organizer for the local and district chapters of the Polish Roman Catholic Union (PRCU) and other civic and fraternal organizations. As a leader in the popular Polish American Political Club, founded in 1919, Swiader conducted an Americanization class for seven years teaching English and aiding new immigrants in preparing for their naturalization exams. He was so successful that he was formally decorated by the Polish government with its "Swords of Haller" award. Among his fraternal duties and positions, Swiader was president of St. Joseph's Lodge No. 213 of the PRCU and president of District Council No. 36. He even served for three years as vice president of the statewide PRCU. He organized community and parish events and was one of the members of the multiethnic committee that helped create and sponsor the annual July 4 "Festival of Nations" celebrations at Oglebay Park. By the time he was relocated to the Pittsburgh Pullman Company office in June 1935, Swiader was an exemplar of the paths available for social mobility from within the Polish ethnic community.[2]

While the 1920s provided some opportunities for advancement, the decade was also a trying one for many Polish families. Like Albert Swiader, Łukasz Piechowicz emigrated from a similar area of Galicia to the United States in 1907 with his wife Katherine and young son Jan. Working as a coal miner, Piechowicz moved for some time through eastern Ohio. By 1913, he lived near Caldwell, Ohio, with his wife and four children. Sometime after 1920 Piechowicz changed professions and got work as a millworker at Wheeling Steel, and the family relocated again to Benwood by 1924. However, the next few years were very difficult. On April 9, 1924, Łukasz Piechowicz died at Wheeling Hospital of chronic myocarditis at age fifty-three. His wife Katherine suffered more grief only nineteen days later when her sixteen-year-old son Jan Piechowicz died in the Benwood Mine Disaster.[3] Katherine Piechowicz struggled to maintain her family's economic security and her own psyche. To supplement the small income from workmen's compensation, her sons Joseph and Stanley found work at the steel mill and the Wheeling Can Factory on Forty-Eighth Street. However, on June 26, 1926, tragedy struck the family again when Stanley Piechowicz fell from a truck on the corner of Twenty-Seventh and Main Street and fractured his skull when he was crushed by a heavy falling box. He was only sixteen years old. By 1930 the remaining family members rented a small home in Benwood for fifteen dollars a month, and Katherine's two remaining sons both worked for Wheeling Steel. While terrible, the story was not without hope. Early on Katherine Piechowicz instilled in her children a love of music and ethnic culture. Anton (Andy) was the most musically inclined. As a young man he performed tap dance at the Capitol Music Hall in downtown Wheeling and paid for his lessons by working in the steel mill. He also played a variety of instruments, especially the piano, which he learned from his mother. Even with his family's tragedies, he was known for years as a "happy, jovial man and was very family-oriented."[4]

The 1920s saw pressure put on ethnic communities to assimilate into life in the United States. Lizabeth Cohen suggests that ethnic culture did not totally break down in the 1920s since ethnic small businesses, Catholic parishes, and ethnic clubs remained the pillars of community allegiance throughout the decade. These institutions acted as an intermediary "not so much [to] tear ethnic youth from their roots as help them reconcile foreign pasts with contemporary American culture."[5] Thus this chapter will focus on the 1920s, a time of increasing cultural tensions but also growing interethnic interactions. Wheeling's Polonia witnessed more modest social mobility, often only with Poles rising from unskilled to semiskilled positions in the steel mills. Steelworkers did find greater stability with the formation in 1920 of the Wheeling Steel Corporation, which merged several independent firms. The new company possessed abundant blast furnaces, tinplate mills, plate and skelp mills, open-hearth works, sheet and fabricating mills, tube works, and coal mines to provide fuel. Becoming the largest employer in the region (17,631 by 1929), Wheeling Steel provided steadier wages during the 1920s.[6]

For Wheeling's Polish community, the 1920s were a transition period but one when the community's institutions grew and flourished. Some minor migration from Polonia occurred, but most moved for work on the periphery of Ohio County to the region's expanding coal mines or between mill towns within Wheeling Steel's orbit. Along with better streetcar traffic and more bridges over the Ohio River, the region became more interconnected. A Polish steelworker living in South Wheeling could very easily ride a streetcar or drive with coworkers to Martins Ferry, Ohio, while still living in Polonia. This diffusion aided in the growth of Polish communities in Martins Ferry and Lansing, Ohio, and in the coal camps in Triadelphia, West Virginia. Rather than declining, the ethnic community expanded its reach, the parish assumed a larger role in everyday life, and those early fraternal societies increased their memberships.

A more worrisome change was the increasing interactions between the children of immigrants on a citywide and regional basis. Attending ethnically integrated high schools, going to movie theaters and department stores in downtown Wheeling, and playing on sports teams undercut some of the community's hold on the entire Polish population. However, the interwar period witnessed both a revival of ethnicity and interethnic interaction. Following the Benwood Mine Disaster of 1924 that devastated families on the South Side and Benwood, diverse immigrant families worked together. By the end of the decade, regional festivals also celebrated the immigrants' cultures. Unlike earlier festivals that catered only to specific ethnic communities, these events were opened up to the public by the late 1920s culminating in the annual summer "Festival of Nations" held at Oglebay Park. While these events gave middle-class leaders a venue to promote the benefits of ethnic heritage, the high participation of working-class Poles shows that the power of ethnicity remained strong.

Benwood Mine Disaster April 1924

For the neighborhoods of South Wheeling and Benwood, the disaster at Wheeling Steel's Benwood Mine was the darkest moment during the 1920s. At 7:08 a.m. on April 28, 1924, a massive explosion took place during a torrential rainstorm. Occurring minutes after the start of the morning shift, a pocket of methane gas set off an explosion in the 8-North section. The state department of mines later learned the company used open safety lamps. Even with minimal methane gas, this was still dangerous because a small fall of slate could lead to an explosion. Coal diggers used black powder for "shooting" the coal face then sprinkled water during the extraction of the coal. One onlooker noted that the mine's "fan should have been in operation continually so that no gas would have been permitted to generate." The blast demolished motors and secondary entry rooms, dislodged timber supports, and caused numerous roof collapses that killed many men. The destruction was so vast that it took several days before crews reached the bodies in Entry Shaft No. 8. It would take at least six months to repair the mine.[7]

The Benwood Mine had a questionable safety record prior to April 28, 1924. In operation for over sixty years, it was a three-entry, room-and-pillar mine. Recently mechanized, the company employed nine underground electric mining machines. Fire bosses checked each room at 3:00 a.m. before the morning shifts. However, the company had a minor gas explosion on September 20, 1923, that killed a boss and two Italian miners. Afterwards, the Wheeling Steel Corporation provided another intake to air out the rest of the mine. Even with the improved ventilation, the mine's roof was "weak and treacherous" with support timbers needed every two feet, and miners left six inches of coal above them.[8] The explosion led to calls for better safety. State mine inspector R. M. Lambie noted that all mines releasing any amount of gas should be termed "gaseous" and use only "approved electric cap lamps, explosion proof motors and also permissible explosives." He also argued for better rock dusting regulations. Lambie was bothered by how coal companies used loopholes to evade the weak regulations. In particular he informed Governor Ephraim Morgan of "rumors that Benwood Mine was not inspected."[9]

The 119 coal miners killed represented a cross section of the new immigrant workforce common in northern West Virginia's mechanized mines. The Polish community suffered the worst loss—39 of the 119 killed. In total, 103 were immigrants from eastern and southern Europe.[10] Word spread quickly of the explosion, and hundreds flocked to the Brown's Run shaft. Women "frantic with fear" ran through the torrential downpour praying for survivors. One observer noted that some women roamed through the Benwood mill yards and streets "haggard of expression and wandering about aimlessly." For two days, wives gathered on the nearby hillside around fires awaiting word. When rescuers announced that those not killed immediately suffocated from "afterdamp," a reporter noted how their cries "caused a moaning sound that could be heard for a considerable distance." The conditions of the dead bodies were appalling. In one pit they found two Italian brothers clasped together in their last moments. A makeshift morgue was first set up at the mine's washroom, but later bodies were "too gruesome to describe." A *Wheeling Intelligencer* newsman noted one unidentified man who was "practically baked. He was swollen to almost twice his normal size." Relatives slowly began to identify their loved ones as best as they could.[11]

Fig. 7.1. Closeup of Benwood Mine Disaster, mass burial, Mt. Calvary Cemetery, May 5, 1924. Courtesy of the Diocese of Wheeling-Charleston, Wheeling, WV.

Ethnic communities formed relief organizations along with St. Ladislaus and St. John's Parishes, the Catholic diocese, and city governments. Benwood Mayor James Cox set up a donation fund through the Bank of Benwood, and Donald Liberatore, head of the bank's foreign department, made sure to distribute the money to the various families. Within a day the local Italian and Polish societies made significant contributions. In Wheeling, Mayor Thomas Thoner also set up a committee and made arrangements to have all local motion picture houses sponsor a benefit performance for the following Sunday matinees. Even the Italian government via its New York City consulate sent word to Father Schoenen to ascertain the number of Italians killed or directly affected. They then sent appropriate funds to provide for their countrymen.[12]

The two major Catholic parishes served as key grieving centers for victims' families. Father Schoenen of St. John's and Fr. Emil Musial of St. Ladislaus arranged for bodies to go to Coocy Bentz or ethnic-owned funeral parlors to be prepared for internment. Beginning on April 29, an endless line of funeral corteges ran through the two cities on their way to mass burials at Mt. Calvary Cemetery east of Wheeling. For Schoenen and Musial, images of grief-stricken families were not new. Bishop Donahue sent both priests to aid in the aftermath of the Monongah Mine Disaster in December 1907. Some of the men who were identified were sent to the Bartscky, Olsztla, and Stolarski Polish funeral parlors on the South Side.[13] Father Schoenen held a triple service for three natives of Szany, Hungary: Istvan Vargo, Ignac Orban, and Sandor Horvath. Father Musial had a particularly trying time on the morning of May 2. Felix Lisak and Lenard Levicki's service was at 8:00 a.m. followed at 8:30 by a private funeral for Jan Golebiewski. A half hour later, a dual service was held for Adam Długoborski and Walter Oblizajek. At 9:30, Carlo Caneva's service took place at the Polish church. Finally, at 11:00 a.m., a triple funeral for Izydor Shalayka, Mike Kazemka, and Jozef Kolodziejski occurred. Afterwards the entire community went to a mass burial at Mount Calvary Cemetery.[14]

The blast left many families without a breadwinner. Father Schoenen found "32 widowed foreign women" in one single block in Benwood and between fifty and sixty widows in a larger two-block area on Main Street. Throughout, "Crying women and weeping children [were] found on every door step."[15] The Catholic Sisters of St. John's Parish along with the diocese's Catholic Women's League canvassed Benwood to locate all needy families. At a time when the South Side Catholic community would have been gearing up to celebrate the annual May processions, the community instead set about to provide food and shelter to the needy. Immigrant societies increasingly received aid from outside sources, like the Associated Charities and especially the Red Cross. The Poles began working with the Red Cross during World War I. In December 1917, the Polish women on the South Side, led by Anna Ronewicz, organized a Polish Ladies National and Army Relief Committee, which operated like the Red Cross. These women took great interest in the organization, assisting in several citywide wartime campaigns. After the war, the Red Cross continued to aid ex-soldiers while also addressing public health and relief for the destitute. Thus, by 1924, the women of the community already had a relationship with the Red Cross and appreciated the services they provided during their time of grief. Steelworkers at Wheeling Corrugating in East Wheeling raised $515, and workers at the Martins Ferry plant also contributed another $510. In the oddest act, considering the immigrant and Catholic background of the victims, the Wheeling Klan No. 1 of the Ku Klux Klan sent $50 for relief.[16]

The tragedy brought together many different immigrants. After doing an investigative piece on twin Italian brothers killed, a local reporter noted her surprise to find in a neighboring Italian woman's home how "many Polish friends of the family, came to view the remains." Mixed immigrant audiences wept together and tried to identify their relatives at the morgues at Cooey

Bentz and Benwood's Blue Ribbon Hall. After visiting grieving residents, she concluded: "The only ray of light for the living was seen in the wonderful fellowship prevailing between all the stricken families, it is a community sorrow which is tying the whole town into big family, into a bond which even the variation of languages, is no account, they speak not to each other by the tongue, but by the language of the heart."[17] During a mass burial of twenty-four miners on May 5 at Mount Calvary an observer noted how the awful scene "melt[ed] away all trace of racial barriers." Widows yelled in desperate anguish as they watched their husbands' bodies placed within the earth. One grieving mother collapsed, screaming in her native language, "My boy, my boy!"[18]

Even with all the public goodwill, many worried about the long-term livelihood of the victims' dependents. Under the West Virginia Workmen's Compensation Act, every widow would receive thirty dollars a month for the rest of her life along with five dollars a year for each child (until they turned sixteen) who lost a father. As part of their company pension plan, Wheeling Steel paid widows a lump sum of $500 from the employee insurance fund and $150 to help cover funeral expenses. However, many men were married before coming to America thus requiring the women to provide official marriage certificates. The Red Cross helped get the necessary documents sent from their home countries.[19]

The grief caused by this tragedy devastated South Wheeling families for years to come. Living in dilapidated and decaying housing, the Polish immigrants also lacked adequate and functioning utilities. On May 3, 1924, Fr. Emil Musial submitted a letter to the newspaper to shed some light on the "bigger" solutions needed for his people. Praising the city's generosity, he wanted to voice his concerns that "the disposition of the fund subscribed for the stricken to their real and lasting benefit." After reading newspaper accounts, Musial targeted something deeper that bothered him and many Poles. Noting how those killed "were hard working and industrious men, and perhaps their pride would suffer if offered aid" directly, Musial stressed that "they are not starving." While this may sound like a leader trying to defer any criticism that his community was poor, Musial was worried about long-term effects of the mine disaster: "What they do need, however, is alleviation from the sufferings and burdens of the future. Many of them, having permanently established their homes in our mist [sic], bought humble homes, but their homes are, without exception, burdened with heavy mortgages, which were expected to be paid from the wages of the victims. The widows and orphans will lose their homes without some outside assistance."[20] Musial suggests how many of these immigrant families, after years of struggling by on lower wages, were finally able to purchase modest homes. Without the hopes of better economic conditions, and now without male breadwinners, families might lose their homes, and that loss, in turn, could lead to the destruction of the ethnic community. Musial left open the idea that some government or organized assistance was needed to guarantee the future stability of the community rather than leaving families to fend for themselves. This approach also suggests a subtle evolution in Musial's thinking. Rather than just a closed-off ethnic community, Polonia would need to reach out to other ethnic groups throughout the city to continue to thrive.

Americanizing and Integrating the Second Generation: High School Football

Much of this cultural association outside the ethnic neighborhood was already beginning to happen among younger Polish Americans. As the children of immigrants reached maturity, they began interacting more with those outside their ethnic group. Adolescents could see Hollywood films in several movie houses, go to Wheeling Park for a day of fun, shop in one of the downtown department stores, or play pick-up baseball at one of the urban ball fields. One of the best venues for socialization occurred in the high schools. While most attended the local parish school, after the eighth grade they had to attend a public or Catholic diocesan high school. Unlike prior generations, many young people were attending high school in the 1920s and 1930s. The growing popularity of high school football in the upper Ohio Valley greatly aided interactions. With so many teams, mill towns were pitted against rival mill towns, and Wheeling's neighborhoods played against other neighborhoods. However, a football team could unite second-generation ethnic groups for a common purpose. Football's popularity grew in the 1920s with regular radio broadcasts of games. In the upper Ohio Valley, games provided some of the most exciting public events during the fall season.[21]

The 1920s and 1930s were a high point for the area's football programs in terms of statewide success. While most teams were composed of native-born residents, the new emerging programs were those that integrated more second-generation ethnic ball players. The two successful programs were Benwood Union and Wheeling High Schools. Benwood Union's rise to prominence came thanks to the popularity of their coach Everett Brinkman. "Brinkie," as he was affectionately known, was born in South Wheeling in 1902 and was a standout letterman at Wheeling High School. He then went on to success with small-school powerhouse West Virginia Wesleyan, winning the WVIC title in 1925. After graduation he entered coaching with his first stint coming for Benwood Union (1927–1932). Known as a disciplinarian, he was a master coach compiling an impressive record of 40–9–4.[22]

Benwood Union's success showed the benefits of integrating second-generation ethnics. In 1926, the team won the West Virginia State Championship with an 8–0 record comprised of mostly native-born or Irish American players. Coach Brinkman built a team using the multiethnic mill town's athletic talent. By 1928, he led the team to another 8–0 season and state championship but with a team possessing more Slavic and Italian American players.[23]

The star on Benwood Union's 1928 squad was team captain and quarterback Dick Matesic, a son of Croatian parents. At the end of the season, Matesic was named First Team All-Valley. As noted in the end-of-season write-up, Matesic was a "190 pounder standing 6 feet one inch, who strikes like dynamite." Based on his stellar play, the *Wheeling Register*'s sportswriters asserted Matesic was "the greatest offensive threat seen in this district during the past five years."[24] In the running-dominated style of offense of the era, Matesic was a perfect fit as a "shifty and fast" back. As a runner, he was a nightmare for opposing defenses running primarily off tackle, often breaking tackles and continuing the "remaining distance unmolested." The quarterback also led one of the valley's most potent "aerial" passing attacks. The team was truly dominant, scoring 224 points in its first six games while holding its opponents to just 21 points. Matesic had amazing games against Linsly, Warwood, and Moundsville. Against Wheeling High, he intercepted a pass and skirted forty yards for a key touchdown. In a win over Wellsburg, he scored every touchdown, and most came on very long runs. Other Benwood Union players to receive All-Valley honors were left guard Dicola and right halfback Blake (for Second Team honors) and left tackle Hartwig and center Mussilli. While Bellaire and Martins Ferry had other notable ethnic players, Benwood Union's quarterback was the star.[25]

The growing popular interest in Brinkman's multiethnic team and his star player Matesic's talents were on full display during their annual rivalry game with Moundsville High. Regular starter and triple threat tackle Kramer, guard Mamick, and fullback Blake were unable to start from injuries suffered against Linsly. Coach Brinkman also sidelined speedy halfback Kopec for the rest of the season. Thus, Benwood entered the game no longer heavy favorites to win on the road.[26] While their usual offensive output was down, Benwood Union won a tough game in a light drizzling rain 19–7. This was a major victory as it was only the second time Benwood had ever beaten their Marshall County rivals. In a thrilling game, the "shifty backfield giant" scored three touchdowns. The newspaper spoke of Matesic's play using implicit ethnic stereotypes of Slavic Americans as large, powerful, and mean. During the win, Matesic "by brute force broke down the stubborn resistance." After beating up on the Moundsville defense, in the second quarter Matesic "the slippery demon from Union resumed his assault" leading to the team's first score, followed by another impressive thirty-five-yard touchdown run. The quarterback was truly a "workhorse" running the ball on 90 percent of Benwood's plays and registering fourteen first downs to Moundsville's two.[27]

Coach Brinkman had another stellar state championship team in 1931, and the squad represented the continued success of integrating the various ethnic groups in Benwood. Finishing with a perfect 9–0 record, Benwood Union's earned its third state title in six seasons. After their first six games, they outscored their opponents by 124 points to 0, and "Brinkman's machine" was already heralded as "Valley champions of 1931." Benwood Union finished the season as one of only two state programs undefeated and untied.[28] With the onset of the Great Depression and the closure of the Wheeling steel mills, the players' immigrant parents and the Benwood community as a whole most likely saw their sons' success as a major source of pride.

Benwood Union's success was having an effect on other area football teams. When the *Wheeling Intelligencer* announced its All-Conference Team in December 1931, the comparison between the First and Second Team squads reflected the growing prominence of ethnic football players. Including stars from Union, Linsly, and Tiltonsville, Ohio, the First Team included players named Cucculelli, Hudacek, and Motto, while the Second Team was made up of mostly Irish, German, and native-born players named Jones, George, Farmer, Beck, and Dorris.[29] The leading point scorers from Wheeling also reflected ethnic players' growing success. Jacob Hudacek of Linsly (9 TDs and 7 extra points) was of Slovak descent, Kopec of Benwood Union (6 TDs and 2 extra points) was of Polish American descent, Kahayada of Benwood Union (3 TDs) was of Czecho-Slovak descent, and Thomas Symansic of Triadelphia (5 TDs) was of Polish American descent.[30] Junior Tommy Symansic in particular was a key dual sports player in football and basketball for Triadelphia High School. The team drew on many immigrant families whose fathers worked for the coal mines in Elm Grove and Triadelphia. Symansic was a talented halfback. During the annual Thanksgiving Day game between rivals Triadelphia and Warwood, Symansic had a key "85-yard dash for a touchdown" on the second half opening kickoff that broke the game open. He was the game's "individual Triad star" scoring all three touchdowns. As a well-known school athlete, Symansic, as noted by the high school yearbook, was "very popular with the ladies."[31]

After his success at Benwood, coach Everett Brinkman was hired to coach the struggling Wheeling High football team in 1933. The following year he followed the same formula he used with Benwood, turning Wheeling High into a state champion with a record of 9-0-2 with another undefeated team and state champion in 1937. His 1934 squad was noted as a "hard driving club" that "tackles so hard" it makes past teams "resemble a pink tea party." While not as prolific a scoring offense as his Benwood Union teams, the 1934 Wheeling High Blue and Gold teams in their first seven games allowed just twelve total points.[32]

By 1934 the transformation in the composition of the Ohio Valley's football teams was complete. The majority of the starting lineups consisted of second-generation ethnics. A good example was the high-profile game between Wheeling High and Triadelphia at Wheeling Island Stadium. Wheeling High came into the game in first place (6-0-1) with Triadelphia in third place (4-2) in the Ohio Valley Athletic Association (OVAA). It was a solid 19-0 victory for Wheeling. Some thought Triadelphia might pose a threat, since they would "have their fullest power and weight available" with "Hacskaylo back at guard" and "Gregorsky [would] take over the left tackle job."[33] References to girth and strength as distinctive Slavic traits had long been a stereotype, but in the case of football matchups this was often true. When Wheeling High took on Bellaire, Ohio, later that season, the *Wheeling Register* noted Bellaire's advantage on the offensive line outweighing the Wheeling High line by eighteen pounds per man. However, Wheeling made up for it with two sizeable Polish American offensive lineman, center Frank Wojcik (185 pounds) and right tackle George Venskoske (210 pounds). Likewise Wheeling possessed the advantage in the backfield with powerful halfbacks like Greek American Stefanow (164 pounds).[34]

A survey of some Wheeling football teams for 1934 suggests this growing multiethnic composition. Benwood Union's offensive line included Polish Americans with left end Leon Leeczak, left tackle Kurlinksi, left guard Rudolph Hodulik (Slovak American), right guard Horvat (Croatian American), right tackle Pelosi (Italian American), and in the backfield Walter Helenski (Polish American).[35] The same was true with the Triadelphia team, comprised of players left end Paul Bobick (Russian American), left tackle Gregorsky

(Polish American), right guard George Hacskaylo (Czech American), right end John Shinsky (Polish American), and the backfield led by quarterback Joseph Figaretti (Italian American), fullback Rapaswich (Polish American), and left halfback Symansic (Polish American).[36] Even Wheeling Central Catholic followed the trend. To match Benwood Union's heavily ethnic team during a November 1934 contest, Wheeling Central boasted players such as left end Malandrakis (Greek American) and Kamierczak (Polish American) at center.[37]

Games like football, baseball, and basketball helped Americanize the various communities throughout Wheeling by pulling kids of the second generation out of their ethnic enclaves. Unlike larger metropolitan cities, Polish American kids could not avoid Croatian Americans in Benwood or German Americans in Center Wheeling. Even for children, sites of play within neighborhoods provided spaces for interethnic cooperation to take shape. Mary Lou Henderson, who grew up in the German American neighborhood in Center Wheeling, played with a variety of young boys growing up. Tackle football games took place in the middle of the brick street between Chapline and Eoff near Twenty-Fifth Street. Henderson also remembered baseball games at nearby Webster School and the Hubbard Playground near Twenty-Sixth Street. Grace Karcher, another German American whose family lived in the same neighborhood, remembered the 1920s and 1930s fondly. She noted that "I played ball of all sorts. . . . When I got older, I played with the neighborhood kids. There were a lot of them—Greek, Lebanese, Serbian, Italian, and Polish." For her and her other male and female friends, their ethnic differences "never entered into our minds. . . . After all, everyone was from someplace else."[38]

Those peer interactions at an early age provided bonding experiences that matured as these children grew up to be teenagers playing on various high school sports teams and later as they became working adults. In addition, the city as a whole looked on with pride as their high school sports teams received regional and statewide recognition and championships throughout the period. Adolph Campiti of Wheeling Island, like many of his generation, was active in various sports. Joining the multiethnic teenagers attending Wheeling Central Catholic High School, Campiti and his fellows won three Catholic state basketball championships in the late 1930s and early 1940s. Many who played football and other sports later found work in the Wheeling District's factories, and their earlier interactions on the gridiron and basketball court would greatly assist in their mutual solidarity to forge the CIO unionism in the 1930s and 1940s.[39]

Ethnic Catholic Parishes and Culture
in the 1920s and early 1930s

The interwar period also witnessed a flowering of the Catholic Church in Wheeling as the diocese continued its "brick-and-mortar" Catholicism by constructing new parishes and allowing existing parishes to extend their influence. During the 1920s, ethnic parishes and fraternal lodges preserved and refashioned ethnicity in local neighborhoods, largely helping to determine what it meant to be Polish, Ukrainian, Italian, Croatian, Czech, and Slovak. However, the era also witnessed tension as many of the immigrant generation's children reached their teen years and adulthood. While they still lived at home and attended mass and parochial school, the temptations of the New Era were appealing. Movies, automobiles, dancing, and jazz music greatly worried immigrant parents. The decade was also one of rising xenophobia against immigrants and their culture. Immigration restriction cut off the continued flow of new migrants into the region. As a result, ethnic Catholic parishes exerted more direct influence over promoting ethnic culture in the 1920s. Community leaders publicized ethnic festivals and parish events for not only native-born critics but their children as well.[40]

St. Ladislaus weathered the cultural changes quite well. Father Musial and the parish had virtual autonomy over shaping the cultural, religious, and economic lives of those of Polish heritage. As a local priest noted of the Polish Americans of St. Ladislaus, "Much of their spirituality is grounded in their race as Polish people."[41] Earlier ethnic festivals continued to grow in the 1920s and early 1930s and attracted a wider audience. The two seminal events each year were the May processions and the crowning of a May Queen along with the newer and much larger "Polish Day" festivals held at Oglebay Park or in Lansing, Ohio. Street fairs tied to Polish Catholic events were crucial for raising funds for parish renovations and fraternal lodges as well. Polish women made homemade pierogies, cabbage, noodles, and kielbasa available for purchase. While these initially were Polish-only events, by the 1920s they were open to all eastern European groups and even native-born residents of the Ohio Valley. They also remained a popular form of entertainment that Polish American children waited for with anticipation. Frank Kogut noted how "we really like processions around here. That's one of things that makes me really love this church."[42] Even non-Polish events attracted a variety of eastern Europeans. Joe Bazo recalls the Hungarians had an annual picnic in the summer at Valley

Grove. It became very popular by the 1930s for its Hungarian dancing and fiddle music, so popular that Polish, Ukrainian, and Slovak immigrants came from the mining camps and steel towns. Another experience that kept Polish Catholic traditions alive were the Forty Hours Devotions in early October, during which children would be sent over to the parish every hour so the parish would never be empty. Once the forty hours ended, the whole community would celebrate mass together.[43]

These events brought the community together across class lines as well. While middle-class residents living in South Wheeling played a key role in organizing events, working-class families were the backbone of the community and prominent in cultural events. Take the May processions, whose May Queen often came from one of the working-class households and was probably a blue-collar worker herself. On May 6, 1934, the community's May Queen was Mary Kuca leading a parade of over three hundred school children, members of the Blessed Virgin Sodality, the parish altar boys, and Father Musial around the South Side. Twenty-five girls from the eighth-grade class bore "a figure of the Blessed Virgin with ribbons leading to each of the girls."[44] The event brought out everyone in the larger Polish community in Wheeling, Benwood, Fulton, and towns on the Ohio side. Kuca herself was a working woman's May Queen. Born in 1912, she lived with her family and started working in the late 1920s as a seamstress for a clothing factory on the South Side. By 1932, she and her sister worked as machine operators at the Wheeling Tile Factory.[45]

Vibrant ethnic Catholic communities, like that at St. Ladislaus, also bred resentment from Wheeling's native-born population. The 1920s were a period of intense xenophobia highlighted by immigration restriction legislation passed by Congress in 1921 and 1924. Native-born white Protestants worried about economic competition with immigrants and the eroding of their traditional culture. By late June 1921, tensions were high, and Wheeling's citizens were introduced to the Ku Klux Klan. In a formal letter to the city planning committee and Mayor Thomas Thoner's office prior to the Fourth of July parade, the Klan "respectively" asked that the city "discourage and prevent the use of any other than the American flag. . . . This [applied] to British, French, Italian, Greek, or any other foreign power." Mayor Thoner (1919–1925), a leading German American Catholic, disagreed, arguing that immigrants turning out "have the right to carry the flags of their own country, provided the American flag is carried" in the front.[46]

The appearance of Wheeling Klan No. 1 in June 1921 was not an aberration. The Klan re-emerged beyond its Southern boundaries throughout the early 1920s in industrial areas across the Midwest. Appealing to native-born

Fig. 7.2. May procession, Mary Kuca May Queen and Father Emil Musial, 1934. Courtesy of the Paul Cihy Family Collection, Phoenix, AZ.

Protestants discontented by continued immigration, modern urban culture, and political corruption in the postwar United States, the Klan called for law and order and a "Christian" revival of true-blooded Americans. As the appeal of the wartime "100 Percent Americanism" campaign continued in the early 1920s, the Klan gained many new members. They also crafted their message to appeal to the particular resentments felt by a local community.[47] In urban areas, the Klan was dominated by members of the Protestant lower-middle class and blue-collar factory workers fearful of the rapid changes taking place. The Klan of this era was increasingly anti-Catholic, and the Catholic Church was excoriated in the Klan's vitriolic rhetoric. They often blamed immigrant "clannishness" on the bondage of Roman Catholicism, especially parish priests, who "retain control of the minds of these victims."[48]

Wheeling Klan No. 1 was quite active in the early 1920s even though it remains difficult to analyze their membership. In a letter reprinted in the *Wheeling Intelligencer*, the local klavern stressed that it was composed of "civic enthusiasts . . . occupying positions of great responsibilities [who were] seen and recognized as gentlemen upon the streets."[49] Wheeling's Klan actively publicized their efforts. On June 29, 1922, four local newspapermen were allowed to attend the Klan initiation for 229 new members at a farm two and a half miles from West Liberty. Calling the event really "Creepy Stuff," the *Wheeling Intelligencer* reporter estimated that a crowd of about 1,000 from several klaverns in the region took part in the ceremony.[50]

With its growing fears of ethnic Catholics, Wheeling's Klan stressed "absolute Americanism" at the same time the local civic elite sought to instill those values among the city's diverse population. The Klan first appeared in Wheeling during the summer of 1921 in a direct challenge to the right of immigrant groups to participate as equals during the Fourth of July festivities. The irony though was that city officials were far from weak in promoting patriotism.[51] The celebration in 1921 was the brainchild of the American Constitutional Association (ACA), which was a pro-business entity promoting Americanization and the anti-union, open shop movement in the state. "America First Day" was held each Sunday around July 4 in the early 1920s throughout West Virginia. The ACA approached ministers and civic officials to promote American ideals while working alongside groups like the Rotary, American Legion, and Chamber of Commerce. On the inaugural America First Day in 1921, Mayor Thomas Thoner called upon the people to "renew their pledges of patriotism and their covenants of loyalty" and to defeat forces that "threaten the very existence of organized society."[52] The Klan, however, disagreed with allowing foreign flags in the parade but argued they had no animosity toward those "foreign born citizens who pledge[d] their allegiance to this republic." They were fine with those who in theory had "renounced all allegiances to the countries from which they came." Even with these rebukes, the festivities went off as planned. The Greek and Polish communities had large contingents marching in the parade with two bands and "beautiful floats" marching in the second division behind the veterans of the Spanish-American and First World Wars, the 314th Field Artillery, and the American Legion.[53]

But even after the successful 1921 Fourth of July parade, the Klan continued to focus on the city's immigrant Catholic population. In January 1923, citizens in South Wheeling saw a ten-foot-high fiery cross in Bellaire, Ohio, illuminated by large searchlights to intimidate immigrant residents. Later that year, the Klan scared the children staying at the St. Vincent Orphans Home in Elm Grove by firing "signal bombs" at a rally on a nearby hill. The fact this event took place so near a Catholic institution was not a coincidence. The practice of burning crosses atop the hills in East Wheeling made them clearly visible at St. Joseph's Cathedral, St. Anthony's Italian Catholic Church, and Our Lady of Lebanon.[54]

To counter the xenophobic climate exemplified by the Ku Klux Klan, by the late 1920s Polish, Ukrainian, and other community leaders promoted ethnic culture for the upper Ohio Valley as a whole. Led by parish leaders and lay working-class women, these ad hoc festivals on ethnic holidays served a more visible purpose. Unlike the anti-immigrant sentiment that dominated cultural and political discourse during the early part of the decade, artists, intellectuals, and civic promoters began stressing the positive elements of a multicultural society by the late 1920s leading to an interest in ethnic folk music. This ethnic revival built off the growing appeal of new forms of dance thanks to the Jazz Age craze for the foxtrot and Charleston. Young people, with the aid of social workers and programs sponsored by the YWCA, were energetic to learn the polka, oberek, and czardas. Modeled after the programs started by Edith Terry Bremer and the YWCA's International Institute to teach the benefits of immigrant culture, more than fifty "Y Institutes" existed by the end of the decade sponsoring ethnic dance exhibitions.[55]

As groups interacted on a daily basis at work, in town, and in schools, they became much more interested in the diverse backgrounds all about them. This cultural interaction developed from Wheeling's unique ethnic composition in the state. Wheeling had the highest number and percentage of foreign-born whites and children of foreign-born parents in West Virginia. Over one-third of Wheeling's population was first or second generation foreign-born. While this high immigrant population was not new, the composition had changed. While Germans and their German American children still led, the second-largest ethnic group in Wheeling and Ohio County were the Poles with 732 foreign-born and 1,743 of Polish American heritage. This number did not include many that lived in Benwood or those who recently moved across the Ohio River.[56]

While the renewed interest in eastern European folk culture was a positive development, the Ukrainians, not the Poles, were the first to promote it. This developed partially from their own cultural nationalism as they felt controlled by the much more dominant Poles in eastern Europe but also in immigrant communities in the United States. Often seen as Ruthenians or Rusyns, they were not distinguished from the Poles for years. Many native residents called them Polish. Beginning in the late 1920s, the Ukrainians, through their own parish, Our Lady of Perpetual Help (called locally St. Mary's), began to promote Ukrainian dance and music for neighborhood children.[57] This revival came with the arrival of a new and energetic priest, Fr. Humphrey Kowalsky. Seeking to promote and unite the Ukrainian population, Kowalsky worked with Oglebay Park staffer Ruth McIntire and the All-Nations Council to promote and sell tickets for Ukrainian folk performances. Oglebay Institute organized the

All-Nations Council, representing each ethnic group in the region, to assist in, as the *Wheeling Daily News* noted, "the preservation of much that is picturesque and interesting of the culture of the Old World."[58] In late November 1930, Wheeling High School sponsored "Glimpses of Picturesque Ukraine," featuring a "Cossack sword dance" and "Ukrainian Cossack ballet" of forty dancers. Organizers informed the audience about the meanings of some of the dances of "this oldest Slavic race," like the "Katerina Khersonka," which was "a dance of the Ukrainian steppes, [suggesting] the golden wheat and azure sky which gives the Ukraine its national colors of blue and gold."[59] Thus this event was a staging of Ukrainian cultural nationalism. Father Kowalsky, an authority on Ukrainian folk songs, noted in promoting the culture that "no race is richer in lore" with songs for all daily events: "the men toiling in the fields, the women at work in their homes or gardens usually accompany their labor with songs. The subject of the songs range all the way from the warriors achievements of the Ukrainian Cossacks to the baking of a loaf of bread inn [sic] an humble peasant hut. All are characteristic of Ukrainian life."[60]

The best expression of the region's multiethnic culture was the annual Festival of Nations at Oglebay Park on Independence Day. Community leaders wanted to promote the estate owned by Earl Oglebay. His property had only recently been deeded and accepted by the city in July 1928. One of the main promoters was Samuel "Ry" Rybeck, a key civic leader in Wheeling's Jewish community. Rybeck and his wife Rosalind were crucial in convincing the city to purchase the park and pitched tents with others to highlight the benefits of outdoor recreation. Hoping to highlight Wheeling's ethnic diversity, they worked with the Oglebay Institute to organize folk dancing programs and the Festival of Nations around the park's sunken gardens. For the first event in 1930, Samuel Rybeck served as chairman of the "Dramatic committee."[61] Each of the region's ethnic groups had exhibits, dancers in full costume, ethnic cuisine, and musicians playing traditional folk music. Czech, Slovak, Ukrainian, Romanian, and Polish immigrant groups had the most diverse programs. At the first festival in 1930, over six thousand came to Oglebay Park to view the dancers and exhibitions. Like earlier events, park officials stressed the importance of fostering Americanism. A procession of nations went through the park to meet a symbolic "Miss Columbia" who "received the representatives of each nation as citizens of the United States." Even before the performances, all the participants sang together "America the Beautiful." The 1931 Festival of Nations broadened to include an Italian and a Hungarian contingent from Martins Ferry. Additional features included traditional handicraft displays from Polish, Slovak, and

Hungarian culture. The second annual event garnered what at that point was the largest gathering ever at Oglebay Park. The events were more educational as dance leaders explained the historical and cultural significance of each dance. For example, the Polish group performed the "Mazurka," a dance with a long history among the aristocratic classes. In contrast, the Ukrainian dancers did a wider array of rural peasant dances, including the "Hopak Holom" ("the whirling dance of village youth") and the "Kolomeyka" ("an ancient wedding and festival dance of the Carpathian Mountaineer") along with the famous sword dance the "Lytsari Zaporozha" ending with the Ukrainian national anthem.[62]

Immigrant women played a leading role in these dance exhibitions. Ukrainian instructor Anna Horeczko had a unique perspective. Born in 1911, she and her father left Torki in southeastern Poland arriving in the United States in November 1923. She grew up in a borderland region during the worst of the First World War, the postwar ethnic conflicts between Poles and Ukrainians, and the Polish–Soviet War. Arriving once these conflicts subsided, her experiences played into her desire to promote her people's unique culture and make sure it was not subsumed by Wheeling's larger Polish population. Cultural productions could thus perpetuate nationalistic tensions coming from Europe. In late 1930, Wheeling's Polish community refuted claims that their native country treated its Ukrainian minority population "with unusual cruelty, permitting officials of Poland to act frivolously and barbaric."[63]

Wheeling's Polish community also sponsored its own dance group made up of girls from working-class families. During the first Festival of Nations in July 1930, the Polish dance team was quite large. All of the Polish American girls were between the ages of twelve and twenty-four. Of the fifteen with available employment information, all but four worked in a factory. Assistant instructor Anna Winkiewicz was twenty-four and worked at the Warwick China Company. Ten of the dancers worked at unskilled factory jobs, primarily at the Wheeling Tile Company on the South Side. Only one saw any sort of social mobility during this time. Anna Januszewski, born in 1910, was working as a lacquerer at the Wheeling Can Company at age sixteen but by her early twenties had gone to vocational school and was a typist and then a clerk at Wheeling Corrugating.[64]

Teaching traditional Polish dance was important in several ways. During a time of Americanized mass culture, ethnic dance helped preserve the old-world traditions for a second generation growing up listening to jazz and other American music. Promoting this culture also suggests the strong support for maintaining ethnic heritage among both working- and middle-class Polish households. While middle-class Polish actors were crucial in sponsoring events like the Festival of Nations, ethnic dancing provided a role for working-class members of the community as well. Finally, these dances helped bridge the gaps between ethnic communities and the wider native-born population by promoting a level of cultural awareness and tolerance.

The Poles also exerted much influence in popularizing Polish culture for a mass audience. Led by Alexander Oszustowicz, a series of popular Polish bands serenaded the Poles during community functions. Originally a musician in the Wheeling Orchestra, Oszustowicz formed his own symphonic orchestra, the Moniuszko Orchestra; however, only drawing Polish listeners, he revamped its repertoire. Reorganized as the Polish American Rhythm Kings, they played a variety of dance-band music, especially polkas. This gave them more recognition as they played for regional Polish fraternal events and had a Sunday program via WWVA radio.[65]

No matter the changes in the 1920s, St. Ladislaus remained the center of the community and expanded its reach. Polish ethnic fraternal organizations involved many immigrant men and their children, and women saw new roles in lay parish governance and societies. Father Musial and the parish lay councils took great concern in growing and attracting activities for the children of Polish families as the high birth rate between 1906 and 1925 put pressures on the small parochial school. Father Musial exercised his authority in 1925 by taking out a twelve-thousand-dollar loan from the South Side Bank & Trust to make upgrades to the school and the Felician Sisters' residence.[66] With an increased parish population, which also served those in eastern Ohio and Triadelphia's coal mining areas, the parish saw a golden era in the 1920s. While tuition costs, usually fifty cents a month, could cut into tight family budgets, parochial schools expanded because of the pervasive piety and regard for parochial schooling among working-class Polish men. Parochial schools also instilled cultural values such as deference to authority, familial and national loyalty, and accepting the limits of personal and monetary desires. For the majority of the community's population, the parochial school protected traditional cultural norms and was crucial in "inventing ethnicity" for a new native-born generation.[67] Parish confirmations show as well how much the parish grew. Available records for 1922 and 1928 show that Polonia's center remained in the area from Fortieth Street south through North Benwood. The number of children reaching confirmation age grew from 140 (1922) to 249 (1928) before declining to 176 (1931).[68] Table 7.1 suggests how the parish school continued to grow. While baptisms peaked in 1925, the school-age population remained large until World War II.

Table 7.1. Souls at St. Ladislaus and Children in Parochial School, 1920–1930

	Souls	Students	Births
1920	1300	336	–
1921	1500	306	–
1922	1500	356	–
1923	–	–	–
1924	–	410	112
1925	1350	421	110
1926	1600	430	93
1927	1300	402	76
1928	1600	432	58
1929	1600	420	86
1930	–	390	40

Source: St. Ladislaus Annual Reports, 1921–1930, DWC.

Beginning with Father Musial as the sole instructor and continuing for decades with the Felician nuns at the helm, Polish Catholics received an education that could rival that of any Wheeling school. Students spent rigorous hours learning about an array of subjects but colored by the nationalist principles promoted by Musial. The curriculum included full instruction in Polish language, history, politics, and religion as well as U.S. history, English, and civics. Mary Martinkosky recalled how "We had Polish and English. English in the morning and the Polish in the afternoon. We [second-generation Polish children] could still speak pretty fluently." [69] Blanche Resczynski also stressed the rigors of this ethnic education: "Also we had geography—English geography in the morning and Polish geography in [the] afternoon. History even your English and your Polish." [70] Likewise, the report cards (*swiadectwo miesieczne*) of Mary Anna Kaczor for the 1934–1935 and 1938–1939 school terms show that students were graded on a regular scale each month in twelve subjects—religion, Polish reading, Polish history, English reading, spelling, grammar, arithmetic, general science, American history, penmanship, Polish grammar, and "attitude." [71]

The types of fraternal and sporting activities also grew during the 1920s. While in larger cities Polish communities saw a significant decline in fraternal groups, Wheeling and the upper Ohio Valley saw male organizations proliferate.

The two largest, the Polish National Alliance (PNA) and Polish Roman Catholic Union (PRCU), maintained their early roles within the community. Both groups by the mid-1930s had Boy Scout troops along with the insurance programs developed in the first decades of the century.[72] The number of lodges just within the Wheeling area expanded. The Woodrow Wilson Lodge No. 2725 of the PNA formed in Elm Grove in October 1933 with the increase of Poles working in the coal mines east of Wheeling. St. Casimir Society No. 282 of the PRCU was organized in November 1922 for the Poles of Fulton. Providing fraternal insurance, sick benefit fund, and a juvenile department, St. Casimir also purchased the peninsula playground for children's recreation activities. Secular clubs also grew including the Polonia Club for Polish American boys and the Polish American Political Club formed in 1919.[73] Young women could be involved in a variety of lay societies that worked with the church, such as St. Mary's Sodality, the Holy Rosary Society, the Children of Mary, or the popular St. Cecelia Chorus.[74] The Rosary Society saw the largest expansion in the 1920s among Polish women as the most popular female pious organization. Meeting regularly for prayer services, it also gave married and unmarried women a place to meet and discuss political and social issues in an approved Catholic setting. The society also sent members to care for those who were sick and assist families in hard times. Women's groups, such as the Polish Women's Alliance No. 414 (formed in 1924) were also crucial in the annual ethnic festivals and raising funds through regular bazaars.[75]

Lay fundraising events were very important to the economic health of the parish during this time. After World War I, Catholic dioceses got more heavily involved in financial oversight of their ethnic, national parishes. Centralizing of diocesan bureaucracies required ethnic parish priests to submit more detailed annual financial reports. Every request for repairs or other budget items needed to be signed off by the chancery, including even sacramental wine forms once Prohibition commenced. This centralizing process cut into the discretionary power of the priests like Father Musial, meaning that collecting pew rents (the primary monetary collection) and private giving and fundraising events grew in significance. Much of this money from fundraising needed to be reported to the chancery but could be used for a wider range of discretionary purposes. Ethnic festivals and bazaars were thus quite popular and profitable. In 1925, St. Ladislaus raised $3,425.94 from fairs and bazaars. While not a majority of the parish's income, the importance of those cultural events took on greater financial significance as the Great Depression loomed. Even in 1929, parish fairs only raised $1,774.16, and in 1930 the amount raised declined again to $978.08.[76] As table 7.2 shows, even while this was a time of increasing

Table 7.2. Financial Records of St. Ladislaus Church, 1921–1930

	Receipts	Pew Rents	Expenses	Debt
1921	$15,021.92	–	–	$11,650
1922	$11,175.02	–	–	$11,150
1923	–	–	–	$9,050
1924	$10,290.35	$2,257.25	$10,219.37	$8,450
1925	$25,721.65	$7,116.65	$23,564.57	$20,100
1926	$13,260.32	$6,346.60	$13,260.32	$18,100
1927	$10,508.35	$6,108.45	$10,471.30	$18,100
1928	$16,856.94	$7,614.78	$16,436.93	$18,100
1929	$11,358.35	$5,424.93	$11,358.35	$18,000
1930	$10,365.20	$4,580.45	$10,346.74	$17,900

Source: St. Ladislaus Annual Reports, 1921–1930, DWC.

affluence and prosperity for the parish as a whole, much of the parish's growth came from increasing debt to diocesan and local banking sources.

With their growing cultural presence in the city, the Polish community exerted its power over defining public space as "Polish American." Through the efforts of a Polish American Political Club petition drive to the city council, the Forty-Seventh Street playgrounds were renamed "Pulaski Field" in October 1930. Founded to aid local Poles in becoming U.S. citizens, the club's building and numbers expanded during the 1920s. Of all the local fraternal associations, the PAP Club was most active in civic affairs to get municipal improvements in South Wheeling. They funded extensive improvements to the park's recreational facilities and also had gates erected and a guard posted at the railroad crossing at Forty-Fifth and McColloch Streets. This action eased what was for years a constant worry of many Polish parents with children getting hit and killed by fast-moving railroad cars. The PAP Club was also instrumental in its successful protest against a city proposal to install gasoline tanks in South Wheeling near many homes.[77] The vote to change the park's name came about a week after the mayor and other city officials joined community leaders and over 1,200 Poles for the fiftieth anniversary of the PNA and banquet at the PAP Club.[78]

By this point the Polish community could exert itself on a wider level and with cross-class support from the community. The PAP Club aided both middle- and working-class men. In 1930, Secretary Stanley Owoc and President Walter Zdanowicz were instrumental in the community's improvements. While Owoc ran a successful barbershop, Zdanowicz was a steelworker throughout the decade but by 1930 was working at the local junkyard.[79] Russian Polish immigrant Bernard Klimazewski, president of St. Joseph's PRCU branch, and Joseph Kupski, president of the local PNA, were both laborers in the tin mill.[80] Along with the PAP Club's political presence, and the local chapters of the PNA and PRCU, the community also had its own newspaper, the *Polish News*, edited by Kazimerz Obecny to disseminate local and international news of Polish concern. Reflecting the overwhelming blue-collar nature of the community, there was even a Polish Workers Association led by Joseph Gosztyla.[81]

Conclusion

Many Polish American children who came of age in the 1920s and 1930s recalled a world that was full of vigor. Two of Adam Pietras's descendants recalled the working-class existence of South Wheeling with fondness. Mary Pietras Robbins remembered growing up near the Ohio River and swimming in it during the hot summers; when it froze, she recalled, "we would skate and ride down the river bank in cardboard boxes from Freismuth's Packing Company." As a child, one could go a few blocks and enjoy the delicious tastes of the Royal Bakery (owned by the Lukaszewicz brothers), especially their "devil dogs," and bring home fresh bread for family members who "ripped off chunks and ate it on the spot." Not far away, she could stop off at Alex Habak's general store, where he made his own Polish sausage. Upon returning home, Robbins and other Polish wives could pick up some fruit and vegetables from Mr. Dzinglski's pushcart as he came by shouting "Apples, peaches!" As children, she recalled they could get free entertainment by playing in the street or go to the nearby Marsh Theater for a dime (even though you could sometimes sneak through a "rat-hole" in the back for free). And if you saved some extra money from your factory job, you could shop for the latest consumer items from the Cooey Bentz Department Store. Regardless of their poorer circumstances, Mary Pietras Robbins recalled "everyone was glad to get whatever they could."[82]

This description is not presented to overly romanticize the difficult trials faced by Polish immigrants. With their own ethnic village, Polish Americans could recall with great candor the united feeling of the community. Mary

Fig. 7.3. Helen Kazmierczak in South Wheeling, ca. 1930. Courtesy of the Paul Cihy Family Collection, Phoenix, AZ.

Martinkosky's parents emigrated from Lublin in the early 1910s, and Mary recalled growing up in the block between Forty-Seventh and Wetzel Streets: "I wouldn't trade my childhood for nothing. We were poor but we didn't know the difference. . . . We had grocery stores on every block, beer joints on every block. I would say there was about fifty businesses from here to Thirty-Third Street. That's only about thirteen blocks. . . . The playground [Pulaski Field] was always full of people. You had to stand in line to get a swing."[83] This account best summarizes much of the sentiment and common experiences of Polish community life in Wheeling's Polonia.

While still united in a lively community promoting Polish Catholic culture throughout the wider upper Ohio Valley, Wheeling's Polish population underwent a transition during the 1920s. The expansion of their ethnic culture was in some respects a defensive reaction to the drastic changes of the post–World War I years. While they wanted to maintain their robust Polonia, as this chapter has shown, Polish immigrants, and especially their children, were being pulled into encounters outside their tight-knit neighborhood. Thus, this was an era of both reinforced ethnic and religious identity tied to St. Ladislaus and increasing interethnic interactions. While the Poles had dealt with living in a crowded and dangerous industrial neighborhood for years, the devastation of the Benwood

Mine Disaster cut across ethnic communities, forging bonds of grief and mutual assistance. Likewise, the second generation was coming of age in a time of mass culture, and group interactions like high school football were breaking down older cultural barriers between ethnic groups. Finally, in response to the anti-immigrant climate of the "Tribal Twenties" and a strong Ku Klux Klan presence locally, the Poles worked with others to highlight the benefits of a diverse, ethnic Wheeling in events such as the Festival of Nations. Even with these cultural exchanges, however, Wheeling's ethnic populations would suffer the brunt of anti-immigrant sentiment, best exemplified by the targeted enforcement of Prohibition.

CHAPTER 8

Moonshiners and Bootleggers: New Immigrants and the Selective Enforcement of Prohibition in Wheeling

On the morning of March 23, 1924, federal prohibition officers patrolling the South Side "caught a strong scent of ripe mash . . . unmistakably arising from cauldrons used in the manufacture of moonshine liquor." After securing a search warrant they, along with state prohibition agents, raided the second-floor home of Polish grocer John Marchlenski and discovered "the largest distilling plant ever unearthed in Wheeling." Realizing the nature of the space and its capacity for producing moonshine on an industrial level, the agents found a fifty-gallon still, seven hundred gallons of mash, and almost one hundred gallons of liquor. Marchlenski claimed he only recently purchased the property. Still, police arrested and held him under a thousand-dollar bond.[1] In the early 1920s, Marchlenski ran a grocery at 2624 Market Street and even after the raid was still operating a small grocery store at his residence. Why would he engage in such an illegal operation? He had immigrated from Przasnysz in Russian Poland in early 1902, and by the early 1920s he was a homeowner. He also had a growing family to take care of including his wife Amelia and their nine children. To feed so many in a working-class neighborhood often meant finding other sources of income, and in the 1920s liquor was very lucrative in Wheeling.[2]

While the arrest of a middle-class grocer like Marchlenski was unique, working-class Polish immigrants also engaged in the illegal trade. Noted rum-runner Alex Cybulski had just served ten months in the Washington County, Pennsylvania, jail. After a subsequent arrest on May 10, 1924, federal authorities only fined him one hundred dollars, even though agents implicated him in a "conspiracy" to bring further amounts of "booze" into Ohio County. Local barber and community leader Stanley Owoc even guaranteed a thousand-dollar surety on Cybulski's bond.[3] Another Russian Pole, Cybulski was emboldened by the potential profits from bootlegging. He lived in the heart of Polish South Wheeling working as a coal miner at the notorious anti-union Hitchman Coal

Company. By 1920, he was an unskilled laborer in the Benwood steel mills taking care of a family of five, and in 1921 he began running a poolroom at his home address.[4]

Bootlegging operations frustrated state and federal enforcement agents. Marshall County Sheriff Clayton expressed his anger after arresting Vinson Gabinist, a Russian Pole, and others in a rooming house in Benwood. Finding four-and-a-half gallons of moonshine whiskey, Clayton noted there had been fifty to sixty prohibition arrests in Marshall County in the prior four months. When assessing blame, Clayton reiterated a point becoming common in the area: "In practically every instance they were foreigners. Less than 1 percent of the arrests have been Americans. The foreigners are for the most part Russian-Poles."[5]

Sheriff Clayton's assessment and the stories of daring raids on urban moonshine stills highlights how Wheeling's immigrant populations were the targets of what Lisa McGirr has dubbed "selective enforcement." Prohibition officers patrolled crowded ethnic neighborhoods hoping to "catch the smell of ripe mash." Coming from an overwhelmingly white Protestant state, West Virginia's Yost Law (1913) and the federal Volstead Act (1919) reflected the desire of reformers to end the saloon and Americanize immigrants. Linking rising crime and urban crowding to Wheeling's numerous saloons and "fake hotels," middle-class Protestant reformers promoted Sunday closing laws and high-priced liquor licenses to close saloons. Escalating frustration led them to advocate for stronger government power to remake new immigrants into their own image. By 1920, local members of the Anti-Saloon League along with state and federal officers used tactics of surveillance and coercive pressure to "Americanize" the multiethnic population.[6]

Immigrants were those most often arrested by dry agents because they disobeyed a law they saw as discriminatory. Coercive Americanization attacked their Catholic and ethnic culture. Enforcement also hit blue-collar neighborhoods, where working-class immigrants moonshined in their homes and bootlegged to supplement their meager income during the area's weakened postwar economy. By focusing on one of the most targeted groups—the Polish—this chapter will highlight how Wheeling's new immigrants responded to state and federal prohibition enforcement.

Recently scholars have examined Prohibition from various local contexts, highlighting how local and regional conditions played into the failures of enforcement. The types of illegal booze, the nature of local government corruption, and the presence of particular ethnic groups affected how enforcement was deployed. For New York City, Michael Lerner found Prohibition "was marked by blatant displays of religious intolerance, class bias, and outright bigotry," the main purpose of which was to "police the habits of the poor, the foreign-born, and the working class." Thus, immigrant communities shared a common language of protest and fused together their identity as part of a wider culture war in the 1920s.[7] The localized nature of Prohibition is vital. As Julien Comte notes in his recent analysis of Prohibition in Pittsburgh, "authors too often obscure the role local actors played in resisting a law imposed on them from above. Observing these dynamics requires reducing the scale of analysis in order to place local actors within their social, political, and cultural context."[8] This case study demonstrates the nature of "selective enforcement" and its effect on Wheeling's Polish American community. Their response to Prohibition was a crucial component of their assimilation process as well. Selective enforcement provided a common experience affecting all of the city's ethnic communities, forging ties that inspired increased political involvement and support for unionization efforts in the 1930s.

Local and State Enforcement

By the turn of the century, Wheeling was renowned as a "wide-open town." With a long history of organized vice, Wheeling's saloons were increasingly attacked by reformers. The dry advocates' main institutional arm was the Anti-Saloon League (ASL). Created in 1893 in Westerville, Ohio, the ASL was led by Protestant ministers and professional political advisers. Growing out of the Committee of One Hundred's local efforts around 1900, as discussed in chapter 2, the ASL in attempting to enforce Sunday closing laws aggressively used the courts, police, and public relations campaigns to attack the beer business. To oust the saloons, the local ASL forced the city council to raise liquor taxes and even ban the "free lunch."[9]

With continued violations of local prohibition statutes, the movement shifted to relying on state-level enforcement. The ASL strategy of lobbying state legislators and working with women's suffrage leaders, such as Lenna Yost, finally paid off when state voters passed a prohibition referendum in 1912. Although the prohibition law named for Lenna Yost's husband, State Senator Ellis Yost, did not go into effect until July 1, 1914, the ASL got started early to "Make Prohibition Prohibit."[10] The ASL worked closely with the district and prosecuting attorney's offices. These public officials hoped Wheeling would become a model moral city. With the support of Republican Mayor Harvey Kirk (1913–1917), ASL member and prosecuting attorney R. M. Addleman closed gambling houses and many saloons, stepping over the head of the police department. Kirk's administration supported a series of raids in the summer of 1913 that closed many speakeasy clubs and gambling rooms. For Addleman, these efforts meant "there will be no coming back to life in this case, for we stuck a knife in the corpse to make sure of death."[11]

When the state went dry on July 1, 1914, members of the ASL in Wheeling were joyous. But within months, numerous problems developed highlighting the inherent flaws in enforcement. Awakening on the morning of July 1, a *New York Times* reporter saw big signs on the hills of Belmont County "in plain view of everybody" advertising intoxicating drinks. This same reporter noted how the Yost Law would drastically hurt the city's businesses and laborers. Immediately the city lost $105,000 in tax revenues, and eight hundred to nine hundred men were thrown out of work.[12]

The Yost Law itself was one of the most "bone dry" state enforcement laws, banning all intoxicants over 0.5 percent alcohol. Stiff penalties were enforced: a first offense incurred a $100–$500 fine and two to six months in the county jail, a second offense was one to five years in the state penitentiary, and a third offense brought life imprisonment. However, like the later Volstead Act, the Yost Law was full of a sea of problems. First, to speed up prosecutions, the law allowed for municipal ordinances to try cases by local courts. However, on several occasions, Wheeling City Council voted down any local prohibition law. Second, the law permitted medicinal and sacramental wines approved via a state internal-revenue-service permit. Many who applied for retail liquor dealer authorization were former saloonkeepers. Fred Bischoff of 4143 Jacob Street applied for a permit starting July 1915. State special undercover agent Tony Mainfort reported to Charles Earhart, attorney for the Wheeling Anti-Saloon League, that a man "in his auto hauls booze to this place" and Bischoff's mother sold regularly to the men working at the nearby Wheeling Traction Company powerhouse. Undercover agents often disguised as workers went to known speakeasies, purchased drinks, then returned to raid the place. Mainfort made twenty-five purchases from April 12 to July 28, 1916. The speakeasies he entered were spread throughout Wheeling, with 40 percent run by African Americans and 25 percent by immigrants or ethnic minorities.[13]

The start of World War I in Europe intensified tensions and prohibition enforcement against immigrants. Deputy sheriffs noted how by September "bootlegging [was] on the increase in Wheeling." Angry over their excessive case load, deputies testified in court against those "with almost unpronounceable names" noting that the majority "in the speakeasy cases [were] foreigners." To send a message, the district attorney's office passed mass indictments against those violating the Yost Law and organized a series of raids based off undercover agent testimony.[14] John Kobus's case shows the difficulties in prosecuting these immigrant violators. Kobus was one of the first arrested under the Yost Law. A twenty-six-year-old from Myszyniec, Russian Poland, he was a grocer living at 4525 Jacob Street, where he allegedly ran a speakeasy. A fellow Pole, Peter Rusky, testified that he bought from Kobus on several occasions and that Kobus kept "wet goods secreted under the floor of the dining room, in a secret vault." The trial was a test case for the ASL, and Charles Earhart and Addleman personally led the prosecution. Kobus's attorney consistently asked jurors if they belonged to any organization formed to enforce the Yost Law or if they harbored anti-immigrant attitudes. In the end, the jury found Kobus not guilty since the ASL could not prove the wet goods were for sale and not just for personal consumption.[15]

From 1914 until the start of national prohibition in 1920, prohibition officials grew frustrated by immigrants' willful violation of the law. Fred Blue, state commissioner of prohibition, linked the dangers of immigrants and bootlegging as the situation worsened by 1916: "The greatest present-day problem of immigration to this country is that of assimilating these outlanders." Blue noted that American freedom and liberty would not be "surrendered to suit the personal habits or notions of the foreigner." As Ronald Lewis summarized the sentiment, "Here was progressive West Virginia's attitude toward immigrants in a nutshell: become like us, that is, socially and economically reliable, or leave."[16]

Prohibition enforcement became a culture war in the state, a battle over Americanism. Apathy toward the law got to such a point that Governor Henry Hatfield claimed in a speech in late September 1915 that he might declare martial law and send the national guardsmen to Ohio County to stop bootlegging. Both the "wets" and "drys" used pageantry to gain public approval. In mid-October 1915, Governor Hatfield, Fred Blue, ASL Chief Counsel Wayne B. Wheeler, and five hundred ASL supporters attended a law enforcement conference at the Market Auditorium. The state president of the ASL asserted that disregarding the sanctity of the law would lead the United States down the path of the German kaiser state.[17] At the same time, a counterdemonstration "Wet Parade" marched throughout downtown. The event was led by the National German-American Alliance's local president Fidelius Riester, who called on all immigrants to participate. Each city ward had a contingent in a parade of over three thousand people with another thirty thousand in attendance. Marchers carried umbrellas with empty beer bottles attached and colorful signs attacking the drys: "Why are workmen leaving Wheeling?"; "Sherman said 'War is Hell'"; and "Freddy Blue will soon be through—Boo Hoo, Boo Hoo."[18]

The efforts of the undercover ASL agents highlights the selective nature of prohibition enforcement toward working-class immigrant neighborhoods. Charles Earhart provided a constant stream of undercover reports to the prosecuting attorney detailing where undercover men purchased illegal booze. From these sources it becomes apparent how undercover men used the threat of arrest to force immigrants to inform them about illegal beer sales and transportation networks. Tony Mainfort reported on purchases he made between April 12 and July 28, 1916. Near a stable in South Wheeling, he saw a man who "hauls booze from Ohio for Gus Schultz" enter the Coy Corner Restaurant on Thirty-Third and Chapline Streets. Uptown, Mainfort got numerous Lebanese workers at the Wheeling Stamping Company to report on the "Bachmann place" across Main Street. One observer saw a woman come out of the joint with three bottles of beer under her sweater.[19] State prohibition chief Bert Phillips was concerned about beer imports from Ohio breweries. On November 19, 1915, he arrested prominent labor leader and socialist Valentine Reuther after he came across the river on the Twenty-Fourth Street ferry. Phillips watched Reuther stop his wagon at the rear of Harry Vogler's restaurant at 2516 Main Street. Inside, Phillips discovered fifteen baskets of beer, ten dozen pints, and two gallons of whiskey. Phillips soon began using a small boat to intercept bootleggers along the shorelines.[20]

The proliferation of immigrant speakeasies caused concerns. The case of Steve Kacinski highlights how immigrant small businessmen operated. Born in Russian Poland in 1877, Kacinski emigrated in the early 1890s and naturalized in 1896. He was a popular saloonkeeper on South Marshall Street catering to steelworkers and coal miners for over a decade, and he spoke Polish, Russian, and Lithuanian. However, the Yost Law forced him to convert his old saloon into a poolroom and restaurant. The adjoining property was converted to a barbershop and "up-to-date pharmacy." Kacinski did not attain a retail liquor permit and within a year was arrested for the first of many violations for operating a speakeasy. After getting out of jail, Kacinski moved his family across the river to Bellaire, where he operated a small automobile repair garage. However, by the mid-1920s the family was back in Benwood. In 1926, Kacinski was a watchman for Wheeling Steel and rented a small house for sixteen dollars a month. By the late 1920s, his family would again find themselves in court for violating the federal Volstead Act.[21]

State and Federal Selective Enforcement in Wheeling

The onset of national prohibition merged with the wartime Americanization campaigns and the general fear of immigrants during the Red Scare but also an increasingly precarious economy for Wheeling's working class. In 1922, the state commissioner of prohibition noted that the two greatest problems of the decade remained: "general disregard of law" and the "organized efforts of moonshiners and bootleggers to intimidate officers of the law and good citizens by threat and acts of violence."[22] Even during the xenophobic "Tribal Twenties," immigrants responded to Prohibition by continuing to distill their own moonshine alcohol as part of their strategy to make do and survive. Moonshining built off a series of self-help strategies immigrant families had employed since arriving in the upper Ohio Valley and was crucial to their working-class identity.[23]

Illicit moonshining enabled many working-class immigrants to supplement their income as living conditions fell during a sharp downturn in the economy from 1920 to 1922. Wheeling Steel began running its mills part-time in the fall of 1920. By January 1921, over thirteen thousand men were out of work in the region including seven thousand just in Wheeling. In addition, there was a shortage of one thousand apartments, while rents rose over 20 percent (as high as 75 percent) in a year. Streetcar fares rose over 60 percent, and food prices remained high. Charities sought to encourage "self-help," but reformers failed to realize that many immigrants were making do distilling moonshine and bootlegging.[24]

National prohibition only continued the numerous problems dry agents had in trying to enforce the law in Wheeling's diverse ethnic communities. In the first year of concurrent enforcement, the state commissioner of prohibition noted a major decrease in the amount of moonshine liquor and home brew statewide, but it was "still frequently found in Wheeling." For example, while the number of stills confiscated dropped by 8.2 percent from 1922–23 to 1923–24, during the same time Ohio County saw a spike of 55.6 percent of stills confiscated.[25] Initially, state officials complained most about the lack of coordination between local, state, and federal entities, especially the state police. By 1924, it was clear "inadequate co-operation of federal authorities to prevent 'rum-running' from bordering states" was a major problem in Wheeling.[26]

Another enforcement dilemma was that one of the most common ways to get some good "spirits" in Wheeling was going to church. Both the Yost and Volstead Acts had loopholes allowing for "sacramental wine" for religious purposes, which greatly benefitted those of the Catholic faith. Priests just had to fill out Treasury Department forms and for a given year tabulate their wine requests, their remaining stockpile, and their future requests. West Virginia was the only state, according to one manufacturer, where these Treasury Department forms had to "be approved by the State Prohibition Commissioner before the shipment is actually made."[27] These forms protected the diocese and Bishop John Swint from attacks by anti-Catholic groups that "Romanists" were too often imbibing during mass. Chancellor Edward Weber kept a firm control over these requests. Father William Hall of Immaculate Conception Parish at Thirty-Sixth Street made a series of large requests from 1920 to 1927. In 1920, he asked for one hundred gallon bottles of wine from a Rochester, New York, firm but also every six months asked for an additional fifty-two gallons, usually from the A. J. Hammer Company of Cleveland.[28]

The hierarchy worried that priests would order more wine to boost their popularity and their numbers during mass. Big fluctuations often drew scrutiny, and the chancellor paid special attention to immigrant parish priests. Father Emil Musial initially forgot to get his application form signed off by the chancellor's office. While usually never needing more than fifteen gallons at a time, Fr. Paul Abraham of Our Lady of Lebanon in October 1925 made two orders for a twenty-gallon keg and then an additional twenty-two gallons of wine.[29] More trouble came from Fr. Francis Bahoric of St. Catherine's Croatian Mission. Only in Benwood for several years, his tenure was full of complaints from Croatians, other priests, and the diocese. Even with a small Croatian congregation, Bahoric consistently requested twenty to twenty-six gallons of wine every six months, about the same amount as a larger parish. Bahoric asserted no wrongdoing and claimed that he was "taking good care that sacramental wine doesn't go into improper hands." Father Bahoric had many problems with his parishioners in the 1920s and argued he was acting as a bulwark against threats from the Communist Party with "some communistic papers coming daily to Benwood."[30] In Bahoric's mind, having a strong mission and ample sacramental wine was one strategy to entice working-class Croats to attend mass and not be tempted by communism. His stockpiling of sacramental wine was just one example of the challenges enforcement agents faced in Wheeling as the immigrant communities pursued their own interests despite the law.

State and federal prohibition agents selectively enforced the Volstead Act in targeting the South Side, continuing the wartime surveillance begun by the Federal Bureau of Investigation. Particular immigrant neighborhoods were targeted on a regular basis. The April 1922 court docket included thirteen liquor cases, of which eight of the violators were Polish. Others targeted multi-ethnic regions, especially the area between Twenty-Fifth and Twenty-Seventh Streets.[31] The key region was near the Centre Market House, referred to as the Greek "coffeehouse district," and Main Street near the Belmont Steel Mill. Both were within the unofficially sanctioned vice district. On March 10, 1923, agents raided 2622 Main Street, arresting several Polish men. Joe Fraczknivicz pleaded guilty and paid a three-hundred-dollar fine after possessing one and a half gallons of moonshine whiskey.[32]

The extensive arrests by dry agents led to prohibition violators overwhelming the federal court docket. To ease the situation, federal judges began accepting mass plea bargains in exchange for small fines. In a similar fashion to Pittsburgh, Julien Comte notes these fines meant "judges were in effect creating an informal licensing system."[33] However, the federal court in Wheeling tended to punish prohibition violators, often setting heavier fines of hundreds of dollars or short prison time in the Ohio County jail as punishment. During the May 1922 term of the U.S. district court, Judge W. E. Baker had 35 felony and 158 misdemeanor cases returned by the grand jury. At the time this was one of the largest criminal dockets in the court's history with almost one hundred of the misdemeanors being prohibition violations. Judge Baker was surprised that fifty-one of those defendants pleaded not guilty. While the docket included many Irish and German Americans, most were newer immigrants, including a good number of Polish residents.[34]

Examining the federal court's handling of the May 1922 court docket sheds light on the uneven application of justice. As Judge Baker progressed through defendants, fines ranged from four hundred to nine hundred dollars in the initial cases, while others were thrown out due to a lack of evidence.[35] Sentences were quite arbitrary. Millworker John Schrader pleaded guilty and was fined just fifty dollars. Judge Baker explained Schrader got off easy on account of "his aged mother." Riley Vucelic of Benwood was acquitted following a three-hour deliberation by the jury stemming from a raid on a house behind his. Judge Baker was stern, saying Vucelic "should consider himself very lucky" and learn his lesson "to keep away from places where liquor is made."[36] Greek American William Lias (Liakakos) was not as lucky. Found guilty of manufacturing moonshine liquor, Lias was fined five hundred dollars and court costs and sentenced to six months in the Ohio County jail.[37]

Judge Baker took stronger action against the Polish immigrants. Agents discovered a fifteen-gallon copper still and one hundred gallons of rye mash at John Belawa's house. Belawa lost his case and had to pay a $250 fine and serve four months in the Ohio County jail.[38] A more interesting case was that of John Rogalski, who lived on Twenty-Seventh Street. In December 1921, federal agent Thomas Arrington discovered a ten-gallon copper still, forty gallons of corn mash, and four ten-gallon lard cans for transporting illegal whiskey. Rogalski pleaded not guilty, and his case went to trial. Three fellow Polish neighbors testified on his behalf. In a strange twist, the jury failed to return a verdict, upon which Judge Baker instructed the district attorney to enter a charge against Rogalski's wife. The court reasoned that illegal liquor and mash was in the home and "someone [was] guilty of violating the law." As the *Wheeling Register* noted, "Not one Federal liquor violator [would] escape punishment if Judge W. E. Baker [could] prevent it." Baker issued a bench warrant for Mrs. Rogalski. She pleaded guilty at first and was released on five-hundred-dollars bond; however, she then changed her mind appearing in court "with two small children clinging to her skirts, another in her arms."[39] Even with his strict sentencing, by 1926 the violations of the law were becoming overwhelming, and Judge Baker was more willing to accept plea deals. On the morning of May 5, 1926, he dispensed with about thirty liquor cases in an hour and a half, imposing fines totaling $7,175 (about $240 per violation). However, he was still willing to take hard stances with Polish violators. Bruno Malarski, a Russian Pole nicknamed "Bruno the liquor king," was fined five hundred dollars and sentenced to eight months in the county jail for a second violation. An earlier violation led the court to deny his petition for citizenship in 1922.[40]

One of the worst examples of this form of judicial selective enforcement occurred during the May 1922 court term involving Michael Sawa. Charged for possessing two gallons of moonshine liquor, two large stills, and a quantity of mash, Sawa claimed the items were left in his home by another "foreigner who sailed almost a year ago for the old country." His son Adolph initially claimed the alcohol as his father's but later changed his mind trying to accept responsibility. The court became suspicious, thinking the nineteen-year-old boy was "being made the goat" by his father. During his trial, attorneys realized Michael was "foreign, and apparently was unable to understand the English language."[41] After appointing several attorneys to assist him, Sawa "apparently" pleaded guilty saying "Yah" to both charges. He was fined five hundred dollars and sent to the county jail. The real dilemma occurred when Judge Baker inserted into one of the charges the phrase "and did unlawfully manufacture two gallons of moonshine whiskey." Without Sawa present to plead, Baker added a four-month federal prison sentence. When instructed of this illegality under the Volstead Act, Judge Baker furiously stated, "The man ought to be in jail."[42] Attorneys on both sides of the case quickly notified the Department of Justice of the judge's biased opinion. Assistant District Attorney William

Grimes noted Sawa "could not understand the English language well, and in any event that was not a legal way to send a man to jail." Luckily Sawa received sympathy. After the attorney general did a full review, President Warren G. Harding issued Sawa a full pardon.[43]

Moonshining, Speakeasies, and "Rum-Running" in Polonia

As enforcement intensified, Polish families continued operating small moonshine stills in their homes. State prohibition agent Alonzo Prince found sixty-two quarts of "home beer" when he raided the home of John Wieneski, who lived a couple blocks from St. Ladislaus. Wieneski became a small-time brewer as a "sideline" to his day job in the nearby steel mill.[44] After the incident in March 1924 described at the start of the chapter, John Marchlenski was arrested again on October 16, 1925, for possessing "one-half pint" of moonshine whiskey along with the discovery of a fifty-gallon still with about "400 gallons of mash" on his property. This second charge was in violation of Section 21 of the National Prohibition Act. Finding Marchlenski guilty, the U.S. district court sentenced him to a six-month term in the Ohio County jail to be followed by another one-year term.[45]

Polish women also played an active role operating moonshine stills. They had an important economic role in the household often managing male boarders and the family budget. However, with the decrease in foreign immigration, they often found it more lucrative to supplement the family economy by bootlegging themselves. One of the most aggressive was "Pretty Katie Lipski" (or Lipsky). Living with her husband near the Belmont Mill district, "fizz ferrets" Tom Arrington and Fred Clayton discovered a "liquor distributing headquarters" at 2618 Main Street. Officers described the beverages as "garnished with a setting of maggots, stale butter, and garbage bowels resting close to the kitchen door." Katie, later referred to as "Polish Mary," often defended her reputation in court. In November 1923, she pleaded guilty to another violation but was only fined ten dollars. By 1925, Katie was fighting the federal court's injunction on their new place at 2622 Main Street after her and her husband violated an older injunction.[46]

Polish women operating home-sized stills built off rural traditions of canning and growing gardens. This home work was vital for working-class households as seen with Katie Haleski. Born in Galicia in 1884, she immigrated to the United States in January 1903. Katie and her husband Anthony had quite difficult lives by the 1920s, often moving from one rental property to another with their five children. Like many Polish women in South Wheeling, Katie began producing her own alcohol for illicit sale. She was first arrested for making home-brew beer on March 27, 1928, and then again on July 28, 1928, for possessing "74 quarts of Home Brew Beer" and another thirty gallons "in the course of manufacture." After she pleaded guilty in October, the court sentenced her to sixty days in the county jail.[47] By 1930, the family rented a home for twelve dollars a month in a poorer neighborhood near the Belmont Mill surrounded by Polish households and African American families who migrated from Alabama.[48]

Gendered assumptions of immigrant women's proper roles could lead to harsher treatment. Stella Groski was arrested for operating a small still. Summoned to Marshall County court, she was, according to the *Wheeling Register*, "surrounded by a weeping group of small children." Heartbroken about her guilt and unable to speak sufficient English without an interpreter, Mrs. Groski asked for sympathy. After her husband's death in a coal mine in August 1921, her children were entirely dependent upon her. About thirty-three years old and arriving in the area in 1910, Groski had five young children, who "clamored about her" leaving her "weeping bitterly and hugging her babies close to her." The judge felt no sympathy for the widow, admonishing her for not applying for aid and thinking it "her privilege to violate the law to gain a living." He set her bond at one thousand dollars, and she and the children were all taken to the county jail.[49]

Wheeling saw a proliferation of various speakeasies and clubs that came in different guises. Throughout the 1920s, these working-class speakeasies were often located in small "soft-drink parlors" or "confectionaries." Andy Przelenski converted his saloon into a confectionery, which was raided in February 1919. Agents in November 1923 found at Mike Rudzake's soft-drink parlor at 71 Forty-Sixth Street what they called "three gallons of 'coffin varnish.'" Joe Skazinski's soft-drink place at 13 Marshall Street was also found to be selling "pop bottle[s] of moonshine."[50] Like in major cities, Judge Baker issued injunctions to "padlock" notorious speakeasies for one year. In November 1930, the top closure was the Café of the Allies (operated by Bill Lias) on 2338 Market Street. When they tried to enter, prohibition agents were met by the most sophisticated of Wheeling speakeasy defenses, "equipped with electrically operated doors and barricaded so that the agents were compelled to use tear gas to get in."[51]

Automobiles supplied speakeasies as a lucrative traffic developed along National Road from Pittsburgh. In the press, these violators were dubbed "rum-runners." In one incident, a Buick roadster sped into town "loaded with fifteen five gallon cans containing real rye liquor." The truck was stopped by local, state, and federal authorities in Fulton. I. C. Kuczejuski of 4613 Jacob Street was arrested along with a John Felinczak of Pittsburgh for trying to deliver the illegal liquor from the Smoky City. State agent Alonzo Price, federal officer George B. Heidz, and another officer found in the machine a phony license and Pennsylvania tags and later poured about seventy-nine gallons of "pure red liquor gushing through a sewer opening."[52]

Alex Cybulski is a good example of how a few Polish immigrants continued to press the law. As noted earlier, Cybulski was caught several times for violating the Volstead Act. His most notable arrest came on April 5, 1923, when he and his partner were arrested near Cybulski's garage at the corner of Forty-Fourth and Eoff Streets. Department of Justice Special Agent H. H. Stroud observed the two men transporting "70 gallons of grain alcohol."[53] The two men had been bootlegging from Pittsburgh since at least January 1, 1923. Upon Cybulski's arrest, his garage contained two ten-gallon cans, three five-gallon glass bottles, and one five-gallon keg, and the special agent witnessed the men selling illegal alcohol to a diverse group of people on April 4. After serving a ten-month term in the Washington County jail for his other violation, he still owed the U.S. district court seventy-five dollars by late 1925. It took until June 30, 1926, for the U.S. marshal to locate Cybulski and force him to pay the fine and costs.[54]

Cybulski's life of crime was hard on his family. Alex's brother Konstanty arrived in New York on the SS *Barbarossa* on November 16, 1912. Initially going to Youngstown, Ohio, Konstanty arrived in Wheeling in April 1913. He worked as a coal miner and lived with his wife Clara and their four children. Eventually Konstanty bought his own home valued at $2,500 in 1930.[55] By all estimates, Konstanty was an upstanding community member compared to his brother Alex. When Alex was in court for the April 1923 arrest, Konstanty and his wife Clara served as surety, putting up one thousand dollars on their home and lot at 4606 Wetzel Street. This was significant for a working-class immigrant family, since their home was only valued at $1,000 at the time and the bond guaranteed they would pay if Alex failed to appear before the court on September 20, 1923. With four young children to care for, this was a major risk on the family's security. When Alex broke the law again in 1924, his brother was unwilling to make the same risk.[56] While Konstanty's growing family owned their own home, by 1930 Alex and his family were renting a home for twenty-two dollars a month in Hudson City, New York, where Alex worked as a janitor.[57]

Wheeling's Bootleg King "Big Bill" Lias

By the mid-1920s, the prohibitionists' focus shifted. Individuals producing moonshine and beer remained a problem, but enforcement agents turned their attention to the suppliers of illegal hooch. With a growing traffic in bootleg alcohol from Pittsburgh, in late January 1926 three cars were captured secretly hauling booze in a split section of their gas tanks. After raids discovering a 350-gallon "cutting plant" and massive stills in South Wheeling, residents learned that bootlegging had become consolidated under one figure—William "Big Bill" Lias.[58]

In 1955, William Lias attributed his financial success as a "numbers" king back to Prohibition: "My family was poor and I wanted some of the better things in life. But whatever I've done, I've done it on the square."[59] Lias's business career started at fourteen with driving a bakery wagon to haul alcohol from Bridgeport, Ohio, to Wheeling. On December 11, 1916, following a "Thrilling Race," Bert Phillips searched an automobile Lias drove and crashed on Twenty-Seventh Street, in which he found twenty-two baskets of beer. Lias received a misdemeanor fine for violating the Yost Law, although he would later be acquitted.[60] In his teens, Lias moved to Detroit, where he got involved with the city's infamous "Purple Gang." Having accumulated enough money and influence, Lias went into the "wholesale" bootlegging business. During the 1920s, Lias's empire encompassed a "liquor fleet" smuggling Canadian whiskey and operating throughout the Midwest. The operation included huge liquor inventories throughout Wheeling and fleets of trucks and passenger autos, all "specially built to haul liquor secretly." The size of his business was massive; during one eighteen-month period, he lost fifty-four automobiles and trucks via seizures and accidents.[61]

Lias operated with cooperation from city and county officials. Lias got six months in the Ohio County jail following a bootlegging arrest in 1922. This, however, did not halt his business: "While I was in jail I used to borrow the sheriff's car at night. I'd drive to Pittsburgh and pick up a load. Then I'd drive back to Wheeling and get rid of it and put the car back where it belonged before morning. I was doing a bootleg business from jail."[62] During a February 1923 county-wide dragnet, Lias took the stand to divulge his relationship with then-sheriff Harry Clouse. They were part of a bootleg ring that also included former city councilman Chester G. Thompson, deputy jailers J. William Schultz and Joe Bennett, and businessmen George Seibert and Cecil H. Kerns. During a dramatic trial, the court claimed Sheriff Clouse released Lias from jail to go with several confederates to procure alcohol in Pittsburgh. Agents arrested them in Canonsburg, but Clouse allowed Lias out of jail the next day (and several times in February and March) to go and secure their release.[63]

By 1924 Lias emerged as his own man controlling speakeasies and the National Road "rum traffic" and expanding into gambling and racketeering. That year he opened a gambling space in his White Front speakeasy. With so many customers patronizing the speakeasy for its bootleg whiskey, Lias decided to set up a craps table with a ten-dollar limit and later added slot machines. He opened up similar gambling apparatuses in his other speakeasies at the Yukon Club and the popular Café of the Allies.[64] When the operation was partially uncovered, Lias was indicted along with a group of Polish men from Wheeling, including I. C. Kuczejuski, Mike Rudzake, Walenty Rybicki, and George Slanski, along with John Felinczak and Hyman Darling of Pittsburgh. Darling drew two years in Atlanta's federal prison and a ten-thousand-dollar fine after one of his drivers turned over evidence to implicate his boss. The jury found Bill Lias not guilty.[65]

Two years later, Lias would not be as lucky. Starting in the fall of 1925, a series of dramatic raids revealed a massive rum-running syndicate between Pittsburgh and Wheeling through which Lias and Darling ran a lucrative trading route from one of Darling's Pittsburgh garages. When the raids captured one of the rum-running vehicles in early 1926, the press marveled at the one-of-a-kind auto tank. It carried 280 well-concealed gallons of liquor, and taps were in place to allow the tank to still carry fifty gallons of gasoline. Agents were lucky to discover the hidden tanks estimated to cost five thousand dollars each. Lias, acknowledged as "leader in an extensive bootlegging business," pleaded guilty in May 1926 to conspiracy charges and was sentenced to sixteen months in an Atlanta federal prison. His conviction led to a short decline in the rum-running traffic, where Lias's fleet of cars had once dominated.[66]

Gang Beer and Moonshine Wars

The big money to be made in the booze business by 1928 led to attempts to steal shipments and intimidate buyers and sellers, which brought about Wheeling's equivalent of the gangster scene. The height of this activity was from 1928 to 1931, a time of national concern over rising crime rates. Hostilities originated from competition over access to the clubs in Center Wheeling, particularly Greek-owned establishments. A renewed series of raids organized by J. J. Doerr, chief federal prohibition officer, from the fall of 1928 through early 1929 led one thirsty customer to complain, "And just think, I went to a couple of coffee houses and they were actually serving coffee."[67] Personal animosities led one faction to tip off agents against their competitors. On November 17, 1928, a man named "Little Joe" was beat up in front of a poolroom at Twenty-First and Main Streets. A large dragnet followed with Doerr noting his men would target "the persons handling large supplies of liquor for profit." Federal agents busted into a series of alleged speakeasies on December 11, 1928, only to be disappointed, except for their stop at the White Front at 2351 Market Street, where they needed their sledge hammers to get past an electrically locked door and heavy partition. Charles Blaxos, Joseph Cicari, and William "Big Bill" Lias were arrested. A day later, onlookers watched as agents poured fifteen gallons of moonshine down the drain from an empty house at 2521 Market Street. Likewise, two Greek men, George Pappas and Joe Perri, were taken into custody at 2329 Market Street, where agents discovered a large amount of bonded liquor. Throughout the week, "several caches of moonshine liquor and cut alcohol [were] found in vacant dwellings on the South Side."[68]

All the men brought to court were operatives of Bill Lias. While their cases were postponed until the May 1929 federal court term, the undue harassment got the best of "Big Bill." In "wordy exchanges" he told Alonzo Prince he "would not always be wearing a prohibition agents' badge."[69] Raids yielded access into Wheeling's more impregnable clubs, like the Produce Club at 11 Fourteenth Street. Raids on other vacant buildings mostly in South Wheeling found at least forty-two separate labels to distribute a variety of beer and whiskey. Agent Doerr was determined to "close every speakeasy in the Northern Panhandle."[70]

South Wheeling's Polish neighborhood also had its own small-time bootlegging family, the Vineskys. John Vinesky and his wife immigrated from Russian Poland in 1886 and by 1900 were living in the "Little Poland" neighborhood on 2500 Main Street. The family constantly moved and in 1910 were living in Monongah, where John and his oldest son Stanley worked in the mines. By 1920, brothers Stanley and Johnny were back in Wheeling, where they began engaging in the illicit bootlegging traffic.[71] Stanley produced moonshine whiskey on a massive scale from his home at 3723 Wetzel Street. On October 2, 1922, federal prohibition agent Walter Bee carried out a search warrant and discovered a one-hundred-gallon still complete with 884 gallons of mash and gallons of moonshine whiskey ready for sale.[72]

More prominent locally was the younger brother Johnny, who was born in 1906. When he was seventeen, Johnny and his brother Joseph were indicted along with a group of men for manufacturing alcohol on George Vance's property off Stone Church Road near Elm Grove.[73] Like many others in the Polish American neighborhood, Vinesky could not escape the law. In July 1928, he was arrested for possession of sixty-five pints of Canadian whiskey, six quarts of gin, and forty gallons of moonshine whiskey at 2822 Chapline Street. Prohibition agents were keeping closer tabs on Vinesky's distribution activities. They had just caught him violating the Volstead Act on December 17, 1927, when he pleaded guilty and received sixty days in the Ohio County jail.[74]

Vinesky's bootlegging operation also made him a target of rivals. In February 1926, Walter Kowalsky attempted to rob Vinesky's home on Twenty-Seventh Street. During his hearing, Kowalsky claimed he was minding his own business at a nearby pool hall when he was chased by Vinesky and the police. Kowalsky lived in Wheeling in 1914 and later served in the 150th Infantry (Mexican Border Campaign). He returned to Wheeling only to be arrested in 1921, serving five years in the Moundsville penitentiary. After his release, he worked as a "liquor runner" from Pittsburgh. In 1926, Kowalsky pleaded guilty to grand larceny and was sentenced to seven years back in the Moundsville penitentiary.[75] While Kowalsky's motives were in doubt, it seems likely he was sent by a rival of Vinesky's. Two years later, three armed Italian men tried to steal one of Vinesky's automobiles. It appeared someone was trying to send Vinesky a message.[76]

After numerous warnings and raids, Wheeling's version of the Chicago "Beer Wars" exploded in the streets of Center and South Wheeling. The *Wheeling Register* reported on Sunday, December 23, that a "nitroglycerin" bomb exploded at 5:30 a.m. the night before in front of Nick Frank's Coffee House at 2355 Market Street, blowing out the windows of the White Front and nearby homes. Frank's business was next door to one owned by Bill Lias, and the two men had fought over turf for several years. Police surmised the "open warfare was brought on by a series of raids in which one faction is reported to have suffered heavily [Lias] while the other went scot free [Frank]." It appears the Lias faction was in a "price war," underselling Frank, and the latter tipped off prohibition agents about Lias's establishments. A week before the bombing, a truckload of men had bombarded Frank's place with rocks.[77]

Police patrols put the South Side on curfew for months during the winter of 1928–1929. About a week after the bombing at Nick Frank's, a black-powder bomb exploded in the side alley of Sam Grossfield's place on Twenty-Fifth Street, wrecking the interior. He was aligned with Nick Frank. On New Year's Day 1929, a bomb was found in a truck near the corner of Twenty-Third and Market Streets. Immediately city police ordered closure of all coffeehouses and poolrooms at midnight to prevent further violence. For several months, tensions remained heightened as federal agents hoped to "Nip Hi-Jacking" of cars carrying illegal hooch, believing this might "precipitate warfare among the rum runners."[78]

Violence did indeed escalate throughout the spring of 1929 following a series of automobile hijackings along National Road. Prohibition agents then tried to raid Nick Frank's business but only confiscated two ounces of whiskey. On March 15, a group of Italians engaged in "gunplay" near a series of vacant buildings along Twenty-Sixth Street where moonshine was being stored. Then, on the evening of March 21, a member of Frank's faction, Nick Terkes, was attacked by two men closely associated with Bill Lias in front of Frank's coffeehouse. Both Nick Frank and Bill Lias went to see the men at police headquarters and on their way out "indulged in a bitter verbal battle" when Lias accused Frank of carrying a gun in his automobile.[79] Wheeling's gangland violence was increasing. The city coroner found that Ohio County had 132 violent deaths in 1928, with twenty involving automobiles.[80]

A terrible example of this trend occurred on Sunday, April 7, 1929, when four men associated with Bill Lias were involved in a high-speed crash on National Road. Driving a Cadillac coupe and traveling east at a speed of at least seventy miles an hour, the men struck an iron utility pole with such force the car was demolished after it "side-twisted" the pole. All were thrown from the automobile, killing George Pappas and James Amien immediately with Andrew Pirso dying later at Ohio Valley General Hospital and Mike Russell suffering serious wounds to his body. They were supposedly delivering a "message" to some enemies at the Acme Pool Hall. The car was registered to "Big" Charlie Kupchak, a Polish man who worked for Lias at the Pirate Café. Inside the car, police found a secret compartment to carry three hundred gallons of liquor.[81] Almost a week later, J. J. Doerr's prohibition agents busted into Nick Frank's coffeehouse as "Sledges Swung," and for the first time the agents were finally able to capture some illegal liquor.[82]

After a respite from violence, Wheeling's "Rum War" flared up again in 1930. In January, federal agents led by J. J. Doerr used a "heavy sledge" to break through barbed wire and a partition wall at Bill Lias's establishment at 2351 Market Street. The next day a bomb exploded a block away near Nick Frank's business. Four of Lias's men were immediately arrested.[83] On June 23, Lias, Joe "Little Shorty" Fragale, and Spiro Petrakis were arrested after state prohibition agents and state police raided Lias's White Front Café and the Owl's Club at 1531 Market Street. The tensions between the Lias and Frank factions reached a peak in mid-July when Frank's Oldsmobile was hit by submachine-gun fire from a group of Lias's men, who seemed to want to put Frank "on the spot." Frank escaped death but got the message, suggesting to authorities he might go to Europe for his own safety. Ohio County Sheriff Ambrose Habig set up patrols of the Greek coffeehouse district after this escalation.[84]

Bill Lias eventually went to federal prison again following harassment by prohibition agents and a late September 1930 raid on his Café of the Allies.[85] During the dramatic trial, Ray Highland, an undercover prohibition agent who purchased alcohol with Lias present, narrowly escaped death when a Buick sedan touring car drove up to his home and opened fire with a submachine gun. People suspected Lias's men, but no charges were brought. When it came time for him to testify, Highland claimed he could not positively identify Lias or any of his associates being present during his undercover visit.[86] Regardless, the largely native-born jury found Bill Lias and two associates guilty of violating the Volstead Act in November. This was Lias's fourth time punished under the law, and each time he received a stiffer sentence.[87] Lias appealed the conviction, but in December 1931 it was upheld by the U.S. Supreme Court. Lias paid a ten-thousand-dollar fine and was sentenced to two years in the Atlanta federal prison.[88]

Prior to going to the Atlanta penitentiary and with the Great Depression worsening, Bill Lias once again was involved in a distribution rivalry with the independent Polish American faction led by Johnny and Walter Vinesky. Agents raided Vinesky's home in October 1930, finding a fifty-gallon still in full operation.[89] Their rivalry reached a head after an attempted hijacking on Fifteenth Street by Lias's men. Afterwards, Lias and Vinesky got into a tense meeting at the Roosevelt Club before both gangs battled it out in the street. Vinesky's liquor distribution network was also under attack from hijackings by a Polish American teenage street gang, who stole liquor stored in a vacant building and then tried to sell it on the street.[90] Vinesky later organized a "liquor vendor's union" after Bill Lias was sent to federal prison, which had a "brief but brilliant reign" until Vinesky's arrest in October 1932 in a large trap laid by federal agents.[91]

Conclusion

During the Prohibition era, prominent bootleggers like Bill Lias and his rivals, as well as working-class immigrants and their children, suffered under constant enforcement. In early January 1929, Pauline Kacinski appeared before Judge Baker and entered a plea of "not guilty," demanding an immediate trial, since her family was "in destitute circumstances." Unable to afford an attorney, she noted her husband was again in jail for violating the Volstead Act. When questioned about him and the charge that one hundred pints of home brew were found in their home, she angrily stated, "He runs his business and I run my own."[92] By mid-January, Mrs. Kacinski was released from custody after it was proven that "her children were in destitute circumstances."[93] However, the Kacinski family continued to suffer under the Volstead Act. Undercover men Roy Hundley and Ray Highland bought one pint of moonshine at Steve Kacinski's establishment on September 4, 1930. Steve pleaded guilty and received a six-month term in the Ohio County jail. Lasting into early 1931, the family was without their main breadwinner as the Great Depression worsened. In May 1932, Kacinski died at the age of fifty-five.[94]

While Prohibition is often portrayed as a fun era with wild dancing in speakeasies and the sound of tommy guns between rival bootleg gangs in the air, the era was also a time of coercive Americanization. All immigrants and their children, whether they operated a small still in their basement or ran a fleet of trucks along National Road, were targeted by federal and state enforcement. By the fall of 1930, federal agents made it clear they would arrest anyone where they found more than one-half of 1 percent alcohol. In October 1930, federal agents rounded up fifty-nine people, mostly immigrants, in just a few days for home distilling.[95] One was Frank Lewandowsky, a prominent leader at St. Ladislaus Parish and in the Polish community. He was caught selling moonshine whiskey by an undercover agent, which led to the discovery of a twenty-gallon still in his home. It was not that shocking when J. J. Doer learned Lewandowsky's family had been "manufacturing liquor for eight or ten years."[96]

Their defiance of prohibition laws may have frustrated native-born, middle-class reformers who had a particular idea of what it meant to be American, but as this local story in Wheeling shows, the defiance on the part of Polish Americans was rooted in their struggles as workers to get by and maintain their ethnic culture. Like many in his working-class neighborhood, earning some extra cash from distilled spirits was part of a continued and wider strategy of making do, a tactic that would have to continue as the Great Depression made matters even worse.

CHAPTER 9

Polonia in the Great Depression and the Rise of the CIO at Wheeling Steel

In 1945, with World War II coming to a close and men away fighting in Europe and the Pacific, many Polish American women fought the Wheeling Steel Corporation. They filed grievances for unfair treatment and exerted leadership within their local union. When Genevieve Urlinski filed a grievance after her foreman refused her sick leave, John Oshenski defended her successful appeal before the department's grievance committee. Later that year, after getting overheated on the shop floor, Edith Vitale, Emma Shust, and shop steward Violet Stazenski in the drum press department "were suspended by [their] immediate supervisor for changing clothes during their ten minute rest period," even after they returned to work. Their grievance appeal was successful, and each received back pay for the lost time after they "stripped" their clothes.[1]

This union consciousness grew among many second-generation factory workers in the 1930s and 1940s as they fought for a better livelihood. A good example was Agnes Helenski. Born in Monessen, Pennsylvania, in 1917, her father Teofil worked in the town's steel mill or coke plant, but in the 1920s the family relocated to Benwood. By 1930, Teofil was a coal miner, but he increasingly needed the labor of his children. While the family's rent was only sixteen dollars a month, the hardships of the Great Depression required Agnes to quit school after the seventh grade to find work. By 1935, she was laboring as a drum press operator at Wheeling Corrugating in East Wheeling.[2]

While at the plant, Helenski was caught up in the unionization drive led by the Steel Workers Organizing Committee (SWOC) in 1936 and 1937. Attaining union recognition in the spring of 1937, SWOC Local 1248 was a mixed-gender local. By June 1937, the Ohio Valley Trades and Labor Assembly observed of Local 1248, "The fair sex has no say at our meeting and . . . we ought to have a few lady delegates." For female union members, male foreman could be very intimidating. While still trying to recruit members throughout the summer of 1937, an Italian American representative noted that the girls were "afraid to wear their badges because they [would] be picked on or get fired."³ However, Agnes Helenski was among many union women in the female departments who demanded the end to harassment by foreman, the maintenance of contract guidelines, and the establishment of seniority lines for female workers. She was joined by Polish American women like Stella Sulek, Mary Kuca (1934's May Queen at St. Ladislaus), Stella Stazenski, and Josephine Lakomy, along with Mildred Visnic (whose family was Yugoslavian), who all started working in the same drum press department in September 1933. Visnic drafted Local 1248's bylaws and later served on the union grievance committee for her department.⁴

To help promote union solidarity, Local 1248's male and female members also backed certain popular union women as candidates for the coveted title of "Miss Wheeling Factory" in the late 1930s. An annual popularity contest created by the company, it helped bridge the gaps between workers from various ethnic communities as well as men and women on the shop floor. For 1938, SWOC backed winning candidate Mildred Visnic. The following year, the title of "Miss Wheeling Factory of 1939" went to Agnes Helenski. For the Polish Americans in the factory and in Wheeling this was a great honor.⁵

For ethnic steelworkers in the upper Ohio Valley, SWOC and the United Steelworkers of America (USWA) gave a collective voice to those who started working at the company in the 1920s and 1930s under arbitrary workplace conditions. The company's largely ethnic workforce fostered a union consciousness from the 1930s through the mid-twentieth century. The union gave Wheeling's ethnic steelworkers a sense of pride, citizenship, and shop-floor democracy through things that never existed at the company—collective bargaining agreements that provided security, the formalized shop-floor steward, and grievance procedures. Subsequent scholars have argued that as the labor movement grew increasingly bureaucratized, unions like the USWA became less responsive to grassroots demands and by the 1960s were undemocratically controlled.⁶ However, for the earlier generation, those who filed grievances, upheld contracts, or joined a picket line saw the union as the best way to bring about a better standard of living for all steelworkers, as well as something not to be taken for granted.

Lizabeth Cohen notes in *Making a New Deal* how Chicago's industrial workers who joined the CIO held clear ideological goals. They supported a "moral capitalism," one where the state and union would forge a more just society. As in Chicago, Wheeling's ethnic working class likewise demanded a moral capitalism based on their shared suffering during the Great Depression and their involvement in local politics and local union and grievance committee meetings. All the while, they sought to maintain close ties to their ethnic community.[7]

Polish American Politics in the Depression Era

With the economic situation deteriorating, Wheeling residents struggled to find their way out of the worsening Depression. By the early months of 1930, the area was shaken by mass layoffs in all factories and mines. In November 1930, Wheeling Steel's massive Benwood plant shuttered, laying off over 1,200. Many remained out of work until the mills restarted in 1932 and 1933. By November 1930, county administrators were concerned about the highest unemployment being in Webster and Ritchie Districts, where everyone was dependent on blue-collar factory jobs. Between 1931 and 1932, those on poor relief rose by 200 percent.[8] Private charities tried to alleviate the suffering as soup kitchens popped up throughout the county. The St. Vincent de Paul Society worked with the Emergency Relief Committee of Wheeling and other female and religious societies to provide hot meals. In Benwood, the winter of 1931 was particularly difficult. By January 18, St. Vincent de Paul had served thirty-two thousand meals in just six weeks.[9] However, by the following winter of 1931–1932, even local charities faltered.

Wheeling's Polonia tried to weather the economic storm and help St. Ladislaus stay afloat. In December 1930, the PAP Club organized a Polish welfare committee "to assist the needy during the winter months."[10] St. Ladislaus maintained its membership, peaking at two thousand members in 1937, but parish incomes took a hit, from $16,856.94 in 1928 dropping to $6,468.09 for 1932. They did not rebound until 1936 with $15,557.02 but dipped again in the late 1930s, falling to under $8,000 in 1941.[11] Father Emil Musial cut his salary from $1,200 a year down to $250 in 1932, but this did not help the parish's debt obligations, which actually increased over the decade from $17,900 to $21,300. Parish societies early in the Depression also donated more money. During 1932, motion picture showings, societal donations, and direct loans from parishioners amounted to almost $1,000. Donations to fund the parish school brought in almost $1,500. This kept the parish above water but could only pay down $300 on its debt.[12] Trying to maintain the parish as a social outlet for the community put great strains on Father Musial.

With the precarious nature of work during the Depression, Wheeling's immigrant families wanted to see their children move up the economic ladder. While work relief was necessary, local politicians promoted classes at McKinley Trade School in South Wheeling as a way for second-generation ethnics to rise above the unskilled factory jobs of their parents. The first of its kind in West Virginia, McKinley opened in 1926–1927 and offered classes to students who completed the seventh grade while still allowing them to earn their high school requirements. Classes included electrical construction, automobile mechanics, mechanical drafting, shop mathematics, printing, and acetylene welding.[13] Robert Plummer argued for higher levels of funding since the school's training programs took young men off the WPA and relief rolls and helped fill needed skilled positions.[14]

Polish Americans took advantage of the trade school. Following the May 1936 graduation, the school acknowledged that of its ninety-seven-member class, none had been on work relief and all were placed at a variety of good paying jobs, particularly at Wheeling Steel, Wheeling Tile, and Continental Can. Thirty-two were Polish or Ukrainian Americans. Edmond Okulanis got a job at the Wheeling Tile Company and earned one thousand dollars in 1939. George Kabala got a job driving a truck for H. L. Seabright Company, while William Oberle got hired at Continental Can Company. Frank Browsky started out at Wheeling Tile in 1936 but by 1939 was working as a skilled pipe cutter for Wheeling Steel earning $1,309. Some also got jobs outside of skilled factory work. Louis Fialkowski was hired at Ohio Valley Hospital, Edward Chmiel got a job at the Hub Department Store, and Fred Templin worked at the Commercial Print Shop.[15] Many of these Polish Americans did quite well. For the fall 1937 class, the school recognized the perfect attendance of Frank Kaminski, Casey Janetski, and Steve Sofca in the electric class and Paul Jurek, Joseph Kuca, Michael Pappas, and John Nakoniczny in the auto mechanics class. The fact so many took advantage of the trade school shows their willingness to improve their situation during the Great Depression.[16]

As the Great Depression continued, Wheeling's Polish community realized they needed to participate directly in the political process. Galvanized by their opposition to Prohibition and Al Smith's 1928 presidential campaign, second-generation ethnics began mobilizing locally. Following the 1932 election, Wheeling's ethnic communities organized formally within the Democratic Party. Their efforts proved vital to shifting Ohio County from a stronghold of the Republican Party since the Civil War to a key county in the Democratic New Deal coalition of the Northern Panhandle.[17]

Wheeling's Polish Americans took the lead in fostering ties between Polish political and fraternal groups throughout the wider tristate region. On

January 27, 1935, twelve lodges met in the St. Ladislaus auditorium under Council No. 36 of the Polish Roman Catholic Union (PRCU). South Wheeling's St. Joseph Lodge No. 321 was the largest and took a major role planning for the following year. The leadership of Council No. 36 also reflected the prominent role of Wheeling's Poles, including Bernard Klimaszewski as president, Stanley Duplaga as treasurer, and Albert Swiader as secretary. PRCU Council No. 36 represented lodges from Washington, Pennsylvania; Wheeling and Fulton, West Virginia; and Neffs, Lafferty, Fairpoint, and Yorkville, Ohio.[18] Likewise, PNA Council No. 133 created in 1915 helped form PNA lodges in Weirton, Moundsville, Fulton, Warwood, Elm Grove, Benwood, and Short Creek during this period.[19]

Polish fraternal events also began attracting the attention of politicians eager for Polish support. The January 1932 celebration of Polish Roman Catholic Union Day held by PRCU District Council No. 36 and thirteen local branches featured keynote speaker Frank S. Barch, editor of all PRCU publications from Chicago. Mayor Thomas Beckett and Republican State Senator George Beneke attended a banquet in the Polish school auditorium.[20] The general election was going to be difficult for incumbent Republicans, and appealing to Polish American patriotism was common. Wheeling Republican Congressman Carl Bachmann gave the keynote address on Pulaski Day in October. Highlighting the role of Casimir Pulaski during the American Revolution as the "father of the United States cavalry," Bachmann noted, "The success of our Revolution is largely due to men of his caliber and quality."[21] Speeches by local politicians emphasized that Poles made good American citizens. Even with his speech, Bachmann lost in the Democratic wave of 1932 to Robert Ramsey of Brooke County.

Following the 1932 election, Wheeling's Polish community increased its political engagement with the Democratic Party. In May 1934, the Ohio County Democratic Club was reorganized, led by George Smudski. A young Polish American in his late twenties, Smudski was a printer who lived in Triadelphia. He quickly reduced the dues from fifty cents a month to one dollar a year to expand membership, hovering around four hundred, with the goal of reaching five thousand members by the 1934 primary election.[22] The fact he was the only Slavic county and district leader was noteworthy and suggests the concerns of reaching out to the growing ethnic population. By July, county officials noted the "unprecedented turnover in political affiliations." In 1932, Ohio County had 28,756 registered Republican voters to just 13,408 registered Democrats. By 1934, that number tightened with 22,369 Republican voters to 18,230 Democratic voters. Smudski's efforts were successful, registering almost five thousand more voters, while the Republican Party had lost over six thousand registered voters. The *Wheeling Register* attributed this turnover to President Franklin Roosevelt's New Deal. Most Democratic gains came from Republican registration losses in the county's coal-mining districts.[23]

The Polish community slowly gained a role in Democratic Party county politics, first as precinct captains and commissioners during primary and general elections. During the 1934 Democratic Party primary, Poles were precinct commissioners in the Richland mining district (Third Precinct Walter Kupsky) and the Ritchie District of South Wheeling (Seventh Precinct Frank Blinsky; Eighth Precinct Clara Gibulski, John Tolpa, and Amelia Czaplinski).[24] For the 1935 city elections, while most ward-level precincts were located in private homes, the concentration of Polish Americans voters allowed for two to be held at the PAP Club (Eighth Ward, Eighth Precinct) and the Polish Hall on National Road in Fulton (Tenth Ward, First Precinct).[25]

The Polish American community's inclusion in local politics spread to other ethnic groups with the Polish taking a leading role in promoting interethnic organization. In August 1935, led by Wheeling's PAP Club, local communities formed the Slavic Voters League. Dr. Gaydosh, a city councilman, described the need for a Slavic organization "to get more recognition in the political life of this state." All of the league's leaders were Poles from Wheeling, led by Anthony Szczypinski, Richard Olszta, John Gornik, and Paul Jurczak. They also chose vice presidents from the nearby communities of Weirton, Moundsville, and Fulton and delegates from each of the Slavic fraternal societies between Weirton and Moundsville. Even while incorporating Polish, Lithuanian, Ukrainian, and Slovak groups, several years later the Slavic Voters League was still a predominately Polish-led organization.[26]

Polish Americans became more active after the 1936 elections, and some were elected to local offices. Years of Americanizing activities paid huge dividends. In the traditional Republican Party strongholds of Wheeling and Warwood, FDR received 22,448 votes to Alfred Langdon's 13,441. The margin was even higher in the nearby mill towns of Bellaire, Martins Ferry, and Yorkville, Ohio.[27] Many Polish American women like Leonora Czaplinski and Olga Oszustowicz were prominent in the Young Democratic Club of Ohio County in 1936 and took a leading role in the 1940 campaign.[28] All Polish American officeholders in Wheeling and Ohio County were blue-collar Democrats. Leonard Czaplinski was elected justice of the peace in South Wheeling in 1937. He worked as a steelworker in the 1920s and took a job as a guard at the state penitentiary but later returned to the Benwood Steel

Works. Czaplinski was also an active labor leader. In the 1940s, he was a union official at the Benwood Blast Furnace, serving in 1948 and 1949 as president of USWA Local 3814.[29] Frank Schewinski served as constable for Ritchie District in South Wheeling in 1937 and again in 1939. Tobacco worker Evelyn Cappas was chosen as one of the few females on the Democratic Party Executive Committee in 1936.[30]

By the 1940 election, Polish Americans were strong Democrats, even as the political situation in Ohio County began tilting back toward the Republicans. With Republican voter registration (25,150) slightly ahead of Democratic Party numbers (21,699), the 1940 election proved to be very tight. FDR won by a smaller margin in Ohio County, 21,790 to 18,091 for Wendell Wilkie. Democrat Matthew Neely won slightly in the race for governor, 20,081 to 19,586, with the Republican candidates winning in the county in the U.S. Senate and Congressional races. Democrats prevailed in all the state legislative and county races.[31] However, in the five most Polish American precincts, all went by a greater margin for the Democratic Party ticket. This trend is evident in the vote for FDR's third term. The Eleventh Precinct in Fulton (voting at Anton Cihy's residence) went 81 percent for FDR, while Washington district only went 60 percent for him. Webster district supported the president with 62.9 percent of the vote, but in the First and Second Precincts, he won 70.5 percent in "Little Poland." And in the core of Polonia in the Seventh and Eighth Precincts in Ritchie District (voting at the PAP Club and Walter Galkowski's home) they gave 86.7 percent to Roosevelt, while he only won the district with 61.6 percent of the vote.[32]

This active political life built off the continued strength of the area's Polish fraternal and cultural organizations in the 1930s. Even with the continued assimilation of the second generation, fraternal lodges and the PAP Club continued to exert a major influence while new Polish American societies formed, especially in Fulton. In May 1939, the community formed the Polish Political and Educational Club, which met in Duplaga Hall on National Road. Organized by working-class Poles Michael Bober (the first president), Frank Cihy, Stanley Rzepka, Stanley Szymanski, John Boginski, and Joseph Gosztyla, the club built off the efforts started by the PAP Club in South Wheeling twenty years earlier while also being a clearinghouse for the "advancements of Polish and other Slovonic [sic] peoples of Ohio county." They also supported viable candidates for city, county, and state offices to represent their interests.[33]

At the same time, a rising middle class in the community suggests their differing aspirations during this period. While still tied to the wider, working-class

Polish community, the local elite's identity was evolving. More entrepreneurial, their business success allowed them to escape some of the precarious aspects of working-class life. A large number attained leadership roles in Polonia's fraternal organizations as well. By the 1930s, they formed the Polish Retailers' Association, bringing together local Polish businessmen catering to the majority working-class Polonia. The association was the brainchild of businessman Stanley Duplaga, who was active in the PNA and St. Casimir Society in Fulton. Discussions began in late 1937 for a group that sought "closer cooperation among the grocers and business men of Polish extraction." Over time, the association included all professional men in the wider Polish community. Coming during the height of the CIO labor organizing, it is unclear why this business association was formed. In other cities, these types of ethnic entrepreneurs served, according to William Galush, as a "model of advancement to the coming generation." The timing suggests possible class divides within the community, while members noted the goal was to promote a "feeling of good will" and to encourage entrepreneurial initiative among younger Polish Americans.[34]

By 1939, the group was renamed the Polish Business and Professional Men's Association, and it further unified the upper Ohio Valley Polish American community by staging an annual summer Polish Day at Oglebay Park. Started in 1938, Polish Day set a model for other large ethnic festivals that continue to the present day among the Greek, Italian, and Lebanese communities. Chairman Joseph Lukaszewicz noted the event brought delegations together from the tristate area for a picnic and over two thousand people listened to music by the Polish American Rhythm Kings and other traditional Polish folk music.[35] The group also began sponsoring a large banquet and dance at the Polish Hall in South Wheeling. With the onset of the European war, Polish Day also became a way to rally support for the Polish cause with over eight thousand in attendance during the 1940 event.[36]

Wheeling's Polonia also increasingly served as an outlet for foreign policy concerns following the Nazi invasion of Poland on September 1, 1939. A few weeks later, President Roosevelt spoke before a special session of Congress requesting a repeal of the arms embargo to belligerent nations, as set by the Neutrality Acts of 1935, 1936, and 1937, and instead to apply a "cash-and-carry" principle to both raw materials and armaments. While the policy enraged isolationist groups, Polish American communities roundly supported FDR. Polish American clubs in Brooke, Hancock, Ohio, and Marshall Counties, along with clubs across the Ohio River in Dillonvale and Martins Ferry, sent resolutions to their congressional delegations urging support for FDR's neutrality revision since "America had always been bound to the cause of justice."³⁷ Wheeling's PAP Club acted as a "Clearing House" for regional "Foreign Citizens Clubs" when it came to lobbying Washington. Stanley Owoc, Edward Marchlenski, and Harry E. C. Front worked in an advisory role in drafting resolutions to Senator Matthew Neely, isolationist Senator Rush Holt, and Congressman A. C. Shiffler to support FDR's neutrality revision bill, which were sent by St. Anne's Society PNA Local 2460 and the Thaddeus Kosciusko Lodge No. 1363 of the PNA of Moundsville.³⁸

The plight of their Polish brethren under the Nazi and Soviet occupations sparked regional efforts to aid refugees. In late January 1940, Polish American clubs canvassed the upper Ohio Valley for "discarded clothing and shoes" to be "sent to the destitute of Poland and refugees in Rumania [sic]." PNA Council No. 133 and PRCU Council No. 36 members went door-to-door in Wheeling.³⁹ In February 1940, Wheeling's Polish Refugees Aid Committee held a rally at the Polish school auditorium with Fr. Emil Musial giving the keynote address. By March 6, the canvassing committee raised three hundred dollars and collected over three hundred pieces of clothing and shoes led by Emily Czaplinski, John Gornik, Emily Jurek, Olga Oszustowicz, Josephine Skrypek, and Rose Rosanski, the Tobacco Workers Union leader and PCRU Council No. 36 trustee.⁴⁰

The Union Comes to Wheeling Steel

The story of unionization at Wheeling Steel was successful thanks to the political and cultural interactions of second-generation ethnic workers. With the passage of the National Industrial Recovery Act in 1933, workers began organizing lodges of the Amalgamated Association in late 1933 through early 1934, beginning a protracted battle against Wheeling Steel. While those at Wheeling faltered, the five lodges at the Portsmouth, Ohio, factory carried on the union drive through the summer of 1936.⁴¹ Following National Labor Relations Board (NLRB) investigations and efforts by the new Steel Workers Organizing Committee (SWOC), the NLRB ruled in May 1936 that the firm illegally forced workers to join their employee representation plan (ERP). Portsmouth steelworkers went on strike in July under newly incorporated local lodges of SWOC.⁴²

The SWOC drive was an exhilarating experience, restarting in late 1936 to early 1937 at the company's mills in the upper Ohio Valley. Packed meetings took place in downtown Wheeling, but SWOC also reached into the ethnic communities. SWOC rallies were held at the Polish Hall in Yorkville, Ohio, and in Martins Ferry's Hungarian Hall along with other ethnic Catholic social spaces. SWOC won both by gaining rank-and-file support and winning over the company union representatives. In early February 1937, a large rally of steelworkers heard how fifty-three company union representatives pledged to help the SWOC campaign, arguing that "the company union is a sham, a farce, and an insult to the intelligence of steel workers." Like what James Rose found in his study of steel unionism at Duquesne, the SWOC in the upper Ohio Valley organized the company union men, who in turn became key leaders in the new SWOC lodges that formed from January to March 1937. At Yorkville and Martins Ferry, the new lodge presidents were chairmen of the company unions, while at Benwood and Yorkville four out of ten officers were prior company representatives. They worked with the SWOC organizers to hold mass meetings in Bellaire, Martins Ferry, Yorkville, Steubenville, and Beech Bottom.[43] By March 1937, the company decided not to engage in a long, bitter fight like at Weirton Steel, and Wheeling Steel signed a collective bargaining agreement with SWOC covering all its mills.[44]

Wheeling Steel's ethnic workforce fostered a "union consciousness" from the late 1930s well into the 1950s. This analysis looks heavily at the local union leadership and the ways they reached out to the rank and file. For that reason, it is slanted toward those most heavily involved in organizing for SWOC and those who served as officers, shop stewards, and grievance committee members in the local unions.[45] These shop stewards were crucial to explaining the positive benefits of unionism to the rank and file. As other scholars have noted, the rank and file at times suffered from strong apathy. Building worker consciousness became difficult as the labor movement itself grew increasingly bureaucratized after World War II. Some historians argue that long-term contracts and complex grievance procedures made local union participation less necessary. In fact their very success meant that the battle would be to constantly remind rank-and-file members why they still needed the union.[46] These union organizers and those rank-and-file members who filed grievances or were involved in shop-floor conflicts saw the USWA as the best way of promoting workplace democracy and a better standard of living for all steelworkers at Wheeling Steel.

Local steelworkers benefitted from a loyal contingent of paid organizers, especially the subregional director of SWOC Paul Rusen. Appointed a district organizer in June 1936, Rusen lived in Smithfield in Jefferson County and spent much of his time at the mills on the Ohio side of the river as well as setting up an office in Wheeling. By the time of the 1937 union contract, local unions cheered Rusen's careful leadership. According to the mixed ethnic Lodge No. 1185 at the massive Benwood Works, Rusen proved to be a "most capable organizer, and has succeeded in organizing the industrial workers of our Valley to a degree heretofore thought impossible."[47] Rusen succeeded by reaching out to the various ethnic groups in the upper Ohio Valley. In late 1936, Rusen utilized Patsy Speen and Frank Jeranko as part-time organizers. He additionally employed Demos Nicas, from the Greek Workmen's Federation, until January 1, 1937, as an organizer who "proved extremely useful in the organizing work among the Greeks in that sub-region."[48] Rusen built off prior efforts during the Amalgamated Association's organizing drive of 1933–1934, which held rallies at ethnic halls throughout the Ohio Valley. In February 1934, Square Deal Lodge No. 145 held regularly meetings in the Hungarian Hall in Martins Ferry. Lodge meetings also mixed with popular dances to attract members and their wives.[49] Following FDR's reelection, SWOC continued using ethnic halls for regional meetings. Appealing to ethnic workers' sense of Americanism, broadsides for a meeting on December 27, 1936, at Martins Ferry's Hungarian Hall asked the second generation "Are you a Free American Citizen and Worker? Do you believe in Your Constitutional and Civil Rights?"[50]

In the years after the successful CIO organizing drive, Wheeling Steel's multiethnic workforce maintained their union culture through shared community and work experiences. While many ethnic groups had developed strong ethnic communities in each of the region's steel towns, by the late 1930s ethnic Catholic steelworkers were becoming increasingly involved in region-wide efforts. These regional fraternal associations maintained a healthy working-class union culture. Popular Slovak Sokol gymnastic clubs held regional sporting, political, and Catholic events throughout the Ohio Valley. In April 1937, the Sokols meet for their annual clinic in Bellaire and held sporting competitions and a region-wide conference with committees from Wheeling, Benwood, and Mingo Junction present.[51]

Building a vibrant culture among the rank and file required forming union locals that reflected the diversity on the shop floor. During the Amalgamated Association organizing drive, Square Deal Lodge No. 145 at Martins Ferry had native-born officers as well as Stanley Shemanski as secretary, Thomas Bella as journal agent, and Andy Petroski as outside guard.[52] As time wore on, most locals were overwhelmingly ethnic in their leadership. In 1948 and 1949, Local 3814 at the Benwood Works had President Leonard Czaplinski, Secretary William Morelli, Treasurer Frank Supan, Guide Patrick Conroy, and inside guard Russell Sivard. For 1952 to 1954, Local 4218 at Continental Foundry

(Warwood) had President George Minyo, Secretary Edward Waszkiewicz, Treasurer Chester Olako, and Guide Ed Broski.[53] Second-generation steelworkers were also very prominent in the statewide CIO. For example, at the Eighth Annual Convention of the West Virginia Industrial Union Council (CIO) held in Wheeling in September 1945, the roster of delegates from the Twenty-Third District was the proverbial melting pot. Led by USWA leader Paul Rusen, the delegation included John Yurkovictch, Frank Cisar, Joseph Agostini, and Florence Decrease (Local 1185); Steve Chervenak, Rose Mary Sanzeri, Joseph Garlowich, Stella Obyc, and Mamie Habdo (Local 1248); Michael Ruza (Local 1240); and Steven Otvenoski and Frank Fularz (Local 1290).[54]

These Catholic steelworkers' support for the labor movement emerged from their own religious viewpoints. Building off the papal encyclicals of Pope Leo XIII and Pope Pius XI, pro-labor Catholic leaders stressed the principle of "subsidiarity," arguing all decisions should be made locally by those directly affected by economic, political, and religious issues. Catholic labor priests and bishops supported the National Catholic Welfare Conference's call for a living wage and collective bargaining rights. With many leading SWOC officials being Catholics, they often spoke to Catholic social teachings and worked with Catholic priests and ethnic fraternal leaders, organizing through both labor and ethnic Catholic social halls.[55] Such connections were evident in Wheeling. In March 1943, the regional meeting of the Catholic Conference on Industrial Labor Problems was held in the city. Bishop John Swint designated Rev. Edmund J. Yahn to chair the conference along with Dr. Joseph Striebach, President of the Wheeling Diocesan Council of the National Council of Catholic Men. David McDonald, treasurer of SWOC, was one of the prominent labor leaders who spoke on "Labor Relations in Production," along with noted labor priest Fr. Charles Owen Rice of Pittsburgh.[56] Bishop Swint highlighted the long tradition of Catholic bishops supporting fairer wages, reduced living costs, minimum wages, social security, and vocational training as part of the "social reconstruction" program. This of course highlighted the need for "participation of labor in industrial management." While not favoring one side over the other, Swint reminded the capitalists that they "must learn wealth is a stewardship" and "the laborer is a human being, not merely an instrument of production."[57]

Catholic dioceses in industrial areas often defended trade unions more explicitly. Pro-labor support was common in the pages of diocesan newspapers like the *Michigan Catholic* and *Pittsburgh Catholic*. While not as vigorous in its support, Wheeling's Catholic *West Virginia Register* defended and reprinted favorable CIO stories from elsewhere highlighting responsible unionism and every worker's right to join.[58] After SWOC won a contract at Wheeling Steel in

1937, the diocesan newspaper began printing more front-page stories on the CIO. The January 29, 1939, issue led with a story of how Detroit's "Archbishop Urges Active Interest in Organizations," noting in bold letters across the masthead "Workers Must Support Unions."[59]

The Wheeling diocese was, however, very favorable to the Association of Catholic Trade Unionists (ACTU), often reprinting stories about the Detroit chapter to promote "Just Unionism." Led by lay Catholics and pro-labor priests, the ACTU worked with Catholic labor leaders and the rank and file to chart a middle ground between fascism and communism.[60] The Catholic Church in Wheeling favored the ACTU because of the growing fear that the SWOC and other CIO unions may have had communist ties. Long before Senator Joseph McCarthy gave his infamous speech at Wheeling's McClure Hotel in February 1950, Wheeling's Catholic working class had developed its own strong anticommunist perspective. Catholic workers sought to foster what labor priests referred to as "Christian Democracy," seeking a religiously informed political culture in America that embraced the hope of the papal encyclicals while rejecting the materialism of both capitalism and communism. The ACTU, in particular, fit this bill.[61]

Rank-and-file steelworkers supported the Catholic Church's anticommunism in a variety of ways. In the spring of 1938, the Knights of Columbus, along with members of the local Italian, Polish, Slovak, and Greek American fraternal organizations, sponsored a "Rally Against Communism" in downtown Wheeling to raise awareness about the church's efforts to combat the communist influence in American society. A month later, a larger rally occurred on Wheeling Island sponsored for the "American citizens of foreign extraction" protesting the influence of both Nazism and communism in America and Europe. Prominent clergy and business leaders sponsored the rally, and doctor and city councilman Michael Gaydosh served as chairman.[62] Workers also expressed these anticommunist sentiments within the local SWOC unions. In early 1939, members of SWOC Local 1248 commended Philip Murray for his stand against "Communism and all other isms." In addition, Betty Pettinato assisted the SWOC local in Yorkville, Ohio, in challenging communist agitation in a town one organizer called the "Hot Bed of Communism in America."[63]

Even with their strong anticommunism, local workers remained active union members. One arena in which to see how Wheeling Steel's multiethnic and largely Catholic rank and file fostered their union consciousness was through the union grievance procedures. As noted by Robert Bruno in his interviews with Youngstown steelworkers, "it is the workers' willingness to use the contract provisions that suggests a conscious reaching for methods of resistance."[64] For the period between April 9 and December 31, 1945, Wheeling steelworkers filed a remarkable 349 separate grievances. Coming in the months prior to the 1946 steel strike, the high number of grievances was obviously unique and did not compare to previous or subsequent years, but they do show how the diverse ethnic workforce took shop-floor complaints seriously and sought to adjudicate what they thought the company rightfully owed them. Those involving immigrant and second-generation steelworkers are most illustrative of the workplace demands. John Juliano of the Steubenville mill asked to be compensated for lost wages due to "his submitting to experiment [by company] to determine cause of unknown rash among employees."[65] Seniority claims for better wages or more favorable jobs were another usual request. John Culdan and Bernard Kopec requested they be placed on the Benwood continuous mill "according to their seniority." Nick Yowich at the Steubenville blast furnace requested to be placed in a job as "furnace keeper" based on his application showing his seniority at the plant.[66] Emma Shust of the East Wheeling plant accused her foreman of "agitating" an operator in a unit of the drum press department.[67] Foremen were commonly accused of unfairly terminating workers who were either too supportive of the union or critical of foremen's arbitrary use of authority. Joe Anaskovich of the Martins Ferry factory claimed he needed reinstatement and compensation for lost time after being unfairly discharged. Leopold Wojtowicz also requested to be reinstated after an unjust termination. Louis Coury complained that he was assigned to a job paying $8.30 but should have earned the wage he earned on his regular union job of $9.50.[68] Finally, workers also filed grievances after being injured. Gus Kariganis asked for compensation after being injured in an accident in the sheet galvanizing department at the Martins Ferry factory and requested the company pay his doctor's expenses.[69]

Union Culture at Wheeling Corrugating's Local 1248

While there are numerous examples of second-generation ethnic steelworkers forming a union consciousness, it is best to examine this process within a single local. Here one sees Wheeling steelworkers continuing to agitate for better work rules on the shop floor and ensuring the company upheld its contract obligations. Local 1248 of SWOC, organized at the Wheeling factory of Wheeling Corrugating, was unique as a metal fabricating plant that employed a large female workforce. While women predominated in the drum press and other related departments, the factory also employed many men as well. These gender dynamics add another element to the problems of forging a strong local union culture.⁷⁰

With the factory located in East Wheeling, many Polish, Slavic, and Italian American women and young men found steady jobs at the plant. Young women worked on presses feeding tin into machines and in the packing ware department at tedious assembly-line work. They also found jobs "flopping tin plate" inspecting it for defects and pin holes. However, as one company executive noted, the work was "endless, tiring, drive you absolutely crazy. Do it hour, after hour, after hour." Although eighteen was the minimum age to work, many teenage girls as young as sixteen lied about their age to get hired. While men earned solid piece rates, at Wheeling Corrugating, female press operators made at least six to seven cents less an hour than men.⁷¹

The company particularly targeted daughters of immigrant families to work as press operators. The work was difficult, made harder by pressure from managers to produce and by fear of breaking the die press. Girls whose presses broke down were often penalized with several days off work even if the breakdown was no fault of their own. New women hired in 1936 earned 37.5 cents per hour for an eight-hour day, while women who started years prior earned only 28.5 cents for a ten-hour day. While women were often segregated by department, better transportation lines allowed many girls from Bellaire, Martins Ferry, and Lansing, Ohio, to work at the East Wheeling plant. The shop floor was a proverbial melting pot of the second-generation immigrant communities in the region, but the daughters of Slavic and Italian families predominated. Polish American women started entering the drum press, drum cover, drum assembly, and ware and trim departments between 1928 and 1936.⁷² A work crew in the furnace pipe department often consisted of three to four girls. Two women put the long metal sheets through shears while one girl tamped it down by pushing on a pedal. It then went through another press where another girl used a perforator to put holes on both sides. After the sheet went through a hemmer, the girls then folded it back over and put rivets in all the holes. Men did the heavier work cutting the metal and forming it into final shapes, but women did most of the production process.⁷³

Initially the union had trouble getting the support of workers at the factory. In May 1937, Sam Carcione urged "all members wear their badges in the plant." This was important because for most of the first year of the union contract, rank-and-file members were constantly harassed by foreman and nonunion businessmen around town for wearing their badges and for being "forced" to pay union dues. Another problem was getting enough members to pay their dues. By January 27, 1938, only 125 workers had paid.[74] To maintain a united front, an organizer reminded the local at an October 1937 meeting, "We ought to forget our troubles and talk nothing but C.I.O. in our plants." The organizer also noted that the "Yorkville girls" had stayed united to stop the company from arbitrarily altering their work schedules to an 11:00 a.m. to 7:00 p.m. shift without the union's consent.[75] By early 1938, the local was considering ways to get Wheeling Steel in the next contract to allow for an automatic dues check-off, although most viewed this as an impossibility with the company.[76] According to one leader, efforts were made in that first year to reach out to the mass of young workers at Wheeling Corrugating to "let them know their advantages and how they have profit by the CIO. We got to educate the younger people because the younger people want everything for nothing." The local union sponsored various dances, a picnic outing following Labor Day, a Halloween dance, and even a basketball team to encourage union solidarity. Continual efforts were made to reach out to the rank and file to warn them that Wheeling Steel would do everything possible to undermine the newly signed contract. Fear and misunderstanding by the rank and file were constant concerns. Even with winning a contract, workers were still at risk. Foreman continued to set workers' shifts, and many female union members could still be treated unfairly. One unionist lamented, "Over half our members do not have the guts to tell their foreman when they are in the right."[77]

Early on, the union's grievance committee sought to protect the jobs and rights of female workers. In January 1938, the committee successfully defended a girl who was terminated for a week.[78] In this early period, grievances themselves tended to be verbal criticisms about working conditions given to shop stewards. After attending the CIO school, Betty Pettinato instructed the local about the proper ways to file grievances in writing with the company and district union.[79] Pettinato was a very active shop steward for the female drum press department, where there were at any time about twenty-five to thirty Polish American Catholics as rank-and-file members. Key female parishioners like Agnes Skrzypek, Josephine Sokolowski, and Sophia Gajewska reported to Pettinato. On one occasion she intervened when the foreman tried to replace a girl with two years' seniority with two younger girls at a lower wage. This senior union member was told if she did not keep up she would "be taken off." Pettinato went to the foreman, who claimed this operator was "back with her dues" thus not a member in good standing. The issue got rectified when she went to the head foreman; however, he still argued that the shop foreman had "the right to take her off her job at any time."[80] Girls in the drum press department consistently asked for "more time" during the recession conditions of 1938 and 1939, but even with a union contract, department foreman still had much control over distributing time.[81] As the recession lingered on, male workers grew angry about the large number of married women working in the factory.[82]

Many more Polish American Catholics began working at the factory and other nearby mills once the United States entered World War II.[83] Most became active members of USWA Local 1248 alongside their involvement in Polish Catholic fraternal organizations and parish activities. Mary Wojewodka was the vice president of St. Kazimer Lodge No. 282 of the PRCU for the Polish community in Fulton, east of town. The lodge was quite active in civic affairs and had a vibrant juvenile department. Wojewodka's children were quite active in the group as well. Daughter Frances spoke at the group's twentieth anniversary celebration in 1942. Her brother Frederick and sister Genevieve started working at Wheeling Corrugating in the summer of 1943. Both quickly became active members in Local 1248.[84] Joseph Gosztyla, who led the local Polish Workers Association and worked in the local meatpacking industry, also served as president of the PRCU in Fulton. His son Frank worked at the Wheeling Mold & Foundry nearby and joined the AFL Patternmakers' local. As photographed by the *Wheeling News-Register*, he would vigilantly serve on the picket line during the 1946 steel strike.[85]

This overlapping membership in Polish civic and fraternal groups helped forge solidarity that translated over into the union. Likewise, the growing participation in the labor movement in the upper Ohio Valley helped spark consistent support for the USWA throughout World War II. Workers at the Continental Can Factory in South Wheeling earned a contract by August 1941, and they requested assistance from Local 1248 in boosting their membership. August 1942 witnessed a union certification election to determine wage increases allowed under the "Little Steel" formula by the National War Labor Board. When the election was held, Wheeling steelworkers voted 11,966 to 577 for USWA recognition in hopes of a forty-four-cents-a-day wage increase.[86] Even with a no-strike pledge endorsed by the leadership, these same local workers were willing to strike during wartime to uphold their collective bargaining contracts. Following the contract expiration after December 24, 1943, area steelworkers walked off the job to seek wage increases to match rising wartime inflation. While proudly patriotic with scores of valley residents serving abroad, they fought to maintain the democratic rights they had struggled so long for at home. As a result of their wartime patriotism, workers made a direct connection between the fight against fascism abroad and the strike for their rights at home in a similar manner to how they viewed World War I. Picket lines formed quickly at mills in East Wheeling, Martins Ferry, and Steubenville.[87] After a short-lived strike "conducted very quietly," the men began returning to work on December 28 under order by CIO President Philip Murray with guarantees of retroactive wage adjustments from the War Labor Board.[88]

On the shop floor, gender discrimination issues were common in the USWA's grievance procedures during the war. Marie Bacue, a second-generation Belgian steelworker at Wheeling Corrugating, filed a grievance in November 1945 claiming her foreman refused to transact her grievance, presumably because she was a woman. Bacue had worked in the drum press department since March 11, 1941. Mary Naples in the drum press department filed a grievance asking "she be paid difference in wages because [she was] placed on [an] other job."[89] Apparently there were many feelings of sex discrimination by both foreman and plant management. Bacue filed another grievance claiming "management attacked her for filing certain grievances." This is an ambiguous statement, but it raises many suggestions as to the climate on the shop floor in late 1945. An unnamed grievance stated a week later that the foreman in the drum assembly department violated the collective bargaining contract by refusing to accept a grievance report.[90] Bacue's efforts to have her and other female workers' grievances heard was apparently being halted by the company after she claimed she was "refused permission to leave to get a pass to transact grievance matters."[91] While these gender-related concerns seem most pronounced at the East Wheeling plant, they also came up at other Wheeling Steel mills. For example, in December 1945, two grievances came from the Yorkville plant from female steelworkers. Jessie Olszeski working on the cold strip mill asked to be placed back on "Roll Bearing job for which she [was] qualified and which her seniority entitle[d] her." Likewise Lahona Marody claimed she was fired unjustly "while women with less seniority [were] still working."[92]

While building union consciousness meant hearing numerous grievances of discrimination by the company, Local 1248 also had to deal with allegations of sex discrimination within the union. Following an election to the grievance committee in October 1945, Betty Piazza Lenore was angry after her appointment to the building material department and not the drum press department. She had been in the drum press department since August 1935 and was elected by the majority female members of that department.[93] A week later, Betty Lenore returned along with 116 members of the drum press department protesting that she was not their representative to the grievance committee.

Most of those present were Polish, Italian, and other second-generation ethnic women who had been working in the department since the early to mid-1930s. In particular, they were angered that the union chose a man to represent them. Lenore noted, "I am the lady who you are fighting for—3/4 of the press line are girls, More confidence on a woman than a man, What could I do with a bunch of men?" When it was suggested that Lenore lacked the seniority, Mary Ciripompa spoke up claiming that "Betty [had] more Seniority, [and the] right to be committeeman in drum Press." With the constant pressure building at the meeting, the chairman finally asked for a vote to change the appointment, and Lenore was elected unanimously.[94] In a department that was overwhelmingly female, women steelworkers expected that a woman represent them.

Local 1248's solidarity was just a part of the budding consciousness of rank-and-file steelworkers, which peaked in late 1945 through early 1946. On October 9, 1945, a craneman at the Benwood mill was suspended for being unwilling to clean slag and cinders out of a pit. While not fired, five fellow cranemen walked out in protest sparking a general work stoppage and idling three hundred workers in the blooming mill and steel works. Local 1185 voted not to return to work until the six men were reinstated, shuttering the plant employing over 1,600 for three weeks. This sympathy strike caused friction for Twenty-Third District officers, since it clearly violated the union contract, leading to a stern rebuke by Paul Rusen. After meeting with members of Local 1185, the union agreed to return to work. Almost a week later, all 320 employees of the nearby Bloch Brothers Tobacco Company in South Wheeling walked off the job after their lunch break, forming a picket line outside the plant. The strike came after the failure of the Tobacco Workers Union and the firm to reach a wage agreement. While known for cordial labor relations, workers demanded all workers, as one picket sign read, "Refuse to Work for Starvation Wages." As the first sustained strike in company history, union members engaged in the unique action of staging a strike parade through downtown Wheeling on October 19.[95]

By the end of World War II, Local 1248's most ethnically diverse departments took a leading role with the looming 1946 steel strike approaching. In August 1944, Local 1248 encouraged members to get more engaged in political action through the CIO Political Action Committee (CIO-PAC). Delegates for the PAC included Stella Obyc, who lived within a block of St. Ladislaus Parish. Violet Stazenski and Josephine Miscuraga were shop stewards for the drum press department, and Polish American Joseph Garlowich was a steward for the shear line and heavy stamping department.[96] With the national strike to commence on January 14, 1946, Local 1248 appointed members for picket duty. All Wheeling Steel plants voted overwhelmingly to go out on strike for a two-dollars-a-day wage increase. A Twenty-Third District study by local union members detailed the rising cost of living since January 1941. Basic consumer staples had risen astronomically, including a 471 percent increase in the price of apples and a 172 percent increase in the price of a dozen eggs. Paul Rusen noted how workers "[were] unable to meet average living expenses at their present rates of pay." Local union leaders promised city officials their members would engage in peaceful picketing, which was expected to include over twenty thousand steelworkers.[97]

The steel strike of 1946 witnessed the culmination of the rising class consciousness among the Wheeling area's ethnic working class. It had been many years since arriving Polish immigrants were referred to as "Polanders" during the late nineteenth century. The Poles slowly entered the labor movement with a strike against the steel companies in 1901 and by joining the local Socialist Party. Young Polish women expanded this solidarity through their strike against the Wheeling Can Company during the summer of 1915, and the Polish and Slavic men working at the city's meatpackers did the same during the strike of 1915–1916. Finally, while not as successful, this ethnic working-class consciousness expanded dramatically during the steel strike of 1919 and in the failed strike against Wheeling Steel in the early 1920s.

Out of these shared experiences, Wheeling's Polish working class increasingly found ways to foster interethnic cooperation. They shared in the grief of losing family members across South Wheeling and Benwood's multiethnic neighborhoods as a result of the Benwood Mine Disaster. Their children found time to interact on the baseball diamond, in downtown social spaces, and on the gridiron as they integrated the various high school football teams. The 1920s and 1930s also saw an expansion of ethnic fraternal organizations connecting Polish Americans throughout Wheeling but also the upper Ohio Valley. These ethnic groups also found ways to respond to the rising xenophobia through events like the Festival of Nations at Oglebay Park, which highlighted the positive benefits of various southern and eastern European cultures. Finally, the area's ethnic working class suffered the brunt of the selective enforcement of Prohibition as agents patrolled their neighborhoods assuming every family had an illegal still in their basement. These interactions greatly assisted in the rising political consciousness of Wheeling's ethnic groups as seen in their shift to the Democratic Party by the 1930s and their active role in supporting the CIO unions trying to improve the quality of life on the shop floor.

Thus by the cold days of 1946, Wheeling's ethnic working class joined over 750,000 steelworkers nationally walking off the job. With Wheeling Steel as the focus, thousands of other workers joined in sympathy strikes. AFL Patternmakers set up picket lines around the Continental Foundry & Machine Company. While a majority of workers at the plant were affiliated with the CIO, the USWA local agreed to respect the AFL picket line, ultimately leading to a group of nine AFL members who "served to stop all the complex workings of the entire plant."[98] Local unions made sure their members were aware of protecting property and picketing peacefully and also that they turned out for picket duty in large numbers. Local 1248 in East Wheeling made sure automobiles were lined up to be used for the "flying squadron" to patrol the factory area and East Wheeling to remind steelworkers not to report to work. When the strike began on January 21, Local 1248 mailed postcards to members notifying them of their turn on picket duty, and names were checked off by picket captains to make sure everyone stood firm. Pickets worked in shifts, maintaining a vigil twenty-four hours a day in "frigid weather." One female operative noted the "girls feel they are being demoralized . . . people are waiting to be called" for strike duty. These women who in their first years in the factory would have been content to earn decent wages, buy desired consumer items, and help support their immigrant parents now felt demoralized that they were not being used enough to do picket duty in the cold weather.[99]

The 1946 strike witnessed a variety of walkouts throughout the upper Ohio Valley with ethnic Catholic working-class residents taking the lead. The day before the steelworkers struck, city officials worried about potential strikes among the AFL building and construction trades, the United Electrical (UE) workers at the Windsor Power Plant, and the packinghouse workers. The latter two could leave families without adequate meat supplies and electric power during a bitterly cold January. Local packinghouses found that their sources of live meat were cut off, and all available meat was already in the hands of local retailers.[100] The day the steel strike commenced, the front page of the *Wheeling News-Register* featured a photograph of men and women of Local 3130 at the Continental Can Company plant at Forty-Eighth Street out on the picket line.[101] Many were Polish Americans whose relatives no doubt had been involved in the heated 1915 strike that raised fears of dividing the immigrant neighborhood. Now, no such fears existed as Polish, Ukrainian, Italian, Lebanese, and Croatian Americans joined the strike. While both sides engaged in what reporter Joe Cullinan called a "frigid politeness," one striker emphasized, "We'll stay here forever before we give an inch."[102]

Conclusion

For Wheeling Steel's multiethnic workforce, the years after unionization brought many new opportunities to express the full range of rights resulting from industrial democracy. They still lived in ethnic communities but increasingly developed a union consciousness through their local unions. With increasing wage rates, benefits packages, and disposable income to spend on desirable consumer items, workers of this generations saw the USWA as the reason for their increasing security. While following generations would begin to criticize the bureaucratic nature of the labor movement, for the generation that brought the union to Wheeling Steel, the USWA was a vital part of their worldview and just as important as their local Catholic parish.

Conclusion

When I was growing up, we had two religions at my house—the Catholic Church and the USWA.

—Jimmy Koprowski in Keith Maillard's *The Clarinet Polka*

Stanisław (Stanley) Biega represents the full arc of life in Wheeling's Polonia. Born in the village of Dębna located on the San River in southeastern Poland on May 8, 1876, he like many from Galicia dealt with the rapid changes to his rural community. By 1900, he had made the overland trip to Bremen, Germany, and purchased a ticket aboard the North German Lloyd's vessel *London* for an almost two-week voyage to the United States. He found work in western Pennsylvania, married his wife Annela Markowicz in 1903, and eventually settled in Wheeling in 1911.[1] The Biega family owned their home at 4404 McColloch Street. While Stanley worked as a millworker, over time his children found jobs to supplement the family's income. By the time he was sixty-four, Stanley was working as a janitor at the Polish St. Ladislaus Parish, and his sons Walter and Frank both worked at the Continental Can Company located a few blocks from their home. Both went through the seventh and eighth grades respectively at the St. Ladislaus Parish school and then went straight into the workforce.[2]

Stanley's son Paul Joseph Biega was born in this Polish community in 1924. Like his brothers, he attended the parish school through eighth grade and then went to several years of high school. By that point, the United States had entered World War II, and in May 1942 Paul found work at the Wheeling Corrugating factory in East Wheeling. Like many other Polish Americans, he joined the United Steelworkers of America through Local 1248 in the drum assembly department.[3] Inspired by duty to his country, Paul left his job to enlist in the U.S. Army on June 4, 1943.[4]

The Biegas lived in a Polish American community held together by a shared Catholic faith tied to St. Ladislaus. However, the community built around the parish and led by Fr. Emil Musial had increasing struggles as well. The Great Depression was difficult on parish finances. Then in both 1936 and 1937, the parish, like the wider region, was hard hit by major floods. Following the 1937 flood, the Diocese of Wheeling organized relief efforts. However, Bishop John J. Swint was disappointed by the Polish community's lack of involvement in the wider city campaign. Noting how he was "fully aware of the misfortunes your parish has met with," the bishop hoped St. Ladislaus would show itself "loyal to the Catholic cause here in the city of Wheeling."[5] By 1940, Father Musial, now in his sixties, noted a variety of frustrations he faced continuing to hold the parish together. By that time, the core of Polonia was just "two hundred polish [sic] families good, bad and indifferent." Many of the older immigrant generation were already in "Mount Calvary cemetery," while many coal miners "were discharged when the coal companies installed machineries one after the other." The second generation, while being successful, did not "consider themselves members of any parish and generally attend[ed] the nearest church they reside[d] to." Father Musial lamented that, unlike the first generation, "You cannot force them to belong to a national [Polish] church." Fewer were also attending the parochial school, which once had over five hundred students but for 1940 had just 190 attending.[6] As he got older, Musial longed for the tighter community he and the original Polish immigrants had forged in South Wheeling.

Even with Father Musial's dour assessment, by the 1930s and 1940s Wheeling's Polish Catholic community had helped its members address the many urban problems of the region. Through religious and cultural events and on the shop floor of the area's steel mills, metal factories, and tobacco plants, Poles and their children worked with other ethnic communities throughout the upper Ohio River Valley. While it is convenient to compartmentalize their lives and beliefs, the Poles and their children did not separate their ethnic, religious, or class identities. Members of Wheeling's Polonia balanced a left-leaning view of the need for a "moral capitalism"[7] with a love of their Polish background and their conservative religious practices, all while finding ways to interact with other ethnic groups on the job, shopping in a local grocery store, walking the picket line, or attending cultural events.[8]

Part of the global labor migrations in the late nineteenth century, Poles gravitated to Wheeling's growing steel industry, coal mines, and diversified manufacturing opportunities. As many Poles settled primarily in South Wheeling, by the 1910s the city had a strong Polonia. However, they arrived in a city with many urban problems as a result of rapid industrialization. Poles lived near the segregated vice district, where saloons were on virtually every corner, and crime and interethnic street fighting predominated. Industrial accidents and even getting killed by a passing railroad car loomed for every new resident. The Poles adapted to this urban environment with the aid of Fr. Emil Musial by creating a unique Polish Catholic space and culture on the South

Side. The parish developed its own parochial school, Polish language organizations, sports teams, and even a Polish American Political Club to aid in the process of becoming U.S. citizens and engaging in the affairs of the community.

This study of Polish Catholic immigrants adds to our understanding of how community building, preservation of their ethnic Catholic religion, and a tendency to support home ownership fostered a tighter group consciousness than among many other immigrant groups. Over time this group consciousness gave them a background to help solve everyday problems and promote union organizing among a diverse ethnic working class. By 1910, the Poles had a strong parish, various mutual-aid societies, and a vibrant culture. As they built their community, they also saw the need to improve local economic conditions. Only a few blocks south of St. Ladislaus, many community members, including mostly young Polish female workers, struck for better wages, safer conditions, and union recognition against the Wheeling Can Company in 1915, organizing in spaces commonly used for Polish Catholic functions. Poles often balanced being at times overly insular, choosing to build and run their own ethnic stores, religious spaces, and fraternal associations, with joining a broader fight for better treatment in the workplace.

However, the Poles' Catholicism and religious devotion were primary elements shaping their identities. They spent their money maintaining the parish and building a home nearby, and they instilled in their children a love for Poland and God, even as they used their ethnic social spaces for political and union organizing activities. Being Catholic, Polish, and a strong union member were not incompatible. "Polishness" in Wheeling meant being supportive of your family, your church, your heritage, and your union.

Historians of the immigrant working class have often focused on how the children of immigrants broke from their insular ethnic communities to forge broader working-class coalitions within the CIO and the Democratic Party. Immigrant families were seen as supportive of narrow, realistic goals, initially protected by the ethnic community at the expense of supporting loftier political goals.[9] Establishing themselves in low-wage industrial jobs enabled them to achieve a level of security and allowed for the preservation of the family unit. The story goes that only after breaking away from their immigrant parents' worldview in favor of a mass consumption culture and the New Deal political order could they foster a unified coalition advocating for industrial democracy in the late 1930s.[10]

While this story may be true in places like Chicago, Pittsburgh, and Detroit, Wheeling's Polish immigrants forged a somewhat different path.

For the first generation in the United States, they fostered a community that tried to unify migrants from a variety of geographical backgrounds. The pull of ethnicity, religion, and class were all equally important in providing a secure community. Labor historians too often do not appreciate this lived experience, favoring instead the moments when workers mobilized collectively in support of mass industrial unions. Building parishes and fraternal lodges, providing insurance programs and ethnic entertainments, manufacturing some illegal moonshine in their homes for extra cash, and working twelve-hour days in the steel mill and then returning home to work on needed repairs are just as vital to understanding the immigrant experience and how it laid the groundwork for subsequent political action. As Leslie Tentler argues, the local parish community's response to the everyday needs of its parishioners "are no less important, and no less formidable, than the creation of a class-based opposition to capitalist exploitation. For a good many workers in the United States, the creation of an ethnic identity and the institutions of which that identity was both symbol and product was probably a necessary antecedent to the development of class consciousness."[11]

It was this localized Polish ethnic community that prepared the second generation. Polish immigrants created a home and a community that stressed stability, security, morality, and a sense of justice. At parochial school, in parish lay societies, and in fraternal organizations, Polish Americans learned the values and pride in their culture that gave them a common language and a set of beliefs to forge a better life. If they did come to argue for a "moral capitalism" in the 1930s, Polish Americans learned about what that type of society could look like daily as they grew up in South Wheeling and experienced the bonds and collective strivings of their fellow immigrants.[12]

For Wheeling's Polish community, the sacred world of their parish was never actually divorced from the secular world of the union hall and political campaigns. While it may be hard for historians to comprehend how such a large group of rural, Catholic immigrants could become Americans and be so active in the union movement, by taking a close-up view of their Polonia we can best understand the values that structured their lives. In his book set in the fictional South Raysburg, but inspired by South Wheeling's Polish community, Keith Maillard's third-generation Polish American narrator surveys the work of the Polish immigrants over the years: "They kept the customs they remembered from the old country, and they stuck together and they minded their own business, and they made it through that big ugly strike in 1919, and they made it through the Depression, and they helped build the USWA in the valley, and they hung on to their little bits of property any way they could and kept their houses real nice, and they sent their sons off to war."[13] The Polish immigrants and their children created their own unique world in Wheeling that affected all levels of local culture, religion, politics, and unionism. If Jimmy Koprowski wanted to best understand how the Poles were able to achieve all these things, his grandfather summed up an attitude that many of the immigrant generation shared: "You don't gotta teach Polaks union . . . Polaks stick togedder."[14]

Notes

INTRODUCTION

1. I would like to thank Sean Duffy for his excellent work conducting oral interviews with a variety of people of different ethnic backgrounds in Wheeling. For the Janeczkos, see Sean Duffy, *The Wheeling Family*, vol. 2, *More Immigrants, Migrants, and Neighborhoods* (Wheeling, WV: James Thornton, 2012), 207–17; Mike Janetsky, 1930 Manuscript Census, Wheeling Sixth Ward, Ohio County, WV, Enumeration District 16, Roll 2550, Page 11A, RG 29—Records of the Bureau of the Census, *Fifteenth Census of the United States*, National Archives and Records Administration (NARA), Washington, DC, reprinted via Ancestry.com.
2. St. Ladislaus Church Confirmation Book, 1922, 1928, St. Ladislaus Parish Sacramental Records, Archives of the Diocese of Wheeling-Charleston (hereafter DWC); Duffy, *The Wheeling Family*, vol. 2, 208.
3. Matthew Borgacz and Helen Janeczko Marriage Certificate, August 16, 1927; Henry S. Baranowski and Martha A. Janeczko, Marriage License, May 19, 1938, both from Ohio County, WV, West Virginia State Division of Vital Statistics, West Virginia State Archives and History Center, Charleston, WV (hereafter WVSA).
4. Keith Maillard, *The Clarinet Polka* (New York: St. Martin's Press, 2003), 2.
5. Ed Gorczyca, interview by the author, August 6, 2008.
6. David Javersak, "Ohio Valley Trades and Labor Assembly, 1882–1915" (PhD diss., West Virginia University, 1977); George Fetherling, *Wheeling: A Brief History* (Wheeling, WV: Polyhedron Learning Media, 2008).
7. Leslie Woodcock Tentler, "Present at the Creation: Working-Class Catholics in the United States," in *American Exceptionalism?: U.S. Working-Class Formation in an International Context*, eds. Rick Halperin and Jonathan Morris (New York: Palgrave Macmillan, 1997), 135; these values were crucial to the "subculture of opposition" defined in Richard Jules Oestreicher, *Solidarity and Fragmentation: Working People and Class Consciousness in Detroit, 1875–1900*, 2nd ed. (Urbana: University of Illinois Press, 1989), 60–67.
8. James Connolly, "Bringing the City Back In: Space and Place in the Urban History of the Gilded Age and Progressive Era," *Journal of the Gilded Age and Progressive Era* 1, no. 3 (July 2002): 262, 270–71.
9. Ronald L. Lewis, *Transforming the Appalachian Countryside: Railroads, Deforestation, and Social Change in West Virginia, 1840–1940* (Chapel Hill: University of North Carolina Press, 1998); Ken Fones-Wolf, *Glass Towns: Industry, Labor, and Political Economy in Appalachia, 1890–1930s* (Urbana: University of Illinois Press, 2007).
10. Lou Martin, *Smokestacks in the Hills: Rural-Industrial Workers in West Virginia* (Urbana: University of Illinois Press, 2015), 1–2, 6–11.
11. Allen Dieterich-Ward, *Beyond Rust: Metropolitan Pittsburgh and the Fate of Industrial America* (Philadelphia: University of Pennsylvania Press, 2015), 2–3, 6–8, 13–14.
12. On Wheeling as an industrial hub within the larger Pittsburgh region, see Dieterich-Ward, *Beyond Rust*. Historians of the U.S.-Mexico borderlands have also noted this trend, especially for fostering a multiracial working class, that navigated the unique

localities along the border, like El Paso, Texas, and Cochise County, Arizona. See, for example, Monica Perales, *Smeltertown: Making and Remembering a Southwest Border Community* (Chapel Hill: University of North Carolina Press, 2010), 3, 60; Katherine Benton-Cohen, *Borderland Americans: Racial Division and Labor War in the Arizona Borderlands* (Cambridge, MA: Harvard University Press, 2009).

13. Brian McCook, *The Border of Integration: Polish Migrants in Germany and the United States* (Athens: Ohio University Press, 2011).
14. This study of Wheeling joins with scholars analyzing rural Polish immigrant communities, particularly in the Midwest. John Radziłowski has examined about fifty rural towns that attracted Polish migrants in rural Minnesota and the eastern Dakotas. Most were from the German partition, arriving as family chain migrations from similar villages, not unlike what took place in Wheeling. Likewise, they settled in a heavily German part of the Midwest, creating a familiar rural and ethnic diversity to what they left in Europe. See Radziłowski, "Out on the Wind: Life in Minnesota's Polish Farming Communities," *Minnesota History* 58, no. 1 (Spring 2002): 18–20, quote p. 21; Radziłowski, *Poles in Minnesota* (St. Paul: Minnesota Historical Society Press, 2005); Susan Gibson Mikoś, *Poles in Wisconsin* (Madison: Wisconsin Historical Society Press, 2012).
15. William J. Galush found a similar trend in the Polish communities in Minnesota, Cleveland, Ohio, Utica, and New York Mills, New York. See Galush, *For More than Bread: Community and Identity in American Polonia, 1880–1940* (Boulder, CO: East European Monographs, 2006).
16. Timothy G. Borden, "The Salvation of the Poles: Working Class Ethnicity and Americanization Efforts during the Interwar Period in Toledo, Ohio," *Polish American Studies* 56, no. 2 (Autumn 1999): 20–21, 24, 26.
17. Fones-Wolf, *Glass Towns*.
18. Deborah R. Weiner, *Coalfield Jews: An Appalachian History* (Urbana: University of Illinois Press, 2006).
19. See, for example, Ronald W. Schatz, *The Electrical Workers: A History of Labor at General Electric and Westinghouse, 1923–60* (Urbana and Chicago: University of Illinois Press, 1983); Gary Gerstle, *Working-Class Americanism: The Politics of Labor in a Textile City, 1914–1960* (Cambridge: Cambridge University Press, 1989).
20. Jefferson Cowie and Nick Salvatore, "The Long Exception: Rethinking the Place of the New Deal in American History," *International Labor and Working-Class History* 74 (Fall 2008): 11.
21. "Introduction," in *The Pew and the Picket Line: Christianity and the American Working Class*, ed. Christopher D. Cantwell, Heath W. Carter, and Janine Giordano Drake (Urbana: University of Illinois Press, 2016), 2, 10.
22. For the best new scholarship highlighting these connections between religion and labor organizing, see Jared Roll, *Spirit of Rebellion: Labor and Religion in the New Cotton South* (Urbana: University of Illinois Press, 2010), 4; Richard J. Callahan Jr., *Work and Faith in the Kentucky Coal Fields: Subject to Dust* (Bloomington and Indianapolis: Indiana University Press, 2009), 1–16; Elizabeth Fones-Wolf and Ken Fones-Wolf, *Struggle for the Soul of the Postwar South: White Evangelical Protestants and Operation Dixie* (Urbana: University of Illinois Press, 2015).
23. Matthew Pehl, "'Apostles of Fascism,' 'Communist Clergy,' and the UAW: Political Ideology and Working-Class Religion in Detroit, 1919–1945," *Journal of American History* 99, no. 2 (September 2012): 440, 443–44, 450–52.

24. Heath W. Carter, *Union Made: Working People and the Rise of Social Christianity in Chicago* (New York: Oxford University Press, 2015), 4–6, 75, 83, 99–100, 110, 119, 131, 151.
25. Matthew Pehl, "The Remaking of the Catholic Working Class: Detroit, 1919–1945," *Religion and American Culture: A Journal of Interpretation* 19, no. 1 (Winter 2009): 38–39.
26. Pehl, "The Remaking of the Catholic Working-Class," 46–47.
27. Michael Löwy, *Redemption and Utopia: Jewish Libertarian Thought in Central Europe: A Study in Elective Affinity* (London: Verso, 1992), ch. 1, quotes p. 6. I thank Steve Rosswurm for allowing me to draw on his early thoughts on this relationship for Polish American workers; see "Catholicism and the CIO: An Elective Affinity," paper at the 38th Annual North American Labor History Conference, October 21, 2016, Wayne State University.
28. Pehl, "The Remaking of the Catholic Working-Class," 46; Rosswurm, "Catholicism and the CIO: An Elective Affinity," 2, 5.
29. Leslie Woodcock Tentler, "On the Margins: The State of American Catholic History," *U.S. Catholic Historian* (2003): 82, 84.
30. Joseph A. McCartin, "Estranged Allies on the Margins: On the Ambivalent Response of Labor Historians to Catholic History," *U.S. Catholic Historian* (2003): 119.
31. Evelyn Savidge Sterne, *Ballots and Bibles: Ethnic Politics and the Catholic Church in Providence* (Ithaca, NY: Cornell University Press, 2003), 5.
32. Sterne, *Ballots and Bibles*, 111–92, 255; James P. McCartin and Joseph A. McCartin, "Working-Class Catholicism: A Call for New Investigations, Dialogue, and Reappraisal," *Labor: Studies in the Working-Class History of the Americas* 4, no. 1 (Spring 2007): 106–7.
33. Benedict Anderson, *Imagined Communities: Reflections on the Origins and Spread of Nationalism*, 3rd ed. (New York: Verso, 2006), 1–8.
34. Dominic Pacyga, *Polish Immigrants and Industrial Chicago: Workers on the South Side, 1880–1922* (Columbus: Ohio State University Press, 1991), 4–5.
35. Pacyga, *Polish Immigrants and Industrial Chicago*, quote on p. 6, 121, 128–30, 258–60.
36. Gary Gerstle, *The American Crucible: Race and Nation in the Twentieth Century* (Princeton, NJ: Princeton University Press, 2001).
37. James R. Barrett, "Americanization from the Bottom Up: Immigration and the Remaking of the Working Class in the United States, 1880–1930," *Journal of American History* 79, no. 3 (December 1992): 997.
38. Barrett, "Americanization from the Bottom Up," 997–99, quote 997–98.
39. Roy Rosenzweig, *Eight Hours for What We Will: Workers and Leisure in an Industrial City* (Cambridge: Cambridge University Press, 1983), 65–90; James R. Barrett, *The Irish Way: Becoming American in the Multi-Ethnic City* (New York: Penguin Press, 2012), 10–11; 13–55; 57–103.
40. Joseph McCartin, *Labor's Great War: The Struggle for Industrial Democracy and the Origins of the Modern American Labor Relations, 1912–1921* (Chapel Hill: University of North Carolina Press, 1997); Gary Gerstle, "Liberty, Coercion, and the Making of Americans," *Journal of American History* 84, no. 2 (September 1997): 524–58.
41. John Bodnar, "Immigration, Kinship, and the Rise of Working-Class Realism in Industrial America," *Journal of Social History* 14, no. 1 (Autumn 1980): 45, 49–52.

42. Thomas Gobel, "Becoming American: Ethnic Workers and the Rise of the CIO," *Labor History* 29, no. 2 (Spring 1988), 174–76, 185–86; Lizabeth Cohen, *Making a New Deal: Industrial Workers in Chicago, 1919–1939* (Cambridge: Cambridge University Press, 1990), 5–7, 75, 209, 285, 314–15.
43. Pacyga, *Polish Immigrants and Industrial Chicago*; Sterne, *Ballots and Bibles*, 3–5.
44. William Hal Gorby, "Subcultures in Conflict in Polonia: Class, Religion, and Ethnic Tensions in the Formation of Wheeling's Polish Community, 1895–1917," *West Virginia History* 4, no. 2 (Fall 2010): 1–34.

CHAPTER 1

Chapter 1 Title. Quote from the *Wheeling Daily Register*, August 7, 1876, 4.
1. John J. Bukowczyk, *And My Children Did Not Know Me: A History of the Polish-Americans* (Bloomington and Indianapolis: Indiana University Press, 1987), 35; Alexander Oszustowicz, Request for Certificate of Arrival, September 1923, Preliminary Forms for Petitions of Naturalizations, Box 2, Folder 2, RG 21— Records of the U.S. District and Circuit Courts for the Northern District of West Virginia, Wheeling Division, Naturalization Records, National Archives and Records Administration, Philadelphia, PA (hereafter RG 21, NARA, Philadelphia). A Polonia is a Polish community outside of Poland created during the Polish diaspora of this era.
2. Sean Duffy and James Thornton, *The Wheeling Family: A Celebration of Immigrants and Their Neighborhoods* (Wheeling, WV: Creative Impressions, 2008), 144–45; Unnamed Polish American of St. Ladislaus Church, interview by Michael Kline, October 31, 1994, in "Pierogi Making at St. Lad's," transcript, Wheeling Spoken History Project, Ohio County Library, http://www.ohiocountylibrary.org/wheeling history/4766.
3. Mary Martinkosky, interview by author, August 10, 2008; Antonio Gorczyca, Preliminary Form for Petition for Naturalization, January 1, 1920, Box 2, Folder 11, RG 21, NARA, Philadelphia; for a classic history of the immigration experience, see John Bodnar, *The Transplanted: A History of Immigrants in Urban America* (Bloomington: Indiana University Press, 1985), ch. 1. For an interpretation using the global world systems model, see Ewa Morawska, "Labor Migrations of Poles in the Atlantic World Economy, 1880–1914," *Comparative Studies in Society and History* 31, no. 2 (April 1989): 237–72; for the transnational connections between Polish immigrant communities in Germany and the United States, see Brian McCook, *The Borders of Integration: Polish Migrants in Germany and the United States, 1870–1924* (Athens: Ohio University Press, 2011); for recent work examining the migrants' decisions for leaving but also grounding it in European state efforts to encourage out-migration, see Tara Zahra, *The Great Departure: Mass Migration from Eastern Europe and the Making of the Free World* (New York: W. W. Norton, 2016).
4. Morawska, "Labor Migrations of Poles in the Atlantic World Economy," 237; Dirk Hoerder, *Cultures in Contact: World Migrations in the Second Millennium* (Durham, NC: Duke University Press, 2002), ch. 14.
5. Dominic Pacyga, *Polish Immigrants and Industrial Chicago: Workers on the South Side, 1880–1922* (Chicago: University of Chicago Press, 2003), 23.
6. For Polish migration from the German Reich, see Richard Blanke, *Prussian Poland in the German Empire, 1871–1900* (Boulder, CO: East European Monographs, 1981);

James S. Pula, *Polish Americans: An Ethnic Community* (New York: Twayne, 1995), 14–15; McCook, *Borders of Integration*, 18–19, 187.
7. Peasant landownership lacked any state policy early on that would have rationalized the rural economy. Only after the endless proliferation of subdividing plots did a gradual consolidation of lands and the rise of medium-sized landholders take place in the early twentieth century. Isolated and scattered strips of peasants' lands in and around the traditional villages were consolidated into integrated plots in more than eight hundred villages. For a clear description of the process, see Robert E. Blobaum, "The 'Woman Question' in Russian Poland, 1900–1914," *Journal of Social History* 35, no. 4 (Summer 2002): 802–3; Blobaum, "To Market! To Market! The Polish Peasantry in the Era of the Stolpin Reforms," *Slavic Review* 59, no. 2 (Summer 2000): 407–9.
8. Stefan Kieniewicz, *The Emancipation of the Polish Peasantry* (Chicago and London: University of Chicago Press, 1969), 180–89; Morawska, "Labor Migrations of Poles in the Atlantic World Economy," 242; Blobaum, "To Market! To Market!" 408–10, 417–20.
9. Morawska, "Labor Migrations of Poles in the Atlantic World Economy," 242–44; Blobaum, "To Market! To Market!" 409–10; Keely Stauter-Halsted, *The Nation in the Village: The Genesis of Peasant National Identity in Austrian Poland, 1848–1914* (Ithaca, NY: Cornell University Press, 2001), 22–25; Piotr Eberghardt, *Ethnic Groups and Population Changes in Twentieth-Century Central-Eastern Europe* (Armonk, NY: M. E. Sharpe, 2003), 85–92.
10. Blobaum, "The 'Woman Question,'" 803; Blobaum, "To Market! To Market!" 410–16. For earlier peasant and Russian relations, see Robert E. Blobaum, *Rewolucja: Russian Poland, 1904–1907* (Ithaca, NY: Cornell University Press, 1995).
11. John J. Kulczycki, *The Foreign Worker and the German Labor Movement: Xenophobia and Solidarity in the Coal Fields of the Ruhr, 1871–1914* (Providence, RI: Berg, 1994), 1–10; 71–104; Morawska, "Labor Migrations of Poles in the Atlantic World Economy," 242–45; Hoerder, *Cultures in Contact*, ch. 14.
12. Laura A. Crago, "The 'Polishness' of Production: Factory Politics and the Reinvention of Working-Class National and Political Identities in Russian Poland's Textile Industry, 1880–1910," *Slavic Review* 59, no. 1 (Spring 2000): 18–20, 38–41.
13. Stauter-Halsted, *The Nation in the Village*, 6–10. For the cultural battles over the definition of *Polishness*, see Larry Wolff, "Dynastic Conservatism and Poetic Violence in Fin de Siècle Cracow: The Habsburg Matrix of Polish Modernism," *American Historical Review* 106, no. 3 (June 2001): 735–64.
14. Robert E. Blobaum, "The Revolution of 1905–1907 and the Crisis of Polish Catholicism," *Slavic Review* 47, no. 4 (Winter 1988): 672–75; Stauter-Halsted, *The Nation in the Village*, 173–80; Blobaum, "The 'Woman Question,'" 802–5; Jan Molenda, "The Role of Women in the Polish Migration to the Rhein-Westphalia Industrial Region at the Beginning of the Twentieth Century," *Polish Review* 42, no. 3 (1997); William Galush, "Journeys of Spirit and Space: Religion and Economics in Migration," *Polish American Studies* 59, no. 2 (Autumn 2002), 7, 13–15.
15. Stauter-Halsted, *The Nation in the Village*, 146–51, 185–215.
16. Morawska, "Labor Migrations of Poles in the Atlantic World Economy," 252–53; Ivan T. Berend, *History Derailed: Central and Eastern Europe in the Long Nineteenth Century* (Berkeley: University of California Press, 2003), 136–40, 152; Dominic A.

Pacyga, "Polish Emigration to the United States before World War One and Capitalist Development," *Polish American Studies* 46, no. 1 (Spring 1989): 10–18.

17. Blobaum, *Rewolucja: Russian Poland*; Bukowczyk, *And My Children Did Not Know Me*, 10–11.
18. For Poles applying for naturalization, *Wheeling Intelligencer*, December 30, 1918, 10. The story of Galkowski, who served in various Polish Catholic fraternal societies, is based off several sources where there is corroborating evidence. All sources place his birth around 1895–97 and his arrival from Russian Poland on July 5, 1913 (or July 5, 1912, in the *Intelligencer*'s case). Walter Galkowski, World War II Draft Registration Card, 1942, National Archives and Records Administration, Washington, DC, Wheeling, WV, Microfilm Series M1937, Roll 18; Wladyslaw Galkowski in *Hamburger Passagierlisten* [Hamburg Passenger List], 1850–1934, database, from Staatsarchive Hamburg, Germany; *Hamburger Passagierlisten*, Volume 373–7I, VIII A1, Band 261, Page 2036, Microfilm No. K 1830; Wladyslaw Galkowski in New York Passenger Lists, 1820–1957 database, Arrival 1913, New York, New York; Microfilm Serial T715, Roll 2122, Page 169, all databases in Ancestry.com; *Callin's Wheeling City Directory, 1919–1920* (Wheeling, WV: R. L. Polk & Co., 1920), 357.
19. Pula, *Polish-Americans*, 15–17; Berend, *History Derailed*, ch. 4; Konstanty Lapinski, in *Hamburger Passagierlisten* [Hamburg Passenger List], 1850–1934, database, Band 247, Page 1315, Microfilm No. K 1823; *Callin's Wheeling City Directory, 1921–1922* (Wheeling, WV: R. L. Polk & Co., 1922), 738; *Polk's Wheeling City Directory, 1924* (Wheeling, WV: R. L. Polk & Co., 1924), 607, via Ancestry.com.
20. Galush, "Journeys of Spirit and Space," 5–10.
21. *Ameryka*, April 28, 1900, reprinted in Galush, "Journeys of Spirit and Space," 10–11; Mark Wyman, *Round Trip to America: The Immigrants Return to Europe, 1880–1930* (Ithaca, NY: Cornell University Press, 1993), 21–25.
22. Sean Duffy, *The Wheeling Family*, vol. 2, *More Immigrants, Migrants and Neighborhoods* (Wheeling, WV: James Thornton, 2012), 197–99; Wyman, *Round Trip to America*, 17–18.
23. Quoted in Morawaska, "Labor Migrations of Poles," 261. For conditions around Maszkienice, see Morawaska, "Labor Migrations of Poles," 256–57, 259–61. For a viable travel route to the ports of Bremen and Hamburg, see Dirk Hoerder, "The Traffic of Emigration via Bremen/Bremerhaven: Merchants' Interests, Protective Legislation, and Migrants' Experiences," *Journal of American Ethnic History* 13, no. 1 (Fall 1993): 90–92.
24. Duffy, *The Wheeling Family*, vol. 2, 197–99; "Wicenty Front," in New York Passenger Lists, 1820–1957, database, Arrival 1906, New York, Microfilm Serial T715, Roll 731, 78, Passenger and Crew Lists of Vessels Arriving at New York, New York, 1897–1957; National Archives Microfilm Publication T715, RG 85, Records of the Immigration and Naturalization Service, NARA, Washington, DC, reprinted by Ancestry.com.
25. Hoerder, "The Traffic of Emigration via Bremen/Bremerhaven," 90–92; Michael Sawa Death Certificate, in West Virginia, Deaths Index, 1853–1973; "Michal Sawah," in New York Passenger Lists, 1820–1957, database, Arrival 1906, New York, Microfilm Serial T715, Roll 684, Page 45; "Michal Sawa," in New York Passenger Lists, 1820–1957, database, Arrival 1909, New York, Microfilm Serial T715, Roll1389, p. 191, both in Passenger and Crew Lists of Vessels Arriving at

New York, New York, 1897–1957; RG 85, NARA, reprinted by Ancestry.com; Pula, *Polish Americans*, 15–17; *Callin's Wheeling City Directory, 1913–1914* (Wheeling, WV: R. L. Polk & Co., 1913), 544. For the IWW's role in the Paterson Strike of 1913, see Melvyn Dubofsky, *We Shall Be All: A History of the Industrial Workers of the World*, 2nd ed. (Urbana: University of Illinois Press, 2000), 152–67.

26. "Leokadia Jasienska" Ship Manifest List, SS *Amsterdam*, Holland-American Line, in New York Passenger Lists, 1820–1957, database, Arrival 1905, New York, Microfilm Serial T715, Roll 536, Page 114, Passenger and Crew Lists of Vessels Arriving at New York, New York, 1897–1957, RG 85, NARA, reprinted by Ancestry.com; 1910 Manuscript Census, Wheeling Eighth Ward, Ohio County, WV, Enumeration District 117, Roll T624_1692, FHL microfilm 1375705, Page 16A, via Ancestry.com.

27. Wyman, *Round Trip to America*, 24; "Antoni Bober," Ship Manifest List, SS *Kronprinz Wilhelm*, Bremen-American Line in New York Passenger Lists, 1820–1957, database, Arrival 1905, New York, Microfilm Serial T715, Roll 528, Page 104, in Passenger and Crew Lists of Vessels Arriving at New York, New York, 1897–1957, RG 85, NARA, reprinted by Ancestry.com; *Callin's Wheeling City Directory, 1911–1912* (Wheeling, WV: R. L. Polk & Co., 1911), 105; Tony Bober, World War I Draft Registration Card, 1918, Ohio County, WV, Roll 1993024, Ancestry.com; Antonius Bober and Agnes Laboj, Marriage File, June 1, 1909, St. Ladislaus Marriage Book, 1908–1941, 28, *St. Ladislaus Sacramental Records Collection*, Archives of the Diocese of Wheeling-Charleston (hereafter DWC). Joseph Obloj's petition for naturalization only talks about his time in Wheeling starting in 1914. He was born in 1873 in Golcawa and had a child born there in 1902, then traveled to America and had another child born in 1912 in Golcawa. He arrived in the United States in March 1914, finding work as an unskilled steelworker. See Joseph Obloj, Preliminary Form for Petition for Naturalization, January 27, 1927, Box 3, Folder 2, RG 21, NARA, Philadelphia.

28. Sample of marriages listing birth locations in St. Ladislaus Marriage Book, 1902–1908; St. Ladislaus Marriage Book, 1908–1941, 28, *St. Ladislaus Sacramental Records Collection*, DWC.

29. Richard Franklin Bensel, *The Political Economy of American Industrialization, 1877–1900* (Cambridge and New York: Cambridge University Press, 2000), 19–23, 47–50; Ken Fones-Wolf, *Glass Towns: Industry, Labor, and Political Economy in Appalachia, 1890–1930s* (Urbana: University of Illinois Press, 2007), 59–80; John Alexander Williams, *West Virginia and the Captains of Industry* (Morgantown: West Virginia University Press, 1976), ch. 5.

30. U.S. Census Bureau, *Tenth Census: Social Statistics of Cities (1880)*, pt. 2, *Southern and Western States* (Washington, DC: Government Printing Office, 1887), 87–92; U.S. Census Bureau, *Report on Manufacturing Industries in the United States at the Eleventh Census (1890)*, pt. 2 (Washington, DC: GPO, 1895), 606–613; U.S. Census Bureau, *Thirteenth Census (1910)*, vol. 3, *Population* (Washington: GPO, 1913), 1011–15.

31. Ken Fones-Wolf, "Caught Between Revolutions: Wheeling Germans in the Civil War Era," in Ken Fones-Wolf and Ronald L. Lewis, *Transnational West Virginia: Ethnic Communities and Economic Change* (Morgantown: West Virginia University Press, 2002), 20–26; Fones-Wolf, *Glass Towns*, ch. 2.

32. U.S. Census Bureau, *Thirteenth Census (1910)*, vol. 3, *Population*, 1011–15.

33. U.S. Census Bureau, *Twelfth Census (1900)*, pt .1, *Population* (Washington, DC: Government Printing Office, 1901), 800–3, 876–77.
34. U.S. Census Bureau, *Fourteenth Census (1920)*, vol. 2, *Population* (Washington, DC: Government Printing Office, 1922), 1036–37.
35. Theodore Warsinsky, Passenger Lists of Vessels Arriving at Baltimore, MD, 1820–1891, Arrival 1876, Microfilm Publication M255, Roll 25, RG 36, Records of the U.S. Custom Service, NARA, Washington, DC; Theodore Warsinsky, 1880 Manuscript Census, Wheeling Eighth Ward, Ohio County, WV; Theodore Warsinsky, 1900 Manuscript Census, Union District, Marshall County, WV; Theodore Warsinsky, 1910 Manuscript Census, Benwood, Fourth Ward, Marshall County, WV, all at Ancestry.com; *Benwood Enterpriser*, August 7, 1913, 4.
36. August Kubsky Death Certificate, in West Virginia, Deaths Index, 1853–1973, database via Ancestry.com; *Callin's Wheeling City Directory, 1888* (Wheeling, WV: W. L. Callin, Co., 1888), 267; *Callin's Wheeling City Directory, 1890–91* (Wheeling, WV: W. L. Callin, Co., 1890), 259; *Callin's Wheeling City Directory, 1892–93* (Wheeling, WV: W. L. Callin, Co., 1892), 262; *Callin's Wheeling City Directory, 1894* (Wheeling, WV: W. L. Callin, Co., 1894), 262; *Callin's Wheeling City Directory, 1896* (Wheeling, WV: W. L. Callin, Co., 1896), 315; Gibson Lamb Cranmer, *History of Wheeling and Ohio County, West Virginia and Representative Citizens* (Wheeling, WV: 1902), 674.
37. See Morawska, "Labor Migrations of Poles in the Atlantic World Economy," 250 for her figures.
38. Hoerder, *Cultures in Contact*, 334–44; Morawska, "Labor Migrations of Poles in the Atlantic World Economy, 238, 242; Kulczycki, *The Foreign Worker and the German Labor Movement*, 18–26.
39. Manuscript Census Schedules, 1910 and 1920 for Wheeling, Ohio County, WV, WVRHC.
40. Pacyga, *Polish Immigrants and Industrial Chicago*, 123–24.
41. Manuscript Census Schedules, 1910 and 1920 for Wheeling, Ohio County, WV, WVRHC.
42. Duffy and Thornton, *The Wheeling Family*, 151.
43. Duffy and Thornton, *The Wheeling Family*, 151–53.
44. Pacyga, *Polish Immigrants and Industrial Chicago*, 40–41.
45. 1910 Manuscript Census, Wheeling Ritchie District, Ohio County, WV, Enumeration District 117, Sixth and Seventh Precincts, WVRHC. Ritchie district's Sixth and Seventh Precincts started at the 4100 block of Jacob Street, which is near the southern end of the Bloch Brothers Tobacco Company, down to Forty-Fourth and Wood Streets.
46. In his study of Detroit's immigrant families, Oliver Zunz found high levels of Polish homeownership by 1900, whereas in most Wheeling census tracks the home ownership rate was around 25 percent. See Oliver Zunz, *The Changing Face of Inequality: Urbanization, Industrial Development, and Immigrants in Detroit, 1880–1920* (Chicago: University of Chicago Press, 1982), 177–95.
47. The unskilled occupations were as follows: thirty-four worked as day laborers at the steel mills, six worked on blast furnace crews, six were coal miners, and four were laborers at Hoffman's Tannery on Twenty-Eighth Street. The white-collar heads were as follows: two grocers, two in saloons, one musician, one salesman, and the other ran a boardinghouse.

48. 1910 Manuscript Census, Wheeling, Ritchie District, Enumeration District 117, Page 14A, WVRHC; Patricia A. Cooper, *Once a Cigar Maker: Men, Women, and Work Culture in American Cigar Factories, 1900–1919* (Urbana: University of Illinois Press, 1987), 164–65, 191–94; Leslie Woodcock Tentler, *Wage-Earning Women: Industrial Work and Family Life in the United States, 1900–1930* (New York: Oxford University Press, 1979), 14–15, 60.
49. *Callin's Wheeling City Directory, 1904–1905* (Wheeling, WV: R. L. Polk & Co., 1904); *Callin's Wheeling City Directory, 1905–1906* (Wheeling, WV: R. L. Polk & Co., 1905), 459; *Callin's Wheeling City Directory, 1907–1909* (Wheeling, WV: R. L. Polk & Co., 1907), 374, 486, Ohio County Public Library (OCPL); Bukowczyk, *And My Children Did Not Know Me*, 35–38.
50. *Callin's Wheeling City Directory, 1904–1905*; *Callin's Wheeling City Directory, 1905–1906*, 459; *Callin's Wheeling City Directory, 1907–1909*, 374, 486; *Callin's Wheeling City Directory, 1911–1912*, 392, 398, 525; *Callin's Wheeling City Directory, 1917–1918* (Wheeling, WV: R. L. Polk & Co., 1918), 408; *Callin's Wheeling City Directory, 1919–1920*, 546; *Callin's Wheeling City Directory, 1921–1922*, 753, OCPL.
51. *Callin's Wheeling City Directory, 1915–1916* (W. L. Polk & Co., 1915), 747; *Callin's Wheeling City Directory, 1917–1918*, 738; Stanisław Zarnoch, Preliminary Form for Petition for Naturalization, January 1, 1920, Box 2, Folder 12, RG 21, NARA, Philadelphia; Stanislaw Zarnoch, World War I Draft Registration Card, 1917, Ohio County, WV, Roll 1993026; *Callin's Wheeling City Directory, 1919–1920*, 968; *Callin's Wheeling City Directory, 1921–1922*, 1322; *Polk's Wheeling City Directory, 1923–1924* (Wheeling, WV: R. L. Polk & Co., 1924), 1041; *Polk's Wheeling City Directory, 1928* (Wheeling, WV: R. L. Polk & Co., 1927), 1169, OCPL; Stanley Zarnoch, 1930 Manuscript Census, Wheeling Eighth Ward, Ohio County, WV, via Ancestry.com.
52. Manuscript Census Schedules, 1900, 1910, and 1920 for Ohio County, and 1920 for Benwood, WVRHC.
53. 1910 and 1920 Manuscript Census Schedules, Eighth Ward, Ohio County, WV, WVRHC.
54. For updates that aided in employing unskilled immigrants, see *Wheeling Register*, August 2, 1903, 5; for company descriptions, see *Directory to the Iron and Steel Works of the United States, Compiled and Published by the American Iron and Steel Association*, 17th ed., corrected to March 1, 1908 (Philadelphia: J. B. Lippincott Company, 1908), 189–91; Sanborn Insurance Atlas Maps, Wheeling, 1890, 1902, 1921, OCPL.
55. 1910 Manuscript Census, Wheeling, Webster District, Ohio County, WV, Enumeration District 131, First and Second Precincts; 1920 Manuscript Census, Wheeling Sixth Ward, Ohio County, WV, Enumeration District 93, First Precinct, WVRHC. The sample included the heads of households in the precincts with the highest concentration of Polish working-class households.
56. *Wheeling Register*, April 17, 1906, 3; *Wheeling Register*, May 7, 1906, 3.
57. *Directory to the Iron and Steel Works of the United States, 1908*, 189–91; 1900 Manuscript Census, Wheeling, Washington District, Enumeration District 136, Ancestry.com.
58. *National Labor Tribune*, February 21, 1901, 8; *National Labor Tribune*, June 6, 1901, 8; Edward C. Wolf, "Wheeling and the Panama Canal," *Upper Ohio Valley Historical Review* (2004): 13–15.
59. 1910 Manuscript Census, Washington District, Wheeling, Ohio County, WV,

Enumeration District 126 and 144; 1920 Manuscript Census, Washington District, Wheeling, Ohio County, WV, Enumeration District 120; 1920 Manuscript Census, Wheeling First Ward, Enumeration District 75, Ancestry.com.
60. 1920 Manuscript Census Schedules, Ohio County; 1930 Manuscript Census Schedules, Ohio County, WVRHC.
61. Andrej Wojewadka, Preliminary Form for Petition for Naturalization, May 22, 1926, Box 3, Folder 2, RG 21, NARA, Philadelphia.
62. 1920 Manuscript Census Schedules, Ohio County, WVRHC; John J. Bukowczyk, "The Transformation of Working-Class Ethnicity: Corporate Control, Americanization, and the Polish Immigrant Middle Class in Bayonne, New Jersey, 1915–1925," *Labor History* 25, no. 1 (Winter 1984): 55–60.
63. Stanisław Kyrc, Preliminary Form for Petition for Naturalization, February 6, 1925, Box 2, Folder 9, RG 21, NARA, Philadelphia.
64. Stanly Duplaga, Declaration of Intention, March 4, 1919, Wheeling Division, Naturalization Records, Declarations of Intention, 1912–1989, Box 1, vol. 4, RG 21, NARA, Philadelphia; 1910 Manuscript Census, Washington District, Wheeling, Ohio County, WV, Enumeration District 126 and 144; 1920 Manuscript Census, Washington District, Wheeling, Ohio County, WV, Enumeration District 120; 1920 Manuscript Census, Wheeling First Ward, Enumeration District 75, Ancestry.com.
65. United States Selective Service System, *World War I Selective Service System Draft Registration Cards, 1917–1918* (Washington, DC: NARA), M1509, Ohio County, WV, Roll 1993024, Ancestry.com. Using the database in 2008, I searched for those draft cards where the registrant noted their "birth in Poland."
66. Blobaum, "To Market! To Market!" 409–10; thirty-one listed villages with no context on the partitioned portion of the Polish lands; United States Selective Service System, *World War I Selective Service System Draft Registration Cards, 1917–1918*, Ohio County, WV. As seen in later chapters, this data illuminates the diverse regional and village ties that eventually dissipated over time. Most ethnic enclaves first had to forge a strong collective national identity to unite disparate regional loyalties. See Thomas Guglielmo, *White on Arrival: Italians, Race, Color, and Power in Chicago, 1890–1945* (New York: Oxford University Press, 2003), 5–15, 31–34, 60.
67. United States Selective Service System, *World War I Selective Service System Draft Registration Cards, 1917–1918*, Ohio County, WV.

CHAPTER 2

Chapter 2 Title. Quote from *Wheeling Daily Intelligencer*, August 17, 1903, 8.
1. "Out of Work: The North Wheeling Polanders Will Soon Be in Want," *Wheeling Register*, November 12, 1893, 4.
2. "Out of Work," *Wheeling Register*, November 12, 1893, 4.
3. My arguments benefit from the amazing social history by David Rose. See Rose, "The Trial of Alice Bradford: A Study in the Politics of Prostitution in Wheeling, W.VA.," *Upper Ohio Valley Historical Review* 16, no. 1 (Autumn/Winter 1986), 6–22; David W. Rose, "Prostitution and the Sporting Life: Aspects of Working Class Culture and Sexuality in Nineteenth Century Wheeling," *Upper Ohio Valley Historical Review* 16, no. 2 (Spring/Summer 1987): 7–31.
4. James Barrett's insights on the role of public spaces in acculturating interethnic

interaction are crucial to my insights in this chapter; see James R. Barrett, *The Irish Way: Becoming American in the Multi-Ethnic City* (New York: Penguin Press, 2012), 10–11; 13–55.
5. James R. Barrett, *Work and Community in the Jungle: Chicago's Packinghouse Workers, 1894–1922* (Urbana and Chicago: University of Illinois Press, 1987), 65, 100.
6. Elliott J. Gorn, *Mother Jones: The Most Dangerous Woman in America* (New York: Hill & Wang, 2001), 76–77; West Virginia Department of Mines, *Twenty-Third Annual Report, June 30, 1905* (Charleston, WV: Tribune, 1906), 86–87; Edward Slavishak, *Bodies of Work: Civic Display and Labor in Industrial Pittsburgh* (Durham, NC: Duke University Press, 2008), 29–50, quote 50 and 36.
7. For the employment figures, see *Report of the Commissioner of Labor of the State of West Virginia, 1895–1896* (Charleston, WV: Moses W. Donnally, 1896), 318–326; *Ninth Biennial Report of the Bureau of Labor of West Virginia, 1905–1906* (Charleston, WV: Tribune, 1906), 112, 122–24; *Tenth Biennial Report of the Bureau of Labor of West Virginia, 1907–1908* (Charleston, WV: Tribune, 1908), 105, 120–23; *Fifteenth Biennial Report of the Bureau of Labor of West Virginia, 1919–1920* (Charleston, WV: Tribune, 1920), 16, 37–39; Peter Boyd, *History of Northern West Virginia Panhandle, Embracing Ohio, Marshall, Brooke and Hancock Counties*, vol. 1 (Topeka, KS: Historical Publishing Company, 1927), 291–99.
8. Herbert Gutman, "Work, Culture, and Society in Industrializing America, 1815–1919," *American Historical Review* 78, no. 3 (June 1973): 531–88.
9. Barrett, *Work and Community in the Jungle*, ch. 4; Slavishak, *Bodies of Work*, ch. 1.
10. *Wheeling Intelligencer*, February 3, 1908; for the Depression's effect on common wage rates, see Peter R. Shergold, "Wage Rates in Pittsburgh during the Depression of 1908," *Journal of American Studies* 9, no. 2 (August 1975): 161, 165, 172; John A. Fitch, *The Steel Workers* (New York: Russell Sage, 1911), 159–60; *Wheeling Register*, January 12, 1908, 7 and January 19, 1908, 6.
11. *Wheeling Register*, March 1, 1908, 17; *Benwood Enterpriser*, February 12, 1914, 4; *Benwood Enterpriser*, April 30, 1914, 4; *Benwood Enterpriser*, June 4, 1914, 4.
12. Shergold, "Wages Rates in Pittsburgh," 182–85; *National Labor Tribune*, August 20, 1908, 1.
13. *Wheeling Register*, January 3, 1908, 10; January 7, 1908, 8
14. *Wheeling Register*, January 10, 1908, 10; January 12, 1908, 7.
15. *Wheeling Register*, January 13, 1908, 7.
16. *Wheeling Register*, January 23, 1908, 5; January 24, 1908, 4; January 25, 1908, 6; February 2, 1908, 18.
17. *Wheeling Register*, January 25, 1908, 6; January 31, 1908, 2, 9; February 15, 1908, 1; February 17, 1908, 3.
18. *Wheeling Register*, June 8, 1909, 1. For reporting on immigrants, see Matthew Frye Jacobson, *Barbarian Virtues: The United States Encounters Foreign People at Home and Abroad, 1876–1917* (New York: Hill & Wang, 2000), 105–138.
19. *Benwood Enterpriser*, April 30, 1914, 4; *Benwood Enterpriser*, December 17, 1914, 4. For descriptions of tramps and the poor, see *Wheeling Majority*, December 10, 1914. By early 1915, there were about five thousand unemployed at the National Tube Company; see, *Wheeling Majority*, January 14, 1915, January 21, 1915. For arrests of tramps and streetwalkers, see *Wheeling Majority*, October 15, 1914; January 28, 1915, 1; February 4, 1915, 1; February 11, 1915, 6.
20. *Benwood Enterpriser*, February 12, 1914, 4; April 8, 1915, 4; July 15, 1915, 4;

July 29, 1915, 4; March 9, 1916, 2; *Wheeling Majority*, July 8, 1915; *Benwood Enterpriser*, January 22, 1914, 4; February 12, 1914, 4.
21. *Wheeling Register*, September 15, 1907; September 20, 1907.
22. *Wheeling Register*, September 15, 1907.
23. *Amalgamated Journal*, October 20, 1910, quoted in Slavishak, *Bodies of Work*, 160.
24. *Wheeling Register*, January 25, 1905, 11; March 5, 1905, 5, 20; March 11, 1905, 3; March 3, 1905, 10.
25. *Wheeling Intelligencer*, August 3, 1906, 3.
26. *Wheeling Intelligencer*, April 15, 1907, 6; March 8, 1907, 6; *Benwood Enterpriser*, April 15, 1915, 4.
27. *Benwood Enterpriser*, September 16, 1915, 4; June 19, 1913, 4; July 2, 1913, 4; January 22, 1914, 4.
28. David Alan Corbin, *Life, Work, and Rebellion in the Coal Fields: The Southern West Virginia Miners, 1880–1922* (Urbana: University of Illinois Press, 1981), 10; West Virginia, Department of Mines, *Twenty-Fourth Annual Report, Coal Mines in the State of West Virginia, for the Year Ending June 30, 1906* (Charleston, WV: Tribune, 1907), 166–67, 211; *Wheeling Intelligencer*, April 18, 1907, 6; *Wheeling Daily News*, January 30, 1907, 3.
29. "As They Say in Wheeling," The Final Report of the Wheeling Spoken History Project (Wheeling, WV: Wheeling National Heritage Area Corporation (WNHAC), 1995), 97–98.
30. "As They Say in Wheeling," WNHAC, 131–22; Slavishak, *Bodies of Work*, 57–58; West Virginia, *Annual Report of the Department of Mines, for the Year Ending June 30, 1907* (Charleston, WV: Tribune, 1908), ix.
31. Sean Duffy and James Thornton, *The Wheeling Family: A Celebration of Immigrants and Their Neighborhoods* (Wheeling, WV: Creative Impressions, 2008), 162–63.
32. "As They Say in Wheeling," WNHAC, 159–60; West Virginia, *Annual Report of the Department of Mines: For Fiscal Year Ending, June 30, 1915*, pt. 2 (Charleston, WV: Tribune, 1915), 40; *Benwood Enterpriser*, July 15, 1915, 4.
33. *Wheeling Register*, December 30, 1897, 8; December 13, 1896, 1; *Wheeling Intelligencer*, September 4, 1906, 8.
34. *Wheeling Register*, January 26, 1903, 2; Victor G. Reuther, *The Brothers Reuther and the Story of the UAW: A Memoir* (Boston: Houghton Mifflin Co., 1976), 12, 29–30; *Benwood Enterpriser*, May 8, 1913, 4.
35. John Bodnar, "Immigration, Kinship, and the Rise of Working-Class Realism in Industrial America," *Journal of Social History* 14, no. 1 (Autumn, 1980): 45, 49–52.
36. Joseph Kowalski, 1910 Manuscript Census, Wheeling, Webster District, Ohio County, WV, Enumeration District 131, First Precinct, Page 13A, West Virginia and Regional History Center (WVRHC).
37. For the role of "semi-public" spaces, see Perry Duis, *The Saloon: Public Drinking in Chicago and Boston, 1880–1920* (Urbana and Chicago: University of Illinois Press, 1983), 1–8, quote 86.
38. *Wheeling Daily Register*, February 24, 1895, 4; *Wheeling Register*, November 1, 1897, 5.
39. *Wheeling Register*, December 13, 1896, 1; December 12, 1897, 20. The newspaper misspelled Anton's name as Cienkwsz. According to city directories, his father was named Anton Czenkus; *W. L. Callin Wheeling City Directory, 1898–1899* (Wheeling, WV: W. L. Callin, 1898), 161; the proper name is taken from the official death

record. See Anton Cienkurski Jr., Death Record, December 11, 1897, 92, Division of Vital Records, West Virginia State Archives and History Center, Charleston, WV (hereafter WVSA).

40. *Wheeling Majority*, November 19, 1914; see sample of eighty households from 1920 Manuscript Census Schedules, WVRHC. These descriptions come from Ohio County, Wheeling City Tax Map, 1901, Ohio County Courthouse, Ohio County Clerk's Office, Wheeling, WV (hereafter OCCO). I thank Ginger Kabala and Fr. John Byrd of the South Wheeling Preservation Alliance for this amazing document; Sanborn Insurance Atlas Maps, Wheeling, 1884, 1890, 1902, and 1921, OCPL.
41. *Wheeling Register*, June 6, 1909, 4; June 2, 1909, 4.
42. *The History of West Virginia, Old and New* (American Historical Society, Inc., 1923), 460 and at http://www.lindapages.com/wags-ohio/trolley/trolley-train.htm. There were two main lines starting at Twenty-Sixth Street going south. For a map showing the dense network, see Wheeling City Tax Map, 1901, OCCO.
43. *Wheeling Daily Intelligencer*, April 1899; David Javersak, "The Ohio Valley Trades and Labor Assembly: The Formative Years, 1882–1915" (PhD diss., West Virginia University, 1977), ch. 2.
44. Wheeling City Tax Map, 1901, Plates 9, 14, and 15, Ohio County Courthouse; Sanborn Insurance Atlas Maps, Wheeling, 1890, 1902, OCPL.
45. *Report of the Health Department of City of Wheeling, West Virginia, for the Two Years Ending June the Thirtieth Nineteen Hundred & Thirteen* (Wheeling, WV: City Health Department, 1913), OCPL, 12–13, 16–17; *Wheeling Register*, July 1, 1912, 5.
46. *Wheeling Daily News*, January 7, 1907, 4.
47. *Wheeling Daily News*, January 7, 1908, 1; *Wheeling Intelligencer*, August 5, 1909, 12; *Report of the Health Department of City of Wheeling*, 1913, OCPL, 16–17.
48. *Wheeling Register*, August 30, 1914, 12; *Wheeling Daily News*, January 6, 1907, Section 4, 8.
49. *Wheeling Daily News*, May 3, 1906, 3. For Schmulbach Brewery, see *Wheeling Majority*, September 5, 1912.
50. Schmidt served as president of the Board of Public Works for eight years and as councilman for the Fourth Ward for twelve consecutive years. See Thomas Condit Miller and Hu Maxwell, *West Virginia and Its People*, vol. 2 (New York: Lewis Historical Publishing Company, 1913), 596–97. For efforts of similar urban mayors and reformers, see Robert D. Johnston, *The Radical Middle Class: Populist Democracy and the Question of Capitalism in Progressive Era Portland, Oregon* (Princeton, NJ: Princeton University Press, 2002).
51. For Schmidt's policies, see *Wheeling Intelligencer*, March 13, 1907, 1; April 19, 1907, 2.
52. See *Wheeling Intelligencer*, April 10, 1907, 1 for Health Officer's report.
53. *Report of the Health Department of City of Wheeling*, 1913, OCPL, 32–35.
54. *Report of the Health Department of City of Wheeling*, 1913, OCPL, 41, 45, 49.
55. James S. Pula, "The Progressives, the Immigrant, and the Workplace: Defining Public Perceptions, 1900–1914," *Polish American Studies* 52, no. 2 (Autumn 1995): 58–59, 62; *Wheeling Register*, July 3, 1912, 5; July 4, 1912, 5.
56. *Wheeling Register*, May 26, 1915; *Wheeling Daily News*, July 11, 1915, Part 5, 1. The spelling of the names is based on that reported in the press, even though misspellings were common.
57. Ronald L. Lewis, *Transforming the Appalachian Countryside: Railroads, Deforestation,*

and *Social Change in West Virginia, 1880–1920* (Chapel Hill: University of North Carolina Press, 1998), 269–73.

58. There were fifteen massive floods between March 1903 and March 1913, and 1908 was a year of extremes. There were large floods in February (42.8 feet) and March (39.6 feet); however, by October 1908, the Ohio River was in the midst of a major drought with the river measuring only two inches on October 12, 1908. See "Wheeling Floods: 1762 to the Present" via the OCPL, http://wheeling.weirton.lib.wv.us/history/events/floods/floods.htm.
59. *Wheeling Intelligencer*, March 14, 1907, 1, 9; March 15, 1907, 1.
60. *Wheeling Intelligencer*, March 14, 1907, 9.
61. *Wheeling Intelligencer*, March 15, 1907, 6, 8; *Wheeling Daily News*, March 29, 1913, 4–5, 7; March 28, 1913, 1–2, 8; March 29, 1913, 4–5, 7.
62. *Wheeling Intelligencer*, March 20, 1907, 7–9; *Wheeling Daily News*, March 28, 1913, 1–2; March 28, 1913, 8; March 29, 1913, 4–5, 7.
63. In the early twentieth century, the group was referred to as "Syrians," even though they were from Lebanon.
64. *Wheeling Daily News*, March 16, 1907.
65. *Wheeling Daily News*, March 16, 1907; *Wheeling Intelligencer*, March 20, 1907, 12; March 21, 1907, 1; March 22, 1907, 1.
66. *Wheeling Daily News*, March 30, 1913, Section 4, 5.
67. *Wheeling Daily News*, March 30, 1913, Section 3, 2; Section 4, 5; March 30, 1913, 1; March 31, 1913, 3.
68. Rose, "The Trial of Alice Bradford," 17–18; *W. L. Callin's Wheeling City Directory, 1903–1904* (Wheeling, WV: R. L. Polk & Co., 1904), 27–28; *W. L. Callin's Wheeling City Directory, 1904–1905* (Wheeling, WV: R. L. Polk & Co., 1905), 29; *W. L. Callin's Wheeling City Directory, 1905–1906* (Wheeling, WV: R. L. Polk & Co., 1906), 31; *W. L. Callin's Wheeling City Directory, 1907–1909* (Wheeling, WV: R. L. Polk & Co., 1909), 34, OCPL.
69. Rose, "The Trial of Alice Bradford," 17–18. For crime statistics, see *Bulletin of the Department of Labor: Statistics of Cities*, vol. 30 (Washington, DC: September 1900), 935; *Bulletin of the Department of Labor: Statistics of Cities*, no. 36 (Washington, DC: September 1901), 840; *Bulletin of the Department of Labor: Statistics of Cities*, no. 42 (Washington, DC: September 1902), 916. Cases of drunkenness remained the highest crime (1900, 433; 1901, 735; 1902, 511; 1914, 1,101). For 1914, see *Wheeling Register*, July 10, 1914, 6.
70. Rose, "The Trial of Alice Bradford," 6; Rose, "The Committee of One Hundred," 2–3. A similar arrangement existed in St. Paul, MN, where the "physical terrain of the city acted to maintain the invisibility of its poor." City leaders developed a licensing system for saloons, which by 1905 provided $384,000, the top source of city revenues. See Mary Lethert Wingerd, *Claiming the City: Politics, Faith, and the Power of Place in St. Paul* (Ithaca, NY: Cornell University Press, 2003), 79–84, quote on 82, 112.
71. *Wheeling Daily Intelligencer*, April 7, 1900; Rose, "The Committee of One Hundred," 5–6. For an example of another religious-led movement, see Daniel Czitrom, *New York Exposed: The Gilded Age Police Scandal That Launched the Progressive Era* (New York: Oxford University Press, 2016).
72. Rose, "The Committee of One Hundred," 3; *Wheeling Daily Intelligencer*, May 14, 1902, 5; October 7, 1903, 6.

73. *Wheeling Register*, January 7, 1905, 4.
74. *Wheeling Register*, March 5, 1905, 3; Mara L. Keire, "The Vice Trust: A Reinterpretation of the White Slavery Scare in the United States, 1907–1917," *Journal of Social History* 35, no. 1 (Autumn 2001): 5–6, 12–15. The region was also referred to as "Paper Mill Alley."
75. Rose, "The Trial of Alice Bradford," 7–9; *Wheeling Register*, March 5, 1905, 3.
76. *Wheeling Intelligencer*, March 23, 1904; March 25, 1904; *Wheeling Register*, June 26, 1904; for quote, see *Wheeling Register*, July 19, 1904.
77. Rose, "The Trial of Alice Bradford," 10–17.
78. *Wheeling Register*, January 12, 1906, 9; *Callin's Wheeling City Directory, 1903–1904*, 677–79; *Callin's Wheeling City Directory, 1905–1906*, 707–8.
79. *Wheeling Daily Register*, May 12, 1891, 3.
80. Madelon Powers, *Faces along the Bar: Lore and Order in the Workingman's Saloon, 1870–1920* (Chicago: University of Chicago Press, 1998), 49–50, 51–54; Duis, *The Saloon*, 233–34, 282.
81. *Wheeling Daily Intelligencer*, October 10, 1891, 9; *Wheeling Daily Register*, November 4, 1893; December 23, 1893; February 6, 1895; February 8, 1895; *Wheeling Register*, January 10, 1908, 10; for the banning of the free lunch, see *Wheeling Register*, June 29, 1909, 10.
82. For more on "universals," see Duis, *The Saloon*, 145–46; *Callin's Wheeling City Directory, 1905–1906*, 708.
83. *Wheeling City Directory, 1888* (Wheeling, WV: W. L. Callin, 1888); *Wheeling City Directory, 1890–1891* (Wheeling: W. L. Callin, 1891); *Wheeling City Directory, 1892–1893* (Wheeling: W. L. Callin, 1893); 1880 Manuscript Census, Wheeling Fifth Ward, Ohio County; 1900 Manuscript Census, Wheeling, Fifth Ward, Ohio County, Ancestry.com; *Sanborn Insurance Map*, Wheeling, WV, 1884.
84. *Callin's Wheeling City Directory, 1905–1906*, 708; *Callin's Wheeling City Directory, 1907–1909*, 703–4; *Callin's Wheeling City Directory, 1913–1914* (Wheeling, WV: R. L. Polk & Co., 1913), 747–48.
85. Roy Rozenzweig, *Eight Hour for What We Will: Workers and Leisure in an Industrial City, 1870–1920* (New York: Cambridge University Press, 1983), 49.
86. For a fine explanation of Schmulbachism, see Rose, "Prostitution and the Sporting Life," 20–23.
87. Peter C. Boyd, "Old Mozart Park Popular Hilltop Spot," *Wheeling News-Register*, August 26, 1951; "Ancient Cellars Once Used to Store Beer May Serve Wheeling as Air Raid Shelters," *Wheeling News-Register*, February 8, 1942, 8. For the commercialization of working-class leisure, see Rosenzweig, *Eight Hours for What We Will*, 171–90.
88. Jon Kingsdale, "The 'Poor Man's Club': Social Functions of the Urban Working-Class Saloon," *American Quarterly* 25, no. 4 (October 1973): 474, 482–84; Daniel Okrent, *Last Call: The Rise and Fall of Prohibition* (New York: Scribner, 2010), 27–29; *Wheeling Daily Intelligencer*, February 28, 1903, 5; March 25, 1903, 3.
89. *Wheeling Register*, May 6, 1905, 3; May 20, 1905, 3; see *Wheeling Daily Intelligencer*, March 25, 1903, 5, for the list of "coffeehouses." The immigrants included, for example, Ciukus and Shiligusky at 4421 Jacob Street, John Prezelenski at 4504 Jacob Street, August Dueker at Twenty-Sixth and Chapline Street (used as a German and trade union hall), and Agnic and Visnich at 2514 Main Street.
90. *Morning Herald* (Baltimore), December 13, 1898, 4; *National Labor Tribune*,

August 21, 1902, 5; Rose, "The Committee of One Hundred," 6; *Wheeling Daily Intelligencer*, April 30, 1902, 5.

91. The subject of early twentieth century vice and the various moral reform movements against them have attracted a long interest for scholars of Progressive Era reform. See Zane L. Miller, *Boss Cox's Cincinnati: Urban Politics in the Progressive Era* (New York: Oxford University Press, 1968); Ruth Rosen, *The Lost Sisterhood: Prostitution in America, 1900–1918* (Baltimore: Johns Hopkins University Press, 1982); Paul S. Boyer, *Urban Masses and Moral Order in America, 1820–1920* (Cambridge, MA: Harvard University Press, 1978); for New York City, see Michael A. Lerner, *Dry Manhattan: Prohibition in New York City* (Cambridge, MA: Harvard University Press, 2007), 23–24.

92. Michael J. Buseman, "Vending Vice: The Rise and Fall of West Virginia State Prohibition, 1852–1934" (PhD diss., West Virginia University, 2012), ch. 4; John Alexander Williams, *West Virginia and the Captains of Industry* (Morgantown: West Virginia University Press, 2002), 210; *Wheeling Daily Intelligencer*, February 1, 1901; *Wheeling Daily Intelligencer*, February 24, 1903, 1; April 29, 1902, 8; April 30, 1902, 5.

93. Hearing, Indictments, *State v. Hofreuter, Eberhard*, November 16, 1902, Ohio County Criminal Court, envelope 384E-1, OHI 781; *State v. Driehorst, L. C.*, November 16, 1902, Ohio County Criminal Court, envelope 384E-7; *State v. Przelenski, John*, March 23, 1902, February 26, 1901, March 1, 1901, Ohio County Criminal Court, envelope 384E-7, Ohio County Court Records, Ohio County, WV, A&M 31, WVRHC.

94. For surveillance of saloons in New York, see Czitrom, *New York Exposed*, 15, 114–15; Lerner, *Dry Manhattan*, 22–27. For Worcester, Massachusetts, see Rosenzweig, *Eight Hours for What We Will*, 94–101, 117–26. Further instances of surveillance of Wheeling's immigrants are discussed in chapters 5, 6, and 8.

95. *Wheeling Daily Intelligencer*, November 3, 1903, 3; *Wheeling Intelligencer*, December 26, 1905, 3.

96. *Wheeling Intelligencer*, December 26, 1905, 2; December 18, 1905, 12; *Wheeling Register*, February 14, 1908, 8; *Wheeling Daily Intelligencer*, November 3, 1903, 4.

97. Indictments, *State v. Christos, George*; *State v. Horatagis, Angelo*; *State v. Markis, Pete*, July 11, 1917, Ohio County Court Records, envelope 400A-3, OHI 789, Ohio County Court Records, A&M 31, WVRHC; *Wheeling Daily News*, July 14, 1913, 4; *Wheeling Intelligencer*, July 12, 1917, 5.

98. *Wheeling Register*, May 15, 1905, 3.

99. *Wheeling Daily Intelligencer*, May 13, 1891, 4; Rose, "The Trial of Alice Bradford," 18.

100. *Wheeling Daily News*, July 29, 1913, 3; Rose, "The Trial of Alice Bradford, 18; *Wheeling Daily Intelligencer*, May 27, 1902, 1; October 7, 1903, 4.

101. *Benwood Enterpriser*, April 15, 1915, 4; May 27, 1915, 4; June 17, 1915, 4; September 23, 1915, 4; October 28, 1915, 4.

102. *Benwood Enterpriser*, December 23, 1915, 2; January 27, 1916, 2; February 10, 1916, 2; *Wheeling Register*, January 26, 1916, 10. For Mike Kostolich's confectionery at 352 Market Street in North Benwood, see 1920 Manuscript Census, Benwood, Marshall County, West Virginia, First Ward, Ancestry.com.

103. David R. Roediger, *Working Toward Whiteness: How America's Immigrants Became White, the Strange Journey from Ellis Island to the Suburbs* (New York: Basic Books, 2005), 37–39, 41–43.

104. David Brody, *Steelworkers in America: The Nonunion Era* (New York: Harper

Torchbooks, 1969), 120–21; James R. Barrett and David Roediger, "In-between Peoples: Race, Nationality and the 'New Immigrant' Working Class," *Journal of American Ethnic History* 16 (Spring 1997): quotes 7, 16.
105. *Wheeling Intelligencer*, August 20, 1906, 2; *Wheeling Daily Intelligencer*, September 21, 1903, 6. The creation of the Polish Catholic parish will be the focus of chapter 3.
106. Barrett and Roediger, "In-between Peoples," 15–16; *Wheeling Daily Intelligencer*, March 3, 1903, 3.
107. *Wheeling Daily Intelligencer*, March 17, 1903, 1; April 3, 1903, 3.
108. *Wheeling Register*, January 17, 1906, 8; *Wheeling Daily Intelligencer*, October 15, 1903, 2.
109. *Wheeling Intelligencer*, January 17, 1906, 3. While they would add more to the narrative, there are few examples of Polish immigrant voices in the newspapers at this time.
110. J. W. Werninger, "Defense of the Foreign Element," *Wheeling Register*, January 22, 1906, 4.

CHAPTER 3

1. Sean Duffy and James Thornton, *The Wheeling Family: A Celebration of Immigrants and Their Neighborhoods* (Wheeling, WV: Creative Impressions, 2008), 146–47, 157–60; Mary Martinkosky, interview by author, August 10, 2008.
2. Robert Anthony Orsi, *The Madonna of 115th Street: Faith and Community in Italian Harlem, 1880–1950* (New Haven and London: Yale University Press, 1985), xiii–13. For Polish Catholic practices, see "Wladyslawa, Kosciol Sw.," in *Memories of a Church Still Loved: St. Ladislaus Catholic Church*, in *Parish History File, Wheeling, WV, St. Ladislaus (1902–1995)*, Archives of the Diocese of Wheeling-Charleston (DWC).
3. Dominic Pacyga, *Polish Immigrants and Industrial Chicago: Workers on the South Side, 1880–1922* (Chicago: University of Chicago Press, 2003), 1–4; 5–6.
4. For the Americanization effort within the Catholic Church at this time, see Jay P. Dolan, *In Search of an American Catholicism: A History of Religion and Culture in Tension* (New York: Oxford University Press, 2002), 90–94, 130–46; James R. Barrett, *The Irish Way: Becoming American in the Multiethnic City* (New York: Penguin Press, 2012), ch. 2; James Barrett and David Roediger, "The Irish and the 'Americanization' of the 'New Immigrants' in the Streets and in the Churches of the Urban United States, 1900–1930," *Journal of American Ethnic History* 24, no. 4 (Summer 2005): 17–26; James M. O'Toole, *The Faithful: A History of Catholics in America* (Cambridge, MA: Harvard University Press, 2008), 94–144.
5. John McGreevy, *Parish Boundaries: The Catholic Encounter with Race in the Twentieth-Century Urban North* (Chicago: University of Chicago Press, 1996), 8–15.
6. Keith Maillard, *The Clarinet Polka* (New York: St. Martin's Press, 2003), 2. Many places used by Maillard in his novel are fictionalized but based around real locations in Wheeling.
7. Unnamed St. Ladislaus Parish history, in *Parish History File, Wheeling, WV, St. Ladislaus (1902–1995), incorporated into St. Alphonsus*, DWC.
8. Evelyn Savidge Sterne, "Bringing Religion into Working-Class History: Parish, Public, and Politics in Providence, 1890–1930," *Social Science History* 24, no. 1 (Spring 2000): 155, 159.

9. Unnamed parish history, *Parish History File, St. Ladislaus*, DWC. For the early mission at Immaculate Conception Parish, see *Wheeling Daily Register*, June 18, 1892, 4; July 4, 1892, 5; August 26, 1893, 5; June 11, 1896, 5. For more on the role of these types of Polish fraternal organizations, see William J. Galush, "Polish Americans and Religion," cited in John J. Bukowczyk, ed., *Polish Americans and Their History: Community, Culture, and Politics* (Pittsburgh: University of Pittsburgh Press, 1996), 83–84.
10. Father Miskiewicz's comments are cited in *Wheeling Daily Register*, June 11, 1896, 5. For the St. Stanislaus Society's role in purchasing the property, see *Church Calendar*, December 1, 1901, 4.
11. Tricia T. Pyne, *Faith in the Mountains: A History of the Diocese of Wheeling-Charleston, 1850–2000* (Eckbolsheim, France: Editions du Signe, 2001), 29. For the anti-Catholic politics of the 1890s, see John Higham, *Strangers in the Land: Patterns of American Nativism, 1860–1925* (New Brunswick, NJ: Rutgers University Press, 1955), ch. 4.
12. John T. McGraw to Governor W. A. MacCorkle, May 8, 1896; MacCorkle to McGraw, May 11, 1896, Box 1, Folder, Jan–June 1896, Bishop Donahue's Correspondence, DWC.
13. Stephen B. Elkins to Bishop Donahue, October 25, 1898, 1898 Box, Folder 5, E, 1898; Elkins to Donahue, July 29, 1900, Box 5, Folder 9, E, 1898, Bishop Donahue's Correspondence, DWC. The first letter is dated 1894.
14. John T. McGraw to Bishop Patrick Donahue, October 28, 1906, Box 24 ("Madz-R"), Folder 2 (Mc 1906), Bishop Patrick J. Donahue Collection, DWC. The diocese's archives have gone through extensive changes since I began this research in 2007. The original sorting of the Bishop Donahue collection was listed as *Bishop Donahue's Correspondence*. As of 2013, his papers are listed as the *Bishop Patrick J. Donahue Collection*. The more recent title will be used for newer materials located after the archives moved and new documents were opened for viewing.
15. Pyne, *Faith in the Mountains*, 29.
16. Executive Committee of Polish Catholic Congress, Chicago, Illinois, to the Archbishops of the Roman Catholic Church in the United States gathered in Washington, DC, November 21, 1901, Bishop Donahue's Correspondence, 1901–1906, DWC. For background on the Polish Catholic Congress and the Polish Independent controversy, see Daniel Buczek, "Equality of Right: Polish American Bishops in the American Hierarchy?" *Polish American Studies* 62, no. 1 (Spring 2005): 9, 11–12; Barrett, *The Irish Way*, 70–71; Victor R. Greene, *For God and Country: The Rise of Polish and Lithuanian Ethnic Consciousness in America, 1860–1910* (Madison: State Historical Society of Wisconsin, 1975), 84, 96, 110, 112–14, 133.
17. Leslie Woodcock Tentler, "On the Margins: The State of American Catholic History," *American Quarterly* 45, no. 1 (March 1993): 106–7.
18. *Diamond Jubilee, Very Rev. Emil Musial, Pastor St. Ladislaus Church, 1901–1951*, in *Parish History File, Wheeling, WV, St. Ladislaus (1902–1995)*, DWC.
19. *Diamond Jubilee, Very Rev. Emil Musial, Pastor St. Ladislaus Church, 1901–1951*, DWC.
20. *Wheeling Intelligencer*, November 22, 1951, DWC.
21. Maillard, *The Clarinet Polka*, 25–26.
22. "Życiorys Wiel. Ks. Prob. Emila Musiała Jubilata 25-Ciolecia Swego Kapłaństwa," in *Pamietnik uroczystosci zlotego jubileusza swiecenn kaplanshich przewielebnego ksiedza*

Emila Musiala, proboszcza parafii Sw. Wladyslawa Krola, Wheeling, W.Va. (Wheeling, WV: 1926), 6, 7, 9, 15, 16, in *Parish History File, Wheeling, WV, St. Ladislaus (1902–1995)*, DWC. This and subsequent passages were translated by the author with the assistance of Donata Blobaum in 2009–2010.

23. *Diamond Jubilee, Very Rev. Emil Musial*, DWC; *"Życiorys Wiel. Ks. Prob. Emila Musiała Jubilata"* (Wheeling, WV: 1926), in *Parish History File, Wheeling, WV, St. Ladislaus (1902–1995)*; "Father Emil Musial," Clergy Record Form, Diocese of Wheeling, August 1944, Deceased Priests Files, DWC.
24. Emil Musial, Detroit, to Right Reverend Bishop, April 27, 1901; Musial to Chancellor Weber from St. Cyril's and Methodius's Seminary, Detroit, June 16, 1901, Bishop Donahue's Correspondence, 1901–1906, DWC.
25. Emil Musial to Father Weber from Polish Seminary, Detroit, September 5, 1901, Bishop Donahue's Correspondence, 1901–1906, DWC.
26. Emil Musial, Detroit, to Rev. Edward Weber, November 1, 1901, Bishop Donahue's Correspondence, 1901–1906, DWC.
27. Legal Statement of Emil Musial signed at Chancellor's Office, Wheeling, WV, November 6, 1901, Bishop Donahue's Correspondence, 1901–1906, DWC. For Musial's ordination at St. Joseph's Cathedral, see *Church Calendar*, December 1, 1901, 1. For laying the cornerstone, see *The Church Calendar*, September 1, 1902, 1, DWC.
28. Rev. Thomas Morys to Bishop Donahue, November 18, 1901, Donahue Folder 5, McF-Mourt, 1901, Bishop Donahue's Correspondence, 1901–1906, DWC.
29. Rev. Thomas Morys to Bishop Donahue, November 18, 1901; Morys to Chancellor Edward Weber, telegram, September 20, 1901, Donahue Folder 5, McF-Mourt, 1901, Bishop Donahue's Correspondence, 1901–1906, DWC.
30. *"Życiorys Wiel. Ks. Prob. Emila Musiała Jubilata 25-Ciolecia Swego Kapłaństwa,"* (Wheeling, WV: 1926), in *Parish History File, Wheeling, WV, St. Ladislaus (1902–1995)*, DWC.
31. Galush, "Polish Americans and Religion," 87–88.
32. *"Życiorys Wiel. Ks. Prob. Emila Musiała Jubilata 25-Ciolecia Swego Kapłaństwa,"* (Wheeling, WV: 1926), in *Parish History File, Wheeling, WV, St. Ladislaus (1902–1995)*, DWC.
33. Jacob Gryczka to Bishop Donahue, January 27, 1903, Donahue Folder 4, GL-GR, 1903; Fr. Joseph Dabrowski to Donahue, January 28, 1903, Donahue Folder 9, DI-DY, 1903, Bishop Donahue's Correspondence, 1901–1906, DWC.
34. Bishop Donahue to Fr. Joseph Dabrowski, January 30, 1903, Donahue Folder 9, DI-DY, 1903, Bishop Donahue's Correspondence, 1901–1906, DWC.
35. Rev. Vitoldus Bukaczkowski to Bishop Donahue, May 26, 1904, Donahue Folder 4, Boy-BU, 1904, Bishop Donahue's Correspondence, 1901–1906, DWC.
36. *Church Calendar*, April–May, 1921, DWC.
37. Emil Musial to Father Weber from Polish Seminary, Detroit, September 5, 1901, Bishop Donahue's Correspondence, 1901–1906; Musial to Right Reverend Bishop P. J. Donahue, Wheeling, February 9, 1906, Box 24, Folder 4, "Mo-My, 1906," Bishop Patrick J. Donahue Collection, Correspondences, DWC.
38. *Church Calendar*, December 1, 1901, 1; January 1, 1902, 3.
39. St. Ladislaus, Baptismal Records, December 22, 1901, to September 2, 1923, Microfilm Roll 10, DWC. Thanks to archivist Jon Erik-Gilot for calling these to my attention.

40. *Church Calendar*, September 1, 1904, 2.
41. Rev. William J. Sauer, Chester, to Rev. Edward Weber, Chancellor, Wheeling, March 10, 1904, Box 18, "P-Z, 1904," Folder 5, "Sa-Sc, 1904," Bishop Patrick J. Donahue Collection, Correspondences, DWC.
42. Rev. William J. Sauer, Chester, to Rev. Edward Weber, Chancellor, Wheeling, March 10, 1904, Box 18, "P-Z, 1904," Folder 5, "Sa-Sc, 1904," Bishop Patrick J. Donahue Collection, Correspondences, DWC; Rev.William J. Sauer to Rev. Edward E. Weber, March 22, 1906, Box 1906, Folder 1, "SA, 1906," Bishop Patrick J. Donahue Collection, Correspondences, DWC.
43. William Sauer to Rev. Edward Weber, Chancellor, March 12, 1904, Box 18, "P-Z, 1904," Folder 5, "Sa-Sc, 1904," Bishop Patrick J. Donahue Collection, Correspondences, DWC.
44. William Sauer to Rev. Edward Weber, April 11, 1907, Box 1907, Folder "S-1907," Bishop Patrick J. Donahue Collection, Correspondences, DWC.
45. *75th Anniversary Book, 1911–1986, Sacred Heart of Mary Parish, Weirton, West Virginia*, 1, Sacred Heart of Mary Parish, Weirton, West Virginia Parish History File, DWC; *Church Calendar*, November 1920, 11.
46. *Wheeling Intelligencer*, November 22, 1951.
47. *Pamietnik uroczystosci zlotego jubileusza swiecenn kaplanshich przewielebnego dsiedza Emila Musiala, proboszcza parafii Sw. Wladyslawa Krola, Wheeling, W.Va.* (Wheeling, WV: 1926), in Parish History File, Wheeling, WV, St. Ladislaus (1902–1995), DWC.
48. For debates on ethnic intraparish conflicts, see Evelyn Savidge Sterne, *Ballots and Bibles: Ethnic Politics and the Catholic Church in Providence* (Ithaca, NY: Cornell University Press, 2003), 111–31; Leslie Woodcock Tentler, *Seasons of Grace: A History of the Catholic Archdiocese of Detroit* (Detroit: Wayne State University Press, 1992), 137–65.
49. *Church Calendar*, March 1, 1903, 1; *Wheeling Intelligencer*, February 23, 1903. It is difficult to know who were members of these specific Polish societies, but based on the evidence it is fair to assume they were mostly living in South and Center Wheeling.
50. "List of Debts and Liabilities of St. Ladislaus Church, Wheeling, W.Va., Rev. Emil Musial, Pastor," December 31, 1902, Bishop Donahue's Correspondence, 1901–1906, DWC.
51. Unnamed Polish American of St. Ladislaus Church, interview by Michael Kline, October 31, 1994, in "Pierogi Making at St. Lad's," transcript, Wheeling Spoken History Project, Ohio County Library (hereafter OCPL), http://wheeling.weirton.lib.wv.us/history/wahp/other/96-021.htm.
52. Contract Fahey Brothers to Bishop Donahue, May 22, 1902, Bishop Donahue's Correspondence, 1901–1906, DWC.
53. Chancellor Weber to Emil Musial, September 10, 1902, Bishop Donahue's Correspondence, 1901–1906, DWC.
54. Chancellor Weber to Emil Musial, April 27, 1904, Bishop Donahue's Correspondence, 1901–1906, DWC.
55. His debts cannot be calculated since the diocese lacks the 1900–1910 *Annual Reports* for Wheeling parishes.
56. Emil Musial to Chancellor's Office, March 8, 1905, Bishop Donahue's Correspondence, 1901–1906, DWC.

57. Bishop Donahue to Rev. Emil Musial, February 9, 1906, Bishop Donahue's Correspondence, 1901–1906, DWC.
58. Musial's dispute with Bishop Donahue was not uncommon for the time. The most extreme example occurred in 1885 when the bishop of Detroit ousted Fr. Dominic Kolasinski at St. Albertus Parish for poor financial accounting. The move led to acts of violence and direct confrontation until his reinstatement. See Barrett, *The Irish Way*, 70; Leslie Tentler, "Who Is the Church? Conflict in a Polish Immigrant Parish in Late Nineteenth-Century Detroit," *Comparative Studies in Society and History* 25, no. 2 (April 1983): 241–76. For other examples of this trend, see Jay Dolan, *The Immigrant Church: New York's Irish and German Catholics, 1815–1865* (Baltimore: Johns Hopkins University Press, 1975), 87–98; Anthony J. Kuzniewski, *Faith and Fatherland: The Polish Church War in Wisconsin, 1896–1918* (South Bend, IN: University of Notre Dame Press, 1980), 47–48, 62.
59. For Italian Catholic seasonal processions, see Orsi, *The Madonna of 115th Street*, 6–8. The late nineteenth and early twentieth centuries were still a time when popular politics were expressed and mobilized in a "politics of the streets." Catholic processions thus served a cultural and a subtle political purpose as well. For the "politics of the streets," see Simon Newman, *Parades and the Politics of the Street: Festive Culture in the Early American Republic* (Philadelphia: University of Pennsylvania Press, 1997), 3–10; for the role of public space and how rapid immigration fostered new types of public display by both men and women in urban areas, see Mary P. Ryan, *Civic Wars: Democracy and Public Life in the American City during the Nineteenth Century* (Berkeley: University of California Press, 1997), 57, 124, 248.
60. Delores Skrzypek, interview by Michael Kline, October 31, 1994, OCPL. I did not find any instances of May processions in Wheeling being done in conjunction with May Day parades by the Socialist Party, as seen in larger cities. However, as in other communities, Wheeling's Catholics would have understood that May 1 was increasingly associated with International Labor Day. For more about the role of the May processions' anti-Socialist context, see Donna Haverty-Stacke, *America's Forgotten Holiday: May Day and Nationalism, 1867–1960* (New York: New York University Press, 2009), 95–96.
61. *Wheeling Register*, May 6, 1905, 7; Pacyga, *Polish Immigrants and Industrial Chicago*, 138–40.
62. *Wheeling Daily Intelligencer*, September 16, 1903, 4.
63. *Wheeling Register*, January 18, 1905, 9; *Wheeling Daily News*, May 7, 1906, 8.
64. Much of this scholarship has focused on Catholic laywomen's roles in diocesan and other Progressive Era reform movements. See, for example, Deborah A. Skok, "The Historiography of Catholic Laywomen and Progressive Era Reform," *U.S. Catholic Historian* 26, no. 1 (Winter 2008): 3–6; Mary J. Oates, *The Catholic Philanthropic Tradition in America* (Bloomington: Indiana University Press, 1995); Maureen Fitzgerald, *Habits of Compassion: Irish Catholic Nuns and the Origins of New York's Welfare System, 1830–1920* (Urbana: University of Illinois Press, 2006); Deborah A. Skok, *More than Neighbors: Catholic Settlements and Day Nurseries in Chicago, 1893–1930* (Dekalb: Northern Illinois University Press, 2007). For laywomen's autonomy at the parish level, see Sterne, *Ballots and Bibles*, 132–52; Sarah Deutsch, *Women and the City: Gender, Space, and Power in Boston, 1870–1940* (New York: Oxford University Press, 2002), 40–42; Mary Lethert Wingerd, *Claiming the City:*

Politics, Faith, and the Power of Place in St. Paul (Ithaca. NY: Cornell University Press, 2001).
65. "*Czescl Pozdrowienie Wielebnemu Ksiedzu Jubilatowi*," in *Pamietnik uroczystosci zlotego jubileusza swiecenn kaplanshich przewielebnego ksiedza Emila Musiala, proboszcza parafii Sw. Wladyslawa Krola, Wheeling, W.Va.* (Wheeling, WV: 1926), in *Parish History File, Wheeling, WV, St. Ladislaus (1902–1995)*, DWC.
66. Jane Murray, interview by Michael Kline, October 31, 1994, OCPL.
67. *Church Calendar*, July 1, 1904, 3. Frank Templin led the St. Ladislaus Society, and A. Matielewicz led the St. Stanislaus Society.
68. Tentler, *Seasons of Grace*, 211–13; Unnamed Parish History of St. John's in Benwood, 22–23, in *St. John's Parish History File, Benwood, WV*, DWC. For more on the church's stance on birth control, see Leslie Woodcock Tentler, *Catholics and Contraception: An American History* (Ithaca, NY: Cornell University Press, 2004).
69. *Pamietnik uroczystosci zlotego jubileusza swiecenn kaplanshich przewielebnego ksiedza Emila Musiala, proboszcza parafii Sw. Wladyslawa Krola, Wheeling, W.Va.* (Wheeling, WV: 1926), in *Parish History File, Wheeling, WV, St. Ladislaus (1902–1995)*, DWC.
70. *St. Ladislaus Annual Reports*, 1915–1916, DWC.
71. *The Church Calendar*, March 1920, 14–15; Unnamed Parish History, *Parish History File, St. Ladislaus*, DWC.
72. "*Historija Tow. Św. Józefa, Grupa 213 Z.P.R.K.*," in *Pamietnik uroczystosci zlotego jubileusza swiecenn kaplanshich przewielebnego ksiedza Emila Musiala, proboszcza parafii Sw. Wladyslawa Krola, Wheeling, W.Va.* (Wheeling, WV: 1926), 41, in *Parish History File, Wheeling, WV, St. Ladislaus (1902–1995)*, DWC. For Polish immigrant insurance programs and fraternal lodges, see William J. Galush, *For More than Bread: Community and Identity in American Polonia, 1880–1940* (Boulder, CO: East European Monographs, 2006), 45–53.
73. Pacyga, *Polish Immigrants and Industrial Chicago*, 144–46.
74. Delores Skrzypek, interview by Michael Kline, October 31, 1994, OCPL.
75. Unnamed Parish History, *Parish History File, St. Ladislaus*, DWC.
76. Pacyga, *Polish Immigrants and Industrial Chicago*, 154–55.
77. Thomas A. Guglielmo, *White on Arrival: Italians, Race, Color, and Power in Chicago, 1890–1945* (New York: Oxford University Press, 2003), 10.
78. Emil Musial to Chancellor Weber, December 20, 1904, in Bishop Donahue's Correspondence, 1901–1906, DWC.
79. St. Ladislaus Marriage Book, 1902–1908, St. Ladislaus Sacramental Records Collection, DWC.
80. Dolan, *In Search of an American Catholicism*, 90–94, 130–46; Barrett, *The Irish Way*, 59. For St. John's, see *Church Calendar*, October 1906, 5.
81. *Church Calendar*, December 1, 1904, 1; Barrett, *The Irish Way*, 76–89.
82. *Church Calendar*; October 1, 1905, 1; February 1, 1906, 1; January 1907, 1; November 1906, 1.
83. *Church Calendar*, April 1907, 1–2; October 1908, 1.
84. *Church Calendar*, February 1, 1906, 1. James Barrett notes while Protestant and Catholic reformers engaged in similar efforts, Catholics addressed the wider economic and social problems people faced and also tended to not see a difference between deserving and undeserving poor. Barrett, *The Irish Way*, 86–88.
85. *Church Calendar*, January 1907, 1; October 1908, 1; January 1909, 1.
86. October 1910–May 25, 1913, *St. Joseph's Cathedral Announcement Ledgers*,

1898–1918, in Parish History File, *Cathedral of St. Joseph, Wheeling, WV (1828–Present)*, DWC.
87. *Wheeling Telegraph*, January 4, 1913, 2; *Church Calendar*, January 1912, 1.
88. November 16, 1913, *St. Joseph's Cathedral Announcement Ledgers*, in Parish History File, *Cathedral of St. Joseph, Wheeling, WV (1828–Present)*, DWC; *Church Calendar*, January 1907, 5.
89. Tentler, *Seasons of Grace*, 208–9.
90. *Church Calendar*, November 1, 1912, 1–2; *Wheeling Register*, October 13, 1912, 5.
91. Undated speech by Bishop Donahue from 1909, 4, 6–10, Box, B. D. Sermons, etc., 1916–1920, Folder 26, Bishop Donahue's Correspondence, DWC. Donahue included divorce in his speech because of the church's growing concern about birth control, its connections to socialism, and the breakup of the traditional family structure. See Tentler, *Catholic and Contraception*, 20–35.
92. Undated speech by Bishop Donahue from 1909, 18, 36, DWC.
93. State Commission Report of P. J. Donahue, et al., to Governor William E. Glasscock, November 27, 1912, 14–15, Box, Bishop Donahue, Finances-Invoices, 1898–1918, Folder 44, Mining Investigation Kanawha County, 1912, Bishop Donahue's Correspondence, DWC.
94. *Wheeling Register*, May 15, 1905, 9.
95. *Callin's Wheeling City Directory, 1917–1918* (Wheeling, WV: R. L. Polk & Co., 1918), 513; *Callin's Wheeling City Directory, 1919–1920* (Wheeling, WV: R. L. Polk & Co., 1920), 681; *Callin's Wheeling City Directory, 1921–1922* (Wheeling, WV: R. L. Polk & Co., 1921), 938, OCPL.
96. *Callin's Wheeling City Directory, 1917–1918*, 441, 517; *Callin's Wheeling City Directory, 1919–1920*, 614, 686; *Callin's Wheeling City Directory, 1921–1922*, 848, 944; *Polk's Wheeling City Directory, 1928* (Wheeling, WV: R. L. Polk & Co., 1927), OCPL.
97. St. Ladislaus Annual Reports, 1911–1919, DWC.
98. St. Ladislaus Annual Reports, 1916, DWC. Mary Martinkosky confirmed the role of small business owners in the Polish American Club; see interview with Mary Martinkosky, August 10, 2008.
99. *Pamietnik uroczystosci zlotego jubileusza*, 2, 10, 18, 30, 42, 58, St. Ladislaus Parish History File, DWC; *Callin's Wheeling City Directory, 1919–1920*, 1020; *Callin's Wheeling City Directory, 1921–1922*, 771, OCPL.
100. *Pamietnik uroczystosci zlotego jubileusza*, 62, 66, St. Ladislaus Parish History File, DWC.

CHAPTER 4

1. *Wheeling Majority*, July 29, 1915.
2. *Wheeling Majority*, July 29, 1915; coverage in *Wheeling Majority*, August 12, 19, 26, September 2, 16, 1915.
3. *Wheeling Majority*, August 26, 1915; for quote, see *Wheeling Majority*, July 29, 1915.
4. *Wheeling Majority*, July 29, 1915. For the importance of immigrant working class social and recreational spaces, see Roy Rosenzweig, *Eight Hours for What We Will: Workers and Leisure in an Industrial City, 1870–1920* (Cambridge and New York: Cambridge University Press, 1983).

5. James P. McCartin and Joseph A. McCartin, "Working-Class Catholicism: A Call for New Investigations, Dialogue, and Reappraisal," *Labor: Studies in the Working-Class History of the Americas* 4, no. 1 (Spring 2007): 99–110.
6. For the "subculture of opposition," see Richard Jules Oestreicher, *Solidarity and Fragmentation: Working People and Class Consciousness in Detroit, 1875–1900*, 2nd ed. (Urbana: University of Illinois Press, 1989), 61–62.
7. David Montgomery, *Workers' Control in America: Studies in the History of Work, Technology, and Labor Struggles* (Cambridge: Cambridge University Press, 1979), 9–31.
8. Lou Martin, "Working for Independence: The Failure of New Deal Politics in a Rural-Industrial Place" (PhD diss., West Virginia University, 2008), 76–82.
9. *Report of the Commissioner of Labor of the State of West Virginia, 1890–1891* (Charleston: Moses W. Donnally Public Printer, 1891), 41–2, 45–52.
10. *Report State Commissioner of Labor, 1890–1891*, 18.
11. *Report State Commissioner of Labor, 1890–1891*, 64–72.
12. *Report State Commissioner of Labor, 1890–1891*, 64–67, 69–70; *Second Report of the State Commissioner Labor of West Virginia* (Charleston, WV: Moses W. Donnally Public Printer, 1892), 30.
13. *Wheeling Daily Register*, August 31, 1893, 2; September 5, 1893, 6; September 7, 1893, 3.
14. What happened in Wheeling and Benwood was also apparent in the mill towns of Pittsburgh. Following the 1892 Homestead Strike, native-born workers and the wider public increasingly viewed the Eastern European steelworkers with animosity in Homestead, McKeesport, and throughout the region. See Paul Krause, *The Battle for Homestead, 1880–1892: Politics, Culture, and Steel* (Pittsburgh: University of Pittsburgh Press, 1892), 315–328.
15. *Second Report of the State Commissioner Labor, 1892*, 30; *Wheeling Daily Register*, September 15, 1893, 5.
16. *Wheeling Daily Register*, September 19, 1893, 6.
17. For viewing crowd actions as "mobs," see Edward Slavishak, *Bodies of Work: Civic Display and Labor in Industrial Pittsburgh* (Durham, NC: Duke University Press, 2008), 85–86. For reporting on the violence near the Riverside Mills, see *Wheeling Daily Register*, September 19, 1893, 6; September 20, 1893, 8; September 23, 1893, 3; October 3, 1893, 5; *New York Times*, October 4, 1893.
18. For the skilled workers' producerism, see Charles Postel, *The Populist Vision* (New York: Oxford University Press, 2007), 205–42; "Justice," "The Iron and Steel Situation," *Wheeling Register*, October 8, 1893, 12.
19. *Wheeling Register*, October 1, 1893, 5.
20. "A Card from Austrians," *Wheeling Daily Register*, September 22, 1893, 5; "A Card," *Wheeling Daily Register*, September 25, 1893, 6.
21. *Wheeling Daily Register*, November 8, 1893, 6; November 12, 1893, 6; November 9, 1893, 6.
22. Montgomery, *Workers Control in America*, ch. 3–4.
23. Ohio Valley Trades and Labor Assembly, Minute Book No. 1, April 22, 1888, 12–13, Ohio Valley Trades and Labor Assembly Records, A&M 1055, West Virginia and Regional History Center (hereafter OVTLA Records, WVRHC); OVTLA, Minute Book No. 1, May 27, 1888, 22–23, OVTLA Records, WVRHC.
24. Gibson Lamb Cranmer, *History of Wheeling and Ohio County, West Virginia and*

Representative Citizens (1902), 363–64; Henry D. Scott, *Iron and Steel in Wheeling* (Toledo, OH: Caslon Co., 1929), 110–13; Lou Martin, "Causes and Consequences of the 1909–1910 Steel Strike in the Wheeling District" (MA thesis, West Virginia University, 1999), ch. 1–2 and 16–17. Those opening tinplate mills included: Wheeling Corrugating (1894), Martins Ferry Laughlin Mill (1895), and LaBelle Iron Works (1895).

25. U.S. Commissioner of Corporations, *Report on the Steel Industry*, vol. 1 (Washington, DC: Government Printing Office, 1911–1913): 1–8; Cranmer, *History of Wheeling and Ohio County*, 364; Martin, "Causes and Consequences of the 1909–1910 Steel Strike," 20–21.
26. Montgomery, *Workers' Control*, 55–63; *Wheeling Daily Register*, January 23, 1898, 5; January 25, 1898, 2, 4; January 27, 1898, 6; January 28, 1898, 5; January 30, 1898, 5. According to Henry Scott, an average heat was one and a half hours long; see Scott, *Iron and Steel in Wheeling*, 65–66. The workers did go out on strike when the new scale went into effect. Soon the helpers reluctantly returned to work at the reduced scale; see *Wheeling Daily Register*, February 21, 1898, 6; March 8, 1898, 6.
27. *Wheeling Daily Register*, March 17, 1898, 4, 6; March 20, 1898, 5; *Wheeling Daily Intelligencer*, October 1, 1900, 8; November 6, 1900, 3; OVTLA, Minute Book No. 3, October 14, 1900, 47; October 28, 1900, 50; January 13, 1901, 65, OVTLA Records, A&M 1055, WVRHC.
28. Martin, "Causes and Consequences of the 1909–1910 Steel Strike," 27–31; *National Labor Tribune*, August 1, 8, 1901; David Brody, *Steelworkers in America: The Non-Union Era* (1969), 61–66; *Wheeling Daily Intelligencer*, August 10, 1901, 1.
29. *Wheeling Daily Intelligencer*, July 26, 1901, 1; July 27, 1901, 1. The first organized were skilled men from the Riverside plate mill (125 in number); *Wheeling Daily Intelligencer*, July 29, 1901, 2.
30. *Wheeling Daily Intelligencer*, August 15, 1901, 1–2; July 29, 1901, 2; I. V. Barton, State Commissioner of Labor to Governor A. B. White, August 12, 1901, Box 14, Folder 2, A. B. White Papers, A&M 110, WVRHC.
31. *Wheeling Daily Intelligencer*, August 8, 1901, 5; August 12, 1901, 2; August 14, 1901, 1.
32. *Pittsburgh Press*, August 10, 1901, 1; August 13, 1901, 1.
33. *Wheeling Daily Intelligencer*, August 19, 1901, 2; August 21, 1901, 8; August 22, 1901, 5; August 23, 1901, 5; August 24, 1901, 5. S. Kolonksy may be A. Kolinskie living near Forty-Eighth Street; see *Wheeling City Directory, 1901–1902* (Wheeling, WV: W. L. Callin Co., 1901), 351. Fred Warceski is more likely Fred Warsinsky, a tinworker living at 4208 Water Street; see *Wheeling City Directory, 1901–1902* (Wheeling, WV: W. L. Callin Co., 1901), 604, Ancestry.com. John Schlanski was not listed in a close spelling in the city directory or 1900 manuscript census.
34. *Wheeling Daily Intelligencer*, August 24, 1901, 5; August 26, 1901, 2; August 31, 1901, 5.
35. Victor G. Reuther, *The Brothers Reuther and the Story of the UAW: A Memoir* (Boston: Houghton Mifflin Co., 1976), 12; 1900 Manuscript Census, Ohio County, Wheeling, WV, Sixth Ward, WVRHC; *Wheeling City Directory, 1901–1902*, 508.
36. Reuther, *The Brothers Reuther*, 12–14.
37. David Javersak, "Ohio Valley Trades and Labor Assembly, 1882–1915" (PhD diss., West Virginia University, 1977), 206–8; OVTLA, Minute Book No. 1, April 7, 1888, OVTLA Records, A&M 1055, WVRHC; *Wheeling Daily Intelligencer*, July 12, 1897, 5;

August 23, 1897, 5; OVTLA, Minute Book No. 4, February 23, 1902, 23–24; April 13, 1902, 52, OVTLA Records, A&M 1055, WVRHC.

38. For the Republican Party's immigrant strategy, see David J. Tichenor, *Dividing Lines: The Politics of Immigration Control in America* (Princeton, NJ: Princeton University Press, 2002), 74–75, 83; *Wheeling Register*, September 20, 1896, 5; December 13, 1896, 3; December 20, 1896, 3; Riverside Laborer, "A Card," *Wheeling Register*, October 25, 1896, 7. By 1900 there was an obvious drop in naturalizations. In 1896, there were over 400, but in 1900 only 175 naturalized. See *Wheeling Register*, November 2, 1900, 3; November 4, 1900, 8.

39. In 1892, five German Poles registered along with seven Russian Poles. In 1894, fifteen German Poles and six Russian Poles registered; *Declaration of Naturalization: Ohio County, West Virginia, 1889–1896*, WVRHC. For the sample, see *Declarations of Naturalization*, 143, 146–47; *Wheeling Register*, December 26, 1897, 9.

40. James R. Barrett, "Americanization from the Bottom Up: Immigration and the Remaking of the Working Class in the United States, 1880–1930," *Journal of American History* 79, no. 3 (December 1992): 997–98; 1000; Stanislaus A. Blejwas, "Polonia and Politics," cited in John J. Bukowczyk, ed., *Polish Americans and Their History: Community, Culture, and Politics* (Pittsburgh: University of Pittsburgh Press, 1996), 121–51.

41. Charles A. Wingerter, *History of Greater Wheeling and Vicinity: A Chronicle of Progress and a Narrative Account of the Industries, Institutions, and People of the City and Tributary Territory*, vol. 1 (Chicago and New York: The Lewis Publishing Company, 1912), 257–58; Tom Dunham, *Wheeling in the 20th Century* (Bloomington, IN: 1st Books Library, 2003), 23.

42. Manuscript Census Schedules, 1910, Ohio County, WV, WVRHC. The sample size for 1910 included 115 Polish households (29 owned, 77 rented, and 9 unknown) of homes in the Eighth Ward.

43. Edward R. Kantowicz, *Polish American Politics in Chicago, 1888–1940* (Chicago: University of Chicago Press, 1975), 38–42, 49–52; Blejwas, "Polonia and Politics," 132–34.

44. OVTLA, Minute Book No. 3, November 25, 1900, 57, OVTA Records, A&M 1055, WVRHC; *Wheeling Daily Intelligencer*, July 9, 1897; July 27, 1897; Albert Bauer address, OVTLA Minute Book No. 3, January 13, 1901, 65, OVTLA Records, A&M 1055, WVRHC. For Debs's role in the early formation of the Social Democracy in Wheeling, see Fred Barkey, *Working Class Radicals: The Socialist Party in West Virginia, 1898–1920* (Morgantown: West Virginia University Press, 2012), 8–10.

45. OVTLA, Minute Book No. 3, May 13, 1901, 101; April 28, 1901, 95–99; OVTLA, Minute Book No. 4, March 23, 1902, OVTLA Records, A&M 1055, WVRHC; Frederick Allan Barkey, "The Socialist Party in West Virginia from 1898 to 1920: A Study in Working Class Radicalism" (PhD diss., University of Pittsburgh, 1971), 13–20, 242.

46. OVTLA, Minute Book No. 4, June 3, 1903, 177; OVTLA, Minute Book No. 4, April 12, 1903, 162–63, OVTLA Records, A&M 1055, WVRHC; *Wheeling Register*, August 7, 1903, 2; August 8, 1903, 5; August 14, 1903, 3; August 16, 1903, 1; August 18, 1903, 5, 9. Various organizing efforts raised substantial strike funds through the summer and fall of 1903; see OVTLA, Minute Book, October 11, 1903, 200, 203; October 25, 1903, 209; November 8, 1903, 210–11, OVTLA Records, A&M 1055, WVRHC.

47. *Wheeling Register*, August 19, 1903, 9; August 21, 1903, 4; August 22, 1903, 4.
48. *Wheeling Register*, April 9, 1906, 1; April 16, 1906, 3; May 6, 1906, 15; May 13, 1906, 16; May 30, 1906, 5. For the Supreme Court case, see *Hitchman Coal & Coke Co. v. Mitchell*, 245 U.S. 229 (1917).
49. Barkey, *Working Class Radicals*, 45–46; Javersak, "The Ohio Valley Trades and Labor Assembly," 110–12.
50. *Wheeling Majority*, December 30, 1909.
51. Barkey, *Working Class Radicals*, 90; OVTLA, Minute Book No. 6, January 9, 1910, 107, OVTLA Records, A&M 1055, WVRHC; Brody, *Steelworkers in America*, 71–72; Martin, "Causes and Consequences," ch. 3, 47–49, 58–59. See *Wheeling Intelligencer*, August 30, 1909, for Eagan incident; for quote, see *Wheeling Majority*, December 16, 1909.
52. Reuther, *The Brothers Reuther*, 12–31; *Wheeling Majority*, January 20, 1910.
53. Barkey, *Working Class Radicals*, 78–79; 105–7.
54. Brody, *Steelworkers in America*, 113–14; Martin, "Causes and Consequences," 55–58.
55. *Wheeling Board of Trade Yearbook for 1911* (Wheeling, WV: Secretary's Office, 1911), 18–21, WVRHC.
56. *Wheeling Board of Trade Yearbook for 1911*, 7, 17.
57. *Wheeling Majority*, March 3, 1910; February 24, 1910.
58. *Wheeling Majority*, February 24, 1910; March 3, 1910.
59. *Wheeling Majority*, July 28, 1910; September 8, 1910.
60. A sample of household heads for Ritchie district's Seventh and Eighth Precincts highlight the ethnic diversity in 1910. In the Seventhth Precinct ethnic household breakdown (N = 236) was as follows: Native U.S. (23.3 percent), German (36.4 percent), Polish (25 percent), English (4.2 percent), Irish (3.8 percent), Ruthenian (3.4 percent), and other ethnicities (3.8 percent). The Eighth Precinct ethnic household breakdown (N = 280) was as follows: German (36.1 percent), Native U.S. (28.6 percent), Polish (21.4 percent), Irish (5.7 percent), French (2.5 percent), English (1.8 percent), and other ethnicities (3.9 percent). Manuscript Census Schedules, 1910, Ohio County, WV, WVRHC.
61. *Wheeling Majority*, December 8, 1910; Meeting Minutes, Local Branch of the Fifth and Sixth Ward Socialist Party, March 21, April 25, 1911, 33, 36, Minute Book, 1910–1911, Ms 2007-006, Wheeling Socialist Party Collection, 1904–1918, West Virginia State Archives, Charleston, WV (WVSA).
62. In 1907 there were twenty-two saloons from Thirty-Third to Forty-Eighth Streets. Over half were run by German patrons, five by Irishmen, and two (John Przelenski and Paul Rudzinski) by Poles. The Polish saloons were located less than a block from St. Ladislaus. *Callin's Wheeling City Directory, 1907–1909* (Wheeling, WV: R. L. Polk & Co., 1907), 526, 740; *Callin's Wheeling City Directory, 1911–1912* (Wheeling: R. L. Polk & Co., 1911), 202, 806, 520, 818.
63. *Wheeling Majority*, January 5, 1911; February 9, 1911; May 11, 1911. There is no membership list for the Polish local itself, as the collection mostly includes correspondence of the Ohio County Party and ward branches. See, MM, Local Branch of the Fifth and Sixth Ward Socialist Party, May 4, 1911, 37, Minute Book 1910–1911, Ms 2007-006, Wheeling Socialist Collection, WVSA.
64. *Wheeling Majority*, July 13, 1911; January 11, 1912; February 15, 1912.
65. Ken Fones-Wolf, *Glass Towns: Industry, Labor, and Political Economy in Appalachia*,

1890–1930s (Urbana and Chicago: University of Illinois Press, 2007), 119–20, 217; Mark Wahlgren Summers, *Party Games: Getting, Keeping, and Using Power in Gilded Age Politics* (Chapel Hill: University of North Carolina Press, 2004), ch. 11.
66. Shelton Stromquist, *Reinventing "The People": The Progressive Movement, the Class Problem, and the Origins of Modern Liberalism* (Urbana and Chicago: University of Illinois Press, 2006), 57–58.
67. *Wheeling Register*, November 2, 1910; November 3, 1910.
68. *Wheeling Register*, November 5, 1910.
69. *Wheeling Register*, May 11, 1909; May 12, 1909; May 23, 1909.
70. *Wheeling Intelligencer*, November 8, 1912. The poor record keeping of the 1912 elections limits any calculation of relative percentages for each party for Ritchie district.
71. Quote in undated speech by Bishop Donahue from 1909, 8–9, Box, B. D. Sermons, etc., 1916–1920, Folder 26, Bishop Donahue's Correspondence, Archives of the Diocese of Wheeling-Charleston (DWC).
72. Jay P. Dolan, *In Search of an American Catholicism: A History of Religion and Culture in Tension* (New York: Oxford University Press, 2002), 90–94, 130–46.
73. *Wheeling Majority*, July 29, 1915.
74. *Wheeling Majority*, August 12, 1915; August 19, 1915.
75. Barrett, "Americanization from the Bottom Up," 997–99; Rosenzweig, *Eight Hours for What We Will*, 65–90; Oestreicher, *Solidarity and Fragmentation*, 30–67, 172–214.
76. *Wheeling Majority*, March 13, 1913, 8.
77. March 6, 1890, Meeting Minutes, Tobacco Workers' Union, Minutes, Local 2 (Wheeling, WV), 1890–1905, A&M 1280, WVRHC; *Building Blochs: The Monthly Bulletin of the Bloch Brothers Tobacco Company*, Wheeling, WV, vol. 3, no. 5, July–August 1954; "An Original West Virginia Product," *The West Virginia Review* (September 1930).
78. *Wheeling Majority*, January 23, 1913, 10; February 13, 1913, 1. For the list of beneficiaries, see October 7, 1915, 2; OVTLA, Minute Book, 1914–1916 (Loose Volume), September 12, 1915, 87, OVTLA Records, A&M 1055, WVRHC. For the later lives of the Polish laborers, see *Callin's Wheeling City Directory, 1915–1916* (Wheeling, WV: R. L. Polk & Co., 1915), 738; 1920 Manuscript Census, Wheeling First Ward; Ohio County, WV; "John Szelegowski," Death Index, West Virginia Deaths Index, 1853–1973, Ancestry.com.
79. For debates between socialists and IWW members, see *Wheeling Majority*, April 10, 1913, 1; April 17, 1913, 7.
80. *Wheeling Majority*, April 17, 1913, 1; May 8, 1913, 1; June 12, 1913, 8; September 4, 1913, 8.
81. *Wheeling Register*, July 19, 1914, 13. For the role of the Tobacco Strippers Union, see *Wheeling Majority*, November 13, 1913, 1; OVTLA, Minute Book No. 16, November 5, 1913, 10, and November 12, 1913, 12, OVTLA Records, A&M 1055, WVRHC; *Wheeling Majority*, December 11, 1913, 1.
82. 1910 Manuscript Census, Wheeling Second Ward, Ohio County; *Callin's Wheeling City Directory, 1915–1916*, 110; *Callin's Wheeling City Directory, 1917–1918* (Wheeling, WV: R. L. Polk & Co., 1918), 108, Ancestry.com.
83. For reaching out to Protestant and Catholic clergy, see *Wheeling Majority*, January 1, 1914, 1; January 15, 1914, 1; OVTLA, Minute Book No. 16,

November 30, 1913, 20–21; December 10, 1913, 23; OVTLA Records, A&M 1055, WVRHC; *Wheeling Majority*, January 1, 1914, 8.
84. *Wheeling Majority*, February 12, 1914, 1; OVTLA, Minute Book No. 16, January 14, 1914, 33; January 21, 1914, 34; February 3, 1914, 38–39; February 24, 1914, 47; March 10, 1914, 51, OVTLA Records, A&M 1055, WVRHC. For organizer frustrations, see Barkey, *Working Class Radicals*, 115; OVTLA, Minute Book No. 16, February 17, 1914, 45; March 17, 1914, 52–53, OVTLA Records, A&M 1055, WVRHC.
85. William Galush, *For More than Bread: Community and Identity in American Polonia, 1880–1940* (Boulder, CO: East European Monographs, 2006), 108–112. Frank Ledvinka would lead the eastern Ohio coal strike of 1914–1915 and was a key Polish-speaking union leader in the Ohio Valley; see *Wheeling Telegraph*, January 4, 1913, 2; *Wheeling Majority*, January 2, 1913, 1; January 9, 1913, 1.
86. For all the union events, see *Wheeling Majority*, March 12, 1914, 1; March 19, 1914, 7.
87. OVTLA, Minute Book No. 16, April 14, 1914, 60, OVTLA Records, A&M 1055, WVRHC.
88. President Charles Huggins Report to the OVTLA, January 23, 1916, 2–4, Box 2, Miscellaneous Folder; OVTLA, Minute Book No. 16, Box 3, February 16, 1916; OVTLA, Minute Book, 1914–1916, Loose Volume, July 25, 1915, 80–81; August 8, 1915, 83; August 22, 1915, 85, OVTLA Records, A&M 1055, WVRHC.
89. OVTLA, Minute Book, 1914–1916, Loose Volume, December 26, 1915, 104–5, OVTLA Records, A&M 1055, WVRHC; *Wheeling Majority*, December 9, 1915, 1; December 16, 1915, 7.
90. *Wheeling Majority*, December 16, 1915, 1; December 23, 1915, 1; December 30, 1915, 1; January 20, 1916, 1.
91. *Wheeling Intelligencer*, April 9, 1918; April 12, 1918.

CHAPTER 5

1. Jeanette Keith, *Rich Man's War, Poor Man's Fight: Race, Class, and Power in the Rural South during the First World War* (Chapel Hill: University of North Carolina Press, 2004), 9–11.
2. *Wheeling Intelligencer*, April 9, 1917; April 14, 1917; May 1, 1917; *Benwood Enterpriser*, June 7, 1917, 2.
3. *Wheeling Intelligencer*, April 9, 1917; April 10, 1917.
4. "Poles Pledge Allegiance to United States," *Wheeling Register*, May 7, 1917, 8.
5. "Poles Pledge Allegiance to United States," *Wheeling Register*, May 7, 1917, 8.
6. Gary Gerstle, *American Crucible: Race and Nation in the Twentieth Century* (Princeton, NJ: Princeton University Press, 2001).
7. William J. Galush, *For More than Bread: Community and Identity in American Polonia, 1880–1940* (Boulder, CO: East European Monographs, 2006), 131–32. Poles in Europe also fought in the German, Austrian, and Russian armies. It was not clear that support for the Entente directly translated into support for Poland until after the Bolshevik Revolution and Wilson's Fourteen Points.
8. Wheeling's Polonia presented a counter space to the dominant, conformist Americanization. Here, the forms of resistance are less overt, hidden in ethnic Catholic cultural productions. See James C. Scott, *Domination and the Arts of*

Resistance: Hidden Transcripts (New Haven, CT: Yale University Press, 1990), 19, 43, 111, 117–19, 172–82.
9. John J. Bukowczyk, *And My Children Did Not Know Me: A History of the Polish-Americans* (Bloomington and Indianapolis: Indiana University Press, 1987), 28–33. For coercive Americanization, see David M. Kennedy, *Over Here: The First World War and American Society* (New York: Oxford University Press, 1980), 45–92.
10. *Wheeling Register*, June 2, 1904, 10; *Wheeling Daily News*, July 21, 1909, 4.
11. Galush, *For More than Bread*, 134–36; Victor Greene, *For God and Country: The Rise of Polish and Lithuanian Ethnic Consciousness in America 1860–1910* (Madison: The State Historical Society of Wisconsin, 1975).
12. *Wheeling Intelligencer*, January 1, 1912, 10.
13. *Wheeling Register*, May 8, 1912, 14; July 3, 1912, 8; July 5, 1912, 2. The Polish Soldier's Day Parade included Poles from Wheeling and other surrounding communities.
14. *Wheeling Register*, July 9, 1914, 12. For backgrounds on the leaders, see *Callin's Wheeling City Directory, 1913–1914* (Wheeling, WV: R. L. Polk & Co., 1913), 374; *Callin's Wheeling City Directory, 1915–1916* (W. L. Polk & Co., 1915), 361; Paul Jurzcak, WWI Draft Registration Card, September 1918, Wheeling, WV, Roll 1993025, in *United States Selective Service System Draft Registration Cards, 1917–1918*, NARA, M1509; Anton Cihy, 1920 Manuscript Census, Washington District, Wheeling, Ohio County, WV, roll T625_1967, Enumeration District 120, Tenth Precinct, Fourteenth Census of the United States, 1920; RG 29, Records of the Bureau of the Census, National Archives, Washington, DC, all reprinted via Ancestry.com.
15. "Class Prepares for Citizenship," *Wheeling Register*, July 22, 1914, 5.
16. *Wheeling Register*, August 1, 1914, 6. The Polish nationalist movement in Poland was pro-Russian in 1914.
17. Christopher Capozzola, *Uncle Sam Wants You: World War I and the Making of the Modern American Citizen* (New York: Oxford University Press, 2008), 174–78.
18. John Hennen, *The Americanization of West Virginia: Creating a Modern Industrial State, 1916–1925* (Lexington: University of Kentucky Press, 1995), 3–4, 82–83.
19. Capozzola, *Uncle Sam Wants You*, ch.1, 4; Governor John J. Cornwell, private and confidential circular, December 12, 1917, Box 57, Folder 1, John J. Cornwell Papers, A&M 952, West Virginia and Regional History Center, Morgantown, WV (hereafter WVRHC).
20. Thomas McK. Hearne, "In re: John Schmelgeski, Suspected Espionage-Wheeling, West Virginia," May 23, 27–28, 1918, Bureau of Investigation Case Files, Old German Files, 1909–1921, "John Schemelgeski," 207754, Record Group 65, Records of the Federal Bureau of Investigation, National Archives, College Park, MD, Footnote.com, hereafter "BI, Old German Files." Documents are now available through the Fold 3 database.
21. Thomas McK. Hearne, "In re: Robert Stolz, Espionage-Wheeling, West Virginia," October 12, 1918, BI, Old German Files, "Robert Stolz," 304366, RG 65, NA, Footnote.com.
22. John B. Wilson, "In re: George Gregofsko and Zefia Gregofsko, Alleged Violation of the Espionage Act," May 31, 1918, BI, Old German Files, 1909–21, 208014, RG 65, NA, Footnote.com.
23. Paul Jurczak, WWI Draft Registration Card, Registration Roll 1993025, NARA

microfilm M1509; 1920 Manuscript Census, Wheeling Eighth Ward, Ohio County, WV, Enumeration District 109; *Callin's Wheeling City Directory,1915–1916*, 361; *Callin's Wheeling City Directory, 1917–1918* (Wheeling, WV: R. L. Polk & Co., 1918), 359; *Callin's Wheeling City Directory, 1921–1922* (Wheeling, WV: R. L. Polk & Co., 1922), 676, Ancestry.com; Austin V. Wood, "In re: Registration Matters," January 6, 1919, BI, Old German Files, "Various," 8000–3657, p. 67, RG 65, NA, Fold3.com.

24. Tomas McK. Hearne, "In re: Konstanty Latinski, Disloyalty," August 5, 8, 10, 1918, BI, Old German Files, "Konstanty Latinki," 255735, Roll 699, Page 1–3, RG 65, NA, Fold3.com. For Wojciech Swiader, see 1920 Manuscript Census, Wheeling Eighth Ward, Ohio County, WV, Enumeration District 109; Albert Swiader, WWI Draft Registration Card, 708, Roll 1993025, NARA microfilm M1509; *Callin's Wheeling City Directory, 1921–1922*, 738, Ancestry.com.

25. Capozzola, *Uncle Sam Wants You*, 26–32; John B. Wilson, "In re: Sale of fire arms to foreigners," March 29, 1917, BI, Old German Files, "Various," 8000–3657, RG 65, NA, Fold3.com.

26. Shemek Wnuck, WWI Draft Registration Card, Roll 1993026, NARA, M1509, Ancestry.com; John B. Wilson, "In re: List of men failing to report to City of Wheeling Exemption Board for examination," August 28, 1917, BI, Old German Files, "Various," 202600–50, RG 65, NA, Fold3.com.

27. John B. Wilson, "In re: List of men failing to report," August 28, 1917, "Jon Mozodewsza, Order 336, Serial 1622, Page 25, BI, Old German Files, "Various," 202600–50, M1085, RG 65, NA, Fold3.com; John Mozedwsza, WWI Draft Registration Card, Registration Roll 1992866, NARA microfilm M1509, Ancestry.com; John L. Dickey, Chairman of Local Draft Board, Ohio County, WV, Local Draft Board, March 6, 1919, 47-1-21, Box 93, Final List of Delinquents and Deserters, Record Group 163, Records of the Selective Service System, National Archives and Records Administration, Philadelphia, PA.

28. Ohio County, Local Draft Board, March 5, 1919, 47-1-21; City of Wheeling, WV, Local Draft Board, February 24, 1919, 47-1-32, Box 93, RG 163, NARA, Philadelphia.

29. *Pittsburgh Gazette Times*, August 12, 1917, 45; *Benwood Enterpriser*, August 16, 1917, 2; *Wheeling Register*, July 14, 1918, 3; June 7, 1917.

30. *Wheeling Register*, September 12, 1917, 4; September 21, 1917, 2. Of the fourteen, four failed to report, two were rejected, seven claimed an exemption as aliens, and one more claimed an exemption for his family; later, the city draft board refused exemptions made by thirty-one men, seven of whom were Poles from South Wheeling. See *Wheeling Register*, September 25, 1917, 10.

31. *Benwood Enterpriser*, January 17, 1918, 2.

32. "Placówka Nr. 82 Hallerczyków w Wheeling, W.Va.," in *Pamietnik uroczystosci zlotego jubileusza swiecenn kaplanshich przewielebnego ksiedza Emila Musiala, proboszcza parafii Sw. Wladyslawa Krola, Wheeling, W.Va.* (Wheeling, WV: 1926), 65, 67, in Parish History File, St. Ladislaus, Wheeling, WV (1902–1995), DWC. For Haller's Polish Army, see Stanley R. Pliska, "The 'Polish-American Army' 1917–1921," *The Polish Review* 10, no. 2 (1965): 46–59.

33. For discussion of the pogroms and violence against Ukrainians, see Andrzej Kapiszewski, "Controversial Reports on the Situation of Jews in Poland in the Aftermath of World War I: The Conflict between the US Ambassador in Warsaw Hugh Gibson and American Jewish Leaders," *Studia Judaica* 7 (2004): 257–304. For

the best history of the involvement of ordinary Poles in the violence, see William Hagen, *Anti-Jewish Violence in Poland, 1914–1920* (Cambridge: Cambridge University Press, 2018), 179, 316–17.

34. "*Placówka Nr. 82 Hallerczyków w Wheeling, W.Va.,*" 65, 67, 69; Teofil Lachowicz, *Polish Freedom Fighters on American Soil: Polish Veterans in America from the Revolutionary War to 1939* (Minneapolis, MN: Two Harbors Press, 2011), 183–85.

35. For their background, see vol. 42, p. 362, Form A, and vol. 62, p. 441, Form C, in *Haller's Army Index*, Database, Polish Genealogical Society of America, 2009, http://pgsa.org/haller.php; Jan Miroslaw in New York Passenger Lists, 1820–1957 database, arrival September 21, 1912, New York, New York; Microfilm Serial T715, Roll 1944, p. 169, Passenger and Crew Lists of Vessels Arriving at New York, New York, 1897–1957, Microfilm, RG 85, Records of the Immigration and Naturalization Service, National Archives, Washington, DC; Wladyslaw Zdanowicz, WWI Draft Registration Card, Registration Roll 1993026, NARA, microfilm M1509, all via Ancestry.com; Władysław Zdanowicz, Preliminary Form for Petition for Naturalization, December 8, 1925, Box 2, Folder 11, Record Group 21, Records of the U.S. District Court for the Northern District of West Virginia, NARA, Philadelphia.

36. *Wheeling Register*, November 15, 1917, 5; *Wheeling Daily News*, November 15, 1917, 13.

37. A. Bruce Bielaski to John B. Wilson, Wheeling, November 26, 1917, "In re: Steffen Hoffman," Investigative Case Files of the Bureau of Investigation, 1908–1922, Old German Files, 1909–21, 97142, p. 4, microfilm M1085, RG 65, NA, Fold3.com.

38. Capozzola, *Uncle Sam Wants You*, 188. For German and Austrian "enemy aliens" registering in Wheeling, see *Wheeling Register*, December 8, 1917, 9. The declaration greatly affected the estimated 1,200 Croatian, Hungarian, and Slovak populations of Benwood, whose sovereign was the Austro-Hungarian Empire. See *Wheeling Register*, December 8, 1917, 11; January 17, 1918, 5; January 19, 1918, 10; February 4, 1918, 10; February 7, 1918, 4.

39. For the confusion in recruiting, see Joseph T. Hapak, "Selective Service and Polish Army Recruitment during World War I," *Journal of American Ethnic History* 10, no. 4 (Summer 1991): 41–43; Telegram of Governor John J. Cornwell, November 21, 1917; John B. Wilson, "In re: Steffen Hoffman, Recruiting Poles for French Army," December 2, 1917, BI, Old German Files, 97142, p. 6, 9, M1085, RG 65, NA, Fold3.com.

40. *Wheeling Register*, December 13, 1917, 5; February 26, 1918, 10; February 21, 1918.

41. Jozef Fitz, Preliminary Form for Petition for Naturalization, March 9, 1926, Box 3, Folder 12, RG 21 NARA, Philadelphia.

42. "Address of Right Reverend P.J. Donahue to the Graduates of Mount de Chantal," June 6, 1917, Bishop Patrick J. Donahue Speeches and Sermons, Miscellaneous, Series V, Folder 24, Bishop Patrick J. Donahue Collection, Archives of the Diocese of Wheeling-Charleston (DWC).

43. *Benwood Enterpriser*, September 20, 1917, 2. Benwood continued to see many immigrant men go off to Camp Petersburg or Camp Lee in Virginia; see *Benwood Enterpriser*, March 28, 1918, 2; April 4, 1918, 2.

44. Konstantz Vendlinski, Military Petition for Naturalization, April 11, 1919, Washington, DC, No. 3172, Military Petitions for Naturalization, 1918–1924, ARC

6051621, RG 21, NARA, Washington, DC, Ancestry.com; Peter Templin, 1920 Manuscript Census, Wheeling Eighth Ward, Ohio County, WV, Enumeration District 109; Peter Templin, WWI Draft Registration Card, No. 24, Union Precinct, Marshall County, West Virginia, Roll 1992732, M1509, Ancestry.com. Background on the men of Battery F was gathered using United States Selective Service System, *World War I Selective Service System Draft Registration Cards, 1917–1918* (Washington, DC: NARA), M1509, Ohio County, WV, Roll 1993024, via Ancestry .com. For the 314th Field Artillery, see Linda Cunningham Fluharty, "History of 314th Field Artillery," and "Memories of Battery F," available at http://www .wvgenweb.org/marshall/314/314th.htm.

45. Fluharty, "History of 314th Field Artillery" and "War Diary, 314th Field Artillery," available at http://www.wvgenweb.org/marshall/314/314th.htm and http://www .wvgenweb.org/marshall/314/314-diary.txt. For a history of the Eightieth Division that somewhat discusses the role of local Wheeling soliders, see *Wheeling Intelligencer*, May 28, 1919, 10–11; for the 314th Artillery's role in the late 1918 campaigns, see Jennifer D. Keene, *Doughboys: The Great War, and the Remaking of America* (Baltimore: Johns Hopkins University Press, 2003), 3–4, 43–44.
46. Evelyn Savidge Sterne, *Ballots and Bibles: Ethnic Politics and the Catholic Church in Providence* (Ithaca, NY: Cornell University Press, 2004), ch. 5, quote on p. 141.
47. Paula Kane, *Separatism and Subculture: Boston Catholicism, 1900–1920* (Chapel Hill: University of North Carolina Press, 1994), 3; James R. Barrett and David Roediger, "The Irish and the 'Americanization' of the 'New Immigrants' in the Streets and in the Churches of the Urban United States, 1900–1930," *Journal of American Ethnic History* (Summer 2005): 5–7.
48. For quotes from the NCWC Handbook, see Evelyn Sterne, *Ballots and Bibles*, 159.
49. Sterne, *Ballots and Bibles*, 158–61; Rev. Henry T. Drumgoole, Chairman of Committee on Historical Record of Catholic War Activities to Rev. Edward E. Weber, Chancellor, Wheeling, July 18, 1918, Records of the Chancery—Chancellor's Office, Administrative Records, General Correspondence Files, Box 23, Folder 3, DWC.
50. Jay P. Dolan, *The American Catholic Experience: A History from Colonial Times to the Present* (Garden City, NY: Doubleday & Company, 1985), 294–303; *Church Calendar*, March 1917, 8.
51. *Church Calendar*, April 1917, 6.
52. *Church Calendar*, May 1917, 1.
53. *Church Calendar*, May 1917, 8. For the growth of parish lay societies at St. John's, see St. John's Parish History in *St. John's Parish History File (Benwood, West Virginia)*, DWC.
54. *Church Calendar*, May 1917, 8; Sterne, *Ballots and Bibles*, 153–73.
55. Sterne, *Ballots and Bibles*, 148.
56. Sterne, *Ballots and Bibles*, 132–52; Gary Gerstle, "Liberty, Coercion, and the Making of Americans," *Journal of American History* 84, no. 2 (Sept. 1997): 525–27; Lizabeth Cohen, *Making a New Deal: Industrial Workers in Chicago, 1919–1939* (Cambridge: Cambridge University Press, 1990), ch. 2–3.
57. *Church Calendar*, July 1917, 8; *Benwood Enterpriser*, June 21, 1917, 4.
58. *Church Calendar*, July 1917, 8; Sterne, *Ballots and Bibles*, ch. 8.
59. *Church Calendar*, October 1917, 1, 5. See Sterne, *Ballots and Bibles*, ch. 7–8 for role of interdiocesan committees.

60. *Wheeling Register*, October 21, 1917, 1; *The Church Calendar*, October 1918, 11. Wheeling organizers followed a similar pattern for the third Liberty loan campaign in April 1918. Each major immigrant group's collection efforts were led by middle-class leaders in the ethnic community. For the Poles, the city was divided in half, with Dr. M. Gaydosh taking north of Wheeling Creek and Fr. Emil Musial organizing the efforts south of the creek. See *Wheeling Register*, April 10, 1918, 14. The ninety-three men that served from St. Ladislaus was fourth overall for the entire West Virginia Diocese; see "Number of Men in Service" by Parishes Reporting, in Chancellor's Office: Administrative Records, General Correspondence Files, Box 23, Folder 3, DWC.
61. *Wheeling Intelligencer*, October 19, 1917, 1, 12.
62. *Wheeling Register*, May 1, 1918, 11; May 11, 1918, 12; *Benwood Enterpriser*, May 16, 1918, 2; May 2, 1918, 2.
63. *Wheeling Intelligencer*, April 8, 1918, 3.
64. *Wheeling Intelligencer*, June 25, 1918, 5; *Wheeling Intelligencer*, July 4, 1918, 4.
65. *Wheeling Register*, July 5, 1918, 11; June 27, 1918, 9; June 28, 1918, 2.
66. *Wheeling Register*, July 2, 1918, 2.
67. *Wheeling Register*, July 5, 1918, 11.
68. *Wheeling Intelligencer*, July 5, 1918, 4; *Wheeling Register*, July 5, 1918, 11; *Callin's Wheeling City Directory, 1917–1918* (Wheeling, WV: W. L. Callin, Co., 1917), 568, 724.
69. *Wheeling Intelligencer*, July 5, 1918, 5.
70. *Church Calendar*, December 1917, 1.
71. *Church Calendar*, December 1917, 1; *Church Calendar*, June 1918, 1, 3.
72. *Church Calendar*, December 1917, 3.
73. *Church Calendar*, December 1917, 3.
74. *Church Calendar*, October 1917, 7.
75. Cohen, *Making a New Deal*, 161, 174.
76. *Church Calendar*, December 1917, 3; *75th Anniversary Book, 1911–1986, Sacred Heart of Mary Parish, Weirton, West Virginia*, Sacred Heart of Mary Parish, Weirton, West Virginia Parish History File, DWC.
77. *Church Calendar*, February 1918, 1, 4–5; *Church Calendar*, May 1918, 6; *Wheeling Register*, September 19, 1918, 4; September 22, 1918, 1; "Bishop Urges More Coal," *United Mine Workers Journal*, October 15, 1918, 5.
78. *Church Calendar*, October 1918, 11.
79. *Church Calendar*, October 1918, 11; *Church Calendar*, November 1918, 2. Also see Sterne, *Ballots and Bibles*, ch. 7. Background of Polish community members derives from Manuscript Census Schedules, 1920, Ohio County, WVRHC; *Callin's Wheeling City Directory, 1919–1920* (Wheeling, WV: R. L. Polk & Co., 1920).
80. *Church Calendar*, October 1918, 9.
81. "Historya Klubu Polsko-Amerykanskiego Politycznego w Wheeling, W.Va," [History of the Polish-American Political Club in Wheeling, W.Va.], translated by John Mysliwiec from *Pamietnik uroczystosci zlotego jubileusza swiecenn kaplanshich przewielebnego ksiedza Emila Musiala, proboszcza parafii Sw. Wladyslawa Krola, Wheeling, W.Va.* (Wheeling, WV: 1926), 57, in Parish History File, Wheeling, WV, St. Ladislaus (1902–1995), DWC.
82. "Historya Tow. Gwiazda Oswiaty: Grupa 2395 Z.N.P.Z., Fulton, Wheeling, W.Va.," [History of the Educational Star Society: Group 2395 of the Polish National

Alliance from Fulton Wheeling, W.Va.], translated by John Mysliwiec from *Pamietnik uroczystosci zlotego*, 77; *"Historya Towarzystwa Oswiata: Grupa 2353 Zwiazku Nar. Polsk, Benwood, W.Va,"* [History of the Education Society: Group 2353 Polish National Alliance, Benwood, W.Va.], translated by John Mysliwiec from *Pamietnik uroczystosci zlotego*, 71.
83. *Wheeling Intelligencer*, January 21, 1919, 5.

CHAPTER 6

1. Joseph Rasanske, 1900 Manuscript Census, Webster District, Wheeling, Ohio County, WV, Enumeration District 131, Roll 1769, RG 29, Bureau of the Census, Twelfth Census of the United States, 1900, National Archives and Records Administration (hereafter NARA), Washington, DC; Josef Rozanski, New York Passenger Lists, 1820–1957 database, Arrival July 5, 1893, via SS *Obdam*, Rotterdam to New York, New York, Microfilm Serial: M237, Roll 613, p. 24, Passenger Lists of Vessels Arriving at New York, New York, 1820–1897, RG 36, Records of the U.S. Customs Service, NARA, Washington, DC; *Callin's Wheeling City Directory, 1901–1902* (Wheeling, WV: W. L. Callin, 1901), 504; *Callin's Wheeling City Directory, 1903–1904* (Wheeling, WV: R. L. Polk & Co., 1903), 494; *Callin's Wheeling City Directory, 1904–1905* (Wheeling, WV: R. L. Polk & Co., 1904), 543; Jozef Rozanski, World War I Draft Registration Card 5469, Ohio County, WV, Roll 1993025, United States, Selective Service System, World War I Draft Registration Cards, 1917–1918, National Archives, Washington, DC, M1509, Ancestry.com. For Rozanski leading the Labor Day parade in 1906, see Evelyn K. Harris and Frank J. Krebs, *From Humble Beginnings: The West Virginia State Federation of Labor, 1903–1957* (Charleston: West Virginia Labor History Publication Fund, 1960), 317.
2. *Church Calendar*, November 1918, 2; Bishop Patrick Donahue, Miscellaneous Correspondence, Box, 1904–1922, Folder 6, Bishop Patrick J. Donahue Collection, Archives of the Diocese of Wheeling-Charleston (DWC); *Amalgamated Journal*, January 11, 1923, 11.
3. The Interchurch World Movement, *Public Opinion and the Steel Strike of 1919: Supplementary Reports of the Investigators to the Commission of Inquiry* (New York: Harcourt, Brace and Company, 1921), 154–55, 167, 170.
4. For the OVTLA, see Frederick Allan Barkey, "The Socialist Party in West Virginia from 1898–1920: A Study in Working Class Radicalism" (PhD diss., University of Pittsburgh, 1971).
5. James R. Barrett, *The Irish Way: Becoming American in the Multiethnic City* (New York: Penguin Press, 2012), ch. 4.
6. *Amalgamated Journal*, October 23, 1919, 11.
7. *Amalgamated Journal*, December 4, 1919, 11; *Wheeling Majority*, November 27, 1919, 1.
8. David Montgomery, "Nationalism, American Patriotism, and Class Consciousness among Immigrant Workers in the United States in the Epoch of World War I," in *"Struggle a Hard Battle": Essays on Working-Class Immigrants*, ed. Dirk Hoerder (DeKalb: Northern Illinois University Press, 1986).
9. David Brody, *Steelworkers in America: The Nonunion Era* (New York: Harper Torchbooks, 1969), 246–62.

10. Henry Dickerson Scott, *Iron and Steel in Wheeling* (Toledo, OH: Caslon Company, 1929), 160, 162; *Benwood Enterpriser*, April 20, 1916, 2; May 25, 1916, 4.
11. David Brody, *Steelworkers in America*, 214–220; *Amalgamated Journal*, October 3, 1918, 1; September 5, 1918, 18, 28; Joseph McCartin, *Labor's Great War: The Struggle for Industrial Democracy and the Origins of Modern American Labor Relations, 1912–1921* (Chapel Hill: University of North Carolina Press, 1997), 94–119.
12. David Brody, *Labor in Crisis: The Steel Strike of 1919* (Philadelphia: J. B. Lippincott Company, 1965), 61–65, 69–74, 78–81; Scott, *Iron and Steel in Wheeling*, 166–68. For problems in the organizing structure in Chicago, see Lizabeth Cohen, *Making a New Deal: Industrial Workers in Chicago, 1919–1939* (Cambridge: Cambridge University Press, 1990), 38–43; Brody, *Steelworkers in America*, 214, 219, quote on 246.
13. Brody, *Steelworkers in America*, 222–23, quote on 241; McCartin, *Labor's Great War*, 94–119.
14. Brody, *Steelworkers in America*, 221–23; Michael Kazin, *The Populist Persuasion: An American History*, rev. ed. (Ithaca, NY: Cornell University Press, 1998), 69–74; McCartin, *Labor's Great War*, 156–66; *Amalgamated Journal*, October 10, 1918, 18; November 7, 1918, 31; December 4, 1919, 11.
15. Brody, *Steelworkers in America*, 232, 236, quote by Foster on 237, 240.
16. For the list of grievances, see Cohen, *Making a New Deal*, 378, footnote 43.
17. *Amalgamated Journal*, December 5, 1918, 17; December 12, 1918, 18; January 9, 1919, 12. Crescent Lodge #8 was the main local organizing force in the Wheeling District, and it had the proud distinction of being one of the oldest lodges of the Amalgamated Association, created on September 6, 1879.
18. *Wheeling Intelligencer*, December 14, 1918, 11; December 16, 1918, 2; December 19, 1918, 9.
19. *Amalgamated Journal*, May 1, 1919, 5; December 12, 1918, 30; December 19, 1918, 25; February 13, 1919, 3; March 20, 1919, 2, 3; January 2, 1919, 2; April 17, 1919, 29; *Wheeling Majority*, January 2, 1919, 1.
20. *Amalgamated Journal*, February, 6, 1919, 7; April 17, 1919, 29.
21. *Wheeling Intelligencer*, January 17, 1919, 6; January 20, 1919, 10.
22. *Amalgamated Journal*, May 8, 1919, 6, 14; May 22, 1919, 26; June 19, 1919, 6.
23. *Amalgamated Journal*, June 19, 1919, 9, 10; July 17, 1919, 9; July 31, 1919, 14; August 7, 1919, 23, 28, 31.
24. *Amalgamated Journal*, August 7, 1919, 9; September 11, 1919, 32. The new lodges were: Nail City #24 (LaBelle Iron Works), Wheeling Lodge (LaBelle tin mill), Fort Henry (LaBelle tin mill), Mountain State (Wheeling Iron & Steel Co., Benwood), Stogie City (Wheeling Iron & Steel, Belmont Mill, Wheeling), and Victory Lodge (National Tube Works, Benwood).
25. William Z. Foster, *The Great Steel Strike and Its Lessons* (New York: B.W. Huebsch, Inc., 1920), 184–85; *Wheeling Intelligencer*, September 15, 1919, 3; September 16, 1919, 11; September 17, 1919, 2.
26. *Wheeling Intelligencer*, September 22, 1919, 1; September 23, 1919, 1; *Amalgamated Journal*, September 25, 1919, 3; October 2, 1919, 25; October 16, 1919, 18.
27. *Wheeling Intelligencer*, September 22, 1919, 1–2; *Wheeling Majority*, September 18, 1919, 1. Fort Henry Lodge #20 also warned its members that the four daily Wheeling newspapers were printing misleading articles claiming steelworkers

received two hundred to three hundred dollars a week; see *Amalgamated Journal*, August 28, 1919, 32.
28. *Wheeling Intelligencer*, October 20, 1919, 3.
29. *Wheeling Intelligencer*, October 23, 1919, 2; October 27, 1919, 12; October 29, 1919, 2; November 5, 1919, 6.
30. *Wheeling Majority*, November 27, 1919, 1; *Wheeling Intelligencer*, November 10, 1919, 5; November 11, 1919, 9. For the National Committee's relief policies, see Foster, *Great Steel Strike*, 213–22. For the Foster meeting, see F. M. O'Donnell, "In re: William Z. Foster Meeting," November 14, 1919, Bureau of Investigation Case Files, Old German Files, 1909–21, "Various," 315819, Record Group 65, Records of the Federal Bureau of Investigation, National Archives, College Park, MD, Footnote.com.
31. James D. Parriott, Prosecuting Attorney, Moundsville, to Governor John Cornwell, November 29, 1919, Box 110, Folder 4, John J. Cornwell Papers, A&M 952, West Virginia and Regional History Center, West Virginia University, Morgantown, WV (hereafter WVRHC).
32. There are several men named William Wagner in the area around this time. One was a foreman at the Riverside, and two others are listed as millworkers. Based on the evidence and tensions as men were being brought in to break the strike, any of them could be the most plausible person. See *Wheeling Intelligencer*, October 7, 1919, 2; November 29, 1919, 5; *Callin's Wheeling City Directory, 1919–20* (Wheeling: W. L. Polk & Co., 1919), 902; William L. Wagner, 1920 Manuscript Census, Union District, Benwood, Marshall County, WV, Enumeration District 55, Roll T625_1953, NARA, Ancestry.com; *Wheeling News Sunday*, November 30, 1919; Mayor Clark Sprouts, Benwood, to Governor John Cornwell, December 3, 1919; James D. Parriott to Cornwell, November 29, 1919, Box 110, Folder 4, John J. Cornwell Papers, WVRHC.
33. *Wheeling Majority*, December 4, 1919, 1; *New York Times*, December 2, 1919, 3; *Wheeling Register*, December 2, 1919, 1; *Amalgamated Journal*, December 11, 1919, 6; James D. Parriott, telegrams to Governor John Cornwell, December 1, 1919, all in Box 110, Folder 4, John J. Cornwell Papers, WVRHC; John B. Wilson, "In re: Riot at National Tube Company's Plant, Benwood, W.Va.," December 9, 1919, BI, Old German Files, 8000-382434, RG 65, NA, Footnote.com; Governor John Cornwell, telegram to J. D. Parriott, December 4, 1919, Box 110, Folder 4, John J. Cornwell Papers, WVRHC.
34. John B. Wilson, "Riot at National Tube Company's Plant, Benwood, West Virginia," January 2, 1920, BI, Old German Files, 8000-382434, RG 65, NA, Footnote.com; *Wheeling Register*, December 2, 1919, 6. The attempt to link Meharlow to the Union of Russian Workers came after the Palmer Raids in November 1919 targeting the URW. See Beverly Gage, *The Day Wall Street Exploded: A Story of America in Its First Age of Terror* (New York: Oxford University Press, 2009), 120–22.
35. Mayor Clark Sprouts to Governor John Cornwell, December 3, 1919; Cornwell to Sprouts, December 4, 1919; Sprouts to Cornwell, December 6, 1919, Box 110, Folder 4, John J. Cornwell Papers, WVRHC.
36. Cornwell to Clark Sprouts, December 4, 1919, Box 110, Folder 4, John J. Cornwell Papers, WVRHC.
37. Mayor Clark Sprouts to Governor John Cornwell, December 6, 1919; Sprouts to

Cornwell, December 4, 5, and 8, 1919; James D. Parriott to Cornwell, December 6, 1919, Box 110, Folder 4, John J. Cornwell Papers, WVRHC.
38. The *Wheeling Majority* says the service was held at the "Polish Catholic Church," while others suggest it was the Ukrainian church. See *Wheeling Majority*, December 4, 1919, 1, 7; *Wheeling Register*, December 2, 1919, 6; December 4, 1919, 5; December 6, 1919, 5; *Benwood Enterpriser*, December 4, 1919, 2; Matej Mateusz Baron, estate appraisal, filed July 26, 1921, in Ohio County Court, Appraisers Record Book, Ohio County, Book 8, 211, Ohio County Clerk's Office, Ohio County Courthouse, Wheeling, WV (hereafter OCCO).
39. *Wheeling Majority*, December 11, 1919, 12.
40. It is unclear from the press coverage of how the union investigated these claims. See, *Wheeling Register*, December 2, 1919, 6; December 3, 1919, 4–5.
41. Scott, *Iron and Steel in Wheeling*, 168; *Wheeling Register*, December 9, 1919, 4; December 10, 1919, 1, 6; December 11, 1919, 9; December 14, 1919, Section 2, 1.
42. *Amalgamated Journal*, November 20, 1919, 25.
43. Brody, *Steelworkers in America*, 223; quote from *Amalgamated Journal*, January 16, 1919, 14.
44. *Church Calendar*, August 1919, 2; April 1920, 10; July 1920, 22; Fr. P. M. Schoenen to Fr. Edward Weber, November 10, 1919; Schoenen to Weber, March 5, 1920, October 15, 1921, Deceased Priests Files, DWC.
45. P. M. Schoenen to Fr. Edward Weber, January 30, 1922, Deceased Priests File, DWC.
46. Fr. P. M. Schoenen to Father Edward Weber, November 18, 1922; Schoenen to Weber, January 23, 1923, Deceased Priests Files, DWC.
47. St. Ladislaus Parish, Annual Reports, 1917–1924; Financial Reports, 1917–1924, DWC.
48. "Steel Concerns May Merge," *Iron Age*, June 3, 1920, 1633; July 17, 1920, 1747; Scott, *Iron and Steel in Wheeling*, 168–69. Company employment figures derive from Wheeling Steel Corporation, Annual Reports, 1920–1929, Wheeling Jesuit University Library (WJU).
49. Alexander Glass, Chairman Wheeling Steel Corporation, *1921 Annual Report of the Wheeling Steel Corporation, Wheeling, W.Va., For the Year Ended December 31, 1921*, WJU; *Amalgamated Journal*, April 1, 1920, 31.
50. "Wheeling Steel Corporation and Its Safety Program," *West Virginia Review* 7, no. 12 (September 1930): 427; *Wheeling Register*, May 27, 1928, 12; Cohen, *Making a New Deal*, 184, 447–48.
51. *Amalgamated Journal*, January 1, 1920, 27; January 8, 1920, 5.
52. *Amalgamated Journal*, August 19, 1920, 14, 28; September 2, 1920, 13.
53. *Amalgamated Journal*, February 26, 1920, 8; March 4, 1920, 8; March 11, 1920, 7; March 18, 1920, 7.
54. *Amalgamated Journal*, July 29, 1920, 8; October 14, 1920, 7; April 14, 1921, 6; July 21, 1921, 11. Peter Klochan was a Slovak worker at the Riverside blast furnace; see 1920 Manuscript Census, Benwood Second Ward, Marshall County, WV, Enumeration District 57, Roll T625_1953, p. 3B. Kalaska was a Slovak American laborer; see 1930 Manuscript Census, Benwood Fourth Ward, Marshall County, WV, Enumeration District 19, Roll 2543, p. 5A, NARA, Ancestry.com.
55. *Amalgamated Journal*, March 4, 1920; July 29, 1920, 8; April 14, 1921, 8.
56. *Amalgamated Journal*, June 23, 1921, 9. For a history of the breakdown of union

contracts, see the history compiled by Harry Farley of Stogie City #25, *Amalgamated Journal*, February 22, 1923, 16–17.
57. *Amalgamated Journal*, April 17, 1921, 7; May 12, 1921, 31; May 26, 1921, 6.
58. *Amalgamated Journal*, June 9, 1921, 1; *Wheeling Register*, June 4, 1921, 6; June 7, 1921, 5.
59. *Amalgamated Journal*, July 28, 1921, 25; August 18, 1921, 1, 2, 25. The main agents used in Wheeling wrote via pseudonym. They were X58, Z22, and Z125; see *Amalgamated Journal*, October 6, 1921, 29; Ohio Valley Trades and Labor Assembly, Minute Book No. 8, January 8, 1922, Box 2, Folder 2, *Ohio Valley Trades and Labor Assembly Records*, A&M 1055, WVRHC.
60. *Amalgamated Journal*, August 4, 1921, 1, 32; September 1, 1921, 9.
61. *Amalgamated Journal*, August 25, 1921, 13, 25, 28; September 1, 1921, 1. These Poles lived in the vicinity of the Belmont Mill, particularly on the 2600 block of Locust and Main Streets; see Leo Sulek, 1920 Manuscript Census, Wheeling Sixth Ward, Ohio County, WV, Enumeration District 93, Roll T625_1966, Fourteenth Census of the United States, NARA; *Callin's Wheeling City Directory, 1921–1922* (Wheeling, WV: W. L. Callin & Co., 1921), 1175; Alexander Sulek, World War I Draft Registration Card 73, WV, Ohio County, Roll 1993025, NARA, M1509; Wladislaw Swek, WWI Draft Registration Card 122, WV, Ohio County, Roll 1993025, WWI Draft Registration Cards, 1917–1918, NARA, M1509, Ancestry.com.
62. *Amalgamated Journal*, October 13, 1921, 32; October 20, 1921, 13, 17; November 10, 1921, 20.
63. *Amalgamated Journal*, January 15, 1920, 17; Thomas A. Guglielmo, *White on Arrival: Italians, Race, Color, and Power in Chicago, 1890–1945* (New York: Oxford University Press, 2003), 39–58; John Bodnar, Roger Simon, and Michael P. Weber, *Lives of Their Own: Blacks, Italians, and Poles in Pittsburgh, 1900–1960* (Urbana: University of Illinois Press, 1982), 55–88.
64. T. Edward Hill, *Report of Bureau of Negro Welfare and Statistics, 1921–22* (Charleston, WV: Tribune, 1922), 15; Sean Duffy, *The Wheeling Family*, vol. 2, *More Immigrants, Migrants, and Neighborhoods* (Wheeling, WV: James Thornton, 2012), 207–17.
65. *Wheeling Intelligencer*, July 23, 1921, 14; T. Edward Hill, *Report of Negro Welfare and Statistics, 1923–24* (Charleston, WV: Tribune, 1924), 9, 46, 77; *Amalgamated Journal*, February 8, 1923, 3; *Wheeling Register*, September 24, 1923, 5. By September, over two hundred migrants purchased railroad tickets to return to the South.
66. James Bumkin, John Calhoun, and William Collins, Employee Cards, Series 12, Box 1, Employee Cards, Wheeling–La Belle Nail Company records, Archives and Special Collections, Ohio County Public Library, Wheeling, WV. I want to thank Laura Carroll for bringing these to my attention.
67. For policy changes at Wheeling Steel, see Scott, *Iron and Steel in Wheeling*, 173–75; Alexander Glass, Chairman Wheeling Steel Corporation, *1923 Annual Report of the Wheeling Steel Corporation, Wheeling, W.Va., For the Year Ended December 31, 1923*, WJU; Raymond-Lynn Boothe, *Fire on the Water: A New History of the Wheeling Steel Corporation* (Raleigh, NC: Lulu Press, 2011), 112–25. For the union's view on hours, see *Amalgamated Journal*, September 6, 1923, 15; September 20, 1923, 13; September 27, 1923, 13.

68. Frank Buchan, Frank Chelminski, Mike Cichowicz, and Andrew Cichowicz, Employee Cards, Series 12, Box 1, Employee Cards, Wheeling-La Belle Nail Company records, Archives and Special Collections, Ohio County Public Library, Wheeling, WV.
69. *Seventeenth Annual Convention of the West Virginia Federation of Labor*, Wheeling, WV, September 8–13, 1924, 102–3, 253–4; OVTLA, Minute Book No. 9, January 13, 1924, March 23, 1924, April 23, 1924, December 14, 1924, Box 2, Folder 4, *Ohio Valley Trades and Labor Assembly Records*, A&M 1055, WVRHC; *Amalgamated Journal*, December 13, 1923, 2.
70. OVTLA, Minute Book No. 9, April 23, 1924, Box 2, Folder 4, *Ohio Valley Trades and Labor Assembly Records*, A&M 1055, WVRHC; *Amalgamated Journal*, January 18, 1923, 5; August 23, 1923, 18.
71. Joe Rozanski, 1930 Manuscript Census, Wheeling Sixth Ward, Ohio County, WV, Enumeration District 15; *Callin's Wheeling City Directory, 1923–1924* (Wheeling, WV: W .L. Polk & Co., 1923), 829; *Callin's Wheeling City Directory, 1926* (Wheeling, WV: W. L. Polk & Co., 1926), 862; *Callin's Wheeling City Directory, 1928* (Wheeling, WV: W. L. Polk & Co., 1927), 777; *Polk's Wheeling City Directory, 1930* (Pittsburgh: R. L. Polk & Co., 1930), 654; *Polk's Wheeling City Directory, 1932* (Pittsburgh: R. L. Polk & Co., 1932), 602; *Polk's Wheeling City Directory, 1934* (Pittsburgh: R. L. Polk & Co., 1934), 589; Joseph Rosanski, 1940 Manuscript Census, Wheeling Sixth Ward, Ohio County, WV, Enumeration District 35–67, Ancestry.com.
72. Bodnar, Simon, and Weber, *Lives of Their Own*, 93–94, 137, 139, 143.
73. Frances S. Hensley, "Women in the Industrial Work Force in West Virginia, 1880–1945," *West Virginia History* 49 (1990): 118–20, 122.
74. Pasquale DiCesare oral history interview, in Wheeling National Heritage Area Corporation, Final Report, Wheeling Spoken History Project (Wheeling, WV: 1994), 10–11, Wheeling National Heritage Area Corporation Records, Wheeling, WV (hereafter, Wheeling Spoken History); Sean Duffy, *The Wheeling Family*, vol. 2, *More Immigrants, Migrants and Neighborhoods* (Wheeling, WV: James Thornton, 2012), 79.
75. Ethelbert Stewart, Department of Labor, to Secretary of Labor William B. Wilson, October 24, 1918; Report of Mary H. Ely to Department of Labor, October 18, 1918, p. 6, RG 174, General Records of the Department of Labor, Selected Material from Chief Clerk's File No. 20/162, Richard Hadsell Collection, A&M 2122, WVRHC.
76. Report of Mary H. Ely, and supplemental explanation of findings, by Elbert E. Peck, DL; Report of Mary H. Ely, October 18, 1918, p. 7, RG 174, Hadsell Collection, WVRHC.
77. Mary Drosieko, *Arts & Advertising of Bloch Bros. Tobacco Co.: The Nation's Favorite Since 1879* (Wheeling, WV: Creative Impressions, 2002); "An Original West Virginia Product," *The West Virginia Review* (September 1930).
78. John Bodnar, *The Transplanted: A History of Immigrants in Urban America* (Bloomington: Indiana University Press, 1985), 71–83; Suzanne M. Zukowski, "From Peasant to Proletarian: Home Ownership in Milwaukee's Polonia," *Polish American Studies* 66, no. 2 (Autumn 2009): 7–8.
79. For Wheeling banks, see Harry P. Corcoran, "Wheeling Today," *West Virginia Review* 1, no. 5 (February 1924): 20; also see the advertisements published in *Callin's Wheeling City Directory, 1921–1922* (Wheeling, WV: R. L. Polk & Co., 1922), 67–75,

OCPL. For Polish bank assests, see the Appraisers Books, Ohio County Courthouse. For specific examples, see Szyman Kowalski, Appraisers Record, September 5, 1918, Ohio County, Book 6, p. 160; Katherine Zombak, Appraisers Record, July 2, 1922, Ohio County, Book 9, p. 165, OCCO.

80. John Kogut, oral history interview, Wheeling Spoken History Project, 356–57, WNHAC.
81. Louis C. Martin, "Working for Independence: The Failure of New Deal Politics in a Rural-Industrial Place," (PhD diss., West Virginia University, 2008), ch. 4; Duffy, *The Wheeling Family*, 151.
82. *Wheeling Intelligencer*, April 13, 1924, 14; 1930 Manuscript Census, Eighth Ward, Wheeling Ohio County, WV. I did a complete counting of all Eighth Ward households in 1930 led by someone of Polish, Ukrainian, Russian, Lithuanian, Czech, Slovak, or Yugoslavian descent. All total, 54 percent owned, and 46 percent rented.
83. 1920 Manuscript Census, Eighth Ward, Wheeling, Ohio County; Benwood First Ward, Marshall County, WV; 1930 Manuscript Census, Eighth Ward, Wheeling, Ohio County, WV.
84. Of the 125 households sampled, 3 were worth respectively $35,000, $18,825, and $10,000. Their inclusion makes the average price $3,570.08. 1930 Manuscript Census, Wheeling Eighth Ward, Ohio County, WV.
85. *Wheeling Register*, April 16, 1924, Section 2, 10.
86. J. W. Meyers and wife to John Zalewski, personal property agreement (ppa), May 10, 1906, Deed Book 122, 23–24; Hannah Hoeke to Jan Zalewski, et al., ppa, July 12, 1916, Deed Book 153, 85–86; John Zalewski and wife to Bolic Bruzdas, ppa, August 3, 1922, Deed Book 183, 212; John Zalewski and wife to William Joseph Zalewski, ppa, November 29, 1924, Deed Book 197, 564–65, OCCO.
87. Ivan Tribe, *Mountaineer Jamboree: Country Music in West Virginia* (Lexington: University of Kentucky Press, 1984), 43; 1930 Manuscript Census, Wheeling Eighth Ward, Ohio County, WV; Cynthia "D'Accione" Thames, oral history interview, WNHAC Final Report, Wheeling Spoken History Project (Wheeling, WV: 1994), 128–29, WNHAC.
88. John "Jack" Fahey, "40 Years on the B&O," Oral History, June 23, 1994, Wheeling Spoken History Project, transcript via Ohio County Public Library (OCPL).
89. Frank Kruszewski to Wincenty Front, ppa, July 30, 1913, Deed Book 144, 118; Paul Rudzinski to Ada Broski, ppa, November 10, 1915, Deed Book 11, 491, OCCO.
90. John Marchlenski to Adam Kwit, ppa, August 22, 1914, Deed Book 148, 101; Adam Kwit to Aniela Marchlenski, ppa, August 28, 1914, Deed Book 148, 118; Frank O'Brien to John Marchlenski, ppa, September 3, 1914, Deed Book 148, 264; Marchlenski to John Manakosa, et al., ppa, March 10, 1924, Deed Book 192, 523, OCCO.
91. George Zuebel to Stanley Duplaga, ppa, February 18, 1922, Deed Book 180, 572, OCCO; *Polk's Wheeling City Directory, 1923–1924*; *Polk's Wheeling City Directory, 1928*, OCPL.
92. John Bukowczyk, *And My Children Did Not Know Me: A History of the Polish-Americans* (Bloomington: Indiana University Press, 1987), 41–43; 47–50.
93. *Callin's Wheeling City Directory, 1917–1918* (Wheeling, WV: R. L. Polk & Co., 1918), 408; *Callin's Wheeling City Directory, 1919–1920* (Wheeling, WV: R. L. Polk & Co., 1920), 546; *Callin's Wheeling City Directory, 1921–1922*, 753, OCPL.

94. Herman Werfele, interview by the author, July 23, 2008.
95. The following comparison derives from Walter Prask, Declaration of Intention, November 22, 1913, Box 2, Folder 3, Naturalization Case Files, District Court, 1912–1932, RG 21, Records of the U.S. District Court for the Northern District of West Virginia, NARA, Philadelphia; Walter Prask, World War I Draft Registration Card, June 5, 1917, 54, Seventh Precinct, Wheeling City; Walter Prask and Tillie (Lekla) Wisniewska, Marriage License, September 21, 1918, Ohio County, WV; Stanislaus Klos and Aleksandra Wyzykowska, Marriage License, February 17, 1903, Ohio County Marriage Book, 444, West Virginia Vital Records, WVSA; 1910, 1920, and 1930 Manuscript Census, Wheeling Sixth Ward; 1920 Manuscript Census, Wheeling Eighth Ward, Ohio County, WV; *Callin's Wheeling City Directory, 1915–1916* (W. L. Polk & Co., 1915), 382; *Callin's Wheeling City Directory, 1917–1918*, 799; *Callin's Wheeling City Directory, 1919*, 712; *Callin's Wheeling City Directory, 1921–1922*, 711, 1462; *Callin's Wheeling City Directory, 1924*, 586, 787; *Callin's Wheeling City Directory, 1926*, 818; *Wheeling City Directory, 1928*, 542, 738; *Wheeling City Directory, 1930*, 456, 1092; Stanislaus Klos, 1940 Manuscript Census, Wheeling Sixth Ward, Ancestry.com.

CHAPTER 7

1. Albert Swiader, WWI Draft Registration Card, 708, Roll 1993025, World War I Selective Service System Draft Registration Cards, 1917–1918, NARA microfilm M1509; 1920 Manuscript Census, Wheeling Eighth Ward, Ohio County, WV, Enumeration District 109, Roll T625_1967, p. 14A, RG 29, Records of the Bureau of the Census, Fourteenth Census of the United States, National Archives and Records Administration, Washington, DC; *Callin's Wheeling City Directory, 1921–1922* (Wheeling, WV: W. L. Callin & Co., 1921), 1179; Albert Swander, Declaration of Intention, September 8, 1913, Wheeling Division, Naturalization Records, vol. 3, RG 21, Records of the U.S. District Court Northern West Virginia, Declarations of Intention, 1912–1989, NARA, Philadelphia; *Callin's Wheeling City Directory, 1924* (Wheeling: W. L. Callin & Co., 1924), 933; *Callin's Wheeling City Directory, 1926* (Wheeling, WV: W. L. Callin & Co., 1926), 976; *Polk's Wheeling City Directory, 1932* (Pittsburgh: R. L. Polk & Co., 1932), 686; 1930 Manuscript Census, Wheeling, Ohio County, WV, Ancestry.com.
2. For Swiader's role in the community, see *Wheeling Register*, June 2, 1935, Section 1, 4.
3. Lucas Piechowicz, 1920 Manuscript Census, Noble, Noble County, OH; *Callin's Wheeling City Directory, 1924*, 777, Ancestry.com; Lucas Piechowicz, Death Certificate 5191, Ohio County, April 9, 1924, District No. 3501–91, Series No. 368; Jan (John) Piechowicz, Certificate of Death 6402, Marshall County, April 28, 1924, District No. 2671, Series No. 138, West Virginia State Department of Health, Division of Vital Statistics, West Virginia State Archives and History Center, Charleston, WV (hereafter WVSA). I would like to thank Julia Zaccagnini for her excellent family history of the Piechowiczs reprinted at http://www.wvgenweb.org/marshall/piechowiczfam.htm.
4. *Callin's Wheeling City Directory, 1926*, 807; Stanley Piechowicz, Death Certificate 8799, Ohio County, June 26, 1926, District No. 3501–91, Series No. 644, WVSA; *Polk's Wheeling City Directory, 1934* (Pittsburgh: R. L. Polk & Co., 1934), 549. For Andy Piechowicz's music career, see Zaccagnini, "Piechowicz Family" History.

5. Lizabeth Cohen, *Making a New Deal: Industrial Workers in Chicago, 1919–1939* (New York: Cambridge University Press, 1989), 145.
6. *Wheeling Steel Corporation, Annual Reports*, 1920–1929, Wheeling Jesuit University Library; Raymond-Lynn Boothe, *Fire on the Water: A New History of the Wheeling Steel Corporation* (Raleigh, NC: Lulu Press, 2011), 112–25. By 1925, Wheeling Steel was a fully integrated steel corporation with six blast furnaces (Belmont Twenty-Sixth Street, Top Mill, Martins Ferry, Benwood, Portsmouth, and Steubenville); steel rolling mills (Benwood, Top Mill, East Wheeling, Beech Bottom, Martins Ferry, Portsmouth, and Steubenville); coke ovens (East Steubenville and Portsmouth); tin mills (Yorkville and Martins Ferry); corrugated steel (Wheeling Corrugating, East Wheeling); steel cans (Forty-Eighth Street); and abundant coal mines.
7. *Wheeling Intelligencer*, April 29, 1924; May 3, 1924, 1; May 5, 1924, 3; Chief of Department of Mines, R. M. Lambie, "Benwood Mine Disaster: Report on Benwood Explosion," AR1533, reprinted by WVSA http://www.wvculture.org/history/this dayinwvhistory/0428A.html.
8. West Virginia Department of Mines, *Annual Report*, 1923 (Charleston, WV: Jarrett Printing Co., 1923), 209; WVDM, *Annual Report*, 1924 (Charleston, WV: Jarrett Printing Co., 1924), 348–49; Lambie, "Report on Benwood Mine."
9. WVDM, *Annual Report*, 1923, 209; WVDM, *Annual Report*, 1924, 348–49; Lambie, "Report on Benwood Mine"; R. M. Lambie, Chief of Department of Mines, to Governor Ephraim F. Morgan, May 2, 1924; Lambie to Morgan, May 8, 1924, Box 24, Folder 4, Ephraim Morgan Papers, A&M 203, WVRHC.
10. "Benwood Mine Disaster, List of Victims, April 28, 1924, reprinted by WVSA, http://www.wvculture.org/history/disasters/benwood02.html; Sean Duffy, *The Wheeling Family*, vol. 2, *More Immigrants, Migrants and Neighborhoods* (Wheeling, WV: James Thornton, 2012), 255–60.
11. *Wheeling Register*, April 29, 1924; *Wheeling Intelligencer*, April 29, 1924, 1, 2; April 30, 1924, 1; *Wheeling Daily News*, April 29, 1924, 1.
12. *Wheeling Intelligencer*, April 29, 1924, 8; April 30, 1924, 6; May 1, 1924, 2; May 3, 1924, 2; *Wheeling Daily News*, April 29, 1924, 5; May 2, 1924, 1. I rely heavily on the work of Joseph Anthony Tellitocci in documenting the actual names, ethnic backgrounds, job descriptions, and addresses of those men killed. See his findings in Duffy, *The Wheeling Family*, vol. 2, 255–60.
13. *Wheeling Daily News*, April 30, 1924, 1; May 1, 1924, 1.
14. *Wheeling Daily News*, May 2, 1924, 12.; Duffy, *The Wheeling Family*, vol. 2, 244; *Wheeling Intelligencer*, May 2, 1924, 1; May 3, 1924, 1.
15. *Wheeling Intelligencer*, May 1, 1924, 2.
16. *Wheeling Intelligencer*, May 1, 1924, 2; *Wheeling Register*, May 4, 1924, 1–2; *Wheeling Intelligencer*, May 5, 1924, 3; *Wheeling Daily News*, May 4, 1924, Section 2, 4. By May 5, the *Wheeling Intelligencer* had collected $3,599.81 from private donations, including the Klan. The community had received outside support previously from the diocese, but getting aid from outside secular entities was rather new. The Polish Red Cross auxillary operated out of Polish Hall, helping in recruiting and supplying men for the Polish Army in France. For the Red Cross's wartime and postwar roles, see *Wheeling Intelligencer*, December 24, 1917, 8; February 27, 1918, 5; November 11, 1920, 5; November 25, 1922, 16.
17. Anne Perry, "Mike Calls Twin Brother Rocco to His Death in Mine," *Wheeling Daily News*, May 1, 1924, 9.

18. *Wheeling Intelligencer*, May 6, 1924, 1.
19. *Wheeling Intelligencer*, May 5, 1924, 11; *Wheeling Daily News*, May 4, 1924, Section 5, 6.
20. "Father Musial Suggests Plan: Stricken Families Not in Immediate Need," *Wheeling Register*, May 4, 1924.
21. Michael Oriard, *King Football: Sport and Spectacle in the Golden Age of Radio, Newsreels, Movies & Magazines, The Weekly & The Daily Press* (Chapel Hill: University of North Carolina Press, 2001), 18.
22. "Wheeling Hall of Fame: Everett Brinkman, 1902–1972," Ohio County Public Library (OCPL), http://www.ohiocountylibrary.org/wheeling-history/wheeling-hall-of-fame-everett-brinkman/4144.
23. "Wheeling Hall of Fame: Everett Brinkman, 1902–1972," OCPL.
24. "Register Names All-Valley High School 1928," *Wheeling Register*, December 7, 1928, Section 2, 1.
25. *Wheeling Register*, November 9, 1928, 10; November 13, 1928, 7; November 12, 1928, 4; December 7, 1928, Section 2, 1.
26. *Moundsville Daily Echo*, November 8, 1928, 3.
27. *Wheeling Register*, November 11, 1928, Section 2, 2; *Moundsville Daily Echo*, November 12, 1928, 3.
28. *Wheeling Intelligencer*, November 30, 1931, 11; November 3, 1931, 11; December 2, 1931, 11.
29. *Wheeling Intelligencer*, December 7, 1931, 8.
30. *Wheeling Intelligencer*, December 2, 1931, 12. The ethnic backgrounds of these players were found looking at the 1930 Manuscript Census for Ohio County, Ancestry.com.
31. "85-Yard Run Features Win of Pike Team," *Wheeling Intelligencer*, November 27, 1931, 13; *The Triadelphian*, vol. 17 (Triadelphia, WV: 1931), 79, 119, Ancestry.com.
32. *Wheeling Register*, November 13, 1934, 6.
33. *Wheeling Daily News*, November 3, 1934, 1, 6.
34. *Wheeling Register*, November 29, 1934, 11.
35. Ethnic backgrounds were checked surveying the 1930 and 1940 Manuscript Census for Benwood, Marshall County, and Wheeling, Ohio County, via Ancestry.com. Those without a first name are those where there were several male family members in a household who could have played on the 1934 team by their age; for starters, see *Wheeling Daily News*, November 3, 1934, 6.
36. 1930 and 1940 Manuscript Census for Wheeling, Ohio County, Ancestry.com; *The Triadelphian*, vol. 20 (Triadelphia, WV: 1934), 74, Ancestry.com.
37. "Union Set for Central Brush," *Wheeling Register*, November 2, 1934, 8.
38. Mary Lou Henderson, "Germans in Center Wheeling," interview by Michael Cline, 96-014, July 7, 1994, Wheeling Spoken History Project, OCPL; Duffy, *The Wheeling Family*, vol. 2, 71–72.
39. Duffy, *The Wheeling Family*, vol. 2, 132.
40. Tricia T. Pyne, *Faith in the Mountains: A History of the Diocese of Wheeling-Charleston, 1850–2000* (Eckbolsheim, France: Editions du Signe, 2001), 50–52.
41. Fr. Pat Condron, oral history interview, in Wheeling National Heritage Area Corporation, Final Report, Wheeling Spoken History Project (Wheeling, WV: 1994), 10–11, Wheeling National Heritage Area Corporation Records, Wheeling, WV, 335.

42. Caroline Lakomy, in Duffy, *The Wheeling Family*, 146–47; Delores Skrzypek and Ann Jurczak, "Pierogi Making at St. Lad's," interview by Michael Cline, 96–021, October 31, 1994, Wheeling Spoken History Project, OCPL; Frank Kogut, oral history interview, Wheeling Spoken History Project, 335–6, WNHAC.
43. Joe Bazo and Gladys Klamut, oral history interview, WNHAC Final Report, Wheeling Spoken History Project, 336–37, 365, WNHAC.
44. "May Procession Held in South Wheeling," *West Virginia Register*, May 20, 1934.
45. Mary Kuca, 1930 Manuscript Census, Wheeling, Eighth Ward, Ohio County, WV; *Polk's Wheeling City Directory, 1932*, 416; *Polk's Wheeling City Directory, 1934*, 403, Ancestry.com.
46. *Wheeling Intelligencer*, June 24, 1921, 2. For background on Thoner's career, see Gibson Lamb Cranmer and S. L. Jebson, *The History of the Upper Ohio Valley*, vol. 1, *With Family History and Biographical Sketches: A Statement of Its Resources, Industrial Growth and Commercial Advantages*. (Madison, WI: Brant & Fuller, 1890), 455.
47. For case studies of the 1920s Klan across the industrial Midwest, see William D. Jenkins, *Steel Valley Klan: The Ku Klux Klan in Ohio's Mahoning Valley* (Kent, OH: Kent State University Press, 1990); Leonard J. Moore, *Citizen Klansmen: The Ku Klux Klan in Indiana, 1921–1928* (Chapel Hill: University of North Carolina Press, 1991); Dana M. Caldemeyer, "Before the Klan: Coal Miners, Labor Conflict, and Community in Evansville, Indiana, 1892–1922" (MA thesis, West Virginia University, 2010). For the local nature of the Klan's agenda, see David J. Goldberg, "Unmasking the Ku Klux Klan: The Northern Movement against the KKK, 1920–1925," *Journal of American Ethnic History* 15, no. 4 (Summer 1996): 32–33.
48. Kenneth T. Jackson, *The Ku Klux Klan in the City, 1915–1930* (New York: Oxford University Press, 1967), 236, 240–42; *Searchlight* (Atlanta, GA), September 30, 1922, 6.
49. *Wheeling Intelligencer*, July 29, 1921, 12.
50. *Wheeling Intelligencer*, June 30, 1922, 1, 14.
51. *Wheeling Intelligencer*, June 25, 1921, 4; June 24, 1921, 2, 13; *Wheeling Register*, June 24, 1921, 6.
52. For the context of the ACA and America First Days, see John Hennen, *The Americanization of West Virginia: Creating a Modern Industrial State, 1916–1925* (Lexington: University Press of Kentucky, 1996), 97–100, 135–36; *Wheeling Intelligencer*, June 30, 1921, 8
53. *Wheeling Intelligencer*, July 1, 1921, 9–10.
54. *Searchlight*, January, 27, 1923, 4; *Wheeling Register*, September 18, 1923, 12.
55. Victor R. Greene, *A Passion for Polka: Old-Time Ethnic Music in America* (Berkeley: University of California Press, 1992), 115–17.
56. *Wheeling Register*, June 14, 1931, 5; *Wheeling Register*, October 16, 1930, 4.
57. Our Lady of Perpetual Help, St. Mary's Ukrainian Catholic Church, *75th Anniversary, 1913–1988: Celebrating the Millennium of Ukrainian Christianity* (Wheeling, WV: 1988), OCPL.
58. "Ukrainian Cossack Ballet to Be Given Monday Night," *Wheeling Daily News*, November 30, 1930, Section 4, 4.
59. *Wheeling Daily News*, November 30, 1930, Section 4, 4; *West Virginia Register*, July 1, 1934.
60. For the quote, see *Wheeling Daily News*, November 30, 1930, Section 4, 4; *West

Virginia Register, July 1, 1934. Ukrainians were Uniate Catholics (loyal to the pope) but had their own liturgy derived from Orthodox tradition.

61. For more on Oglebay Park and Samuel Rybeck's efforts, see *Wheeling News-Register*, April 10, 1938, Part 3, 11; *Wheeling Register*, July 1, 1930, 8; July 4, 1930, 7; Rosalind "Buddy Rybeck," interview by Michael Cline, 96–022, September 27, 1994, Wheeling Spoken History Project, OCPL; Duffy, *The Wheeling Family*, vol. 2, 125–26.
62. *Wheeling Register*, July 1, 1930, 8; July 4, 1930, 7; July 5, 1930, 5; June 23, 1931, 14; June 28, 1931, Section 3, 2; July 2, 1931, 8; July 3, 1931, 7; July 5, 1931, 5.
63. Anna Horeczko, 1930 Manuscript Census, Wheeling Eighth Ward, Ohio County, WV; Anna Horeczko in New York Passenger Lists, 1820–1957, database, Arrival November 6, 1923, New York, aboard the SS *Olympic*, Microfilm Serial T715, Roll 3408, p. 63, Passenger and Crew Lists of Vessels Arriving at New York, New York, 1897–1957; National Archives Microfilm Publication T715, RG 85, Records of the Immigration and Naturalization Service, NARA, Ancestry.com; Michael Horeczko, Preliminary Forms for Petition for Naturalization, May 29, 1929, Box 4, Folder 6, RG 21, U.S. District Court for Northern West Virginia, NARA, Philadelphia. For the postwar devastation in the region, see Norman Davies, *White Eagle, Red Star: The Polish–Soviet War 1919–1920 and the Miracle on the Vistula* (London: Random House, 2003); for the protest meeting, see *Wheeling Daily News*, December 12, 1930, Section 1, 11.
64. For the list of the Polish and other ethnic dancers, see *Wheeling Register*, July 5, 1930, 5; for their employment, see 1930 Manuscript Census, Wheeling, Ohio County, WV; *Callin's Wheeling City Directory, 1926*; *Polk's Wheeling City Directory, 1928*; *Polk's Wheeling City Directory, 1930*; *Polk's Wheeling City Directory, 1932*; *Polk's Wheeling City Directory, 1934*, Ancestry.com.
65. Duffy, *The Wheeling Family*, 144–45.
66. St. Ladislaus, Financial Report, 1925, Archives of the Diocese of Wheeling-Charleston, Wheeling, WV (DWC).
67. William J. Galush, *For More than Bread: Community and Identity in American Polonia, 1880–1940*, East European Monographs (New York: Columbia University Press, 2006), 180–90.
68. Saint Ladislaus Church Confirmation Books, 1922, 1928, 1931, St. Ladislaus Parish Records, DWC.
69. Mary Martinkosky, interview by author, Wheeling, WV, August 10, 2008.
70. Blanche Resczynski, interview by the author, Wheeling, WV, August 10, 2008.
71. Mary Anna Kaczor report cards, "*Swiadectwo Miesieczne-Szkola w. Wladyslawa, Wheeling, W.Va.*," 1934–1935, 1938–1939, Parish History File, St. Ladislaus Parish, Wheeling, WV (1902–1995), DWC.
72. Galush, *For More than Bread*, 168–71; "Historija Tow. Św. Józefa, Grupa 213 Z.P.R.K.," in *Pamietnik uroczystosci zlotego jubileusza swiecenn kaplanshich przewielebnego ksiedza Emila Musiala, proboszcza parafii Sw. Wladyslawa Krola, Wheeling, W.Va.* (Wheeling, WV: 1926), 41, in Parish History File, St. Ladislaus, Wheeling, WV (1902–1995), DWC; *West Virginia Register*, December 16, 1934; February 17, 1935.
73. *Wheeling Intelligencer*, October 30, 1933, 2; *West Virginia Register*, November 8, 1942, 3; "Polish-American Political Club," Certificate of Incorporation, 1919, Incorporation Book 11, 301; "Polish-American Trading Company," CI, 1920, Incorporation Book 11, 385; "The Polonia Club," CI, 1923, Incorporation Book 14, 243, OCCO.

74. *Pamietnik uroczystosci zlotego jubileusza swiecenn kaplanshich przewielebnego ksiedza Emila Musiala, proboszcza parafii Sw. Wladyslawa Krola, Wheeling, W.Va.* (Wheeling, WV: 1926), 47, 49, 51, 55, in Parish History File, St. Ladislaus, Wheeling, WV (1902–1995), DWC; St. Ladislaus Parish, Annual Report, 1928–1929, DWC.
75. *Wheeling Register*, June 24, 1934, Section 1, 3; Galush, *For More than Bread*, 160.
76. St. Ladislaus, Financial Reports, 1925, 1929, 1930. For the growing centralization of parish spending and the strains placed on priests and lay communities by the late 1920s, see Galush, *For More than Bread*, 154–55, 163.
77. *Wheeling Register*, October 29, 1930, 4; July 21, 1934, 12.
78. *Wheeling Register*, October 20, 1930, 11.
79. Stanley Owoc, 1920 Manuscript Census, Wheeling Eighth Ward, Ohio County, WV; *Polk's Wheeling City Directory, 1930*, 597; Walter Zdanowicz, 1930 Manuscript Census, Wheeling Eighth Ward, Ohio County, WV; *Callin's Wheeling City Directory, 1926*, 1092; *Polk's Wheeling City Directory, 1928*, 982, Ancestry.com.
80. Branislaw Klimazewski, Declaration of Intention, December 27, 1911, Volume 2, Box 2, RG 2, Records of the U.S. Circuit Court, Northern District of West Virginia, Wheeling Division, Naturalization Records, National Archives and Records Administration, Philadelphia, PA; 1930 Manuscript Census, Wheeling Eighth Ward, Ohio County, WV, Ancestry.com.
81. *Wheeling Daily News*, December 12, 1930, Section 1, 11. No copies of the newspaper have been found nor any direct sources related to the Polish Working Class Association. For the editor, see Kazimerz Obecny, 1930 Manuscript Census, Wheeling Eighth Ward, Ohio County, WV, Ancestry.com.
82. Mary Pietras, in Duffy, *The Wheeling Family*, 159. Alex Habak was born in the Polish lands but attended St. Mary's Ukrainian Catholic Church; see, *Wheeling News-Register*, July 1, 1943, 2. For the Polish businesses in the region, see *Pamietnik uroczystosci zlotego jubileusza swiecenn kaplanshich przewielebnego ksiedza Emila Musiala, proboszcza parafii Sw. Wladyslawa Krola, Wheeling, W.Va* (Wheeling, WV: 1926).
83. Mary Martinkosky, interview by the author, August 10, 2008.

CHAPTER 8

1. *Wheeling Register*, March 23, 1924, Section 4, 4; March 25, 1924, 8.
2. For background on John Marchlenski, see Declaration of Intention, February 27, 1911, Volume 2, Box 2, RG 21, Records of the U.S. Circuit Court, Northern District of West Virginia, Wheeling Division, Naturalization Records, Declarations of Intention, National Archives and Records Administration, Philadelphia, PA (hereafter RG 21, NARA, Philadelphia); 1930 Manuscript Census, Wheeling Eighth Ward, Ohio County, District 25; 1920 Manuscript Census, Wheeling Sixth Ward, Ohio County, District 95; 1910 Manuscript Census, Wheeling Sixth Ward, Ohio County, District 131, Records of the Bureau of the Census, RG 29, National Archives, Washington, DC, Ancestry.com (hereafter, Manuscript Census).
3. *Wheeling Register*, May 13, 1924, 5; Recognizance for Appearance before U.S. Court, Wheeling, May 12, 1924, and Stanley Owoc, Affidavit of First Surety, both in *The United States of America v. Alex Cybulski* Indictment No. 7060, May 12, 1924, Wheeling Criminal Cases Files, Box 12, RG 21, Records of the U.S. District Court for the Northern District of West Virginia, NARA, Philadelphia.

4. United States Selective Service System, *World War I Selective Service System Draft Registration Cards, 1917–1918*, Washington, DC, NARA, M1509, Ohio County, WV, Draft Board, Roll 1993024 (hereafter "WWI draft registration card"); 1920 Manuscript Census, Wheeling Eighth Ward, Ohio County; *Callin's Wheeling City Directory, 1921–22* (Wheeling, WV: R. L. Polk & Co., 1922), 307, Ancestry.com.
5. *Wheeling Register*, December 22, 1920, 14; November 24, 1920, 5.
6. Lisa McGirr, *The War on Alcohol: Prohibition and the Rise of the American State* (New York: W. W. Norton, 2015), ch. 1–3.
7. Michael Lerner, *Dry Manhattan: Prohibition in New York City* (Cambridge, MA: Harvard University Press, 2007), 16, 96, 118.
8. Julien Comte, "'Let the Federal Men Raid': Bootlegging and Prohibition Enforcement in Pittsburgh," *Pennsylvania History: A Journal of Mid-Atlantic Studies* 77, no. 2 (Spring 2010): 166–92, quote on 168.
9. *Wheeling Register*, June 18, 1909, 5; June 26, 1909, 3; June 29, 1909, 10; *Wheeling Daily News*, July 30, 1909, 6.
10. *Wheeling Daily News*, May 14, 1913, 12.
11. *Wheeling Daily News*, July 20, 1913, 4–2; July 21, 1913, 4; *Pittsburgh Press*, July 20, 1913, 1.
12. *New York Times*, July 1, 1914, 5.
13. Chapter 13: "Prohibition," in House Bill No. 8, *Acts of the Legislature of West Virginia, Thirty-First Regular Session, 1913*, http://www.wvculture.org/history/government/prohibition01.html; Michael J. Buseman, "Vending Vice: The Rise and Fall of West Virginia State Prohibition, 1852–1934" (PhD diss., West Virginia University, 2012). For city council's inaction, see *Wheeling Register*, July 25, 1914, 2; *Wheeling Intelligencer*, September 22, 1915, 9; Treasury Department, IRS Affidavits for Retail Liquor Dealer, F. C. Bischoff, August 30, 1915; Charles M. Earhart to Prosecuting Attorney D. A. McKee, September 2, 1915, Ohio County Criminal Court, envelope 398E-4; "List of Purchases Made by Tony Mainfort, Wheeling, Ohio Co.," "Reports of Officers re: Raids/purchases," undated, Ohio County Criminal Court, envelope 399E-2, Ohio County Court Records, Ohio County, WV, A&M 31, West Virginia and Regional History Center (hereafter Ohio County Court Records, WVRHC).
14. *Wheeling Daily News*, September 3, 1914, 10; September 8, 1914, 10.
15. *Wheeling Register*, August 29, 1914, 12; John Kobus, WWI draft registration card, Ohio County, WV, Ancestry.com; *Wheeling Daily News*, September 20, 1914, Section 3, 7.
16. Frederick O. Blue, *When a State Goes Dry: A Brief Study in Law Enforcement* (Westerville, OH: American Issue Publishing Company, 1916), 98–104; Ronald L. Lewis, "Americanizing Immigrant Coal Miners in Northern West Virginia: Monongalia County between the World Wars," in *Transnational West Virginia: Ethnic Communities and Economic Change, 1840–1940*, ed. Ken Fones-Wolf and Ronald L. Lewis (Morgantown: West Virginia University Press, 2002), 276–77.
17. *Wheeling Intelligencer*, September 28, 1915; October 13, 1915, 1, 8; *Benwood Enterpriser*, October 14, 1915, 4.
18. *Wheeling Intelligencer*, October 13, 1915, 9; October 14, 1915, 14
19. "List of Purchases Made by Tony Mainfort, Wheeling, Ohio Co.," 1916, Ohio County Criminal Court, envelope 399E-2, Ohio County Court Records, WVRHC.

20. *Pittsburgh Press*, June 28, 1914, 9; *Wheeling Register*, July 24, 1914, 16; August 30, 1914, 3; January 6, 1915, 14; D. A. McKee to C. F. Rathbone, Charleston, WV, "RE: Yost Law Violators," March 3 and 20, 1915, Ohio County Criminal Court, envelope 398E-4, Ohio County Court Records, WVRHC; *Benwood Enterpriser*, April 15, 1915, 4.
21. Steve Kacinski, 1910 Manuscript Census, Benwood Fifth Ward, Marshall County, West Virginia, Ancestry.com; *Wheeling Register*, July 3, 1914; *Benwood Enterpriser*, June 17, 1915, 4.
22. *Fourth Biennial Report, State Commissioner of Prohibition, 1921–1922* (Charleston, WV: 1922), 49, Box 29, Folder 1, A&M 203, Governor Ephraim Morgan Papers, WVRHC; David J. Goldberg, *Discontented America: The United States in the 1920s* (Baltimore and London: Johns Hopkins University Press, 1999), xi–xii, 54–57.
23. For an example of this "make do" culture among the immigrants of Hancock County, WV, see Lou Martin, *Smokestacks in the Hills: Rural-Industrial Workers in West Virginia* (Urbana: University of Illinois Press, 2015), 68–69, 75, 150.
24. For the 1920–1921 recession in Wheeling, see *Wheeling Register*, November 21, 1920, 1; January 18, 1921, 6; January 22, 1921, 5; January 28, 1921, 8; February 6, 1921, Section 2, 1; February 13, 1921, Section 1, 3.
25. Letter of Transmittal, State of West Virginia, Office of the State Commissioner of Prohibition, Charleston, WV, p. 26–28, 51–52, September 30, 1924, Box 29, Folder 1, A&M 203, Ephraim F. Morgan Papers, WVRHC.
26. *Wheeling Register*, January 17, 1923, 14; *Fourth Biennial Report, State Commissioner of Prohibition, 1921–1922*, 17, 49, Box 29, Folder 1; State Tax Commissioner to Carl O. Bachmann, Prosecuting Attorney, Ohio County, July 5, 1921, Box 8, Folder 1; Letter of Transmittal, 1924, 83, Box 29, Folder 1, A&M 203, Ephraim F. Morgan Papers, WVRHC.
27. O. L. Boyle, President and Manager, La Salle Wines, Inc., Milwaukee, to Rt. Rev. Edward E. Weber, Chancellor, Wheeling, June 7, 1927, in "William Charles Hall," Deceased Priests Files, Correspondence, 1920–1949, Archives of the Diocese of Wheeling-Charleston (hereafter DWC).
28. William Hall, Application to Procure Wine for Sacramental Purposes and Like Religious Rites, U.S. Treasury Department, IRS, June 7, 1927; October 26, 1927; November 11, 1920; September 16, 1922; May 12, 1924; April 11, 1925; March 18, 1930; October 26, 1931; October 27, 1932; and April 14, 1933, in "William Charles Hall," Deceased Priests Files, DWC.
29. Charles Lively, Treasury Department, IRS, Parkersburg, WV, to Edward Weber, October 30, 1920, "Fr. Emil Musial," Deceased Priests Files, DWC; Paul Abraham, Application, U.S. Treasury, October 1, 1925 with Thomas O'Shaughnessy, Barnston Tea Co., New York City; October 26, 1925 with A. J. Hammer Co., Rev. Paul Khoury Abraham, Correspondence, 1923–1959, Deceased Priests Files, DWC.
30. Francis Bahoric, Application, U.S. Treasury, April 23, 1925; August 4, 1925; October 22, 1925; March 25, 1926; October 17, 1926; April 4, 1927; October 24, 1927, all with A. J. Hammer Co.; Fr. Bahoric to Rev. Edward Weber, November 30, 1926; Bahoric to Rt. Rev. Bishop John J. Swint, February 10, 1928, all in "Francis Bahoric," Deceased Priests Files, DWC.
31. McGirr, *The War on Alcohol*, 71–72; *Wheeling Register*, February 15, 1921, 5; April 16, 1922, 5; April 13, 1924, 5.

32. *Wheeling Register*, March 11, 1923, Section 1, 7; *United States v. Joe Fraczknivicz*, U.S. District Court for the Northern District of West Virginia, Indictment No. 7080, May 18, 1923, Wheeling Criminal Cases Files, Box 12, RG 21, NARA, Philadelphia.
33. Comte, "Let the Federal Men Raid," 170–71.
34. *Wheeling Register*, May 4, 1922, 3; May 5, 1922, 6; May 7, 1922, 16.
35. *Wheeling Register*, May 10, 1922, 5; May 11, 1922, 11.
36. *Wheeling Register*, May 12, 1922, 4.
37. *Wheeling Register*, May 27, 1922, 1; June 10, 1922, 6.
38. *U.S. v. John Belawa*, U.S. District Court for the Northern District of West Virginia, Case No. 6289, May 18, 1922, Wheeling Criminal Cases Files, Box 7, RG 21, NARA, Philadelphia.
39. *U.S. v. John Rogalski*, U.S. District Court for the Northern District of West Virginia, Case No. 6283, May 11, 1922, Wheeling Criminal Cases Files, Box 7, RG 21, NARA, Philadelphia; *Wheeling Register*, May 17, 1922, 5; May 18, 1922, 5; May 21, 1922, Section 1, 8.
40. *Wheeling Register*, May 6, 1926, 5; Bronislaw Malarski, Statement of Facts, Petition for Citizenship, No. 6-23551, May 24, 1934, Preliminary Forms for Petitions, Box 4, Folder 12, RG 21, NARA, Philadelphia.
41. *Wheeling Register*, May 18, 1922, 5; Hearings before the Committee on the Judiciary, House of Representatives, 68th Congress, 1st Session, Pursuant to H. Res. 325, November 25 and 26, 1924, *Charges against William E. Baker, United States District Court Judge for the Northern District of West Virginia* (Washington, DC: Government Printing Office, 1925), 12, 29–31.
42. *Charges against William E. Baker*, 13, 19–22, 24, 42.
43. *Charges against William E. Baker*, 42, 13.
44. *Wheeling Register*, March 22, 1929, 15.
45. *United States v. John Marchlenski*, U.S. District Court for the Northern District of West Virginia, Indictment No. 8324, October 21, 1925, Wheeling Criminal Cases Files, Box 19, RG 21, NARA, Philadelphia.
46. For Katie Lipsky's exploits, see *Wheeling Register*, September 9, 1921, 5; April 8, 1922, 5; April 9, 1922, section 2–7; *United States v. Katie Lipiski*, Case File 897-a, November 7, 1923, Wheeling Criminal Cases Files, Box 11, RG 21, NARA, Philadelphia; *Wheeling Intelligencer*, May 4, 1925, 3.
47. Katarzyna Posobiec, Arrival on January 26, 1903, from Bremen to New York, *Passenger and Crew Lists of Vessels Arriving at New York, New York, 1897–1957*, Microfilm Publication T715, Roll 0318, p. 130, RG 85, Records of the Immigration and Naturalization Service, NARA, Ancestry.com; *United States v. Katie Haleski (alias Kaliski)*, U.S. District Court for the Northern District of West Virginia, File 709-g, October 17, 1928, Wheeling Criminal Cases Files, Box 26, RG 21, NARA, Philadelphia.
48. Katie Haleski, 1930 Manuscript Census, Wheeling, Sixth Ward, Ohio County, WV, Ancestry.com.
49. *Wheeling Intelligencer*, March 24, 1922, 10; *Wheeling Register*, May 24, 1922, 11. For Groski's family, see 1920 Manuscript Census, Moundsville, First Ward, Marshall County, WV; Joseph Groski Death Certificate, 22 August 1921, West Virginia Death Index, 1853–1973, FHL Film, Ancestry.com.
50. *Wheeling Register*, February 26, 1919, 5; November 14, 1923, 7; November 15, 1923, 11.

51. *Wheeling Daily News*, November 12, 1930, 2. George Fetherling calls the establishment the "Allies Café." See Fetherling, *The Big Greek: The Rise and Fall of Bill Lias* (Wheeling, WV: Polyhedron Learning Media and Friends of Wheeling, 2018), 16–17.
52. *Wheeling Register*, April 13, 1924, Section 3, 6; September 29, 1928, 2; January, 27, 1929, 9.
53. W. J. Cotton, U.S. Commissioner, Wheeling, Warrant of Arrest, April 6, 1923; Grand Jury Indictment, Case File of *U.S. v. Alex Cybulski*, Indictment 7060, Wheeling Criminal Cases Files, Box 12, RG 21, NARA, Philadelphia.
54. Arrest Warrant for Alex Cybulski, November 23, 1925; *U.S. v. Alex Cybulski (Capias Pro Fine)*, June 30, 1926, Case File 7060, Wheeling Criminal Cases Files, Box 12, RG 21, NARA, Philadelphia.
55. Konstanty Cubulski, Preliminary Forms for Petitions of Naturalizations, undated, Box 2, Folder 1, RG 21, NARA, Philadelphia; 1920 and 1930 Manuscript Census, Wheeling, Eighth Ward, Ohio County, WV, Ancestry.com.
56. Recognizance for Appearance before U.S. Court; Affidavit of Surety, Konstanty Cybulski and Clara Cybulski, August 9, 1923, Case File 7060, Wheeling Criminal Cases Files, Box 12, RG 21, NARA, Philadelphia.
57. Alexander Sebulske, 1930 Manuscript Census, Hudson, First Ward, Columbia County, New York, Ancestry.com.
58. *Wheeling Register*, February 3, 1926, 1; February 2, 1926, 9; February 16, 1926, 6.
59. *Pittsburgh Post-Gazette*, July 12, 1955, 6.
60. "Phillips and Squad in Thrilling Race; Auto Strikes Car," *Wheeling Intelligencer*, December 12, 1916, 12; January 4, 1917, 5; Complaint against William Lias, December 1916, *State v. Lias, William*, Ohio County Criminal Court, envelope 399A-1, OHI 788, Ohio County Court Records, WVRHC; *Wheeling Intelligencer*, January 30, 1917, 5.
61. *Pittsburgh Press*, October 12, 1947, 36; June 5, 1949, 1; Fetherling, *The Big Greek*, 14–15.
62. *Pittsburgh Press*, February 20, 1953, 1. Lias entered the Ohio County jail on January 12, 1923, and the trials revealed that Sheriff Clouse joined Lias on several trips to pick up whiskey. See Fetherling, *The Big Greek*, 18–19.
63. *Pittsburgh Press*, February 20, 1953, 1; *Washington Reporter*, September 17, 1923, 20; *Wheeling Register*, September 18, 1923, 6; Indictment, *United States v. William Lias, et al., Conspiracy No. 7*, Case File 7056, May 8, 1923, Wheeling Criminal Cases Files, Box 12, RG 21, NARA, Philadelphia.
64. *Pittsburgh Press*, February 20, 1953, 1; *Washington Reporter*, September 17, 1923, 20; William Carney, "The William G. Lias Story," Presentation to Wheeling Area Genealogical Society meeting, February 8, 2003, http://www.lindapages.com/wags-ohio/liasbill.htm; Fetherling, *The Big Greek*, 18–19.
65. *Wheeling Register*, May 5, 1924, 9; May 17, 1924, 12. Names of Polish men checked with 1920 and 1930 Manuscript Censuses, Ancestry.com; for more coverage of the case, see Fetherling, *The Big Greek*, 25–27.
66. *Wheeling Register*, May 5, 1924, 9; May 17, 1924, 12; February 1, 1926, 4; February 3, 1926, 5; May 12, 1926, 5; *Washington Reporter*, July 23, 1926, 1. Lias ended up serving just eight months. See Fetherling, *The Big Greek*, 28.
67. *Wheeling Register*, January 17, 1929, 16; December 28, 1928, 4; September 24, 1928, 4.

68. *Wheeling Register*, November 18, 1928, Section 2, 4; December 11, 1928, 8; December 12, 1928, 1, 13; December 13, 1928, 11; December 24, 1928, 7.
69. *Wheeling Register*, December 14, 1928, 5.
70. *Wheeling Register*, December 16, 1928, Section 2, 7 (for quotes by J. J. Doerr); December 18, 1928, 18.
71. 1900 Manuscript Census, Webster District, Wheeling, Ohio County, WV; 1910 Manuscript Census, Monongah, Lincoln District, Marion County, WV; Stanley Venesky, 1920 Manuscript Census, Wheeling Sixth Ward, Ohio County, WV, Ancestry.com.
72. Affidavit for Search Warrant, October 2, 1922; Temporary Recognizance for Appearance Before Commissioner, Stanley Vineskey, October 2, 1922, *United States v. Stanley Vineskey, alias Stanley Visneskey*, Case File 7011, Wheeling Criminal Cases Files, Box 11, RG 21, NARA, Philadelphia.
73. *Wheeling Intelligencer*, August 31, 1923, 5; *Wheeling Register*, September 27, 1923, 5.
74. *United States v. John Vinesky*, Case File 629-g, October 16, 1928, Wheeling Criminal Case Files, Box 26, RG 21, NARA, Philadelphia.
75. *Wheeling Register*, February 5, 1926, 8; February 1, 1926, Sections 4–5; February 20, 1926, 3. For Kowalsky's background, see *State of West Virginia v. Walter Kowalsky*, Hearing, February 5, 1926, Ohio County Circuit Court, envelope 409B-18, OHI 809 roll, Ohio County Court Records, WVRHC.
76. *Wheeling Register*, June 26, 1928, 20.
77. *Wheeling Register*, December 23, 1928, 1, Section 2, 7; *Wheeling Intelligencer*, December 24, 1928, 3.
78. *Wheeling Intelligencer*, December 31, 1928, 2; *Wheeling Register*, January 2, 1929, 11; January 14, 1929, 4; March 5, 1929, 15; Fetherling, *The Big Greek*, 38.
79. *Wheeling Register*, March 5, 1929, 15; March 9, 1929, 14; March 16, 1929, 14; March 22, 1929, 7.
80. *Wheeling Register*, December 30, 1928, 2.
81. There was a lot of press coverage on young James Amien, age twenty, who came from a middle-class Lebanese family, graduated from the prestigious Linsly Academy, and was a student at West Liberty Normal School. His angry father blamed an unnamed bootlegger for his son's death. See *Wheeling Register*, April 8, 1929, 1; April 9, 1929, 1; Fetherling, *The Big Greek*, 25, 36–41.
82. *Wheeling Register*, April 13, 1929, 12.
83. *Wheeling Register*, January 16, 1930, 16; January 17, 1930, 1; January 18, 1930, 1.
84. *Wheeling Intelligencer*, June 24, 1930, 3; *Wheeling Register*, July 8, 1930, 2; July 14, 1930, 1, 5; July 15, 1930, 4.
85. *Wheeling Register*, October 6, 1930, 4; October 9, 1930, 8.
86. *Wheeling Register*, October 11, 1930, 7; October 25, 1930, 1; October 29, 1930, 1; October 31, 1930, 1.
87. *Wheeling Daily News*, November 7, 1930, 1. Lias's first conviction cost him a five-hundred-dollar fine; his second led to him serving six months in the Ohio County jail; the third came in 1926 and led to him serving a year plus in federal prison. See "Bill Lias to Appeal Sentence to Atlanta," *Wheeling Daily News*, November 12, 1930, 1.
88. *Wheeling Intelligencer*, December 1, 1931, 3. Lias was only incarcerated from December 1931 to July 1933. See Fetherling, *The Big Greek*, 60–61.

89. *Wheeling Register*, October 10, 1930, 10; January 11, 1931, 5.
90. *Wheeling Register*, March 6, 1931, 3; March 8, 1931, Section 3, 5; March 10, 1931, 14; March 11, 1931, 5.
91. *Wheeling Register*, October 7, 1932, 2; *Wheeling Intelligencer*, October 12, 1932, 3.
92. *Wheeling Register*, January 9, 1929, 16.
93. *Wheeling Register*, January 13, 1929, Section 4, 12; January 18, 1929, 7.
94. United States v. Steve Kacinski, Case File 1703, October 21, 1930, Wheeling Criminal Case Files, Box 32, RG 21, NARA, Philadelphia; Steve Kacinski, Death Record, May 12, 1932, West Virginia Vital Records, WVSA.
95. *Wheeling Register*, October 2, 1930, 7, 13, 16.
96. *Wheeling Register*, October 2, 1930, 13.

CHAPTER 9

1. Minute Book, Local 1248, Wheeling Factory, Meeting Minutes, July 14, 1944; November 23, 1945, Box 31, USWA District 23, Records (hereafter Local 1248 Minutes, USWA District 23, HCLA); Grievance Case No. 5-G-661, Wheeling Factory, December 7, 1945, p. 10, Meeting Minutes of General Appeals Committee at Wheeling Steel, 1945, USWA District 23, Box 21, Folder 11, Historical Collections and Labor Archives, Penn State University Library, State College, Pennsylvania (hereafter HCLA).
2. Agnes Helenski, 1930 Manuscript Census; 1940 Manuscript Census, Benwood First Ward, Marshall County, West Virginia, Enumeration District 26-23, Roll T627_4426, p. 5B, RG 29, Records of the Bureau of the Census, *Sixteenth Census of the United States, 1940*, NARA, Ancestry.com; Walter Skrzypek and Agnes Helenski, Marriage License Application, January 28, 1947, Marshall County, West Virginia County Clerk Marriage Book, p. 241, West Virginia Vital Records, West Virginia State Archives (WVSA); Agnes Helenski, Check 1402, October 9, 1935, Wheeling Steel LU 1248, Wheeling Factory, Seniority Lists, 1947, Box 24, Folder 3, USWA District 23 (Wheeling, WV) Records, 1944–1960; Wheeling Steel Locals Union Files, Local Union Lists (hereafter Wheeling Steel LU 1248, Seniority Lists, 1947, HCLA).
3. June 25, 1937, Local 1248 Minutes, USWA District 23, HCLA. Wheeling Corrugating in East Wheeling was a finishing plant that employed a larger number of female workers on various production lines.
4. Jim Rose, "'The Problem Every Supervisor Dreads': Women Workers at the U.S. Steel Duquesne Works during World War II," *Labor History* 36, no. 1 (1995): 23–51. For the women, see Stella Sophie Sulek (Check No. 2452), November 2, 1932; Mary Kuca (Check No. 2423), October 13, 1938; Stella Stazenski (Check No. 1409), July 28, 1933; Josephine Lakomy (Check No. 615), March 12, 1934; Wheeling Steel LU 1248, Seniority Lists, 1947, HCLA; May 28, 1937; January 27, 1938; May 22, 1938, Local 1248 Minutes, USWA District 23, HCLA.
5. For Mildred Visnic, see August 12, 1938, Local 1248 Minutes, USWA District 23, HCLA; "Miss Wheeling Factory-1939," *Wheeling News-Register*, September 3, 1939, Section 2, 7.
6. Nelson Lichtenstein, *Labor's War at Home: The CIO in World War II* (Cambridge: Cambridge University Press, 1982), 178–202.

7. Lizabeth Cohen, *Making a New Deal: Industrial Workers in Chicago, 1919–1939*, 2nd ed. (Cambridge: Cambridge University Press, 2008), 314–5.
8. *Wheeling Intelligencer*, October 3, 1932, 11; *Wheeling Daily News*, November 9, 1930, Section 5, 12; November 20, 1930, 9; *Wheeling Intelligencer*, September 3, 1932, 2.
9. *Wheeling Register*, January 18, 1931, 9, 3.
10. *Wheeling Daily News*, December 2, 1930, 20.
11. St. Ladislaus Annual Reports, 1928–1941, Archives of the Diocese of Wheeling-Charleston (DWC).
12. St. Ladislaus Annual Reports, 1928–1941; St. Ladislaus Financial Report, 1930, 1932, DWC.
13. Robert L. Plummer, "McKinley Trade School Progress Is Checked by Lack of Support," *Wheeling News-Register*, November 22, 1937, 2; May 17, 1936, Section 3, 10; August 26, 1938, 19.
14. *Wheeling News-Register*, November 19, 1937, Section 2, 1.
15. *Wheeling News-Register*, May 17, 1936, Section 3, 10. Professions checked in 1940 Manuscript Census, Ancestry.com.
16. *Wheeling News-Register*, November 7, 1937, Section 3, 2.
17. For ethnic voters shifting to the Democratic Party during the 1928 presidential election, see Lisa McGirr, *The War on Alcohol: Prohibition and the Rise of the American State* (New York: W. W. Norton, 2015), ch. 6.
18. *Wheeling Register*, January 27, 1935, 4; January 28, 1935, 10; *West Virginia Register*, October 20, 1940, 3.
19. *West Virginia Register*, August 25, 1940, 3.
20. *Wheeling Register*, January 31, 1932, Section 1, 4; February 1, 1932, 3.
21. *Wheeling Register*, October 10, 1932, 10.
22. *Wheeling Register*, May 15, 1934, 2; George R. Smudski, 1930 Manuscript Census, Seventh Ward, Wheeling, Ohio County, NARA, Ancestry.com.
23. *Wheeling Register*, July 12, 1934, 1; July 23, 1934, 8.
24. *Wheeling Register*, July 24, 1934, 11.
25. *Wheeling Register*, June 2, 1935, Section 1, 3.
26. *Wheeling Intelligencer*, August 5, 1935, 3; *Wheeling News-Register*, November 18, 1937, 17.
27. Vin Sweeney, Steel Workers Organizing Committee to John L. Lewis President CIO, no date, microfilm reel 12, p. 635–37, The CIO Files of John L. Lewis, Part I: Correspondence with CIO Unions, 1929–1962 (Frederick, MD: University Publications of America, 1988).
28. *Wheeling News-Register*, February 4, 1940, Section I, 10.
29. Benwood Blast Furnace, Wheeling Steel Corp., LU 3814, USWA District 23, Box 22, Folder 24, HCLA. Leonard Chaplinski was also vice president of Local 3814 in 1955 and president in 1956.
30. For the Polish American officers, see Charles Lively, *West Virginia Blue Book, 1936* (Charleston, WV: Jarrett Printing Company, 1936), 285–87; Lively, *West Virginia Blue Book, 1937*, 372–75, 437, 482; Lively, *West Virginia Blue Book, 1938*, 330, 437, 391; Lively, *West Virginia Blue Book, 1939*, 418–21; *Polk's Wheeling City Directory, 1932* (Pittsburgh: R. L. Polk & Co., 1932), 308; Evelyn Cappas, 1930 Manuscript Census, Wheeling Eighth Ward, Ohio County, WV; Leonard Chaplinski, Evelyn

Korsnick, and Frank E. Schewinski, 1940 Manuscript Census, Wheeling Eighth Ward, Ohio County, Ancestry.com.
31. *Wheeling Intelligencer*, November 4, 1940, 3; November 7, 1940, 2. These are based on "unofficial results."
32. For precincts, see *Wheeling Intelligencer*, November 5, 1940, 3; for vote totals, see *Wheeling Intelligencer*, December 7, 1940, 16.
33. *Wheeling Intelligencer*, May 1, 1940, 12.
34. *Wheeling New-Register*, February 17, 1938, 9; March 25, 1938, Section 3, 3; July 2, 1939, Section 2, 11. For the role of the local Polish American elite, see William Galush, "City Societies and Commercial Clubs: Embourgoisment among Second Generation Polish Americans," *Polish American Studies* 56, no. 2 (Autumn 1999): 5–8, 10–12, quote on 8.
35. *Wheeling News-Register*, July 2, 1939, Section 2, 11; July 17, 1939, 9.
36. *Wheeling News-Register*, April 28, 1940, Section 2, 9; May 2, 1940, 9; *West Virginia Register*, August 4, 1940, 3, 7; June 29, 1941, 3.
37. For FDR's "cash-and-carry" speech and local responses, see William E. Leuchtenburg, *Franklin D. Roosevelt and the New Deal, 1932–1940* (New York: Harper & Row, 1963), 291–94; *Wheeling Intelligencer*, September 23, 1939, 2.
38. *Wheeling Intelligencer*, September 28, 1939, 4.
39. *Wheeling News-Register*, January 29, 1940, 11; January 30, 1940, 11.
40. *Wheeling News-Register*, February 2, 1940, 11; March 7, 1940, 9; June 10, 1941, 13; *West Virginia Register*, March 17, 1940, 7; October 20, 1940, 3.
41. J. B. Harris, Secretary, Joint Committee Portsmouth Amalgamated Association to John L. Lewis, June 14, 1936; NLRB to John L. Lewis, May 27, 1936, microfilm reel 12, p. 95–96, 120, CIO Files of John L. Lewis, Part I.
42. Louis C. Martin, "Flopping Tin and Punching Metal: A Survey of Women Steelworkers in West Virginia, 1890–1970," in *Women of the Mountain South: Identity, Work, and Activism*, ed. Connie Rice and Marie Tedesco (Athens: Ohio University Press, 2015), 283–84.
43. James D. Rose, *Duquesne and the Rise of Steel Unionism* (Urbana: University of Illinois Press, 2001); *Steel Labor*, February 6, 1937; February 20, 1937.
44. Harold Ruttenberg, "Experience History of Grievance Negotiations between Wheeling Steel Corporation and the Steel Workers Organizing Committee (CIO), April 1937 to August 1941, Harold Ruttenberg Papers, Box 3, Folder 16, HCLA; *Steel Labor*, May 1, 1937; Martin, "Flopping Tin and Punching Metal," 283–84.
45. This approach is necessitated by a large number of sources from organizers and other local union leaders in the materials on the SWOC and USWA housed at the Labor Archives at Pennsylvania State University.
46. Elizabeth A. Fones-Wolf, *Selling Free Enterprise: The Business Assault on Labor and Liberalism, 1945–1960* (Urbana and Chicago: University of Illinois Press, 1994), 115–17; Lichtenstein, *Labor's War at Home*, 178–202.
47. List of SWOC organizers, appointed in June 1936; William Anderson, President Lodge 1185 et al., "To Be Read at All S.WO.C. Lodges," May 3, 1937, microfilm reel 12, p. 600, 192, CIO Files of John L. Lewis, Part I.
48. Clinton Golden to David J. McDonald, January 23, 1937, USWA President's Office, David J. McDonald, Box 144, File 3, Steelworkers Organizing Committee (January–March 1937), HCLA.

49. *Amalgamated Journal*, February 21, 1934.
50. SWOC broadside, in Harold Ruttenberg Papers, Box 3, Folder 14, HCLA.
51. *Wheeling News-Register*, April 17, 1938, Section 5, 2.
52. *Amalgamated Journal*, February 21, 1934.
53. Benwood Plant Protection, Wheeling Steel, Local Union No. 3814, Officers for 1948–1949, USWA District 23 Box 22, Folder 24, Benwood Blast Furnace, Wheeling Steel Corp, LU 3814, HCLA; Continental Foundry, Warwood, WV, Local Union No. 4218, Officers for 1952–1954, USWA District 23, Box 25, Folder 4, HCLA.
54. Proceedings of the Eighth Annual Convention, West Virginia Industrial Union Council (CIO), Wheeling, WV, September 24, 25, 26, 27, 1945 (Wheeling, WV: 1945), 29–30, WVRHC.
55. Kenneth J. Heineman, *A Catholic New Deal: Religion and Reform in Depression Pittsburgh* (University Park: Pennsylvania State University, 1999), 39–40, 59–61, 72, 97.
56. *Pittsburgh Catholic*, March 4, 1943, 2; March 25, 1943, 2.
57. *Pittsburgh Catholic*, April 1, 1943, 6.
58. *West Virginia Register*, September 8, 1935, 1; August 15, 1937, 1.
59. *West Virginia Register*, January 29, 1939, 1.
60. *West Virginia Register*, January 12, 1941, 1. For more on the ACTU, see Heineman, *A Catholic New Deal*, 150–51, 167, 195; Matthew Pehl, "'Apostles of Fascism,' 'Communist Clergy,' and the UAW: Political Ideology and Working-Class Religion in Detroit, 1919–1945," *Journal of American History* 99, no. 2 (September 2012): 452–54.
61. Heineman, *A Catholic New Deal*, 143, 149, 157. No references were found of how Fr. Emil Musial viewed these developments in the 1930s, but he most likely would have supported the diocese's anticommunism based largely on his earlier views on socialism.
62. *Wheeling News-Register*, March 20, 1938, Section 2, 2; April 10, 1938, Section 2, 7.
63. February 24, 1939, Local 1248 Minutes, USWA District 23, HCLA.
64. Robert Bruno, *Steelworker Alley: How Class Works in Youngstown* (Ithaca and London: Cornell University Press, 1999), 108.
65. John Juliano, Grievance 12-G-772, April 26, 1945, USWA District 23 Records, Box 21, Folder 7, Wheeling Steel, Grievance Cases, 1945 (hereafter Wheeling Steel, Grievance Cases), HCLA.
66. John Culdan and Bernard Kopec, Grievance G-894, April 19, 1945; Nick Yowich, Grievance 12-G-794, August 3, 1945, Wheeling Steel, Grievance Cases, HCLA.
67. Emma Shust, Grievance 5-G-667, May 23, 1945, Wheeling Steel, Grievance Cases, HCLA.
68. Joe Anaskovich, Grievance 9-G-182, June 6, 1945; Leopold Wojtowicz, Grievance 2-G-931, October 11, 1945; Louis Coury, Grievance 5-G-302, July 24, 1945, Wheeling Steel, Grievance Cases, HCLA.
69. Gus Kariganis, Grievance 9-G-168, June 28, 1945, Wheeling Steel, Grievance Cases, HCLA. While these summaries provide insights into how workers utilized the grievance procedures, unfortunately the collections for USWA District 23 did not include the resolutions for these particular grievances.
70. This analysis benefits from a set of Local 1248's meeting minutes from 1937 through the 1946 steel strike.

71. Cynthia "D'Accione" Thames and William W. Holloway Jr., oral history interviews, Wheeling National Heritage Area Corporation, Final Report, Wheeling Spoken History Project (Wheeling, WV: 1994), 116–17, 122.
72. Employment trends derive from Wheeling Steel LU 1248, Wheeling Factory, Seniority Lists, 1947, HCLA.
73. For a description of the production processes, see Thames, Wheeling Spoken History Project, 102–3, 108–9.
74. May 14, 1937, August 6, 1937, and January 27, 1938, Local 1248 Minutes, USWA District 23, HCLA.
75. October 29, 1937, Local 1248 Minutes, USWA District 23, HCLA.
76. March 11, 1938, Local 1248 Minutes, USWA District 23, HCLA.
77. September 17, 1937, November 25, 1937, August 26, 1938, and October 1, 1937, Local 1248 Minutes, USWA District 23, HCLA.
78. January 27, 1938, Local 1248 Minutes, USWA District 23, HCLA.
79. December 9, 1938, Local 1248 Minutes, USWA District 23, HCLA.
80. April 28, 1939, Local 1248 Minutes, USWA District 23, HCLA. Pettinato expressed the concerns of many of the young ethnic women on the drum press department when she mentioned how one girl "tells new people not to join the union because the company don't like it," November 10, 1939, Local 1248 Minutes, USWA District 23, HCLA.
81. January 13, 1939, Local 1248 Minutes, USWA District 23, HCLA.
82. April 26 and May 10, 1940, Local 1248 Minutes, USWA District 23, HCLA.
83. There was a gap in the local's minutes from late 1941 to July 1944, making larger insights on World War II difficult.
84. "St. Kazimer's Society Observes 20th Anniversary," *Wheeling (Catholic) Register*, November 8, 1942, 3; Frank Wojewodka, 1940 Manuscript Census, Wheeling, WV, Enumeration District 35–30, Ancestry.com; Frederick Joseph Wojewodka (Check No. 2232), May 17, 1943; Genevieve Wojewodka (Check No. 1257), July 17, 1943; Wheeling Steel LU 1248, Wheeling Factory, Seniority Lists, 1947, HCLA; May 28, 1937; January 27, 1938; May 22, 1938, Local 1248 Minutes, USWA District 23, HCLA.
85. Joe Gostyla, 1920 Manuscript Census, Wheeling, WV, Center District; Frank George Gosztyla, WWII Draft Cards Young Men, 1940–1947, Ancestry.com; *West Virginia (Catholic) Register*, December 15, 1940, 3; *Wheeling News-Register*, January 12, 14, 1946.
86. August 8, 1941, Local 1248 Minutes, USWA District 23, HCLA; *Wheeling News-Register*, August 27, 1942, 2; August 29, 1942, 1.
87. *Wheeling News-Register*, December 26, 1943, 1, 4; December 27, 1943, 1.
88. *Wheeling News-Register*, December 28, 1943, 1, 8. The NWLB rejected the union's wage request leading to a walkout of over 150,000 steelworkers. President Roosevelt ordered the board to grant the wage increases. For more on the Little Steel Formula and the 1943 walkout, see Lichtenstein, *Labor's War at Home*, 75–76, 171.
89. Marie Bacue, Grievance 13-G-151, November 11, 1945; Mary Naples, Grievance 13-G-157, November 20, 1945; Hilda Ault, Grievance 13-G-158, Wheeling Steel, Grievance Cases, HCLA. For Bacue's seniority, see Marie Halloy Bacue, Check No. 1456, Wheeling Steel LU 1248, Wheeling Factory, Seniority Lists, 1947, HCLA.
90. Marie Bacue, Grievance 13-G-152, November 11, 1945; Wheeling Factory

Grievance 13-G-135, November 27, 1945; Wheeling Factory, Drum Assembly Grievance 13-G-159, November 21, 1945, Wheeling Steel, Grievance Cases, HCLA.
91. Marie Bacue, Grievance 13-G-154, November 16, 1945, Wheeling Steel, Grievance Cases, HCLA.
92. Jessie Olszeski, Grievance 9-G-577, December 12, 1945; Lahona J. Marody, Grievance 9-G-575, December 10, 1945, Wheeling Steel, Grievance Cases, HCLA.
93. October 30, 1945, Local 1248 Minutes, USWA District 23, HCLA; Wheeling Steel LU 1248, Wheeling Factory, Seniority Lists 1947, HCLA.
94. November 9, 1945, Local 1248 Minutes, USWA District 23, HCLA.
95. *Wheeling News-Register*, October 9, 1945, 13; October 13, 1945, 1; October 17, 1945, 1, 9; October 19, 1945, 1; October 22, 1945, 14; October 27, 1945, 1. For the Tobacco Workers Union's demands, see *Wheeling News-Register*, October 18, 1945, 10; October 19, 1945, 14.
96. November 23, 1945, Local 1248 Minutes, USWA District 23, HCLA; Joseph Garlowich (Check No. 1616), July 27, 1933; Wheeling Steel LU 1248, Seniority Lists, 1947, HCLA.
97. *Wheeling News-Register*, January 4, 1946, 1; January 11, 1946, 1, 6; January 12, 1946, 1. A pound of apples in 1941 cost 3.5 cents but rose to 18 cents in 1946, while a dozen eggs sold for 25 cents in 1941 and climbed up to 68 cents in 1946.
98. *Wheeling News-Register*, January 12, 1946, 1; January 14, 1946, 1, 2.
99. *Wheeling News-Register*, January 13, 1946, 1, 10; January 23, 1946, 1; January 11, 1946, January 25, 1946, Local 1248 Minutes, USWA District 23, HCLA.
100. *Wheeling News-Register*, January 19, 1946, 1, 2; January 29, 1946, 1.
101. *Wheeling News-Register*, January 21, 1946, 1, 2.
102. *Wheeling News-Register*, January 23, 1946, 1.

CONCLUSION

1. Stanisław Biega, Preliminary Form for Petition for Naturalization, January 29, 1924, Box 2, Folder 2, RG 21, Records of the U.S. District & Circuit Courts for the Northern District of West Virginia, Wheeling Division, Naturalization Records, National Archives and Records Administration, Philadelphia, PA.
2. Stanley Biega, 1940 Manuscript Census, Wheeling Eighth Ward, Ohio County, WV, Enumeration District 35-32, Roll T627_4436, p. 3B, RG 29, Records of the Bureau of the Census, *Sixteenth Census of the United States*, NARA, Washington, DC, Ancestry.com.
3. Paul Joseph Biega, Check No. 2181, May 27, 1942, Wheeling Steel LU 1248, Wheeling Factory, Seniority Lists, 1947, Box 24, Folder 3, USWA District 23 (Wheeling, WV) Records, 1944–1960, HCLA.
4. Paul Biega, Enlistment Record, World War II Army Enlistment Records, RG 64, NARA, College Park, MD, Ancestry.com.
5. Bishop John J. Swint to Rev. Emil Musial, April 1, 1937, Bishop John J. Swint, Outgoing Correspondence, 1928–1938, Folder "M" 1937, Bishop John J. Swint Papers, Archives of the Diocese of Wheeling-Charleston (DWC).
6. Rev. Emil Musial to Bishop Swint, May 25, 1940, Bishop John J. Swint Correspondence, Box M-N, Folder 1937–1940, DWC. This is based on the older DWC filing system prior to the 2013 reorganization.

7. Lizabeth Cohen, *Making a New Deal: Industrial Workers in Chicago, 1919–1939* (Cambridge: Cambridge University Press, 1990), 209.
8. James R. Barrett, *The Irish Way: Becoming American in the Multiethnic City* (New York: Penguin Books, 2012).
9. John Bodnar, "Immigration, Kinship, and the Rise of Working-Class Realism in Industrial America," *Journal of Social History* 14, no. 1 (Autumn 1980): 45.
10. Cohen, *Making a New Deal*, 5–7, 209, 285, 314–15.
11. Leslie Woodcock Tentler, "On the Margins: The State of American Catholic History," *U.S. Catholic Historian* 21, no. 2 (Spring 2003): 84.
12. John Bodnar, *Workers' World: Kinship, Community, and Protest in an Industrial Society, 1900–1940* (Baltimore: Johns Hopkins University Press, 1982), 184; Cohen, *Making a New Deal*, 365.
13. Keith Maillard, *The Clarinet Polka* (New York: St. Martin's Press, 2003), 13.
14. Maillard, *The Clarinet Polka*, 33.

Bibliography

MANUSCRIPT COLLECTIONS

Archives of the Diocese of Wheeling-Charleston (DWC), Wheeling, WV

Annual Reports, 1897–1899; 1911–1940
    Nationality Survey, 1904
Bishop Donahue's Correspondence, 1894–1922
Bishop Swint's Correspondence, 1917–1962
    Correspondence Donahue and Swint
    Correspondence
    Diocesan Clergy, 1918–1946
    Sermons by Topic
Deceased Priests Files
Diocese Parish History Files
    Cathedral of St. Joseph (1828–Present), Wheeling, WV
    Immaculate Conception Parish History File, Wheeling, WV
    Our Lady of Perpetual Help Ukrainian Catholic Church (1913–Present), Wheeling, WV
    St. Alphonsus Parish History File (1856–Present), Wheeling, WV
    St. John's Parish History File (1875–Present), Benwood, WV
    St. Ladislaus Parish History File (1902–1995), Wheeling, WV
    Sacred Heart of Mary Parish History File (1912–Present), Weirton, WV
Records of the Chancery
    Chancellor's Office Administrative Records
    Institutions and Schools
    Student Records
Sacramental Records, St. Ladislaus Parish
    Birth Book
    Confirmation Book
    Marriage Book
    Internment Book

Historical Collections and Labor Archives (HCLA), Penn State University, State College, PA

David J. McDonald Papers
Harold Ruttenberg Papers
Steel Workers Organizing Committee (SWOC) Records, 1936–1942
United Steelworkers of America, Twenty-Third District Records (Steubenville-Wheeling), 1937–1960

National Archives, College Park, MD
Available via Digitized Archives, Ancestry.com, and Fold3.com

  RG 21—Records of the District Courts of the United States
    Military Petitions for Naturalization, 1918–1924
  RG 29—Records of the Bureau of the Census
  RG 36—Records of the U.S. Custom Service
    Passenger Lists of Vessels Arriving at Baltimore, Maryland, 1820–1891
    Passenger Lists of Vessels Arriving at New York, 1820–1897
  RG 59—Records of the Department of State
    Passport Applications, January 2, 1906–March 31, 1925
  RG 64—World War II Army Enlistment Records
  RG 65—Bureau of Investigation Records
    Old German Files, 1909–1921
  RG 85—Records of the Immigration and Naturalization Service
    Hamburg Passenger Lists, 1850–1934
    New York Passenger Lists, 1820–1957
    Passenger and Crew Lists of Vessels Arriving in New York, 1897–1957
  RG 147—Records of the Selective Service System
    World War II Draft Registration Cards

National Archives and Records Administration—Philadelphia, PA

  RG 21—U.S. Circuit Court Naturalization Records
    Declarations of Intention
  RG 21—Records of the U.S. District Court for the Northern District of West Virginia
    Criminal Case Files, 1887–1957
    Declarations of Intention, 1912–1989
    Naturalization Case Files
    Preliminary Forms for Petitions for Naturalization
  RG 163—Records of the Selective Service System
    Lists of Delinquents and Deserters

Ohio County Clerk's Office, Ohio County Courthouse, Wheeling, WV

  Appraiser's Record Books
  Death Records
  Deed Books
  Incorporation Books
  Wheeling City Tax Map, 1901
  Will Books

Ohio County Public Library, Wheeling, WV

  Callin's Wheeling City Directory, 1903–1904 through 1921–1922
  Kline, Michael and Carrie. *Wheeling's Spoken History: An Interim Report on the Wheeling Cultural Heritage Survey Prepared for the Wheeling National Heritage Area Cooperation and the National Park Service*, 1994.

Polk's Wheeling (West Virginia) City Directory, 1923–1924 through 1940
Report of the Health Department of City of Wheeling, West Virginia, for the Two Years Ending June the Thirtieth Nineteen Hundred & Thirteen. Wheeling, WV: City Health Department, 1913.
Sanborn Insurance Atlas Maps, Wheeling, West Virginia, 1884, 1890, 1902, 1921
"Wheeling Floods: 1762 to the Present," http://www.ohiocountylibrary.org/wheeling-history/statistics-about-ohio-river-floods-at-wheeling/3195
Wheeling-LaBelle Nail Company Records

West Virginia and Regional History Center (WVRHC), West Virginia University, Morgantown, WV

John J. Cornwell Papers
Richard M. Hadsell Papers
Ephraim Morgan Papers
Ohio Valley Trades and Labor Assembly Records, 1882–1951
West Virginia State Industrial Union Council, CIO Archives
Wheeling Tobacco Workers Union, Local 2, 1890–1905
Declaration of Naturalizations, Ohio County, West Virginia
Marshall County Court Records
Ohio County Court Records
Manuscript Census Schedules, 1900, Ohio and Marshall Counties
———, 1910, Ohio and Marshall Counties
———, 1920, Ohio and Marshall Counties
———, 1930, Ohio and Marshall Counties

West Virginia State Archives, Charleston, WV

Birth Records
Death Records
Marriage Records
Wheeling Socialist Party Collection

Wheeling Jesuit University Library, Wheeling, WV

Wheeling Steel Corporation, Annual Reports, 1920–1940

U.S. GOVERNMENT DOCUMENTS

U.S. Congress. House of Representatives. *Charges against William E. Baker, United States District Court Judge for the Northern District of West Virginia: Hearings before the Committee on the Judiciary.* Pursuant to H. Res. 325. 68th Cong., 1st sess., 1925. Washington, DC: Government Printing Office, 1925.

U.S. Congress. Senate. *Report on the Conditions of Employment in the Iron and Steel Industry.* 62nd Cong., 1st sess., 1913. Washington, DC: Government Printing Office, 1913.

U.S. Congress. Senate. *Investigation of the Strike in the Steel Industries: Hearings before* the Committee on Education and Labor. Pursuant to S. Res. 202. 66th Cong., 1st sess., 1919. Washington, DC: Government Printing Office, 1919.

U.S. Department of Commerce. Bureau of the Census. *Twelfth Census of the United States*. Pt. 1: *Population (1900)*. Washington, DC: Government Printing Office, 1902.

———. *Twelfth Census of the United States*. Pt. 2: *Population (1900)*. Washington, DC: Government Printing Office, 1902.

———. *Thirteenth Census of the United States*. Vol. 3, *Population (1910)*. Washington, DC: Government Printing Office, 1913.

———. *Thirteenth Census of the United States*. Vol. 4, *Population (1910): Occupation Statistics*. Washington, DC: Government Printing Office, 1914.

———. *Fourteenth Census of the United States*. Vol. 1, *Population (1920)*. Washington, DC: Government Printing Office, 1921.

———. *Fourteenth Census of the United States*. Vol. 2, *Population (1920)*. Washington, DC: Government Printing Office, 1922.

U.S. Department of the Interior. Bureau of the Census. *Report on Manufacturing Industries in the United States at the Eleventh Census*. Pt. 2, *Statistics of Cities (1890)*. Washington, DC: Government Printing Office, 1895.

U.S. Industrial Commission. *Report on the Relations and Conditions and Capital and Labor Employed in Manufacturers and General Business*. Washington, DC: Government Printing Office, 1901.

U.S. Selective Service System. *World War I Selective Service System Draft Registration Cards, 1917–1918*. Washington, DC: National Archives and Records Administration, M1509, Ohio County, West Virginia, Roll 1993024. *Ancestry Library Edition*.

WEST VIRGINIA STATE DOCUMENTS

Commissioner of Labor. *Biennial Report of the Bureau of Labor*, 1896–1943.
Report of Bureau of Negro Welfare and Statistics, 1921–1928.
Proceedings of Annual Convention, West Virginia Industrial Union Council (CIO), 1938–1945.
West Virginia. *West Virginia Blue Book*, 1928–1940.
West Virginia Commissioner of Labor. *Biennial Reports of the Bureau of Labor*, 1897–1940.
West Virginia State Department of Mines. *Annual Reports*, 1900–1935.
West Virginia State Federation of Labor. *Proceedings of Annual Conventions*, 1906–1940.

NEWSPAPERS, PERIODICALS, TRADE UNION JOURNALS

Amalgamated Journal
Black Diamond
Benwood Enterpriser, 1913–1919
Building Blochs
Church Calendar, 1898–1922
Iron Age

Morning Herald (Baltimore, MD)
Moundsville Daily Echo
National Labor Tribune
New York Times
Pittsburgh Gazette Times
Pittsburgh Post-Gazette
Pittsburgh Press
Searchlight (Atlanta, GA)
Steel Labor
United Mine Workers Journal
Washington Reporter
West Virginia Register (Diocese of Wheeling-Charleston), 1934–1945
West Virginia Review
West Virginia School Journal
Wheeling Daily Intelligencer
Wheeling Daily News
Wheeling Daily Register
Wheeling Intelligencer
Wheeling Majority, 1909–1919
Wheeling News-Register
Wheeling Register

ORAL HISTORIES

By the Author

Gorczyca, Ed. Interview by the author, 6 August 2008, notes.
Martinkosky, Mary. Interview by the author, 10 August 2008, transcript.
Resczynski, Blanche. Interview by the author, 10 August 2008, transcript.
Werfele, Herman. Interview by the author, 23 July 2008, transcript.

Wheeling Spoken History Project, Ohio County Library Archives

Murray, Jane. Interview by Michael Kline, 31 October 1994, transcript.
Skrzypek, Delores. Interview by Michael Kline, 31 October 1994, transcript.
Anonymous Interviews. Interview by Michael Kline, 31 October 1994, transcript.

By the Wheeling National Heritage Area Corporation (WNHAC)

"As They Say in Wheeling," The Final Report of the Wheeling Spoken History Project, 1995.

CONTEMPORARY ARTICLES, PAMPHLETS, SPEECHES

Bulletin of the Department of Labor: Statistics of Cities. Washington, DC: 1900–1902.
The CIO Files of John L. Lewis. Frederick, MD: University Publications of America, 1988.

Commission of Inquiry, the Interchurch World Movement. *Public Opinion and the Steel Strike*. New York: Harcourt, Brace, and Company, 1921.

Directory to the Iron and Steel Works of the United States, Compiled and Published by the American Iron and Steel Association. 17th ed., corrected to March 1, 1908. Philadelphia: J. B. Lippincott Company, 1908.

The Interchurch World Movement. *Public Opinion and the Steel Strike of 1919: Supplementary Reports of the Investigators to the Commission of Inquiry*. New York: Harcourt, Brace, and Company, 1921.

Lambie, R. M. Chief of Department of Mines. "Benwood Mine Disaster: Report on Benwood Explosion." AR1533, reprinted by West Virginia State Archives.

St. Ladislaus Parish. *Pamietnik uroczystosci zlotego jubileusza swiecenn kaplanshich przewielebnego ksiedza Emila Musiala, proboszcza parafii Sw. Wladyslawa Krola, Wheeling, W.Va*. [Fr. Emil Musial twenty-fifth anniversary book], 1926. St. Ladislaus Parish History File, Archives of the Diocese of Wheeling-Charleston.

ONLINE SOURCES

Carney, William. "The William G. Lias Story." Presentation to Wheeling Area Genealogical Society meeting, February 8, 2003. http://www.lindapages.com/wags-ohio/liasbill.htm.

Fluharty, Linda Cunningham. "History of 314th Field Artillery," and "Memories of Battery F." http://www.wvgenweb.org/marshall/314/314th.htm.

———. "War Diary, 314th Field Artillery." http://www.wvgenweb.org/marshall/314/314-diary.txt.

Haller's Army Index. Polish Genealogical Society of America, 2009, http://pgsa.org/haller.php.

House Bill No. 8: Chapter 13, "Prohibition." *Acts of the Legislature of West Virginia, Thirty-First Regular Session, 1913*. http://www.wvculture.org/history/government/prohibition01.html.

Lambie, R. M. "Benwood Mine Disaster: Report on Benwood Explosion." AR1533, West Virginia State Archives. http://www.wvculture.org/history/thisdayinwvhistory/0428A.html.

Ohio County Public Library. "Wheeling Floods: 1762 to the Present." http://wheeling.weirton.lib.wv.us/history/events/floods/floods.htm.

———. "Wheeling Hall of Fame: Everett Brinkman, 1902–1972." http://www.ohiocountylibrary.org/wheeling-history/wheeling-hall-of-fame-everett-brinkman/4144.

———. Wheeling Spoken History Project. http://wheeling.weirton.lib.wv.us/wahp/other/96-021.htm.

West Virginia Northern Community College. "West Virginia Northern Community College and the History of the Hazel Atlas Corporation." http://www.wvncc.edu/alumni/hazel-atlas-glass-history/105.

West Virginia State Archives. "Benwood Mine Disaster, List of Victims, April 28, 1924." http://www.wvculture.org/history/disasters/benwood02.html.

Zaccagnini, Julia Piechowicz. "The Piechowicz Family." http://www.wvgenweb.org/marshall/piechowiczfam.htm.

PUBLISHED CONTEMPORARY BOOKS

Callahan, James Morton. *History of West Virginia, Old and New.* Chicago: American Historical Society, 1923.
Cranmer, Gibson Lamb. *History of Wheeling and Ohio County, West Virginia and Representative Citizens.* Wheeling, WV: 1902.
Cranmer, Gibson Lamb, and S. L. Jebson. *History of the Upper Ohio Valley.* Vol. 1, *With Family History and Biographical Sketches: A Statement of Its Resources, Industrial Growth and Commercial Advantages.* Madison, WI: Brant & Fuller, 1890.
Fitch, John. *Pittsburgh Survey: The Steel Workers.* Edited by Paul Kellogg. New York: Russell Sage Foundation, 1910.
Foster, William Z. *The Great Steel Strike and Its Lessons.* New York: B. W. Huebsch, Inc., 1920.
Mill, Thomas Condit, and Hu Maxwell. *West Virginia and Its People.* Vol. 2. New York: Lewis Historical Publishing Company, 1913.
Wheeling Board of Trade Yearbook for 1911. Wheeling, WV: Secretary's Office, 1911.

SECONDARY SOURCES

Anderson, Benedict. *Imagined Communities: Reflections on the Origins and Spread of Nationalism.* 3rd ed. New York: Verso, 2006.
Arts & Advertising of Bloch Bros. Tobacco Co.: The Nation's Favorite Since 1879. Wheeling, WV: Creative Impressions, 2002.
Barkey, Fred. *Working Class Radicals: The Socialist Party in West Virginia, 1898–1920.* Morgantown: West Virginia University Press, 2012.
Barrett, James R. *Work and Community in the Jungle: Chicago's Packinghouse Workers, 1894–1922.* Urbana: University of Illinois Press, 1987.
———. *The Irish Way: Becoming American in the Multiethnic City.* New York: Penguin Press, 2012.
Bensel, Richard Franklin. *The Political Economy of American Industrialization, 1877–1900.* New York: Cambridge University Press, 2000.
Benton-Cohen, Katherine. *Borderland Americans: Racial Division and Labor War in the Arizona Borderlands.* Cambridge, MA: Harvard University Press, 2009.
Berend, Ivan T. *History Derailed: Central and Eastern Europe in the Long Nineteenth Century.* Berkeley: University of California Press, 2003.
Biskupski, M. B. B., James S. Pula, and Piotr J. Wrobel, eds. *The Origins of Modern Polish Democracy.* Athens: Ohio University Press, 2010.
Blanke, Richard. *Prussian Poland in the German Empire, 1871–1900.* Boulder, CO: East European Monographs, 1981.
Blobaum, Robert E. *Rewolucja: Russian Poland, 1904–1907.* Ithaca and London: Cornell University Press, 1995.
Bodnar, John. *The Transplanted: A History of Immigrants in Urban America.* Bloomington: Indiana University Press, 1985.
———. *Workers' World: Kinship, Community, and Protest in an Industrial Society, 1900–1940.* Baltimore: Johns Hopkins University Press, 1982.

Bodnar, John, Roger Simon, and Michael P. Weber. *Lives of Their Own: Blacks, Italians, and Poles in Pittsburgh, 1900–1960*. Urbana and Chicago: University of Illinois Press, 1982.

Boothe, Raymond-Lynn. *Fire on the Water: A New History of the Wheeling Steel Corporation*. Raleigh, NC: Lulu Press, 2011.

Boyd, Peter. *History of Northern West Virginia Panhandle, Embracing Ohio, Marshall, Brooke and Hancock Counties*. Vol. 1. Topeka, KS: Historical Publishing Company, 1927.

Boyer, Paul. *Urban Masses and Moral Order in America, 1820–1920*. Cambridge, MA: Harvard University Press, 1978.

Brody, David. *Labor in Crisis*. Philadelphia: Lippincott, 1965.

———. *Steelworkers in America: The Non-Union Era*. New York: Harper & Row, 1969.

Bruno, Robert. *Steelworker Alley: How Class Works in Youngstown*. Ithaca and London: Cornell University Press, 1999.

Bukowczyk, John J. *And My Children Did Not Know Me: A History of the Polish-Americans*. Bloomington and Indianapolis: Indiana University Press, 1987.

———. *Polish Americans and Their History: Community, Culture, and Politics*. Pittsburgh: University of Pittsburgh Press, 1996.

Callahan, Richard J., Jr. *Work and Faith in the Kentucky Coal Fields: Subject to Dust*. Bloomington and Indianapolis: Indiana University Press, 2009.

Cantwell, Christopher D., Heath W. Carter, and Janine Giordano Drake, eds. *The Pew and the Picket Line: Christianity and the American Working Class*. Urbana: University of Illinois Press, 2016.

Capozzola, Christopher. *Uncle Sam Wants You: World War I and the Making of the Modern American Citizen*. New York: Oxford University Press, 2008.

Carter, Heath W. *Union Made: Working People and the Rise of Social Christianity in Chicago*. New York: Oxford University Press, 2015.

Cohen, Lizabeth. *Making a New Deal: Industrial Workers in Chicago, 1919–1939*. New York: Cambridge University Press, 1990.

Cooper, Patricia A. *Once a Cigar Maker: Men, Women, and Work Culture in American Cigar Factories, 1900–1919*. Urbana and Chicago: University of Illinois Press, 1987.

Corbin, David Alan. *Life, Work, and Rebellion in the Coal Fields: The Southern West Virginia Miners, 1880–1922*. Urbana and Chicago: University of Illinois Press, 1981.

Czitrom, Daniel. *New York Exposed: The Gilded Age Police Scandal that Launched the Progressive Era*. New York: Oxford University Press, 2016.

Davies, Norman. *White Eagle, Red Star: The Polish–Soviet War 1919–1920 and the Miracle on the Vistula*. London: Random House, 2003.

Deutsch, Sarah. *Women and the City: Gender, Space, and Power in Boston, 1870–1940*. New York: Oxford University Press, 2002.

Dieterich-Ward, Alan. *Beyond Rust: Metropolitan Pittsburgh and the Fate of Industrial America*. Philadelphia: University of Pennsylvania Press, 2015.

Dolan, Jay P. *The American Catholic Experience: A History from Colonial Times to the Present*. Garden City, NY: Doubleday & Company, 1985.

———. *The Immigrant Church: New York's Irish and German Catholics, 1815–1865*. Baltimore: Johns Hopkins University Press, 1975.

———. *In Search of an American Catholicism: A History of Religion and Culture in Tension*. New York: Oxford University Press, 2002.
Dubofsky, Melvyn. *We Shall Be All: A History of the Industrial Workers of the World*. 2nd ed. Urbana: University of Illinois Press, 2000.
Duffy, Sean. *The Wheeling Family*. Vol. 2, *More Immigrants, Migrants, and Neighborhoods*. Wheeling, WV: James Thornton, 2012.
Duffy, Sean, and James Thornton. *The Wheeling Family: A Celebration of Immigrants and Their Neighborhoods*. Wheeling, WV: Creative Impressions, 2008.
Duis, Perry. *The Saloon: Public Drinking in Chicago and Boston, 1880–1920*. Urbana and Chicago: University of Illinois Press, 1983.
Dunham, Tom. *Wheeling in the 20th Century*. Bloomington, IN: 1st Books Library, 2003.
Eberghardt, Piotr. *Ethnic Groups and Population Changes in Twentieth-Century Central-Eastern Europe*. Armonk, NY: M. E. Sharpe, 2003.
Fetherling, George. *The Big Greek: The Rise and Fall of Bill Lias*. Wheeling, WV: Polyhedron Learning Media and Friends of Wheeling, 2018.
———. *Wheeling: A Brief History*. Wheeling, WV: Polyhedron Learning Media, 2008.
Fitzgerald, Maureen. *Habits of Compassion: Irish Catholic Nuns and the Origins of New York's Welfare System, 1830–1920*. Urbana: University of Illinois Press, 2006.
Fones-Wolf, Ken. *Glass Towns: Industry, Labor, and Political Economy in Appalachia, 1890–1930s*. Urbana and Chicago: University of Illinois Press, 2007.
Fones-Wolf, Ken, and Elizabeth Fones-Wolf. *Struggle for the Soul of the Postwar South: White Evangelical Protestants and Operation Dixie*. Urbana: University of Illinois Press, 2015.
Fones-Wolf, Ken, and Ronald L. Lewis. *Transnational West Virginia: Ethnic Communities and Economic Change, 1840–1940*. Morgantown: West Virginia University Press, 2002.
Gage, Beverly. *The Day Wall Street Exploded: A Story of America in Its First Age of Terror*. New York: Oxford University Press, 2009.
Galush, William J. *For More than Bread: Community and Identity in American Polonia, 1880–1940*. Boulder, CO: East European Monographs, 2006.
Gerstle, Gary. *American Crucible: Race and Nation in the Twentieth Century*. Princeton, NJ: Princeton University Press, 2001.
———. *Working-Class Americanism: The Politics of Labor in a Textile City, 1914–1960*. 1st paperback ed. Cambridge: Cambridge University Press, 1991.
Goldberg, David J. *Discontented America: The United States in the 1920s*. Baltimore and London: Johns Hopkins University Press, 1999.
Gorn, Elliot J. *Mother Jones: The Most Dangerous Woman in America*. New York: Hill & Wang, 2001.
Greene, Victor. *For God and Country: The Rise of Polish and Lithuanian Ethnic Consciousness in America 1860–1910*. Madison, WI: The State Historical Society of Wisconsin, 1975.
———. *A Passion for Polka: Old-Time Ethnic Music in America*. Berkeley: University of California Press, 1992.
Guglielmo, Thomas A. *White on Arrival: Italians, Race, Color and Power in Chicago*. Oxford: Oxford University Press, 2003.
Hagen, William. *Anti-Jewish Violence in Poland, 1914–1920*. Cambridge: Cambridge University Press, 2018.

Haverty-Stacke, Donna. *America's Forgotten Holiday: May Day and Nationalism, 1867–1960*. New York: New York University Press, 2009.
Heineman, Kenneth J. *A Catholic New Deal: Religion and Reform in Depression Pittsburgh*. University Park: Pennsylvania State University Press, 1999.
Hennen, John C. *The Americanization of West Virginia: Creating a Modern Industrial State, 1916–1925*. Lexington: University of Kentucky Press, 1996.
Higham, John. *Strangers in the Land: Patterns of American Nativism, 1860–1925*. New Brunswick and London: Rutgers University Press, 1955.
Hoerder, Dirk. *Cultures in Contact: World Migrations in the Second Millennium*. Durham, NC: Duke University Press, 2002.
———. *"Struggle a Hard Battle": Essays on Working-Class Immigrants*. Dekalb: Northern Illinois University Press, 1986.
Jacobson, Matthew Frye. *Barbarian Virtues: The United States Encounters Foreign Peoples at Home and Abroad, 1876–1917*. New York: Hill and Wang, 2000.
Jackson, Kenneth T. Jackson. *The Ku Klux Klan in the City, 1915–1930*. New York: Oxford University Press, 1967.
Jenkins, William D. Jenkins. *Steel Valley Klan: The Ku Klux Klan in Ohio's Mahoning Valley*. Kent, OH: Kent State University Press, 1990.
Johnson, Robert D. *The Radical Middle Class: Populist Democracy and the Question of Capitalism in Progressive Era Portland, Oregon*. Princeton, NJ: Princeton University Press, 2002.
Kane, Paula. *Separatism and Subculture: Boston Catholicism, 1900–1920*. Chapel Hill: University of North Carolina Press, 1994.
Kantowicz, Edward R. *Polish American Politics in Chicago, 1888–1940*. Chicago: University of Chicago Press, 1975.
Kazin, Michael. *The Populist Persuasion: An American History*. Ithaca, NY: Cornell University Press, 1998.
Keene, Jennifer D. Keene. *Doughboys: The Great War, and the Remaking of America*. Baltimore: Johns Hopkins University Press, 2003.
Keith, Jeanette. *Rich Man's War, Poor Man's Fight: Race, Class, and Power in the Rural South during the First World War*. Chapel Hill: University of North Carolina Press, 2004.
Kennedy, David. *Over Here: The First World War and American Society*. New York: Oxford University Press, 1980.
Kessler-Harris, Alice. *Out to Work: A History of Wage-Earning Women in the United States*. New York: Oxford University Press, 1982.
Kieniewicz, Stefan. *The Emancipation of the Polish Peasantry*. Chicago: University of Chicago Press, 1969.
Krause, Paul. *The Battle for Homestead, 1880–1892: Politics, Culture, and Steel*. Pittsburgh: University of Pittsburgh Press, 1992.
Krebs, Frank J. *From Humble Beginnings: The West Virginia State Federation of Labor, 1903–1957*. Charleston: West Virginia Labor History Publication Fund, 1960.
Kulczycki, John J. *The Foreign Worker and the German Labor Movement: Xenophobia and Solidarity in the Coal Fields of the Ruhr, 1871–1914*. Oxford and Providence, RI: Berg, 1994.
Kuzniewski, Anthony J. *Faith and Fatherland: The Polish Church War in Wisconsin, 1896–1918*. South Bend, IN.: University of Notre Dame Press, 1980.

Lachowicz, Teofil. *Polish Freedom Fighters on American Soil: Polish Veterans in America from the Revolutionary War to 1939*. Minneapolis, MN: Two Harbors Press, 2011.
Lerner, Michael. *Dry Manhattan: Prohibition in New York City*. Cambridge, MA: Harvard University Press, 2007.
Leuchtenberg, William E. *Franklin D. Roosevelt and the New Deal, 1932–1940*. New York: Harper & Row, 1963.
Lewis, Ronald L. *Transforming the Appalachian Countryside: Railroads, Deforestation, and Social Change in West Virginia, 1880–1930*. Chapel Hill: University of North Carolina Press, 1998.
Lichtenstein, Nelson. *Labor's War at Home: The CIO in World War II*. Cambridge: Cambridge University Press, 1982.
Löwy, Michael. *Redemption and Utopia: Jewish Libertarian Thought in Central Europe: A Study in Elective Affinity*. London: Verso, 1992.
Maillard, Keith. *The Clarinet Polka*. New York: St. Martin's Press, 2003.
Martin, Lou. *Smokestacks in the Hills: Rural-Industrial Workers in West Virginia*. Urbana: University of Illinois Press, 2015.
May, Earl Chapin. *Principio to Wheeling, 1715–1945: A Pageant of Iron and Steel*. New York: Harper & Brothers, 1945.
McCartin, Joseph. *Labor's Great War: The Struggle for Industrial Democracy and the Origins of Modern American Labor Relations, 1912–1921*. Chapel Hill: University of North Carolina Press, 1997.
McCook, Brian. *The Borders of Integration: Polish Migrants in Germany and the United States, 1870–1924*. Athens: Ohio University Press, 2011.
McGirr, Lisa. *The War on Alcohol: Prohibition and the Rise of the American State*. New York: W. W. Norton, 2015.
McGreevy, John T. *Catholicism and American Freedom: A History*. New York: W. W. Norton & Company, 2003.
———. *Parish Boundaries: The Catholic Encounter with Race in the Twentieth-Century Urban North*. Chicago: University of Chicago Press, 1996.
Mikoś, Susan Gibson. *Poles in Wisconsin*. Madison: Wisconsin Historical Society Press, 2012.
Miller, Zane L. *Boss Cox's Cincinnati: Urban Politics in the Progressive Era*. New York: Oxford University Press, 1968.
Minder, Mike. *Wheeling's Gambling History to 1976*. Wheeling, WV: Nail City Publishing, 1997.
Montgomery, David. *Workers' Control in America: Studies in the History of Work, Technology, and Labor Struggles*. Cambridge: Cambridge University Press, 1979.
Moore, Leonard J. Moore. *Citizen Klansmen: The Ku Klux Klan in Indiana, 1921–1928*. Chapel Hill: University of North Carolina Press, 1991.
Newman, Simon. *Parades and the Politics of the Street: Festive Culture in the Early American Republic*. Philadelphia: University of Pennsylvania Press, 1997.
Oates, Mary J. *The Catholic Philanthropic Tradition in America*. Bloomington: Indiana University Press, 1995.
Oestreicher, Richard Jules. *Solidarity and Fragmentation: Working People and Class Consciousness in Detroit, 1875–1900*. 2nd ed. Urbana and Chicago: University of Illinois Press, 1989.
Okrent, Daniel. *Last Call: The Rise and Fall of Prohibition*. New York: Scribner, 2010.

Oriard, Michael. *King Football: Sport and Spectacle in the Golden Age of Radio, Newsreels, Movies & Magazines, The Weekly & The Daily Press*. Chapel Hill: University of North Carolina Press, 2001.

Orsi, Robert Anthony. *The Madonna of 115th Street: Faith and Community in Italian Harlem, 1880–1950*. New Haven, CT: Yale University Press, 1985.

O'Toole, James M. *The Faithful: A History of Catholics in America*. Cambridge, MA: Harvard University Press, 2008.

Pacyga, Dominic. *Polish Immigrants and Industrial Chicago: Workers on the South Side, 1880–1922*. 2nd ed. Chicago: University of Chicago Press, 2003.

Perales, Monica. *Smeltertown: Making and Remembering a Southwest Border Community*. Chapel Hill: University of North Carolina Press, 2010.

Postel, Charles. *The Populist Vision*. New York: Oxford University Press, 2007.

Powers, Madelon. *Faces along the Bar: Lore and Order in the Workingman's Saloon, 1870–1920*. Chicago: University of Chicago Press, 1998.

Pula, James S. *Polish Americans: An Ethnic Community*. Twayne's Immigrant Heritage of America Series. New York: Twayne, 1995.

Pyne, Tricia T. *Faith in the Mountains: A History of the Diocese of Wheeling-Charleston, 1850–2000*. Eckbolsheim, France: Editions du Signe, 2001.

Radziłowski, John. *Poles in Minnesota*. St. Paul: Minnesota Historical Society, 2005.

Reuther, Victor G. *The Brothers Reuther and the Story of the UAW: A Memoir*. Boston: Houghton Mifflin, 1976.

Roediger, David. *Working Toward Whiteness: How America's Immigrants Became White, the Strange Journey from Ellis Island to the Suburbs*. New York: Basic Books, 2005.

Roll, Jared. *Spirit of Rebellion: Labor and Religion in the New Cotton South*. Urbana: University of Illinois Press, 2010.

Rose, James D. *Duquesne and the Rise of Steel Unionism*. Urbana: University of Illinois Press, 2001.

Rosen, Ruth. *The Lost Sisterhood: Prostitution in America, 1900–1918*. Baltimore: Johns Hopkins University Press, 1982.

Rosenzweig, Roy. *Eight Hours for What We Will: Workers and Leisure in an Industrial City*. Cambridge: Cambridge University Press, 1983.

Ryan, Mary P. *Civic Wars: Democracy and Public Life in the American City during the Nineteenth Century*. Berkeley: University of California Press, 1997.

Schatz, Ronald W. *The Electrical Workers: A History of Labor at General Electric and Westinghouse, 1923–60*. Urbana and Chicago: University of Illinois Press, 1983.

Scott, Henry D. *Iron and Steel in Wheeling*. Toledo, OH: Caslon Company, 1928.

Scott, James C. *Domination and the Arts of Resistance: Hidden Transcripts*. New Haven, CT: Yale University Press, 1990.

Skok, Deborah A. *More than Neighbors: Catholic Settlements and Day Nurseries in Chicago, 1893–1930*. Dekalb: Northern Illinois University Press, 2007.

Slavishak, Edward. *Bodies of Work: Civic Display and Labor in Industrial Pittsburgh*. Durham, NC: Duke University Press, 2008.

Stauter-Halsted, Keely. *The Nation in the Village: The Genesis of Peasant National Identity in Austrian Poland, 1848–1914*. Ithaca, NY: Cornell University Press, 2001.

Sterne, Evelyn Savidge. *Ballots and Bibles: Ethnic Politics and the Catholic Church in Providence*. Ithaca, NY: Cornell University Press, 2003.

Stromquist, Shelton. *Reinventing "The People": The Progressive Movement, the Class*

Problem, and the Origins of Modern Liberalism. Urbana and Chicago: University of Illinois Press, 2006.

Summers, Mark Wahlgren. *Party Games: Getting, Keeping, and Using Power in Gilded Age Politics.* Chapel Hill: University of North Carolina Press, 2004.

Tentler, Leslie Woodcock. *Catholics and Contraception: An American History.* Ithaca, NY: Cornell University Press, 2004.

———. *Seasons of Grace: A History of the Catholic Archdiocese of Detroit.* Detroit: Wayne State University Press, 1992.

———. *Wage-Earning Women: Industrial Work and Family Life in the United States, 1900–1930.* New York: Oxford University Press, 1979.

Tichenor, David J. *Dividing Lines: The Politics of Immigration Control in America.* Princeton, NJ: Princeton University Press, 2002.

Tribe, Ivan. *Mountaineer Jamboree: Country Music in West Virginia.* Lexington: University of Kentucky Press, 1984.

Weiner, Deborah R. *Coalfield Jews: An Appalachian History.* Urbana and Chicago: University of Chicago Press, 2006.

Wingerd, Mary Lethert. *Claiming the City: Politics, Faith, and the Power of Place in St. Paul.* Ithaca, NY: Cornell University Press, 2003.

Wingerter, Charles A. *History of Greater Wheeling and Vicinity: A Chronicle of Progress and a Narrative Account of the Industries, Institutions, and People of the City and Tributary Territory.* Vol. 1. Chicago and New York: The Lewis Publishing Company, 1912.

Williams, John Alexander. *West Virginia and the Captains of Industry.* Morgantown: West Virginia University Press, 1976.

Wyman, Mark. *Round Trip to America: The Immigrants Return to Europe, 1880–1930.* Ithaca, NY: Cornell University Press, 1993.

Zahra, Tara. *The Great Departure: Mass Migration from Eastern Europe and the Making of the Free World.* New York: W. W. Norton, 2016.

Zunz, Oliver. *The Changing Face of Inequality: Urbanization, Industrial Development, and Immigrants in Detroit, 1880–1920.* Chicago: University of Chicago Press, 1982.

SCHOLARLY ARTICLES AND BOOK CHAPTERS

Barrett, James R. "Americanization from the Bottom Up: Immigration and the Remaking of the Working Class in the United States, 1880–1930." *Journal of American History* 79, no. 3 (December 1992): 996–1020.

Barrett, James R., and David Roediger. "In-between Peoples: Race, Nationality and the 'New Immigrant' Working Class." *Journal of American Ethnic History* 16 (1997): 3–44.

———. "The Irish and the 'Americanization' of the 'New Immigrants' in the Streets and in the Churches of the Urban United States, 1900–1930." *Journal of American Ethnic History* 24, no. 4 (Summer 2005): 3–33.

Blobaum, Robert. "To Market! To Market! The Polish Peasantry in the Era of the Stolypin Reforms." *Slavic Review* 59, no. 2 (Summer 2000): 406–26.

———. "The Revolution of 1905–1907 and the Crisis of Polish Catholicism." *Slavic Review* 47, no. 4 (Winter 1988): 667–86.

———. "The 'Woman Question' in Russian Poland, 1900–1914." *Journal of Social History* 35, no. 4 (Summer 2002): 799–824.

Bodnar, John. "Immigration, Kinship, and the Rise of Working-Class Realism in Industrial America." *Journal of Social History* 14, no. 1 (Autumn 1980): 45–65.

Borden, Timothy G. "The Salvation of the Poles: Working Class Ethnicity and Americanization Efforts during the Interwar Period in Toledo, Ohio." *Polish American Studies* 56, no. 2 (Autumn 1999): 19–44.

Buczek, Daniel. "Equality of Right: Polish American Bishops in the American Hierarchy?" *Polish American Studies* 62, no. 1 (Spring 2005): 5–28.

Bukowczyk, John J. "The Transformation of Working-Class Ethnicity: Corporate Control, Americanization, and the Polish Immigrant Middle Class in Bayonne, New Jersey, 1915–1925." *Labor History* 25, no. 1 (Winter 1984): 53–82.

Comte, Julien. "'Let the Federal Men Raid': Bootlegging and Prohibition Enforcement in Pittsburgh." *Pennsylvania History: A Journal of Mid-Atlantic Studies* 77, no. 2 (Spring 2010): 166–92.

Connolly, James. "Bringing the City Back In: Space and Place in the Urban History of the Gilded Age and Progressive Era." *Journal of the Gilded Age and Progressive Era* 1, no. 3 (July 2002): 258–78.

Cowie, Jefferson, and Nick Salvatore. "The Long Exception: Rethinking the Place of the New Deal in American History." *International Labor and Working-Class History* 74, no. 1 (Fall 2008): 3–32.

Crago, Laura A. "The 'Polishness' of Production: Factory Politics and the Reinvention of Working-Class National and Political Identities in Russian Poland's Textile Industry, 1880–1910." *Slavic Review* 59, no. 1 (Spring 2000): 16–41.

Galush, William. "Journeys of Spirit and Space: Religion and Economics in Migration." *Polish American Studies* 59, no. 2 (Autumn 2002): 5–16.

Gerstle, Gary. "Liberty, Coercion, and the Making of Americans." *Journal of American History* 84, no. 2 (Sept. 1997): 524–58.

Gobel, Thomas. "Becoming American: Ethnic Workers and the Rise of the CIO." *Labor History* 29, no. 2 (Spring 1988): 173–98.

Goldberg, David J. Goldberg. "Unmasking the Ku Klux Klan: The Northern Movement against the KKK, 1920–1925." *Journal of American Ethnic History* 15, no. 4 (Summer 1996): 32–48.

Gutman, Herbert. "Work, Culture, and Society in Industrializing America, 1815–1919." *American Historical Review* 78, no. 3 (June 1973): 531–88.

Hapak, Joseph T. "Selective Service and Polish Army Recruitment during World War I." *Journal of American Ethnic History* 10, no. 4 (Summer 1991): 38–60.

Hensley, Frances S. "Women in the Industrial Work Force in West Virginia, 1880–1945." *West Virginia History* 49 (1990): 115–24.

Hoerder, Dirk. "The Traffic of Emigration via Bremen/Bremerhaven: Merchants' Interests, Protective Legislation, and Migrants' Experiences." *Journal of American Ethnic History* 13, no. 1 (Fall 1993): 68–101.

Kapiszewski, Andrzej. "Controversial Reports on the Situation of Jews in Poland in the Aftermath of World War I: The Conflict between the US Ambassador in Warsaw Hugh Gibson and American Jewish Leaders." *Studia Judaica* 7 (2004): 257–304.

Keire, Mara L. "The Vice Trust: A Reinterpretation of the White Slavery Scare in the United States, 1907–1917." *Journal of Social History* 35, no. 1 (Autumn 2001): 5–41.

Kingsdale, Jon. "The 'Poor Man's Club': Social Functions of the Urban Working-Class Saloon." *American Quarterly* 25, no. 4 (October 1973): 472–89.

Martin, Louis C. "Flopping Tin and Punching Metal: A Survey of Women Steelworkers in West Virginia, 1890–1970." In *Women of the Mountain South: Identity, Work, and Activism*, edited by Connie Rice and Marie Tedesco. Athens: Ohio University Press, 2015.

McCartin, James P., and Joseph A. McCartin. "Working-Class Catholicism: A Call for New Investigations, Dialogue, and Reappraisal." *Labor: Studies in the Working-Class History of the Americas* 4, no. 1 (Spring 2007): 99–110.

McCartin, Joseph A. "Estranged Allies on the Margins: On the Ambivalent Response of Labor Historians to Catholic History." *U.S. Catholic Historian* 21, no. 2 (2003): 114–20.

Molenda, Jan. "The Role of Women in the Polish Migration to the Rhein-Westphalia Industrial Region at the Beginning of the Twentieth Century," *Polish Review* 42, no. 3 (1997): 317–38.

Morawska, Ewa. "The Internal Status Hierarchy in the East European Immigrant Communities of Johnstown, PA, 1890–1930s." *Journal of Social History* 16, no. 1 (Autumn 1982): 75–106.

———. "Labor Migrations of Poles in the Atlantic World Economy, 1880–1914." *Comparative Studies in Society and History* 31, no. 2 (April 1989): 237–72.

Pacyga, Dominic. "Polish Emigration to the United States before World War One and Capitalist Development." *Polish American Studies* 46, no. 1 (Spring 1989): 10–18.

Pehl, Matthew. "'Apostles of Fascism,' 'Communist Clergy,' and the UAW: Political Ideology and Working-Class Religion in Detroit, 1919–1945." *Journal of American History* 99, no. 2 (September 2012): 440–65.

———. "The Remaking of the Catholic Working Class: Detroit, 1919–1945." *Religion and American Culture: A Journal of Interpretation* 19, no. 1 (Winter 2009): 37–67.

Pliska, Stanley R. "The 'Polish-American Army' 1917–1921." *The Polish Review* 10, no. 2 (1965): 46–59.

Porter, Brian. "Anti-Semitism and the Search for a Catholic Modernity." In *Antisemitism and Its Opponents in Modern Poland*, edited by Robert Blobaum, 103–23. Ithaca, NY: Cornell University Press, 2005.

Pula, James S. "The Progressives, the Immigrant, and the Workplace: Defining Public Perceptions, 1900–1914." *Polish American Studies* 52, no. 2 (Autumn 1995): 57–69.

Radziłowski, John. "Out on the Wind: Life in Minnesota's Polish Farming Communities." *Minnesota History* 58, no. 1 (Spring 2002): 16–28.

Rose, David N. "Prostitution and the Sporting Life: Aspects of Working Class Culture and Sexuality in Nineteenth Century Wheeling." *Upper Ohio Valley Historical Review* 16, no. 2 (Spring/Summer 1987): 7–31.

———. "The Trial of Alice Bradford: A Study in the Politics of Prostitution in Wheeling, W.VA." *Upper Ohio Valley Historical Review* 16, no. 1 (Autumn/Winter 1986): 6–22.

Rose, Jim. "'The Problem Every Supervisor Dreads': Women Workers at the U.S. Steel Duquesne Works during World War II." *Labor History* 36, no 1 (1995): 23–51.

Shergold, Peter R. "Wage Rates in Pittsburgh during the Depression of 1908." *Journal of American Studies* 9, no. 2 (August 1975): 163–88.

Skok, Deborah A. "The Historiography of Catholic Laywomen and Progressive Era Reform." *U.S. Catholic Historian* 26, no. 1 (Winter 2008): 1–22.
Sterne, Evelyn Savidge. "Bringing Religion into Working-Class History: Parish, Public, and Politics in Providence, 1890–1930." *Social Science History* 24, no. 1 (Spring 2000): 149–82.
Tentler, Leslie Woodcock. "On the Margins: The State of American Catholic History." *American Quarterly* 45, no. 1 (March 1993): 104–27.
———. "Who Is the Church? Conflict in a Polish Immigrant Parish in Late Nineteenth-Century Detroit." *Comparative Studies in Society and History* 25, no. 2 (April 1983): 241–76.
Wolf, Edward C. "Wheeling and the Panama Canal." *Upper Ohio Valley Historical Review* 27 (2004).
Wolff, Larry. "Dynastic Conservatism and Poetic Violence in Fin de Siècle Cracow: The Habsburg Matric of Polish Modernism." *American Historical Review* 106, no. 3 (June 2001): 735–64.
Zukowski, Suzanne M. "From Peasant to Proletarian: Home Ownership in Milwaukee's Polonia." *Polish American Studies* 66, no. 2 (Autumn 2009): 5–44.

PHD DISSERTATIONS, THESES, AND OTHER UNPUBLISHED SECONDARY SOURCES

Barkey, Frederick Allan. "The Socialist Party in West Virginia from 1898 to 1920: Study in Working Class Radicalism." PhD diss., University of Pittsburgh, 1971.
Buseman, Michael J. "Vending Vice: The Rise and Fall of West Virginia State Prohibition, 1852–1934." PhD diss., West Virginia University, 2012.
Caldemeyer, Dana M. "Before the Klan: Coal Miners, Labor Conflict, and Community in Evansville, Indiana, 1892–1922." MA thesis: West Virginia University, 2010.
Javersak, David T. "The Ohio Valley Trades and Labor Assembly: The Formative Years, 1882–1915." PhD diss., West Virginia University, 1977.
Martin, Louis C. "Causes and Consequences of the 1909–1910 Steel Strike in the Wheeling District." MA thesis, West Virginia University, 1999.
———. "Working for Independence: The Failure of New Deal Politics in a Rural Industrial Place." PhD diss., West Virginia University, 2008.
Rosswurm, Steve. "Catholicism and the CIO: An Elective Affinity." Paper Presented at the 38th Annual North American Labor History Conference, October 21, 2016, Wayne State University.

Index

Page numbers in italics refer to figures and tables.

Aetnaville, 156
African Americans, 1, 51, 91, 161, 200
  and migration from Deep South, 66, 161–62
Amalgamated Association, 104–6, 108, 157, 159, 162–63
  Crescent Lodge No. 8, 150, 152, 157, 280n17
  Ft. Henry Lodge No. 20, 150, 280n27
  Mountain State Lodge No. 19, 150, 151–52, 155, 159, 280n24
  Nail City Lodge No. 24, 150, 152, 280n24
  new lodges of, 280n24
  Stogie City Lodge No. 25, 147–48, 150, 159–60
  in the 1930s, 225, 227
  Victory Lodge No. 21, 150, 152, 155–56
  See also labor strikes
Amalgamated Association of Iron and Steel Workers (AAISW), 104–7, 156, 159, 162
Amalgamated Association of Iron, Steel, and Tin Workers (AAISTW), 147, 153
Amalgamated Journal, 46
American Constitutional Association (ACA), 186
American Expeditionary Forces (AEF), 132, 135
  and the Eightieth Division, 135, 277n45
  and the 314th Field Artillery, 135–36, 186, 277nn44–45
  and Polish immigrants, 134–36
Americanization
  and America First Day, 186
  Catholic, 71, 92–93, 125, 136–39, 145
  coercive, 11–12, 125, 198, 203, 216, 273n8

"from the bottom up," 11–13, 118
  and pluralistic Americanism, 15, 125, 139, 145
  and Polish efforts, 171
  and World War I parade, 140–41
  See also First World War
American Protective Association (APA), 73
American Sheet and Tin Plate Company, 112–13, 119, 156
anticommunism, 204, 228–29, 300n61
Anti-Saloon League (ASL), 64, 198–200
anti-union, 100–101, 108–9, 160, 186, 197
Appalachia, 8, 28
Associated Charities, 54, 176
Association of Catholic Trade Unionists (ACTU), 9, 229
Austro-Hungarian Empire, 7, 24, 32, 128, 133, 276n38

Bahoric, Francis, 204
Baker, W. E. (judge), 205, 206, 208, 215
Baltimore & Ohio (B&O) Railroad, 45, 49, 55
  in accidents, 47, 50, 52
  as employer, 43, 48, 66, 111
  in expansion of Wheeling, 2, 183
  and Polish community, 80, 87
  in strikes, 107, 161
Baron, Matija, 155, 156, 159
Bellaire, Ohio, 52, 186, 202, 227, 231
  and football, 179, 181
  and labor activities, 48, 104, 119, 156, 222, 226
  and Polish immigrants, 81, 126, 127
Belmont Bunk, 162

Belmont Mill, 30, 66, 287n6
  and area for Prohibition enforcement, 205, 207–8
  and labor unions, 104–5, 152, 159–62, 280n24
  near Little Polonia neighborhood, 36, 45, 50–51, 91, 109, 131, 147
  workforce of, 36–38, 50, 168
Benwood Blast Furnace, 36, 47, 49, 101, 104, 282n54
  in 1901 strike, 106–7
  and United Steelworkers of America, 223, 230
Benwood mills, 105, 156, 174, 235
Benwood Mine Disaster of 1924, 16, 172, 173–78, 236
Benwood tube works, 1, 26, 37, 107, 172
Benwood Works, 35, *103*, 159, 160, 227
Bessemer (steel process), 38, 104, 105, 159
Black Madonna, 70
Bloch Brothers Tobacco, 30, 56, 252n45
  as employer, 35, 43, 44, 100, 120, 164
  and Jesse Bloch, 118
  in labor strike, 235
Blue, Fred, 201–2
boarders, 33–35, 37, 50
Board of Public Works, 56, 63, 110, 257n50
Boggs Run, 52
  and immigrants, 18, 62, 67, 101, 103, 132
bootlegging, 16, 197–98, 203, 207, 209–13
Boy Scout troop, 88, 192
Bridgeport, Ohio, 48, 52, 97, 127, 210
Brinkman, Everett, 178–81
Brzozów, 27, 32, 39, 134
Bureau of Investigation, 15
  concerns about Polish Army recruitment, 133–34
  general surveillance of immigrants, 129–32, 204, 260n94
  monitoring for draft dodgers and "enemy aliens," 129, 275n30
  monitoring of 1919 steel strike, 153–54, 155

Café of the Allies, 208, 211, 215
Catholic Action movement, 10
Catholic anti-socialism, 93–94, 96, 116–17
Catholic War Relief Service, 139
Catholic Women's League for Protective Work, 93
Center Wheeling, *51*, 56, 165, 182, 211, 264n49
  and "Little Poland" neighborhood, 36–38, 49, 54
Centre Market House, 30, 53, 62, 66
  and prostitution, 38, 61
child labor, 34–35, 44, 48–50, 163–64, 217
  organized labor concerns about, 99–100, 120
Chinese Exclusion Act, 108
city hall, 46, 125
City Health Department, 53–54, 59
Clarinet Polka, The (Maillard), 1, 72, 75, 239, 242, 261n6
coal miners, 9, 94, 197, 202, 209, 217
  and immigrants, 35–36, 68, 74
  and labor actions, 104–5, 111, 119, 122, 149, 158
  in surrounding communities, 80
  in Wheeling, 35–36, 37, 127, 240
  and workplace accidents, 47–48, 171, 174
  in World War I, 127, 131, 135, 144
coffeehouse, Greek-owned, 64, 205, 211–12, 215
Cohen, Lizabeth, 13, 143, 172, 218
coli bacillus, 53
Committee of One Hundred, 59, 64
Congress of Industrial Organizations (CIO), 2, 5, 10–11, 16, 182, 241
  in 1930s and 1940s, 217–19, 221, 223–25, 227–29, 231–37
Cooey Bentz (department store), 30, 175, 194
Cornwell, John, 129, 133–34, 141, 155–56
cut nail industry, 2, 36, 43, 50, 104
Cybulski, Alex, 197–98, 209

Democratic Party
  in the 1890s, 74, 109–10, 115–16, 117
  in the 1930s, 220–23, 236, 241
development faith, 28
Diocese of Krakow, 25, 76
Diocese of Wheeling-Charleston, 10, 15, 69, 239
  and immigrant national parishes, 69, 71–72, 76–78
diseases, spread of, 52–53, 54–55
Donahue, Patrick, 58, 71, 73–75, 91, 176
  and Emil Musial's appointment, 76, 78–80
  and Polish at St. Ladislaus, 82–84, 87
  reform efforts of, 93–94, 120
  during World War I, 134, 137, 138, 139, 142, 144
downtown Wheeling, 29, 58, 225, 229, 235
  urban problems of, 52, 59, 113
  working-class leisure activities in, 166, 172, 173
draft board, 124, 128, 130–34
Driehorst, L. C., 30, 64, 115
Duplaga, Stanley, 30, 39, 95, 96
  and Polish organizations, 221, 223–24
  and successful businesses, 165, 167–68, *169*

Earhart, Charles, 200–201, 202
eastern Ukraine, 23, 26, 132
Eighth Ward, 33, 34, 45, 98, 151, 165–66
  in politics, 108, 110, 116, 117–18, 222
  See also Ritchie District
"elective affinity," 10–11, 16
employee representations plans (ERPs), 159, 225
"enemy aliens," 128–29, 133, 276n38
ethnic community formation, 8, 9, 11, 172
  and Wheeling's Polonia, 4, *33*, 71–72, 96, 98, 137
ethnic middle class, 13, 35–37, 126
  in forming business associations, 223–24
  in opening small businesses, 167–69

ethnic tensions, 55, 65
  anti-immigrant viewpoints, 67–68
  Polish Catholic clergy and Irish Catholic leaders, 71, 74, 91–92, 142, 265n58
  street fighting and turf boundaries, 65–67
Executive Committee of the Polish Catholic Congress, 74

Falcon Society (Polish Falcons), 125, 126–28, 132
fake hotels, 60, 198
Felician Sisters, 89, 144, 190–91
"Festival of Nations," 171, 173, 188–90, 196, 236
First World War
  and Americanization parade, 140–42
  and immigrants needing to prove loyalty, 128–29, 136
  and Polish support for draft and Liberty bonds, 132, 139–40
  in Wheeling, 123–25
  See also American Expeditionary Forces; Bureau of Investigation; Liberty bonds
flooding, of Ohio River, 55–58, 258n58
football
  and Benwood Union, 178–82
  and Dick Matesic, 179–80
  high school teams in upper Ohio Valley, 178–82
  and Tommy Symansic, 180–81, 182
  and Triadelphia High, 180–81
  and Wheeling Central Catholic, 30, 182
  and Wheeling High, 30, 178, 179, 181, 188
Forty Hours Devotion, 87, 142, 184
Foster, William Z., 148, 149, 150, 151, 153
Fourteen Points, 142, 273n7
Fourth Liberty Loan Drive, 144, 149, 278n60
Frank, Nick, 213–15

fraternal organizations (lodges), 7, 14, 92, 121, 173, 183
   and labor unions, 151, 228, 229, 233, 236
   Polish, 73, 88, 96, 98, 171, 190–93
   in upper Ohio Valley, 220–23, 227, 241–42
   in World War I, 125, 126, 145
Front, Harry, 225
Front, Wincenty, 25, 167
Fulton, WV, 30, 43, 52, 184, 209, 233
   Polish neighborhood in, 38–39, 80, 145, 192, 221–24
   and Stanley Duplaga, 165, 167–68
   and Wheeling Mold & Foundry, 43, 52, 122, 127

Galkowski, Wladyslaw, 23–24, 223
Gaydosh, Michael, 139, 222, 229, 278n60
German Americans, 1, 12, 28–29, 51, 66
   and Catholics, 71, 72, 74, 137, 138
   in labor movement, 99, 101, 113, 118, 123, 148
   and Prohibition, 201, 205
   in Wheeling, 151, 182, 187
   in World War I, 3, 15, 124, 128, 129, 131
Gilded Age, 10, 28
glassworkers, 8, 112
Gorczyca, Anthony, 17–18, 19
Gosztyla, Joseph, 194, 223, 233
Great Depression, 167, 180, 192, 218
   and Prohibition, 215–17
   in Wheeling, 219–20, 239

Hallerczy Boys (Polish Army), 131, 132–34, 135, 136
Hamburg-American Line, 23, 24, 25, 26
Hazel Atlas Glass Company, 30, 163
Helenski, Agnes, 217–18
Hilton, Walter
   as Socialist editor of the *Wheeling Majority*, 118, 119, 121, 153
   as Socialist Party candidate and organizer, 98, 114, 123
   See also Socialist Party; *Wheeling Majority*

Hitchman Coal & Coke Company, 43, 47–48, 135
   and accidents, 47–48, 49
   and coal miners, 36, 68, 129, 131, 158, 168
   and labor unions, 111, 119, 197, 271n48
Hobbs, Brockunier Glass Works, 49, 62, 100
Holy Name rally, 93–94, 138, 142
Holy Name Society, 137, 139
Homestead strike, 101, 112, 268n14

immigration
   and anti-immigrant viewpoints, 99–103, 268n14
   effects of late nineteenth-century industrialization on, 18–22, 248n3
   and labor unions, 43, 44, 99–100, 108
   Polish, 3–4, 16, 26, 72
   restrictions on, 108, 183, 184–85, 201
   to rural locales, 246n14
   in Wheeling: family chain migrations, 26–28, 29, 32; settlement patterns, 29, 32–40; *za chlebem* ("for bread") migration to America, 22–26
"industrial democracy," 117, 146, 148, 149–50, 170, 238
Industrial Workers of the World (IWW), 26, 99, 119–20
interethnic interactions, in the 1920s, 172–73, 183, 187, 195
interwar period, 13, 163, 173, 183

Janeczko, Thaddeus, 1, 161
Jasienska, Leokadia, 26–27
Jazz Age, 88, 187
Jurczak, Paul, 127, 129–30, 222

Kacinski, Steve, 202, 215–16
Kazmierczak, Helen, 195
Kirk, Harvey, 56, 199–200
Knights of Columbus, 93, 124, 137, 138–39, 229
   and war fund, 142, 143

Knights of Labor, 104–5
Kowalsky, Humphrey, 187–88
Krakow, 17, 22, 24–25, 27, 33, 76
Ku Klux Klan, 176, 184–86, 196
Kuca, Mary, 184, 185, 218

LaBelle Mill, 43, 105, 162, 269n24, 280n24
   and labor unions, 104, 107, 112, 151, 152–53
labor strikes
   Hitchman Coal & Coke strike of 1906, 111
   machinists' strike (1903), 111
   meatpacking strikes of 1915–1916, 122–23
   steel strike of 1919, 148–57
   steel strike of 1943, 233–34
   steel strike of 1946, 235–37
   and steelworkers (1898–1900), 105, 269n26
   U.S. Steel Corporation strike of 1901, 105–7, of 1909–1910, 112
   and Wheeling Can Company (1915), 122
   Wheeling Steel, 1921–1924 lockout, 160–63
Lakomy family, *19*, 70, 218
Lansing, Ohio, 48, 80, 173, 183, 231
Lapinski, Konstanty, 24, 130
Last Chance Saloon, 62, 65
laypeople, 72, 86, 136
laywomen, 58, 86, 265n64
Ledvinka, Frank, 121, 160, 273n85
Lesser Poland Voivodeship, 25
Lewandowsky, Frank, 35–36, 95, 168, 216
Lias, William ("Big Bill"), 205, 208, 210–11, 295n60, 295n62
   arrests and convictions, 296nn87–88
   Café of the Allies, 208, 211, 215
   White Front, 211, 212, 213, 214
   "Beer Wars," 211, 213–15
Liberty bonds, 3, 129–30, 137, 139, 153, 156
   and Liberty Loan Parade, 140–41

   and Liberty Loan drives, 140–41, 144, 149, 278n60
   See also First World War
lockout, 99, 158, 160
Łódź, 23
Lublin, 2, 17, 23, 39, 195
Lukaszewicz, Joseph, 95, 194, 224
Maillard, Keith
   The Clarinet Polka, 1, 72, 75, 239, 242, 261n6
Mainfort, Tony, 200, 202
Malarski, Bruno, 206
Marchlenski, John, 144, 167, 197, 207
Market Auditorium, 113, 138, 139, 141, 153, 201
Martinkosky, Mary, 70, 191, 195
Martins Ferry, Ohio, 53, 179
   and coal mines, 48
   and labor organizing, 151, 156, 173, 226, 227, 234
   and Polish immigrants, 81, 134, 188, 222, 224
   and steel mills, 5, 52, 80, 176, 230
May processions
   and Polish Catholic culture, 70, 84–85, 183–84, *185*
   in Wheeling, 138, 176, 265nn59–60
McKinley Trade School, 220
meatpacking
   in the city of Wheeling, 30, 38–39, 55
   labor strike, 4, 36, 122–23, 233, 236
   medium-sized city, 3–7, 16, 40, 249
Meuse-Argonne Campaign, 135
Moniuszko Orchestra, 17, 190
moonshine
   production for supplemental income, 16, 165, 216, 242
   and role of women, 207–8
   and targets during Prohibition, 198, 203, 205–7, 210, 212–14
"moral capitalism," 13, 218, 240
Morawsky, Peter, 115, 122
Musial, Emil, 77
   and Benwood Mine Disaster, 175–76, 177–78
   building and ministering at St. Ladislaus, 27, 71, 96, 98, 191–92

Musial, Emil (*continued*)
  early ministry of, in upper Ohio Valley, 3, 15, 79–82
  and finances, debts, and disputes with diocese, 82–84, 87, 95, 165, 219
  and labor issues, 116–17, 158
  in the 1930s and 1940s, 219, 225, 239–40
  process of hiring, 74–78
  relationship of, to the diocese, 93–95, 116–17, 204, 278n60
  role of, during World War I, 125–27, 130, 134, 140, 142–45
  role of, with SS. Cyril and Methodius Seminary, 78–79
  and social and cultural functions at St. Ladislaus, 88–89, 183, 184–85, 190
  views of, on other immigrants, 91–92
  See also St. Ladislaus Parish; Polish Americans

National Catholic War Council (NCWC), 137, 144
National Committee for Organizing Iron and Steel Workers (NCOISW), 149–50
National German-American Alliance (NGAA), 201
National Labor Relations Board (NLRB), 225
National Road
  and immigrants living along or out, 38–39, 131, 222, 223
  during Prohibition, 208, 211, 214, 216
  as transportation route, 2
National War Labor Board (NWLB), 149, 233
native-born people
  in factories and labor movement, 48, 67, 98, 146, 155–57, 227
  and football, 178–80
  population of, in region, 5, 29, 51, 58, 84, 183
  role of, in Americanization, 12, 131, 135, 190
  and xenophobia, 37, 42, 67, 86, 101–2, 184–86

naturalization
  and coercive Americanization in World War I, 124, 140–41
  Polish immigrants applying for, 24, 109–10, 135, 250n18, 270nn38–39
  See also Americanization; First World War
nonunion, 104–6, 111, 149, 151–52, 159, 237
North Benwood, 36, 43, 46, 55, 131, 190
Northern Panhandle
  and industrial development, 5, 28, 82
  and labor, 111, 220
  and Prohibition, 16, 212

oberek, 70, 187
Ohio Valley Trades and Labor Assembly (OVTLA), 30–31
  anti-immigrant viewpoints of, 108, 163
  as craft labor organization, 29, 98, 106–7, 113, 147
  and "Organize the Unorganized" campaign, 115, 118–23
  reaching out to new immigrants, 15, 98, 123, 147–48
  and role of socialists, 97, 99
  and state workmen's compensation law, 118–19
  and steel strike of 1919, 148, 151, 152–53
Oglebay Park, 171, 173, 183, 187–89, 224, 236
  See also "Festival of Nations"
Olszta, Marcel, 95, 96, 165, 222
100 Percent Americanizers, 125, 142
  See also First World War
Oszustowicz, Alexander, 17–18, 19, 190
Our Lady of Perpetual Help parish (Ukrainian), 187
  See also Ukrainian Americans
Owoc, Stanley, 95, 96, 194, 197, 225

Pacyga, Dominic, 12, 14, 33, 71, 90
Paczki Ball, 70, 88

peasants
  and Austrian partition, 22–24
  and Congress Poland, 20–21
  and emigration, 2, 18–19, 40, 69, 249n7
  and Prussian partition, 19–20
Peters, Jack, 151, 153
pew rents, 88, 89, 95, 158, 192–93
pierogies, 70, 87, 183
Poland
  and Catholicism, 70
  changes to rural life in, during nineteenth century, 249n7
  and Galicia, 22–25, 130, 189, 239, 241
  German, 19–20, 29, 35, 49–50, 76, 78
  people born in, 147, 171, 197, 201, 202
  Russian, 17, 21–26, 32, 39, 161, 165
  support for, after Nazi invasion, 224–25
  World War independence of, 125, 132, 139
Polanders
  and anti-immigrant viewpoints, 44, 67–68, 101, 108, 123, 236
  used in newspaper articles, 41–42, 101–2, 126, 128, 254n1
  See also native-born people
Polish American Citizens' League, 127
Polish American Club, 95, 96, 267
Polish American Hall
  celebration of rebirth of Poland, 146
  union rallies, 121–22
  World War I rally, 125, 140
  1919 strike meetings, 148, 150–52
Polish American Political Club (PAP Club), 129, 145, 171, 192–93, 241
Polish American politics
  Democratic Party, 115–16, 220–23
  Republican Party, 108–9
  Socialist Party, 99, 110, 114–15
  See also Democratic Party; Republican Party; Socialist Party
Polish American Rhythm Kings, 17, 88, 190, 224
Polish Americans
  and Americanization, 11–14, 199
  and bootlegging, 212–14, 215
  and football, 178–82
  immigration of, to Wheeling, 17–18, 22–30, 32–40
  during interwar years, 163–73
  in labor movement, 97–109, 123, 217–18, 227–37
  in labor strikes, 147–49, 150–52, 156
  in medium-sized cities, 3–8
  and Polish Catholic culture, 70–71, 84–90, 183–85, 187–94
  and politics, 110, 114–15, 126–28, 219–25
  during World War I, 124–26, 128–36, 140–42, 145
  See also immigration; Poland, Polonia; St. Ladislaus Parish
Polish Army (Haller's Army), in France, 131–36
Polish Army Veterans Association (PAVA), 132–33
Polish Falcons, 125, 126–28, 132
Polish Ladies National and Army Relief Committee, 176
Polish National Alliance (PNA)
  in Ohio Valley, 221, 224–25
  role of, in Wheeling, 88, 137, 140, 145, 192–94
  in United States, 7, 125–26
  See also fraternal organizations
Polishness (Polskość), 21, 27, 84, 126, 241
Polish Relief Committee, 139
Polish Roman Catholic Union of America (PRCU)
  in Ohio Valley, 221, 225
  role of, in Wheeling, 88–89, 137, 171, 192, 194, 233
  and St. Joseph's Lodge No. 213, 88–89, 171, 194, 221, 233
  in United States, 7, 125
  See also fraternal organizations
Polish-Soviet War, 132, 189, 290n63
Polish West Virginian, 95
polka bianca, 85
Polonia
  community-building in, 80, 82–84
  community divisions in, 90–96, 125, 240

Polonia (*continued*)
  community unity in, 71, 126, 190, 192, 242
  economic security in, search for, 64, 147, 163–70, 172
  employment of Poles in, 37
  during Great Depression, 219, 223–27
  immigration to, 17–18, 27–28, 32–40
  and moonshining, 207
  need for, to reach out to other ethnic groups, 178
  and role of Polish culture, 70
  See also Polish Americans; St. Ladislaus Parish
pool hall, 36, 168, 213, 214
poolroom, 127, 131, 155, 168
  during Prohibition, 198, 202, 212, 214
Prohibition
  and politics, 110, 115, 200–201, 220
  and sacramental wine, 192, 203–4
  "selective enforcement" of, in Wheeling, 3, 16, 196, 198–99, 236
  statewide efforts in, 62, 65, 130, 202–4
  and violence over bootlegging turf, 210–15
  in Wheeling, 168, 203–9, 216
  See also Lias, William; saloons; Yost Law
prostitution, 38, 42, 59–61, 63, 65
Pulaski Field, 30, 193, 195

Republican Party, 7
  in West Virginia, 28, 74
  in Wheeling politics, 99, 109, 112, 115–17, 220–23
Rerum Novarum, 10, 94, 98, 112, 116, 136
Reuther, Valentine, 99, 107–8, 113, 114, 202
Reuther, Water, 49, 113
Ritchie District
  as center of Polonia, 29, 33–34
  and Great Depression, 219, 222–23
  home ownership of Poles in, *34*
  voting patterns of, 114–55, 271n60
  See also South Wheeling

Riverside Mill
  as dangerous workplace, 43–47, 50, 119
  and labor organizing and violence, 102–11, 122, 127–29, 154–56
  as major employer, 26, 35, 116, 161
Rozanski, Joseph, 125, 144, 147, 159, 163, 279n1
rum-running, 203, 207, 208–9, 210–11
Russian Revolution of 1905, 23, 32, 36
Russo-Japanese War, 23, 32
Rybeck, Samuel, 188, 290n61

Sacred Heart of Mary Parish, 81–82, 142–44
saloons
  labor union meetings in, 115, 123
  as small businesses, 35, 37, 167–68
  as social spaces, 5, 13, 14, 30, 53, 107
  as sites of vice, 15, 42, 44, 59–65, 68–69, 242
  and Prohibition enforcement, 199–202, 208
  See also Prohibition; prostitution; Schmulbach, Henry; Yost Law
saloonkeepers
  as ethnic small-business owners, 37, 62–64, 200
  and free lunch, 44
  and social halls, 107, 115, 123, 202
Sawa, Michael, 25–26, 206–7
Scherwinski's Hall, 97
Schmidt, Charles, 53–54, 257n50
Schmulbach Brewery, 30, 53, 113
Schmulbach, Henry, 42, 63–64
"Schmulbachism," 42, 63–64, 259n86
Selective Service Act of 1917, 39–40
  and draft in Wheeling, 124, 128–35, 141, 275n30
Slavic Voters League, 222
Social Democracy of America, 110
Socialist Party
  early organizing of, in Wheeling, 96, 97, 109–11
  in local politics, 113, 114–18
  and Polish socialist local, 114–15, 236, 265, n60, 271n63

"Organize the Unorganized" campaign
  of, 118–21
  role of, in OVTLA, 110–13
  See also Hilton, Walter; labor strikes;
    Ohio Valley Trades and Labor
    Assembly
sodality, 86, 87, 184, 192
South Wheeling, *51, 57*
  crowded streets in, 50–52
  immigrants settling in, 25, 27–29, 33,
    39–40
  immigrant turf battles in, 65–69
  industrial zone, 41–43, 161–63
  and labor organizing, 98–99, 106–16,
    121, 151–56, 159, 233, 235–36
  during the 1930s, 220–24
  politics of vice in, 59–65
  and Polonia, 1–3, 15, 17–18, 193–95,
    240–42
  precarious working-class life in,
    43–58, 164–67, 173, 177
  and Prohibition, 197, 202, 208,
    210–13
  and St. Ladislaus's early years, 70–73,
    78, 83, 85, 90–96
  See also flooding; labor strikes;
    Polonia; Ritchie District
speakeasies, 200, 201, 202, 208, 211–12
SS. Cyril and Methodius Polish Seminary of Detroit, 76, 78–79
St. Alphonsus Catholic Church, 1, 30,
  56, 62, 72, 139, 151
St. Hedwig's Society, 70, 73
St. John's Parish, 30, 87, 94–95
  and Benwood Mine Disaster, 175–76
  diverse ethnic congregation of, 68, 92,
    94–95, 137–38, 145
  and effects of 1919 steel strike,
    157–58
St. Joseph's Cathedral
  as center of Catholic reform organizations, 30, 45, 58, 92–93, 267n91
  role of, in larger city events, 139, 153,
    186
St. Joseph's Society of the PRCU, 88–89,
  171, 194, 221, 233
St. Ladislaus Parish, *85*
  baptisms in, *81*
  as center of Polonia, 1, 3, 7, 14–15,
    70–72
  and effects of 1919 steel strike,
    156–58, 170
  and Father Emil Musial, 75, 77, 78–82
  financial records of, *89, 193*
  in the Great Depression, 218–19, 221,
    235, 239–41
  growth of, in the 1920s, 183–84,
    190–95
  and military service, 134–36
  parochial school, *90, 91, 191*
  and relationships within the Diocese
    of Wheeling-Charleston, 73, 90–95,
    137–44
  social and cultural life at, 70, 84–89,
    98, 121
  and tensions within Wheeling, 91–96
  views of, on Poland, 140, 142
  and weddings, 27, 33, 85–86, 168
  and World War I, 123, 126–28
  See also Musial, Emil; Polish Americans; Polish Roman Catholic Union;
    Polonia
St. Ladislaus Society, 73, 83, 137,
  256n67
St. Mihiel (battle), 135
steel strike of 1919, 15, 147–59, 236,
  242
Steel Workers Organizing Committee
  (SWOC), 217–18, 225–30
Sterne, Evelyn, 11, 14, 136
streetcars, 80
  in Progressive Era, 5, 50, 52, 66, 118,
    129, 173
  as sites of strikes and violence, 102,
    104, 154–55, 203
Swiader, Wojciech, 130, 171, 221
Swint, Bishop John, 79, 204, 228, 239

Templin, Frank, 127, 144
Templin, Peter, 135–36
Thoner, Thomas, 175, 184, 186
tinplate mills
  as employers, 30, 43, 62, 99, 105, 144,
    149, 172, 269n24
  and organized labor, 112–13, 119, 156

Top Mill, 27, 29–32, 38–41, 119, 287n6
Triadelphia, West Virginia, 48, 173, 180–81, 190, 221

Ukraine, eastern, 23, 26, 132
Ukrainian Americans
  as immigrants in Wheeling, 14, 80, 84, 135, 183–84, 222
  living and working with Polish Americans, 156, 161, 163–64, 220, 237
  and post–World War I violence in Europe, 132, 275n33
  and Ukrainian culture, 187–89, 290n60
  and World War I in Wheeling, 135, 140
United Mine Workers of America (UMWA)
  and Diocese of Wheeling-Charleston, 94, 144
  and Fifth Ohio Subdistrict, 111–12, 121, 152, 153, 160
United Steelworkers of America (USWA)
  fighting gender discrimination, 234–35
  fostering "union consciousness," 226–31, 235–36, 238
  grievance procedures of, 229–30, 232–33, 234–35, 300n69
  Local 1185 (Benwood), 227–28, 235
  Local 1248 (Wheeling Corrugating), 217–18, 228–37, 239, 301n80
  Local 3130 (Wheeling Can Company), 237
  Local 3814 (Benwood), 223, 227, 298n29
  organizing of, 218 (*see also* Steel Workers Organizing Committee)
  shop stewards of, 217, 218, 226, 228, 232, 235
  World War II–era organizing, 233–34, 301n88
Upper Benwood, 108, 208
upper Ohio Valley
  industrial development of, 5–6, 48, 158, 165
  interethnic culture of, 178, 187, 203

and Polish immigrants, 79–80, 127, 132–34, 171, 191, 195, 240
and union organizing, 16, 151, 218, 224, 226–27, 233–37
U.S. District Court for the Northern District of West Virginia, 205, 207, 209, 215
U.S. Steel strike
  of early 1900s, 99, 105–6, 112–13
  of 1919, 149–57

Vinesky, Johnny, 212–13, 215
Visnic, Mildred, 218
Volstead Act, 198, 200, 202–6, 209, 213–16

Warsaw, 2, 17, 23–26, 39, 161
Warwick China Company, 1, 30, 44, 60, 189
Weirton, West Virginia
  and Polish fraternal societies, 80, 221, 222
  role of, in Ohio Valley, 5, 52
  and Sacred Heart of Mary Catholic Parish, 81, 142, 143
  and Weirton Steel, 80, 226
welfare capitalism, 143
Wheeling, West Virginia
  photographs of, 6, 30–31, 51, 57
  See also Center Wheeling; South Wheeling
Wheeling Can Factory, 30, 43, 49, 56, 120, 162
  as major employer, 43, 162, 172, 189
  1915 strike, 97–98, 117–18, 122, 236, 241
Wheeling Corrugating, 30, 43, 176, 239, 297n3
  and the drum press department, 166, 217–18, 230–35, 301n80
  union culture at, 230–36
  See also United Steelworkers of America
Wheeling Daily News, 56–57, 188
Wheeling Intelligencer, 124, 141, 156, 174, 180, 185–86

Wheeling Island, 56, 106, 127, 181, 182, 229
Wheeling Majority, 97, 112, 118, 148, 153, 156
Wheeling Mold & Foundry
  as major employer, 30, 38–39, 43, 49, 52
  and Polish Americans, 119, 121–22, 127, 131, 233
  See also Fulton, WV
Wheeling News-Register, 50, 102, 115–16, 233, 237
Wheeling Steel Corporation, 3, 15, 158, 172, 174, 287n6
  steel strikes, 148, 160–63, 217
Wheeling Steel & Iron
  as major employer, 29, 30, 43, 45, 101, 104, 280n24
  as site of union activity, 101, 105–6, 119, 122, 149, 151–52, 154, 156, 159
  See also labor strikes; Top Mill
"wide-open" culture
  and Alice Bradford, 61
  in Wheeling, 15, 42
  and "South of the Creek" vice culture, 59–65, 199
women
  as factory workers, 163–64
  and Polish Red Cross auxiliary, 176, 177, 287n16
  and saloon culture, at turn of twentieth century, 61–65, 258n70
  See also labor strikes; Ohio Valley Trades and Labor Assembly; St. Ladislaus Parish
working-class life
  mechanization, 43–44, 48, 99, 100, 103, 119
  unemployment, 23, 32, 44–46, 62, 67, 102, 116, 118, 149, 219
  workplace accidents, 46–49, 59, 88–89, 119, 159, 230
  See also coal miners; Riverside Mill; South Wheeling
Workmen's Compensation Act, 118–19, 159, 177
World War I. *See* First World War
WWVA, radio, 17, 166, 190

Yorkville, Ohio
  and Polish immigrants, 81, 221, 222
  and steel mills, 5, 52, 149, 160, 287n6
  and SWOC, 225, 226, 229, 232, 234
Yost Law, 198
  local and state enforcement, 130, 198, 199–203, 210
  "Wet Parade" protest, 201–2

Zimmermann Telegram, 124

www.ingramcontent.com/pod-product-compliance
Lightning Source LLC
Chambersburg PA
CBHW031722230426
43669CB00007B/208